LIVING
JEWISH

LIVING
JEWISH

*The Lore and Law
of Being a Practicing Jew*

by

Michael Asheri

SECOND EDITION

DODD, MEAD & COMPANY
New York

First published as a Dodd, Mead Quality Paperback in 1983
Copyright © 1978 by Everest House, Publishers; additional material copyright © 1980 by Everest House, Publishers
All rights reserved
No part of this book may be reproduced in any form
without permission in writing from the publisher
Published by Dodd, Mead & Company, Inc.
79 Madison Avenue, New York, N.Y. 10016
Distributed in Canada by
McClelland and Stewart Limited, Toronto
Manufactured in the United States of America
Designed by Sam Gantt

Library of Congress Cataloging in Publication Data

Asheri, Michael, 1924-
Living Jewish.

Originally published: 2nd ed. New York : Everest
House, 1980, c1978.
Includes index.
1. Jews — Rites and ceremonies.   I. Title.
[BM700.A74 1983]   296.4   83-14148
ISBN 0-396-08263-7 (pbk.)

For my children, Gabriel, Suzana, Miriam,
Daniel and Dina and for their children: *ken yirbu*

Contents

PART V   Daily Jewish Life

PART VI   Prayer: Private and Communal

PART VII   The Holidays

PART VIII   Just for Jews

Preface to the Second Edition

WHEN *Living Jewish* appeared last year, I was concerned with the possibility that Conservative and Reform Jews, for whom it was essentially written, might feel looked down upon, since my approach to our common heritage is an Orthodox one.

Happily this has not happened and I am not convinced that it is due to any particular virtue of my own as an author. Rather, I feel that it is a gut reaction of Jews at the innermost level of their being.

Put simply, I believe that no matter what label they may wear: Orthodox, Conservative, Reform, there is a certain impermeable core in Jews which is capable of resisting pressure from any side and which recognizes, through all the smokescreens and ecumenism, that *Israel am kodesh*: Israel is a holy people, the chosen of God.

That Jews whose eyes see a radically different Judaism than mine fail to resent my vision of the central fact of their lives and even, at times, find in it the beginning of a new-old path to follow, I can ascribe only to the "homing instinct" of the Jewish soul they all possess.

Living Jewish is dedicated to my children, whose Judaism ranges from the ultra-Orthodoxy of Jerusalem's Kiryat Mattersdorf to the left-wing, secular Zionism of a Hashomer Hatzair kibbutz in the Negev. To this second edition I would like to add another dedication, to their mother and my wife, Doña Tzippora, *acharona, acharona chaviva*.

MICHAEL ASHERI

Rehovot, 5739

xi

Preface

Where should I place a mezuza?
Can I name my son after my father if my father is still alive?
What day does Passover start this year?
Is the Sephardic custom different from the Ashkenazic?

A knowledgeable Jew, living among less well-informed Jews, is asked questions like these so often he comes to consider them part of his daily life. More often than not, after the question has been answered, the questioner will ask, "Isn't there a book somewhere that just plain tells what being Jewish is all about?"

This is an attempt at such a book. It tries to give the facts about being Jewish with no preaching and no moralizing. The book can be read from beginning to end, if the reader wishes to, or used as a reference work for answering most of the common questions that crop up in the course of Jewish life. Non-Jews as well will find their understanding of Jews and Jewish life enhanced by this book.

As for the point of view taken by the author, the reader is not exhorted to follow any particular path, since the purpose of the book is not to preach but to teach. Nevertheless, the facts regarding law and custom are in accordance with the practices and beliefs of Orthodox Jews. Orthodoxy has been taken as the criterion of observance, because, whether followed or not, it is acceptable to all Jews, whereas some Conservative and Reform practices are not. Where Sephardic custom differs from Ashkenazic custom, both variations are usually given.

In reality there is an even more important reason for describing the laws and customs of Judaism in Orthodox terms: completeness. In my experience, when a Jew asks a question that touches on his Jewishness, he wants as full an answer as can be given within the limits of practicality. All Jews know that the traditions of their people are the inheritance of every one of them, but many, rightly or wrongly, feel themselves unable to accept this inheritance as a whole. Their solution is to take as much as they think they can handle, but they want to know about the rest of it too.

So, at no place in this book will the Jewish reader be told how Jewish he *should* be: every Jew in the world makes his own decision regarding that. What he *will* be told is how Jewish he *can* be. If he has already made his decision, the author is not going to ask him to change it.

After all, what would be the use? There is a Yiddish proverb that says: "When all Jews hold the same beliefs, Messiah will long since have arrived!"

Until that time comes, I hope this book will tell both Jew and non-Jew what "living Jewish" is all about.

Michael Asheri

NOTES ON TRANSLITERATION OF HEBREW WORDS

Throughout this book, Hebrew words are transliterated in the pronunciation heard in Eretz Israel today. There are inconsistencies from time to time, but that is the general rule. Where it is felt necessary, the Ashkenazi pronunciation is given in parentheses following the Israeli-Sephardic form.

As for spelling, the Hebrew letters chet and chaf are rendered by "ch," which is pronounced as in German; "ei" is also pronounced as in German. Thus, "mein" would be pronounced as if it were *mine* in English ("ch" and "ei" spellings apply to Yiddish as well).

Abbreviations used are:

(A.) - Ashkenazic
(S.) - Sephardic
(Y.) - Yiddish

What we are is what we are
We are Jews, is what we are.
Blessed are we and our world,
Sweet as sugar is our life.

. . . Yiddish folksong

PART
I

The
Jewish
People

1

Who Is a Jew?
Cohen, Levi and Israel

BOOKS on Judaism usually start off with a discussion of religious concepts. This book will not, because it is possible to be Jewish without being religious in any accepted sense. Obviously then, the first thing we have to do is determine, *who is a Jew?*

The full answer is that to be Jewish you either have to be born Jewish or undergo religious conversion to Judaism. The percentage of Jews accounted for by conversion is a fraction of one percent; most Jews are born that way. But what does "born Jewish" mean?

ANYONE BORN OF A JEWISH MOTHER IS
JEWISH BY BIRTH

In the case of a mixed marriage, if the mother is Jewish and the father is not, the children are born Jews. If, on the other hand, the father alone is a Jew, the children of such a marriage are not Jewish and if they wish to be Jewish must undergo a religious conversion the same as any other Gentile.

3

The reasons given for this unalterable law are many; one is that children derive their Jewishness from their mother because they are under her influence in their earliest, formative years. This may be a supporting reason, but it is not the legal reason. The legal reason is found in the Torah (Deut. 7:3-4): "Neither shall you make marriages with them. Your daughter you shall not give unto his son nor his daughter shall you take unto your son. For he will turn away your son from following Me."

Rashi (Rabbi Sh'lomo Yitzchaki, France, 11th century), the author of the basic commentary on the Torah, says regarding this last verse that its plain meaning is that if the son of the Gentile (the final "he" of the verse) marries your daughter, he will turn away *your* son, which your daughter will bear him, from following God. From this we learn that your daughter's son (who has a Gentile father) is considered *your* son, that is, he is considered a Jew. However the son of your son who has a Gentile mother is not considered your son, i.e. a Jew, but *her* son, because nowhere in the Torah is there given as a reason for not giving your son a non-Jewish wife that she will turn *your* son (that is, her son whose father is your son) away from God.

So it should be clearly understood that it is not enough to say, "I feel Jewish, I consider myself to be Jewish, other people consider me Jewish, so I am Jewish." If one is not born of a Jewish mother or formally converted to Judaism one is not Jewish. A good parallel is the case of a person who is brought to the United States at the age of a few days and who grows up there. As American as he may look, act and feel, he is not a citizen of the United States until he has gone through the legal process of naturalization.

So much for who is a Jew. Our interest at the moment, however, is not so much the individual Jew as the Jewish people. For a starter, let's take a look at the word "people."

THE JEWISH *What?*

Are the Jews a race, a religious group, a linguistic group, a nationality or what? A race they are not: there are blond and blue-eyed Jews, black Jews, brown Jews, yellow Jews, and all shades in between. A religious group they most certainly are, although there are atheists who are, nonetheless, Jews. A linguistic group? Jews speak scores of different languages. Nationality? Jews are citizens of many countries; there are Jews in both houses of Congress in the United States and in both Lords and Commons in England. France has had two Jewish Prime Ministers.

No, the Jews are none of these things. The Jews are a *people* just as, for example, the Armenians are a people; the Irish, a mixture of many races, two languages and two religions, are a people; the Basques, racially indistinguishable from their French and Spanish neighbors, are a people. The Jews, however, are a people quite unlike any other in the world and what makes them so will be discussed in the second part of this book; for the moment we are interested in the actual physical makeup of the Jewish people.

To begin with, not all Jews are the same. In fact, like Caesar's Gaul, all Israel is divided into three parts: all male Jews are either *Cohen, Levi* or *Israel.*

WHAT IS A COHEN?

A *Cohen* is a priest and a descendant of Aaron, Moses' brother. The Aaronites, or *Cohanim* (the plural of Cohen), served as the officiating priests in the Temple in Jerusalem. They blessed the congregation on occasion and redeemed the firstborn, as they do to this day. They were specifically named by God to this office when He told Moses, "And bring thou near unto thee Aaron thy brother and his sons with him, from among the children of Israel, that they may minister as priests unto me" (Exod. 28:1). Thus, among the Jews, the priesthood is hereditary.

Today there is no Temple in Jerusalem and of course the priests do not function there. Nonetheless, they still have certain privileges and obligations which set them apart from other Jews. There are five principal things:

- A Cohen is the first man to be called up when the Torah is read publicly in the synagogue.
- On certain occasions the Cohanim bless the congregation.

(This blessing, called *Birchat Cohanim*, is discussed in
chapter 28.)
- A Cohen redeems the firstborn sons of Jewish women.
  (This ceremony, called *Pidyon Ha-ben*, is described in
  chapter 9.)
- A Cohen may not marry a divorced woman or a *chalutza*
  or a convert.
- A Cohen may have no contact, even indirectly, with the
  dead. He may not belong to a burial society (chapter 16),
  may not enter a house in which there is a corpse, nor a
  morgue or cemetery except for the burial of a member of
  his own family or that of a *met mitzva* (an unclaimed
  body whose burial becomes the responsibility of the community).

The reason for his being called to the Torah first is to honor
him. The blessing of the congregation and the redemption of the
firstborn sons are specific duties which God assigned him. The
reason he may not marry a divorced woman or a *chalutza* (see
chapter 13) is that, as a priest, this would be considered demean-
ing. He is prohibited from any contact with the dead because
according to Jewish law, a human corpse defiles and makes
ritually unclean anyone coming into contact with it, even indirectly, and a priest must not risk such defilement unless it is
absolutely necessary.

How does a Cohen know he is a priest, a descendant of Aaron?
He knows because he has been told so by his father and he by his
father before him, and so on into antiquity. A Cohen is easily
identified by his Hebrew name; an ordinary Jew named Samuel,
whose father's name is Isaac, will be called in Hebrew, "Shmuel
ben Yitzchak," or Samuel son-of Isaac. A Cohen with the same
name would be called "Shmuel ben Yitzchak Ha-Cohen," or
Samuel son-of Isaac, the Priest.

A Cohen need not have the last name Cohen in ordinary life;
indeed, a great many Cohanim do not. The first modern Chief
Rabbi of the Holy Land, Rabbi Abraham Kook, was a Cohen.
Most people named Rappaport (or Rappoport, etc.) are Cohanim
because the founder of their family line, Rapa of Porto (Italy),

was a Cohen. People named Cohen, Kahn, Cogan, Kahan, Ka-
gan, Kaganovitch, Kohn, Kaplan or Katz are almost always
Cohanim although there are rare exceptions and occasionally a
man will be found named Cohen who is not only not a priest, he is
not even a Jew.

HOW DOES A PRIEST DIFFER FROM A RABBI?

A rabbi stands in a special relation to the rest of the congregation. Put simply, the rabbi knows more than anyone else about
Jewish law and is named by the congregation as its judge in matters of Jewish law and custom. He receives his authority to decide
questions of law (called *s'micha*) from another rabbi or court of
rabbis. This is, of course, a simplification, but in its essentials
describes the position of the rabbi within a congregation.

The priest, on the other hand, stands in a special relation to
God. He is, in a sense and for certain purposes only, the interme-
diary between the congregation and the Lord. In this he is similar
to priests of other religions. Catholic priests, for example, are
supposed to possess a faculty enabling them to forgive sins and
administer sacraments, which only they can do. The difference is
that the Catholic priest receives this supposed power from another human being; another priest. To the Jewish way of thinking
this is not possible; such a faculty cannot be given by one human
to another but must be received directly from God, as is the case
with the Cohanim who inherit their priestly status from the
ancestors named by God in the Torah; Aaron and his sons and
descendants.

THE LEVIIM

The second category of Jew is the *Levi*. These are descendants
of the tribe of Levi, as were Moses and Aaron, but unlike Aaron
and his descendants were not chosen by God to be priests, but
rather assistants to the priests. During the time of the Temple
they served in that capacity. They are also distinguished by having the name Ha-Levi attached to their Hebrew names. Rabbi
Kook's successor as Chief Rabbi of the Holy Land was Rabbi

Isaac Herzog, a Levi. The second man called to the Torah, after the Cohen, is always a Levi, and it is the duty of the Leviim to help the Cohanim wash their hands prior to giving the Priestly Blessing. Most people with the names Levy, Levi, Levine, Levis, Levitt, Loewy, Halevy and Segal (or Siegel, Segall, etc.) are Leviim.

ISRAEL

The third and by far the largest category of Jews is people who are neither Cohen nor Levi. These are called *Israel*, or just plain Jews.

In most Orthodox (and Conservative) congregations, particularly the smaller ones, a stranger appearing in the synagogue on a day when the Torah is being read publicly (Monday, Thursday or Saturday), will be asked if he is a Cohen or a Levi so that he may be given the honor of the first or second *aliya*, the Hebrew term for being called up to the Torah. Often, if he is neither, he will answer humorously, in Yiddish, "K'mat a Yisroel" (barely a Jew).

2

Ashkenazim, Sephardim and Others

APART from their individual differences as Cohen, Levi or Israel, all Jews fall into one of three categories, based on their historical and geographical origin. These three groups are *Ashkenazim*, *Sephardim*, and a third category comprising all Jews who come under neither of the two main classifications. For convenience sake we will call them *"Others."* With the exception of occasional visitors, all Jews in Europe and the Americas are either Ashkenazim or Sephardim.

WHO ARE THE ASHKENAZIM?

Although historically the Hebrew name *Ashkenaz* is taken to mean Germany, in our times the word *Ashkenazi* has come to mean any European Jew not specifically of Spanish or Portuguese origin or descent. The term applies equally to their descendants in the Americas and elsewhere. In more specific terms, the Ashkenazim are descendants of Yiddish, German, French, Hungarian and Russian-speaking Jews, as well as most of the Jews of

Scandinavia, Finland, England and Holland. By and large, anyone whose parents, grandparents or great-grandparents spoke
Yiddish, German or Hungarian is almost sure to be an Ashkenazi.

WHO ARE THE SEPHARDIM?

The name *Sepharad* is originally taken to mean Spain, and the
Sephardim are Jews of Spanish or Portuguese origin. Actually, in
our times, the term Sephardic has been extended to include many
Jewish communities in Arabic, Persian and Turkish-speaking
parts of the world who are in reality not of Spanish descent at all,
but who have adopted the Spanish ritual in their prayers and
synagogue services. Many of the ancient Jewish communities
calling themselves Sephardic today are probably descendants of
Jews who left their Homeland during the Babylonian exiles (721
B.C.E., Israel, and 586 B.C.E., Judah) and later (70 C.E., the
destruction of the Second Temple, and 135 C.E., following Bar
Kochba's rebellion).

Today Sephardic Jews are found in Holland and England,
where they are recognizable by their Spanish and Portuguese
surnames, Turkey, Greece, Eastern Romania, Eastern Yugoslavia (Serbia and Bosnia), Bulgaria, North Africa and, of course,
Israel and the Americas. The Jews of Italy are partly of Sephardic origin, particularly those in the North, but many, such as
those of Rome, belong to the ancient Italian community which
has existed for well over two thousand years.

The Jews of England and Holland, with largely Portuguese
names like Henriques, Cardozo, Pereira, Mendes, Seixas and
Gaster (derived from Castro), have dropped the use of Spanish as
a vernacular and speak the language of their country of residence. The Sephardim of the United States, with similar names
but also with names like Allport, Hendricks, Hayes and Brandon,
have done the same. The Jews of Turkey, the Balkans and
Greece, with the exception of the city of Yoanina, speak an archaic and corrupt form of Spanish to this day, as do many of their
descendants in the United States. This dialect, which the linguists call Judeo-Spanish, is called by the Sephardim themselves,

Ladino or *Judezmo*. In North Africa it is called *Jaquetía* (pronounced Hock-et-*ee*-ya).

Other Jews, classified as Sephardic but in their great majority not of Spanish origin, are those of Syria, Lebanon, Egypt, Iraq and other Arab nations. The common language of all these Jews is Arabic. The Persian-speaking Jews of Iran and Bokhara are commonly called Sephardic (although they are not of Spanish origin), because they have adopted the Spanish prayer ritual. Spanish and French-speaking Jews of North Africa are mostly of genuine Spanish extraction, while the Berber and Arabic-speaking Jews may be classified either as Sephardic or as members of that third category, "Others."

WHAT ARE THE DIFFERENCES BETWEEN ASHKENAZIM AND SEPHARDIM?

The real difference is that the two groups *think* of themselves as different. They live in separate quarters in many cities, have separate synagogues, schools, kosher butchers and other community services. Their food is different, the languages they speak at home are different and there are differences in their prayers, religious ceremonies and customs. One of the most obvious differences is the way in which each group pronounces the Hebrew language (chapter 4).

One difference in custom which has caused dissension in mixed Ashkenazic-Sephardic marriages is that of naming a child after a living relative, particularly a grandparent. Sephardim will but Ashkenazim won't. (This is discussed in chapter 7.)

And there are further differences which amount to actual variations in religious law as it is accepted today. In the chapter on Passover you will notice that certain foods prohibited by Ashkenazim are permitted by Sephardim. Another, now more or less theoretical, difference is in the laws concerning marriage. Theoretically, Sephardim may have two wives, while Ashkenazim are bound by the *cherem* (ban) of Rabbenu Gershom and must observe monogamy. This is discussed more fully in chapter 11.

As for other major religious differences, there are almost none. The book on which most decisions in Jewish law are reached on an everyday basis is the *Shulchan Aruch* (chapter 25), which was compiled by a Sephardic rabbi, supplemented with a gloss by an Ashkenazi rabbi, and is used with equal confidence by both communities. The responsa (chapter 25) of Sephardic rabbis are often quoted in the legal decisions of Ashkenazic rabbis and the same is true of Ashkenazic responsa in the decisions of Sephardic *chachamim* (as the Sephardim call their rabbis).

RELATIONS BETWEEN ASHKENAZIM AND SEPHARDIM

While each community maintains its own identity, both are well aware that they are all and equally Jews. While a Sephardi may not feel at home in an Ashkenazi synagogue because of the differences in ritual and the pronunciation of Hebrew, he is quite conscious of being among fellow Jews, and if there is no Sephardic congregation near where he lives, he will join an Ashkenazi congregation. And the reverse is true as well. In Panama, for example, the only important orthodox synagogue is that of the large Arabic-speaking community. Many orthodox Ashkenazim pray in it as well. In Manila, Philippines, one congregation serves both the Arabic-speaking and Ashkenazi communities, which have in reality merged until today there is only one Jewish community in the Philippines, containing elements of both traditions.

As might be supposed, the two groups have always tended to marry within their own communities, and "intermarriage" between Ashkenazim and Sephardim was at one time quite bitterly opposed by parents on both sides. In recent times these objections have tended to disappear and marriage between young people from these differing traditions is accepted by everyone without reserve. (Marriage customs differ, however, and there is still some squabbling about whose ritual will be used at the wedding!)

When, in this book, differences in custom and ritual or other aspects of Judaism are described as "Sephardic," the reference is to the "Oriental" Sephardim from Turkey, Greece, the Balkans and the Arabic-speaking countries, unless otherwise noted. These Jews constitute the immense majority of the Sephardim in the

Americas. The Sephardim mentioned earlier, with names like Brandon and Hendricks, are a small, highly assimilated group without influence in the Sephardic world community.

Nevertheless, a certain romantic image clings to these "Old Families"—many of which have lived in America since before the Revolution—due to the fact that they are, in good part, descendants of *Marranos*, Jews who converted to Catholicism in Spain to save their skins or, more often, their fortunes, and then managed to return to Judaism, sometimes generations later. The majority of the Jews in Spain, when faced with a choice between baptism and exile, unhesitatingly chose exile, misery and, often, death.

In *The Grandees*, a recently written book about "America's Sephardic Elite," the author, Stephen Birmingham, gave his own explanation of the difference between the "old" Sephardic families of the United States and the Ladino-speaking immigrants from Greece and Turkey. Referring to the latter he said:

> "Being poor, they could not afford to become Marranos who had to live by paying bribes. Being poor they also lacked the sophistication and poise it took to lead the Marrano's double life. Finally, being poor and unsophisticated, they lacked the adaptability that would have allowed them to accept conversion."

It is difficult to imagine how more misinformation could be packed into three short sentences. Birmingham says that, in his opinion, it is only ignorance that keeps any Jew from giving up his people and his faith to adopt Christianity.

As to poverty being the only reason these heroic people made the choice they did, it is evident that the Jewish attitude toward apostasy on the one hand and martyrdom on the other has never entered Mr. Birmingham's field of knowledge. The fact is that, far from being an "elite," the old Sephardic families that Mr. Birmingham writes about are believed by most Jews, perhaps unfairly, to be in danger of losing what Judaism they still possess. The Rabbis have laid down a legal ruling that no Jew may reproach a Marrano who returns to Judaism for having converted in the first place. That is the law, but in practice Jews tend to look down on these "old families" for precisely that reason. Cecil Roth, commenting on a letter (doubtfully ascribed to Maimonides) in which temporary false conversion to Islam (not to Christianity) was defended in order to save one's life, said:

> "This is not the place to discuss the ethical or the legal aspects of the problem. So much, however, may be said. A contemporary French or German Jew would not have spoken in this fashion. To the north of the Pyrenees, a spirit of greater fortitude prevailed. The Jews of the Rhineland who 'sanctified the Name of God'* to the man rather than abjure their faith, were more heroic if less picturesque than their Andalusian brethren."

This same heroism was demonstrated by many Jews in Spain who preferred death or exile with loss of everything they had, to accepting idolatry. The "Oriental" Sephardim are their descendants and to ascribe their love of God and the Torah to poverty and lack of sophistication is a calumny. I cannot believe that any responsible member of the "Sephardic Elite" that Mr. Birmingham writes about would agree with him.

WHO ARE THE "OTHERS"?

As explained above, all European Jews and their descendants are either Ashkenazim or Sephardim and the Arabic-speaking Jews are usually classified as Sephardim. If we except Australia and the Americas, whose Jewish population is European or Levantine in origin, we are left with Africa and Asia. It is in these two continents and the sub-continent of India that the Jews who are neither Ashkenazim nor Sephardim were or still are to be found.

While most of the Jews in Africa are either Ashkenazim, such as the large and important colony in South Africa, or Sephardim, as in North Africa, Egypt and the Congo, there is one community

*Died as martyrs

in Ethiopia which appears to have originated in Africa. They are black in color, speak the Semitic languages, Tigré and Tigrinya, claim descent from King Solomon and the Queen of Sheba, and are called *Falashas*. They do not use Hebrew but Ge'ez or Old Amharic as a religious language, are strict observers of the Sabbath and the dietary laws and beyond doubt are Jews, even if their long isolation from the rest of the Jewish people has raised a question as to their religious eligibility to marry other Jews. These Negro Jews are classified as "Others."

India contains four quite distinct Jewish communities. Best-known, perhaps, are the Bene Israel of Bombay. These are dark-skinned Jews whose daily tongue is Marathi, an Indo-European language, and whose daily life differs little from that of the Hindu population surrounding them, except, of course, for their religion.

In the south of India, in Cochin on the Malabar Coast, are the famous "Black Jews." They speak Malayalam, an important Dravidian language spoken by the original inhabitants of India prior to the Indo-European invasions. Also in Cochin is a different community which maintains separate synagogues, forbids intermarriage with and holds itself superior to the Black Jews. These are the *Pardesi*, who are much lighter in color.

Finally, the Jews calling themselves *Baghdadi* are found in Calcutta, Bombay and other places in India. As their name indicates, they are descendants of Jews from what is today Iraq, and speak Arabic among themselves.

Burma has a small Jewish community, almost entirely of Indian origin, in which both Baghdadi and Bene Israel Jews are represented.

There have been, in the past, doubts about accepting both the Bene Israel and the Black Jews as full members of the Jewish people and thus eligible to marry by Jewish law. These doubts were laid to rest by the Chacham Moses Gaster, Chief Sephardic Rabbi of England, and by the even more eminent Sephardic Rabbi, Benzion Uziel. They both made formal declarations to the effect that the Bene Israel are to be considered full Jews. This was done to settle a dispute between the Baghdadi and the Bene Israel Jews in Burma. In more recent years, following their emigration to Israel, the Ashkenazi and Sephardi Chief Rabbinates have reached the same conclusion about both the Bene Israel and the Black Jews.

In China there have been Jews for many centuries who are indistinguishable from the rest of the population, either in appearance or in language. Their center was the city of Kai Feng Fu, capital of the province of Honan. Today a mere handful (if that) of survivors of the community still live there, but it appears that Chinese Jews continue to be found in such cities as Shanghai and Hong Kong where they are distinguished by their double family names (instead of the one-syllable clan or family name used by most Chinese). From what historians have been able to determine, the community of Kai Feng Fu is well over one thousand years old and in all probability of distant Persian or Mesopotamian origin.

As a result of the Russian revolution and the two world wars, a large number of Ashkenazic and Sephardic (mostly Arabic-speaking) Jews settled in Harbin, Manchuria, Shanghai and Hong Kong. These Yiddish, Russian and Arabic-speaking Jews are known among themselves collectively as *Yotzei Sin* ("those who have gone out of China") and are now scattered all over the world, with sizable colonies in Hong Kong, Tokyo and San Francisco.

Finally, there are among the European Jews two exceptions to the rule that they are all either Ashkenazic or Sephardic. These are the Tatar-speaking *Krimchaks* of the Crimea (not to be confused with the Karaim, chapter 3) and the Caucasian Jews of Georgia and other countries in the Caucasus. Both these groups are totally Jewish, but neither can be called either Ashkenazic or Sephardic.

The Krimchaks were almost entirely wiped out by the Germans in the Second World War, but a few families survive in the Crimea and in Israel. The Caucasian Jews emigrated in considerable numbers to Israel, having been permitted to leave by the U.S.S.R. In their native countries most of them live in patriarchal, clan-like villages and, until quite recently, were polygamous. These "Mountain Jews" speak *Tat*, a dialect of Persian with many Hebrew, Turkish and Caucasian words. The city-dwelling Jews of Tiflis and other cities in Georgia speak Georgian, one of the many Caucasian languages.

WHAT TYPES OF JEWS LIVE IN THE AMERICAS?

Most of the Jews in North America are Ashkenazim, although there are important Sephardic colonies in New York, Atlanta, Seattle, Indianapolis, and Chicago, and in several towns on Long Island and in California. Scattered Sephardic families are also to be found all over the United States as well as Canada, most of whom are of Turkish, Greek or Serbian extraction with Ladino as their native tongue. There is also a large Arabic-speaking community, mostly of Syrian origin, centered in the Bensonhurst section of Brooklyn, as well as other Arabic-speaking congregations in Chicago and New Jersey.

In Latin America too, most of the Jews are Ashkenazim, but the proportion of Sephardim is much higher. South of the border, however, the Sephardim are predominantly of Moroccan, Algerian and Tunisian origin although there are a good many Ladino and Arabic-speaking congregations.

3

Offshoots of the Jews

THERE are a few communities who are, or were, considered Jews because they are Jewish in origin, and, in some cases, still think of themselves as Jews, although they have cut themselves off from the main body of the Jewish people. In essence this means that Jews may not marry them, eat at their tables (because their food is not kosher), or, in the case of the now-extinct Frankists, have anything at all to do with them. These groups are as follows.

THE KARAIM

The *Karaim*, also called *Caraites*, broke away from the main body of Israel in the 8th century C.E. They accept only the Bible and reject the Oral Law (chapter 6), which is the basis of actual working law for Jews in general. They use Hebrew in their religious services and even in their business and personal correspondence. The main groups were located in Cairo where there were some 3,000 Karaim, most of whom have emigrated to Israel—and the Soviet Union, where there are several thousand in the

Crimea and in colonies in Lithuania (Vilna), Poland (Lutzk and Halisz) and Russia. There is also a small but important community in Istanbul and there was a colony in Hit, Iraq, but almost all have gone to Israel. The Karaim who live in Europe all speak a dialect of Tatar among themselves and are supposed by many to be descendants of the Khazars, a Turco-Tataric kingdom which converted to Judaism around 800 C.E. The State of Israel recognizes the Karaim as Jews for immigration purposes and there are several Karaite settlements there. Marriage to Jews is forbidden by rabbinic decision because their divorces are considered not valid, but exceptions have been and continue to be made.

THE SAMARITANS

This ancient group, called *Shomronim* in Hebrew, are mostly resident in Holon, Israel, and in Shechem (Nablus) in what was the West Bank territory of Jordan. They practice a biblical form of Judaism, the most notable feature of which is their recognition of Mount Gerizim instead of Jerusalem as the center for worship. They celebrate the Passover on Mount Gerizim in a colorful, night-long ceremony with the sacrifice, cooking and eating of lambs and the singing of special services. They recognize only the Torah, that is to say, the first five books of the Bible, and have an oral tradition of their own which differs from that of both the Jews and the Karaim. They are also recognized as Jews by the State of Israel, and marriage to them is also forbidden by Jewish law.

THE DOENMEH OR SABBATEANS

In the 17th century C.E., a false messiah arose and preached in Turkey, and within a relatively short time immense numbers of Jews became his followers and believed him to be the Messiah (chapter 41). His name was Sabbatai (Shabtai) Zvi and it has been said that at the height of his influence, over half the Jews in Europe acknowledged him as Messiah. Eventually he became a convert to Islam and immediately all but a handful of his followers rejected him. The small group that stuck by him also converted to Islam but maintained themselves, at least in their own estimation, as secret Jews, marrying only among themselves and keeping their faith in Sabbatai Zvi. They were to be found in Salonika and other cities in Greece but are now existent only in Turkey, where they live outwardly as Moslems but secretly as "Jews" with many odd and divergent practices, including the use of Ladino as a sacred language alongside Hebrew. Occasionally a Doenmeh will declare his intention to return to the Jewish people, but these postulants have not been accepted since there is a serious question as to their legitimacy. It is known that during one annual ceremony of theirs there is, or was, an exchange of wives. (For an explanation of legitimacy see chapter 11.)

THE FRANKISTS

One of the followers of Sabbatai Zvi was a man named Jacob Frank who became the leader of those few Jews who remained Sabbateans in Eastern Europe. Eventually he converted to Roman Catholicism in Poland and some of his followers (not all, as is commonly thought) converted with him. For a time they maintained themselves as secret "Jews," to their way of thinking, and had customs which went even further than the wife-exchanging of the Doenmeh. Hidden groups of them probably existed until the end of the last century, but it can be safely assumed that there are no more Frankists left alive. They eventually abandoned their hidden lives and disappeared into the Catholic population of Poland. There are today many Poles of excellent family who have Frankists among their ancestors.

THE PORTUGUESE MARRANOS

In recent years it was discovered that there are sizeable groups of people, ostensibly Catholic, living in several mountain villages in northern Portugal, who are descended from Jewish converts-by-force. These people have apparently never stopped considering themselves Jews, marry only among themselves and are sworn to assist each other. They know one or two words of Hebrew and have made it clear, once they were convinced there was no danger in doing so, that their rejection of Christianity is complete and has always been so. Missionaries have been sent them in an effort to bring them back to formal Judaism, possibly through emigration to Israel.

THE CHUETAS

This is a group of people, Roman Catholic in religion, who live on the Spanish island of Majorca. They are descendants of converted Jews, live in special quarters of Majorcan towns, marry only among themselves and are generally despised by their Christian neighbors. No one has ever been able to discover any trace of loyalty to Judaism among them, although such claims have been made. Apparently they are faithful Roman Catholics.

4

The Languages
of the Jews

THE one possession a man acquires after his birth which no one can take away from him is his language. The Jews have, over the centuries, sired or acquired various languages and put their stamp on them to the extent that they can be considered Jewish languages.

Of course, in most of the countries in which they live, the Jews speak the language of the land, although this has not always been so. In reality, more Jews speak English than any other language, but English cannot be considered a Jewish language; not only is it spoken by more non-Jews than Jews, but there is not even a Judeo-English dialect, as there is a Judeo-Persian or a Judeo-German dialect. There are, however, languages which, even though spoken by other people to some extent, have become intimately identified with the Jews. The most important of these languages—either totally Jewish or shared with non-Jews—are Hebrew, Aramaic, Yiddish and Ladino. There are others, but let us look briefly at these first.

HEBREW

Hebrew is a Semitic language, which means that it belongs to a large family of languages, all related to each other and all of which form most of their words on a stem consisting of three consonants. Other languages in the same family are Arabic, Aramaic, Amharic (the official language of Ethiopia), Tigré and Tigrinya, as well as other dialects spoken in Somaliland and other parts of Ethiopia, and the extinct languages, Canaanite and Phoenician as well as others of less importance, both living and dead.

Hebrew is, of course, the language in which the Bible is written. It is the language of prayer in almost all synagogues the world over, and the language in which the immense majority of books on Jewish law are written. It has been the preferred language for religious writing of all sorts with the Jews since biblical times because it is the one language which learned Jews everywhere know. It is the official language of the State of Israel and the common household speech of most Israelis.

Scholars distinguish four main types of Hebrew:

- Biblical Hebrew (the oldest form).
- Mishnaic Hebrew, the language in which the Mishna and parts of the Midrash (chapter 25) were written. (This form was strongly influenced by Aramaic.)
- Medieval or Rabbinical Hebrew, the language used by the commentators and respondents during the entire Middle Ages and the language in which most rabbis still write their books and responsa.
- Modern Hebrew, as it is spoken in Eretz Israel. (One would expect it to be closest to Medieval Hebrew but it is closest to Biblical Hebrew.)

Written and Printed Hebrew

Several forms of script are used for writing Hebrew by hand, among them the "soletreo" or Sephardic script at one time used throughout the Near East, but the Ashkenazi script has been adopted officially in Israel and is taught in all schools there and in the Americas.

Hebrew is printed in one of two alphabets, which are fairly similar to each other. These are "block letter," in which most prayerbooks, Bibles, etc., are printed, and *Rashi*, or "Rabbinical" letters, in which the commentaries of Rashi to the Bible and Talmud are printed, as well as much other rabbinical writing, minor observations and instructions in the prayerbook, etc. Traditionally, Yiddish is always printed in block letter and Ladino in Rashi.

Spoken Hebrew

Once a Jew leaves his home grounds, one of the first things he notices is the different way Ashkenazim and Sephardim pronounce Hebrew in the synagogue services. The Sephardic pronunciation has several regional variations, all of them quite close to each other, one being the pronunciation used in daily speech in Eretz Israel. Among the Ashkenazim, the main variations are the Polish-Ukrainian, the German, the Lithuanian-White Russian and the Russian forms. This last is the one that used to be commonly taught in *cheders* and Hebrew schools in the United States; today the tendency is to teach the Israeli Sephardic pronunciation. The main differences lie in the way several of the vowel sounds are pronounced as well as one of the consonants, the letter tav, which can be pronounced like "s" or "t" (depending on the word) by the Ashkenazim, but is always pronounced like a "t" by Sephardic Hebrew-speakers.

The accent is also quite different: Ashkenazi Hebrew is accented usually on the penultimate syllable, whereas Sephardi Hebrew is accented on the last syllable. All of these differences add up to the point that a Polish Jew, when praying at a Moroccan synagogue, for example, will have extreme difficulty in following the service, and the reverse, a Moroccan in a Polish *shul*, will be in even worse shape.

ARAMAIC

This is a Semitic language, closely related to Hebrew, and spoken in two main dialects, which became the daily speech of both the Jews and most of their neighbors in Asia Minor during the Babylonian exiles. It survives to this day as the spoken language of a few Christian villages on the Syrian-Lebanese border. In another dialect, which some linguists insist is not Aramaic but the closely related Syriac, it is the speech of several thousand people in Iran, Turkey and Iraq. Among these modern Aramaic-speakers are to be found a number of what are often referred to as "Kurdish Jews," that is to say, Jews from Kurdistan.

Aramaic is thought of, by the Jews at least, as a Jewish language, because three extremely important works were written in it (as well as many less important writings, prayers and hymns). These are the *Targum Onkelos*, an Aramaic translation of the Pentateuch which is found in many printed editions of the Torah; the *Gemara*, which is the completion of the *Mishna* and the basis of the Oral Law (chapter 6) and the *Zohar*, the most important work of the *Kabbala*, the Jewish mystic tradition. Aramaic is often called *Lashon Targum* among Jews and is always printed in Hebrew letters.

YIDDISH

Yiddish is, or was, the common language of Ashkenazi Jews, with the exception of those who spoke German, French or Hungarian. It is a Germanic language, derived historically from the Franconian dialect of 14th century German, and today contains about twenty percent Hebrew and ten percent Slavic and other words in its vocabulary. It is the language the Jews took with them when they left Germany for Poland in the 14th century and was spoken by some ten million people, before the Germans murdered six million of them between the years 1939 and 1945. It is always printed in block letter Hebrew type and possesses a rich and varied literature and folklore.

There are several dialects of Yiddish but their differences lie mainly in pronunciation. In the United States Yiddish is heard far less than formerly, but is still widely spoken in such Orthodox neighborhoods as Williamsburg, Crown Heights and Borough Park in Brooklyn, and, indeed, wherever there are Chasidim. Yiddish is still more or less the official language of the wholesale diamond and fur businesses as well as the language of instruction in most Ashkenazic yeshivas, even in Israel.

The last great stronghold of the Yiddish language is Latin America, where it continues to be a living tongue in which most community affairs and functions are carried out.

LADINO

Ladino or *Judezmo* is the language of the Sephardim of Greece, Turkey, Serbia and Bulgaria, and, in the sub-dialect called *Jaquetía*, of those in parts of North Africa. It is basically a dialect of 15th century Castilian Spanish which has undergone considerable changes in the 500 years since the Jews left Spain. The vocabulary is still mostly Spanish, but many Hebrew and not a few Arabic, Turkish and French words have entered it. With the wartime annihilation of the Serbian and Greek communities, it survives mostly in Turkey, Israel and the United States. In Latin America it tends to disappear quickly since its speakers adapt themselves to modern Spanish and drop the older Judezmo. Ladino is usually printed in Rashi letters, although the Turkish government forbids the use of any but the Latin alphabet for serial publications and Ladino newspapers there are printed in Latin letters, as is at least one newspaper in Israel read by Turkish Jews.

JEWISH DIALECTS

In addition to the four main languages described above, there exist several dialects which are basically non-Jewish languages, which the Jews have, over the centuries, colored with Hebrew words and phrases and written and printed in the Hebrew alphabet. Among others are Judeo-Persian, spoken in Bokhara; Judeo-Tat in the Caucasus, among the Mountain Jews; Judeo-Arabic, at one time important in North Africa; Judeo-Italian, now almost extinct but at one time spoken in Leghorn (Livorno), Italy; Judeo-German, formerly spoken in the Rhineland and still to be heard among Orthodox German Jews in the United States and

Latin America, and Judeo-Tatar, spoken by the Krimchaks of the Crimean Peninsula.

In addition, there are certain areas where the Jews speak a different language than the surrounding populace. This is, or was, the case in most of Slovakia, Sub-Carpathia, Transylvania and parts of Yugoslavia, where the non-Jewish populations speak Ruthenian, Slovakian or another Slavic language, and the Jews speak Hungarian. In the large city of Czernowitz (Cernauti), Romania, the Gentiles speak either Romanian or a dialect of Ruthenian and the Jews speak a dialect of German.

PART
II

The Jewish
Religion

Introduction

Up till now, we have said little about the Jews that could not conceivably have been duplicated in one form or another by any people possessed of the inner strength to hang onto their identity over two thousand years of exile from their spiritual and physical homeland.

The Jews, however, are a unique people, unlike any other that has ever existed. They have a single characteristic which must be understood, because unless it is, there can be no understanding of the customs, laws, signs and observances that set the Jews apart from their neighbors. In truth, there is not a single distinctively Jewish aspect of life which does not derive its meaning from this one, central fact: *The Jews are the chosen people of God.*

5

One God and the Chosen People

WHAT DO WE MEAN BY "GOD" AND BY "THE CHOSEN PEOPLE"?

JEWISH religion, which cannot be separated from Jewish life as a whole, is based on two fundamental beliefs. Once these are grasped, all aspects of Jewish belief and religious practice reveal their meaning and the reason for their existence. If they are not understood, the religion of the Jews cannot be understood. The two pillars upon which the entire edifice of Judaism rests are:

The unity of God.
The election of Israel.

Neither of these concepts is difficult to grasp, but in spite of this they are often misunderstood. They must be clearly explained, because acceptance of them is by no means an individual foible; it is, rather, both the foundation upon which Judaism stands and the cement that holds it together.

ONE GOD

When the Jews say, "Hear, O Israel, the Lord our God, the Lord is One," it is to the word "One" that particular attention must be paid. In the Jewish concept, the "One" that is God is not like any other "one" in existence. This is because any other "one" can be divided into fractions: halves, quarters or, to use a more familiar example, thirds, while the One that is God is totally indivisible. It cannot be further reduced. Thus God is One in two senses: He is alone—there is none other beside Him—and He is *one*, complete and unique, a *one* that shares the characteristics of the largest unit possible in that it has no limit, and the smallest, in that it cannot be further reduced.

This concept of the unique and indivisible God is also held by the Moslems and the Christian Unitarians, both of whom got it from the Jews.

THE CHOSEN PEOPLE

The earth knows many nations and has known many more; common to them all is mortality. To the Jews, who alone among them all have survived, they are known as the *umot ha-olam*, the peoples of the world. As for the Jews, they too are of the world, but, unlike the others, are of more than the world: They are the people God chose to be His own.

It is sometimes stated by those who know no better that Israel's concept of itself as a chosen people means the Jews believe that only they are righteous, only their path the true one and they only are destined for a share in whatever world may exist after death on this earth. The phrase found in the Talmud, "*Tzadikei umot ha-olam*" (The righteous of the peoples of the world) shows how alien to Jewish thought this is.

The chosenness of Israel does not consist of a hereditary place in Heaven; it consists in this: *that God chose Israel to be the people that would receive His Law, study and understand His Law and obey the commandments contained in His Law.*

And the choosing was mutual. Israel Zangwill said, "A chosen people is really a choosing people. Not idly does the Talmudical legend assert that the Law was offered first to all other nations and only Israel accepted the yoke." As much as the Lord chose Israel, Israel chose the Lord.

What does all this mean in terms of actual practice and belief? First we must examine the nature of the way Israel was chosen and how Israel accepted her election.

The Bible, our basic source of knowledge concerning the origins of the Jewish people, tells us that the first to be chosen was Abraham who, in consequence, is always referred to as *Avram Avinu*, Abraham, our Father. Abraham was told by God, "Get thee out of thy land, from thy kinfolk and from thy father's house to the land which I shall show thee." And Abraham, whose own father was a worshiper (and according to Jewish tradition also a manufacturer) of idols, rejected his father's idol worship, recognized the truth of the oneness of God, accepted His command and set the pattern for Jewish life in all the generations succeeding him, up to and including the generation that reads this book.

Further on in the Bible, God spoke even more specifically when He told Moses: ". . . and I will take you unto me for a people" (Exod. 6:7), and again in Lev. 20:26, "You shall be holy unto Me for I the Lord am holy and have set you apart from the peoples of the world to be Mine."

Thus the descendants of Abraham, the Jews, were actually chosen by God to worship Him and to follow His commands, even before the entire law was given them. This was done generations later when the Law, called by Jews the Torah, was given to Abraham's descendants in the desert of Sinai on the way to the land which God had promised their forefather. It was at this time that the *second choosing* took place. This was the true test: when God had given Moses the Torah and Moses told the Jewish people what they had been given, the people all said as one: "All that the Lord has said, we will do and obey."

The import of these words we will examine later, but their plain sense is immediately apparent. Israel had been offered the Torah and had responded by willingly "taking the yoke of the Torah" on their shoulders, in full cognizance of what they were doing. They too had a choice to make and they chose God and the path God had shown them, just as God had chosen them to follow His path.

The means by which the Torah they accepted was given them is so intimately bound to Israel's choosing by God and their choice of God's commandments that it is totally inextricable: the Torah was *revealed* by God to Moses.

REVELATION

Judaism is a *revealed* religion. This means that according to Jewish belief, the Torah, containing the laws and commandments by which the Jewish people live, was not the product of the mind of a leader nor that of the holy men of a tribe. It was not even the product of the mind of a prophet under direct divine inspiration. Quite the contrary; the Torah was given directly by God to Moses who in turn handed it down to the Jewish people without changing a word or letter of what God had revealed to him. The Torah is indeed referred to in both English and Hebrew as Mosaic law, but never lost sight of is the fact that Moses as a lawgiver simply gave that which in turn had been given him. The Torah was given the Jewish people by Moses, but it is not *of* Moses; it is of God.

Once these two basic points are understood; that there is only one, indivisible God and that He chose Israel to worship Him and to obey the commandments contained in His Torah, there is little in Judaism that is hard to understand. Now we must examine more closely what the Torah is.

6

What Is the Torah?

To start with, there are two Torahs, or more accurately, two parts of the Torah. The first is the *Written Torah*, called in Hebrew the *Torah Shebiktav* or *Mikra*. It consists of the first five books of the Bible and is also called the Pentateuch, a Greek word meaning "five books," or the *Chumash*, which has the approximate meaning of five-fold. When we say Torah in this book, it is the Pentateuch we are talking about, if no further classification is given.

In the Torah there are 613 commandments or *mitzvot*. The first of these commandments is found in verse 28 of the first chapter of Genesis, "Be fruitful, multiply and replenish the earth." It tells us that it is man's duty to marry and beget children. The 613th *mitzva* is in the 19th verse of the 31st chapter of Deuteronomy, almost at the end of the Torah: "Now, therefore, write ye for you this song . . ." which informs us that it is the duty of every Jew to own a *Sefer Torah*, or Torah scroll, a commandment that can be observed by belonging to a congregation that possesses such a scroll; that is to say, any Jewish congregation.

The second part of the Torah is the *Oral Torah*, called in Hebrew the *Torah Sheb'al peh*. It consists, in the words of a famous modern authority, Rabbi Zvi Hirsch Chayes, of the "expositions and interpretations which were communicated to Moses orally as a supplement to the [Written Torah]." It is commonly referred to in English as the *Talmud*.

This Oral Torah, which is in no sense inferior in value or authority to the Written Torah, was handed down faithfully from one generation to the next and was not put into writing until after the Bar Kochba rebellion in 135 C.E., when it was edited by Rabbi Yehuda Ha-Nasi and his colleagues. The editing was completed about 219 C.E. and the Oral Law which was then compiled in writing is called the *Mishna*. This Mishna, together with its completion, the *Gemara* (see below), form what is commonly called the Talmud, although to be quite accurate, that term refers to the Gemara alone. The Talmud, as we will call it, was completed in the 5th century C.E. and remains the basic source of all legal decisions affecting a Jew's existence.

Here we should define more closely Mishna and Gemara. The Mishna contains the Oral Law as defined by Rabbi Chayes above. It is written in Hebrew which was strongly influenced by Aramaic. The word *Mishna* itself has the general meaning of "second." The Gemara, which means "completion," is an enormous compendium of the discussions of the rabbinical judges regarding the laws set forth in the Mishna and the decisions which were reached concerning them. Some were unanimous, but many were "split decisions." These actual legal sentences and renderings, both in the Mishna and the Gemara, are the basis of the Jewish law and its application to daily problems. The Gemara is written in Aramaic, the language the rabbis spoke at that time.

In a sense, the Written Torah can be compared to the Constitution of the United States. It is the skeleton of the body of Jewish law just as the Constitution is the skeleton of the body of American civil law. And, just as the huge number of decisions of the United States courts—case law—puts flesh on the skeleton of the Constitution, so does the Talmud put flesh on the bones of the Written Torah. It is the Oral Torah, as found in the Mishna and the decisions of the rabbis—on the exact application of the laws—both in the Mishna and its completion, the Gemara, that gives us the Jewish law as it is observed today.

For example, the Written Torah contains a prohibition against cooking a kid in its mother's milk. The Oral Torah teaches us that this extends to all meat and all milk; no meat may be cooked in milk. The discussions and subsequent decisions of the rabbis have set up a series of laws designed to protect this statute which is considered especially important since it appears not once but three times in the Written Torah. In the end, we are forbidden even to use for meat, plates which have been used for milk and vice-versa.

Many similar examples can be found in the law of the United States. The Constitution gives the Federal Government the right to regulate interstate commerce. Congress passed a law making it a Federal offense to transport a woman across a state line for immoral purposes since this was, by extension, a part of their right to control interstate commerce, even though such an act might have no commercial intent. This law, the Mann Act, was later interpreted to apply to any person who sent a woman in one state a train ticket to travel to another state for "immoral purposes" or even the money to purchase such a ticket.

To continue our comparison, what is legal in one state (the sale of liquor for instance) may be illegal in an adjoining state. The same is true of certain Jewish laws which are observed by one Jewish community but either not observed or observed in a different form by other Jewish communities. One such law is the regulation concerning how long after eating meat, milk products may be eaten. The Eastern European Jews wait six hours, whereas the German Jews, equally observant, wait only three. Another such law is the one prohibiting Ashkenazim from eating peas, beans, rice and certain other grains on Passover. This law does not apply to many Sephardim, who may quite legally eat all of them.

The explanation lies in the fact that not the law itself, but the interpretation of certain details of the law has taken different directions in different parts of the world due to the wide variety of conditions in which Jews live, as well as the gradual develop-

ment of local tradition and the emergence of prominent legal figures—rabbis—who have grown up in these traditions.

This is a process which has been at work in post-Biblical Jewish law since its beginnings: different authorities will hand down
differing decisions on the same subject. For example, the entire
Oral Torah contains only one short chapter of the Mishna which
records no differences of opinion among the Sages.

Modern questions as well have been the subject of totally
opposing decisions by rabbinical authorities of equal eminence.
On the question of whether it is permitted to turn on electric
lights on a Holiday that does not fall on Shabbat, the author of
one of the most widely used super-codes to the Shulchan Aruch
(chapter 25) has said that it is, while an equally learned and
respected rabbi forbids it. Both are Ashkenazim and, while many
observant Jews "hold with" him who forbids, others equally
observant "hold with" him who permits.

Quite obviously, Jewish law is not stagnant; decisions are made
constantly, in our own times, which affect the way Jewish law is
applied to daily life in changing conditions. Nevertheless, the
basic Law as it is set forth in the Written and Oral Torahs is not
subject to change because it was not created in response to tem-
poral conditions. It was not *created* at all, in any way we can
understand, but was revealed directly by God to Moses for His
chosen people to observe.

What should always be kept in mind is that the Jewish law is a
corpus juris the same as any other code of justice or legal system.
It contains enactments based on the fundamental revealed law of
the people, elaborated and refined by the decisions of courts and
judges, many of them in our own generation. Nothing could be
more false than to believe that Judaism, by any definition, gives
to the individual the right to act according to his own whim or
conscience in matters where there is a law governing his actions.
Certain Jews may not choose to observe the laws, but only the
ignorant among them will deny that the laws exist.

And they do exist. You can find them by looking into any one
of several books or by asking a knowledgeable Jew. More than
this, they are not simply a series of platitudes, telling us Jews to
be just to our fellow men, but a detailed schedule of laws telling

us how that justice is to be put into effect, not only toward our fellow men, but to God, who chose us to be His own special people. The fact is that you can't be a good Jew without being a good human being, but you can be a good human being without being a good Jew. In the Jewish view, one is as important as the other.

The Torah itself makes this clear. In Lev. 19:18 we read, "Thou shalt love thy neighbor as thyself." In the very next verse we are told, "Thou shalt not sow thy field with two kinds of seed." The first of these commandments is fundamental to human morality and applies to all peoples at all times. The second commandment applies only to Jews, is obligatory only in the Holy Land and has no reason of a moral or other nature that it is possible to determine. Is it reasonable to suppose that these two verses appear side-by-side purely through chance? On the contrary, the commentators are quick to point out that their propinquity is designed to show that while being a good human being is a requisite of being a good Jew, there are many commandments which it is necessary to observe in order to be a good Jew which have no connection at all with being a "good human being."

Of course there are always people who try to justify their actions. Jews have them too. They are the ones who say, "It isn't necessary to pay attention to the Torah. What counts is to have a good Jewish heart. If you have a good Jewish heart and act accordingly, that's all that's needed." This is known as "Cardiac Judaism." It is something like saying that as long as you are a patriotic American and salute the flag every day, you don't have to pay taxes or serve in the armed forces if you are drafted.

Being a United States citizen is a privilege few people ever wish to give up. Even when living overseas, away from the United States, every American citizen is required to file an income tax return. An American company operating overseas is required to abide by the anti-trust laws, even if the country in which it operates does not have such laws. All of this is taken for granted. Being a Jew is also a great privilege and there are certain obligations attached to that privilege which we are not free to reject, any more than the American citizen is free to refuse to pay income tax.

The fact is, as we all know, that observance of Jewish law is a matter of choice, since there is no physical compulsion. Just as a citizen may leave his country or take other measures to avoid paying his taxes, so may a Jew choose to avoid the responsibilities attached to being one of God's chosen people.

It is true that there are many laws which appear to our understanding to have no practical value and no discernible reason. The traditional Jewish view is that there is no reason given for any of the commandments, but that many of them are such that their reason is obvious to any intelligent person. The others, whose reason is less apparent, are not the less valid because of this. In reality, all Jewish laws can be understood if we remind ourselves of the one basic condition of being Jewish: that the Jews are the chosen people of God and that it is precisely to obey His commandments—all of them—that God chose them and they, in turn, chose Him.

Once we understand the two bases of Judaism, it is easy to see why Judaism has been called a " 'People' centered" culture. Without the Jews' concept of ourselves as a chosen people, few of our laws make sense. With it, all are clear.

Perhaps we should stop a moment and note that what can only be called aberrations do exist within the Jewish people; Jews are not exempt from the self-destructive forces that seem to operate within all cultures to some degree. One movement in particular, the so-called "Reconstructionists," seem to be attempting a definition of Judaism without revelation and, finally, without God, based only on an undefined peoplehood of Israel. As might be expected, the position of the founder of the movement is clearly defined in regard to the election of Israel. He states: "We advocate the elimination from our liturgy of all references to the doctrine of Israel as a chosen people."

Ordinarily the discussion of such bizarre manifestations would be outside the scope of this book, whose purpose is to explore what being Jewish means to normal Jews, but I bring this up to point out that, in spite of their denial of everything basic to Judaism, it should not for a moment be thought that these people are no longer Jews. The reason is clear and has already been pointed out: Judaism is more than a religion. The Jews are a *people*. And the Reconstructionists have made it clear that they have not cut themselves off (as the Karaim did). If they have not cut themselves off, we cannot cut them off.

What is really significant here, to be exact, is that they have not adopted another religion in place of Judaism or, as the early Christians did, created another religion. As for those few people who, having accepted or even solicited baptism, continue to maintain that they are Jews, and, in that guise, attempt to win over faithful Jews to their religion, we should not hesitate to classify them not only as no longer Jews but as active enemies of Israel, deserving of our unceasing opposition and scorn.

Having made this brief examination of the religious principles underlying Judaism, we can now return to the actual form they take in our present-day world. After having discussed, in condensed form, the physical and cultural variations within the Jewish people, we can now begin consideration of how the commandments of the Torah look as "Jewish law and custom."

PART
III

The
Jewish Life
Cycle

7

Birth and Names

BIRTH

THERE are no special laws among the Jews concerning birth itself except those stating that a woman must, after giving birth, immerse herself in the mikva to cleanse herself, since the blood accompanying birth has made her ritually unclean, just as does menstrual blood. The laws governing this will be found in chapter 14.

Any woman in labor or childbirth, or for (at least) seven days thereafter, is considered dangerously ill and it is permitted to violate the Sabbath or other holidays for her sake. This is discussed more fully under *illness*, in chapter 15. During pregnancy a woman is also considered dangerously ill in the sense that her "cravings" for certain types of food must be catered to by her husband or family, even if this means violating the dietary laws. Pregnant women are also exempt from fasting if they experience discomfort.

Among the Orthodox, it is customary to recite psalms for a

woman in childbirth, particularly if delivery is difficult. This is often done by going to a synagogue or yeshiva, where the Torah is studied at all hours, and requesting those present to recite the proper psalms for the benefit of the woman. Every tradition has its own ideas about which of the psalms are most appropriate, but in reality all are considered good.

As noted earlier, only a child born of a Jewish mother is Jewish by birth.

NAMES

A girl is given a name in the synagogue during the public reading of the Torah, usually on the Sabbath following her birth. Her father is called to the Torah (chapter 28) and after his portion is read, a special prayer is recited by the reader for his wife and for the daughter she has borne. At this point the phrase, "and let her name be called in Israel" is said, followed by the name her parents have decided to give her. It is customary for the father to give a *kiddush* after the morning service on this occasion.

A boy is given a name at the time of his circumcision (chapter 8).

Customs concerning the name given a child vary from community to community, but in all places it is considered necessary to give a child a "Jewish name," by which he or she will be known for purposes of Jewish law. This includes being called to the Torah, marriage contracts, divorce documents, etc. The Jewish name may or may not be the one used in daily life. In the United States and many other countries, it is common to find that the name by which a man is called to the Torah is not the name which appears on his birth certificate or by which he is ordinarily known.

For example, a man named Morris in the United States or Mauricio in Latin America, will probably be called to the Torah by the Hebrew name of Moshe or Moishe (Moses) and may well be called that by friends and members of his family.

Even in the case that the Hebrew and English names are the same, or the standard equivalent of the Hebrew name is used in English, a Jewish nickname may be commonly employed. Thus a man named Shmuel in Hebrew would quite properly be called Samuel in English but could perfectly well be called "Shmeelik" (a Slavic diminutive) by his friends. And in many cases he may have a Hebrew name in the synagogue, an English name on his birth certificate but be called by quite another name, going back to his national origin. Some years ago I knew a young man whose Hebrew name was Sholem and his English name Lester. His contemporaries, however, called him Laszlo which was his Hungarian name and the one we first knew him by when he arrived as an immigrant. In another country I knew a young woman named Miriam in Hebrew, whose English name was Mary. Her family and friends called her Merima, which is the equivalent of Miriam in Arabic.

The fact is that the "Hebrew" name given a child is often not really Hebrew at all, but a name which has been traditionally accepted as a Jewish name, suitable for a Jew to be known by. Thus, while a child could not be called Robert, for example, because Robert is not considered a Jewish name, he could easily have the name Feivish, which is actually derived from the name of a Greek god, Phoebus!

What is important is that the name be accepted as Jewish in the community in which one lives. Quite naturally, Ashkenazim and Sephardim have different traditions in this regard. The Sephardim use many genuinely Hebrew names which Ashkenazim as a matter of custom do not use. Such names as Nissim and Shemtob for men, and Rachman and Mazal for women, are simply not found among Ashkenazim, any more than Simcha for men and Chaya for women are found among Sephardim, although all these names are Hebrew.

In Eretz Israel many names are appearing which are Hebrew words that have never been used as names in the past or which, if used, had fallen into disuse. The name Ilana for women is common in Israel and is derived from a Hebrew word meaning tree. Previous to its appearance there it was considered not Hebrew but Slavic or Hungarian. Subsequent to its adoption there has appeared a male equivalent, Ilan.

Of course favorite names have a way of surviving all kinds of language changes. The woman whose name in Cracow was Zlatte would probably have a granddaughter in Chicago named Goldie and she in turn will be likely to have a granddaughter in Tel Aviv named Zehavit. By the same token, Oro in Tangiers becomes Aurea in Caracas and Zahava in Ashdod. All have the same meaning: gold.

And of course there are Hebrew names belonging to idol worshipers (Terach), traitors (Datan) or demons (Lilith) which are not acceptable and could never be used. Other names such as Adam, Abel and Seth are possibly permissible, but almost never encountered because custom dictates that names appearing in the Bible before that of Noah are not used. Ishmael, one would suppose, would not be used by Jews, but I know a learned Sephardic rabbi with that name.

A list of commonly used "Jewish" names for men and women will be found in appendix I. As far as English or Spanish names go, it is felt that Jews should avoid those names which are identified with other religions, such as Christine, Christopher, René, Renée, Mary, María, Fatima, Mohamed, etc.

As for the actual form of the Jewish name, among both Ashkenazim and Sephardim, the Jewish name as it appears on a marriage contract or a divorce document consists of the man's name, followed by the word "ben"—meaning "son of"—plus his father's name, and the word Ha-Cohen or Ha-Levi, if he is a Cohen or a Levi. Following these names will come his family name, and, in the case of a divorce document, the name or names by which he is known commonly—his English name, for instance. This "civil" name is called the *kinui* in Hebrew.

Thus, a man named Maurice Greenberg, for example, whose father's name is Jack and who is a Cohen, will probably show up on a marriage contract as *Reb Moshe ben Reb Yaacov Ha-Cohen Mimishpachat Greenberg.* "Reb" is a title of respect, equivalent to the Spanish "Don" and *mimishpachat* means "of the family of." A woman's name follows the same rules, except that *bat* ("daughter of") is substituted for *ben* before her father's name.

Among the Ashkenazim, when a man is called to the Torah, only his name and his father's name are used. The Sephardim ordinarily use the first and family name omitting the father's name. A peculiar custom exists in this connection: if a man has changed his family name in America, he is called up to the Torah not by the new name, but by the family name as it was before he changed it. Thus a man named Jack Gorman, shall we say, would be called up as Yaacov Gormezano, if that was the original form of his last name in Turkey or Greece.

A convert to Judaism, or *ger*, takes a Hebrew name at the time of his conversion, and where his father's name would ordinarily go, uses *ben Avram*, son of Abraham, since all Jews are descendants of Abraham, including converts. Women converts usually take the name of Ruth, herself a convert, although this is not obligatory, and are also called *bat-Avram*, daughter of Abraham.

There is a custom which should be mentioned since it is still practiced. If a couple loses several children in early childhood, the next child born to them will often be named *Alter* if a boy or *Alte* (sometimes *Alterke*) if a girl. This name means "old one" in Yiddish and is given in the hope that the Angel of Death will not recognize the child nor be able to identify him without a name. In reality, the child has no name until he or she is grown up and ready to be married, at which time a name is given. This used to be the custom, but today it is obligatory in most countries to register a child at birth. This being the case, a name is given for legal purposes but kept a secret from everyone, including the child himself, until he is married. Until then he is known as Alter. Alter is, incidentally, an acceptable "Jewish" name for a child, but is usually combined with another name, the child being called Israel Alter or Chaim Alter—the two names most commonly used. The custom itself is of considerable antiquity and has been called superstitious.

Strangely enough, considering the strictness and formality of so much of Jewish law, the laws concerning names are remarkably few and free and easy. A man who wishes to add another name to the one he already has may do so by the simple process of having himself called up to the Torah in the synagogue on Shabbat by that name and having the *mi-sheberach* recited afterward. From that point on, the new name is his. The custom of adding a name in adult life during serious illness will be found under *illness* in chapter 15.

As to the choice of the name itself on the part of the parents, it is a common practice among Jews everywhere to name a child after one of its grandparents. The Ashkenazim, by a custom so strong many mistakenly believe it to be a law, will not name a child after a living person. Accordingly, if the grandparent is alive, the child will not have his or her name. The Sephardim have no such custom and are usually anxious to name a child after a living grandparent. In an Ashkenazi-Sephardi marriage this often creates a problem between the parents. What should be remembered is that there is no Jewish law against naming a child after a living relative. Although among Ashkenazim it is not proper to do so (because custom must be respected as well as law), in the case of an Ashkenazi-Sephardi marriage, if the Sephardic spouse wishes to name a child after one of his or her parents, there is no reason for opposing such an action. Theoretically, it is possible to name a child after its mother or father, but this is almost unheard of either among Ashkenazim or Sephardim, and is definitely not a Jewish custom. There are very few Jews walking around with "Junior" after their names.

It is the custom among many Jews, however, to name a posthumous child after its father. Among Ladino-speaking Jews, such a child had the additional name of Chilibon if a boy or Chilibona if a girl, but this custom is in decline today.

Concerning family names, attitudes differ. The Ashkenazim, with rare exceptions, did not ordinarily possess fixed family names, and did not use them until they were forced to for the first time in 1782 by the Austro-Hungarian Empire for the purpose of collecting taxes from them. At that time they took names usually from the Yiddish, German, Polish and Russian languages. In many cases these names reflect trades or occupations, such as Zimmerman (carpenter), Blecher (tinsmith), Melamed (Hebrew teacher). In others they were derived from the place of origin, Hollander, Litvak, Frank (usually meaning of Sephardic descent), etc. Often the father's name was used in the form of Isaacs (Isaac's) Samuels, Davids or Jacobs. These patronymics also took the form of names like Davidson, Davidow, Davidovitch, Davidescu, Davidowski and so forth. Occasionally, if the mother rather than the father was the more notable member of the family, the children would be known by her name: Pereles (Pearl's), Bayles (Bayla's), Chanelles (Hanna's), etc.

Other Jews took any name that seemed pleasing to them and that they were permitted to use, such as Mandelbaum (Almond-tree), Rosenberg (Rosehill), Blumenthal (Flowervale), and still others had names arbitrarily assigned them by antiSemitic Gentile officials. Many of these names were ludicrous—Ochsenschwantz (Oxtail), for example—while others were obscene. As a result, Ashkenazic Jews have no particular attachment to most of their family names and are quite willing to change them once they arrive in a new homeland, usually to a new form that is easier to pronounce and spell in their new language. This does not (or should not) apply to such names as Cohen, Katz, Levy or Segal, which are names indicating the priestly descent of the bearer.

The Sephardim, on the other hand, have in many cases had the same family names for many generations and take a certain pride in them. This is particularly true of English, American and Dutch Jews with names like Henriques, Cardozo, Pereira and the like. Ladino and Arabic-speaking Sephardim do not feel nearly so strongly and take simpler forms of their names when they emigrate. Thus Farhi becomes Farr, Gormezano becomes Gorman and, in Brasil, Zaituni becomes Oliveira (olive tree).

Finally, immigrants to Eretz Israel are encouraged to drop their "foreign" names and take Hebrew last names and a great many of them do so. Often they simply translate their "foreign" names into Hebrew and Stein becomes Tzur, Gold becomes Zahav, etc.

8

Circumcision

CIRCUMCISION, the initiation of the Jewish male into full membership in the Jewish people, is practiced in obedience to the second of the 613 commandments of the Torah: "This is My covenant which you shall keep, between Me and you and your seed after you: every male among you shall be circumcised" (Gen. 17:10).

The word "covenant" shows us immediately what the significance of circumcision is; it is our signature on the contract (covenant) that God made with us when He chose us as His people. Through circumcision, every Jewish male actually signs that contract with God with his own blood and the seal of his signing is evident in his flesh as a constant and non-erasable reminder.

The ceremony of circumcision, called *Brit Mila* or *Briss*, is celebrated on the eighth day after the boy's birth. Accordingly, it is always on the same day of the week (Tuesday, Wednesday, etc) that the boy was born. It is not permissible to postpone the briss for as much as one day, unless, of course, the child is ill and either the *mohel* (ritual circumciser) or the child's physician advises that the operation be put off until he is in better health.

On the eighth day, then, a boy is circumcised. It is required that a religious quorum or *minyan* of ten adult males be present if this is humanly possible. If not, the briss must proceed without a minyan. The operation itself is performed by the mohel, who may or may not be a rabbi, but must be an expert in the laws and techniques of circumcision and a practicing and observant Jew. If no such person is available, a Jewish physician can do the operation, and in the case that no Jewish physician is available, it is perfectly permissible for a non-Jewish physician to do it, with the father or some other Jew reciting the appropriate blessings. The important thing is that the boy be properly circumcised on the eighth day.

The ceremony is brief. The minyan is assembled, together with the father, the godfather (called in Hebrew the *sandek*) and the mohel. The child is usually with its mother in another room and it is not permitted for the mother to be present at the moment the circumcision is performed. The child is then brought, by a man designated by the father, into the room where the minyan are waiting. This man is called the *kvatter*, a Yiddish word. It is customary that the child be taken from his mother by the kvatter's wife, called the *kvatterin*, who hands him to her husband, whereupon he is taken into the room.

When the kvatter arrives with the child, all present rise, and, with the exception of the sandek, remain standing throughout the ceremony. The mohel says, in a loud voice, "Baruch Ha-Ba!" (Blessed be he who comes), takes the child from the kvatter and places him briefly on a chair put there for that purpose, called the "Chair of the Prophet Elijah" (Kiseh shel Eliyahu Ha-Navi), since it is said that Elijah, who will announce the arrival of the Messiah, is present at all Jewish circumcisions. Blessings are then recited by the mohel (or by another man if the circumcision is being performed by a physician who does not know the proper blessings). The mohel hands the child to his father who in turn hands him to the sandek. The sandek alone may remain seated since he holds the child in his lap during the entire ceremony. It is not uncommon these days for the child to be placed on a table for the actual operation, but this is not really proper; he should be held by the sandek. Of course if the operation is performed by a physician instead of a mohel, the doctor's wishes must be followed.

At this point the actual operation is performed, after the recitation of a blessing by the mohel. Immediately after the foreskin is cut off, the father recites a blessing, thanking God for having commanded us to "enter into the covenant of our father, Abraham." When the father's blessing has been said, all those present say in a loud voice, "K'shem shenichnass labrit, ken y'kaness latorah ul'chupah ul'maasim tovim." (Just as he has entered into the covenant, so may he enter into the [study of] Torah, marriage and [the performance of] good deeds. If the child's father is not present, the father's blessing is recited by the sandek.

After the circumcision itself, the mohel proceeds to uncover completely the head of the boy's penis, making sure that no adhesions are causing what is left of the foreskin to adhere to the glans. The penis is then bound with a bandage in such a way that the glans is completely exposed and if this is not done, the circumcision is not considered valid. This uncovering and binding is called p'riah.

The mohel then takes a cup of wine and recites a blessing during which the boy's name is proclaimed. It is customary that the name not be made known to anyone but the father and mother, who have chosen it, prior to this blessing. For this reason it is not uncommon that the father whispers the name to the mohel when that part of the blessing is reached, so that the mohel is the first to say it out loud.

After this blessing the mohel puts a little wine in the child's mouth (usually by dipping a piece of cotton in the wine and letting the baby suck it) and continues with the remaining blessings and the ceremony is over. The foreskin itself is placed in a box or vessel containing sand or earth. It is customary in most communities for the sandek to hand the child to his wife, who returns it to its mother.

There is one part of the ceremony which is not practiced commonly any more and this is the m'tzitza, or sucking of the blood from the wound left by the circumcision to speed healing. These days it is done by the mohel symbolically by means of a sterile glass tube or other means by which actual contact between the child and mohel's mouth is avoided, for hygienic reasons.

Greatest care must be taken not to circumcise a child who is ailing or weak since all commandments must be postponed if they involve danger to life; the Torah is to live by, not to die by. If a briss is postponed, however, it may not take place on a Sabbath or holiday.

If a woman has given birth to two sons who have died following circumcision, succeeding sons may not be circumcised in infancy, but must wait until grown up and in good health. If a woman loses a child because of circumcision and the same thing happens to one of her sisters, all succeeding sons born to her or to any of her sisters must wait until they are grown up to be circumcised.

The briss may be performed at any time between sunrise and sunset on the eighth day, although it is customary to have it in the morning or around noon. As to determining the day of the child's birth, the Jewish law states that the day begins at sunset, so a child born after sunset on Monday, for example, is considered to have been born on Tuesday and the briss would be held on Tuesday of the following week. If a child is born at twilight and it is not certain whether before or after sunset, the eight days are counted from the following day. In other words, care is taken that the child not be circumcised a day early although he may be circumcised a day late in case of doubt (but only in case of doubt).

In places such as Alaska, Northern Sweden, etc., where there is no real division of the day by sunset, Jews use the equivalent hour in a designated place to the south. Jews in Alaska use Seattle. In other words, when the sun sets in Seattle, Jews in Alaska consider the day to have begun. This is discussed more fully in chapter 23.

A briss may and indeed must be held on the Sabbath or any holiday, including Yom Kippur, if it happens that the eighth day falls then. On Yom Kippur or other fast days no feast is held following the briss, and the wine blessed by the mohel is not drunk by him but given to minor children to drink so that the blessing will not have been said in vain. On any day not a fast day, the briss is followed by a joyous feast.

The custom of bringing gifts for the baby to a briss has received a particularly enchanting explanation from the rabbinical commentators. They tell us that it is a continuation of the custom initiated by God Himself, who, at the briss of Abraham, the first Jew to be circumcised, gave him and his descendants eternal title to the Land of Israel as a gift to honor the occasion.

While it is not customary to invite Goyim (Gentiles) to a briss, exceptions can be made, particularly in the case of the mother's physician, if he will be honored by being invited. It is not customary for women to be present at the moment of the circumcision itself, although it is not prohibited, whereas it is prohibited for the mother of the child to be present.

In the case of a man who is a Jew by birth but who was circumcised in infancy or later by a non-Jewish physician, without the proper blessings being said, he must, on reaching maturity, seek out a mohel and have a drop of blood taken from the place where his foreskin was. This blood is called the *dam ha-brit*, or blood of the covenant. A child born without a foreskin also has a drop of blood taken in the same manner but it need not be on the eighth day, and, as in the case of the mature man, no blessings are said.

What about mixed marriages in which the mother is a Gentile and the father a Jew? May the son of such a marriage be circumcised on the eighth day by an Orthodox mohel according to Jewish law at the father's request? The answer is an unqualified yes. In such cases the child is, if the father requests it, circumcised *l'shem gerut*—for the purpose of conversion—although this alone will not make him a Jew. For that he will require the rest of the conversion ceremony (see chapter 45), of which circumcision is only the first step. This ceremony must await his reaching the age of reason, since the conversion of a child is not permitted in most cases.

Many people have the custom of celebrating with a small feast on the Friday night preceding a circumcision, after the Sabbath meal has been eaten. This feast is called *Shalom Zachar*, or "peace to the male child"; friends are invited, toasts are drunk and rejoicing is general.

Circumcision is a commandment of such importance that even the most aggressively reformed Jews insist on it, although they may not be particular about who does it or on what day.

9

Pidyon Ha-Ben— Redemption of the Firstborn Son

IF a woman's first child is a boy, her husband, the boy's father, is under an obligation to redeem the child on the thirty-first day after his birth.

This commandment is found in the Torah (Exod. 13:2 and 13:13). "Whosoever openeth the womb among the children of Israel, both of man and of beasts, it is Mine," and ". . . all the firstborn of man among thy sons shalt thou redeem." How this redemption is to be accomplished is stated in Num. 18:15, where God told Aaron, His high priest, "Everything that opens the womb shall be thine, however . . . the firstborn of man you shall surely redeem. . . ."

What this means is that God set aside the firstborn of all species to be His and dedicated to His service. Then He announced that all these firstborn would be given to Aaron and his descendants in payment for their service to Him as priests, but that the firstborn of man did not belong to Aaron, but to God, and that he must be redeemed from that service through Aaron.

To make this even clearer, He took the Levites, i.e. the

descendants of the tribe of Levi, which includes the Cohanim, in the place of these firstborn sons. This is stated clearly in Num. 3:12: "I have taken the Levites from among the children of Israel instead of every firstborn that opens the womb among the children of Israel."

Accordingly there are two reasons why the firstborn son must be redeemed through the Cohanim. The first is that God told the Cohanim that it is their duty to make possible the redemption of the firstborn sons, just as He told all Jews that it is their duty to redeem them. This is the plain instruction of the Torah as we have seen above. Secondly, since God took the Levites, which includes the Cohanim, instead of the firstborn, what we are really doing is compensating the Cohen who is serving in the firstborn's place.

The wording "which opens the womb" makes it clear that this refers to the firstborn of a woman. Accordingly, if a man marries more than once, he is obliged to redeem the firstborn of each of his wives if, of course, the firstborn is a male: If, on the other hand, he marries a woman who has already borne a child, he is not obliged to redeem a son born to him, even though this is *his* firstborn.

The firstborn son of a Cohen or Levi or of the daughter of a Cohen or Levi need not be redeemed.

The obligation to redeem the firstborn male is exclusively that of the father. Accordingly, if a child is posthumous, it is the duty of the *bet din*, or rabbinical court, or in its absence, of the community, to see to the redemption. If for any reason the father is away from home on the thirty-first day after the child's birth, he should go to a Cohen in whatever place he finds himself and redeem the child there, even though the child himself is not present. A firstborn son whose father did not redeem him, must, when he is grown up, seek out a Cohen and redeem himself. The same applies to the son of a Jewish woman and a non-Jewish man, even if in this case the Jewish woman is the daughter of a Cohen or a Levi, because by marrying a non-Jew she loses her status as a member of a priestly family. Any Orthodox Cohen knows the procedure in such cases, which in any event is found in most Orthodox prayerbooks.

Now, how is the firstborn son redeemed? Arrangements must be made to have a Cohen come to the house where the baby will be when he is thirty-one days old. If possible a minyan should be present, and all, including the Cohen, sit down at the table and after washing their hands, say the blessing and eat a piece of bread, starting the feast off. The father then brings in the child and holds in his own hands coins to the value of five *selaim*. In the United States it is customary to use five half-dollars; other countries use whatever coins are available—paper money is not permitted—and the idea is that it must be current, spendable coin of the realm. If no coins of sufficient value are available, other objects with the value of five selaim are substituted.

The father then says to the Cohen, in Hebrew, that the boy is his son and must be redeemed. The Cohen asks the father if he would rather give him the child or redeem him for five selaim. The father answers that he wishes to redeem his son and that he has the necessary money in his hand. He then recites two blessings and gives the money to the Cohen. The Cohen holds the coins over the infant's head and states that the money stands in place of the child and that the child is redeemed. He then places his hands on the child's head and blesses him with the Priestly Blessing (see chapter 28). After this he takes a cup of wine, says the blessing and he and the guests enjoy the feast that has been laid out for them. If no wine is available, any liquor can be used, but no blessing is said because the blessing for bread, which has already been pronounced, makes all other blessings unnecessary, except for that for wine.

It is proper to try to find a Cohen who is an observant Jew. If the Cohen is not poor, he will invariably return the money to the father, usually with the stipulation that it be used to buy something for the child. Often the Cohen will keep one of the coins since it is felt that if he returns all the money, the redemption might be doubtful; the coin he keeps he gives to charity. It is considered best of all to find a Cohen who is needy and agree with him that he will keep all the money. Among the Sephardim, the Cohen keeps all the money, but usually gives it to charity later.

It is a common custom, after the ceremony, to place a gold coin or some other gold object in the child's hand or in his cradle so that he may be blessed with wealth in later life. This is a pleasant folk custom, like throwing wheat (the Jewish custom) over a bride, which if nothing else, serves as a link between our generation and those that preceded it.

The Torah states that the child must be redeemed when he is one month old (Num. 18:16), which we take to mean when he has completed thirty days. Accordingly we perform the ceremony on the thirty-first day after his birth during daylight hours unless, of course, it happens to be a Sabbath or holiday on which the handling of money is forbidden. In such a case we do not wait for the following day, but perform the ceremony at night, right after sundown when the Sabbath or holiday has ended.

In the case that the firstborn son is delivered by Caesarian section, the child is not redeemed since it is held that Caesarian section does not constitute "opening the womb." In the unlikely circumstance that the mother should bear her next child normally and the child is a male, he must be redeemed since it is he who "opens the womb." Medically it is extremely rare for this to take place, since once a woman has had a Caesarian section, ordinarily all succeeding births must be effected by the same operation.

In the case that a woman has had a miscarriage or an abortion previous to her first child being born, if that child is a male an Orthodox rabbi must be consulted as to whether the pidyon ha-ben is necessary. By and large, if the abortion or miscarriage occurs after the fortieth day of pregnancy, no pidyon ha-ben is required for a son born thereafter.

The Sephardim, particularly those of the Arabic-speaking countries, have made the pidyon ha-ben into a very picturesque ceremony. Among the Syrian Jews, the child's mother, dressed again in her bridal gown, begs the Cohen for the child. The Cohen haughtily refuses and she must beg again and again until the Cohen reluctantly allows the child's father to redeem him. The Morroccan Jews go through a similar ceremony in which the mother gives up all the jewels she is wearing, one by one, to the Cohen before he will consent to the redemption ceremony. It goes without saying that the Cohen's reluctance to give up the child and the mother's pleading are all part of a sort of traditional play, acted out for those present, who enjoy its histrionics and rejoice at its "happy ending."

Even if the child has not been circumcised, due to the postponing of the operation for reasons of health, he must be redeemed on the thirty-first day.

Pidyon ha-ben, the redemption of the firstborn son, is another important reminder of the Jews' unique position as the chosen people of God.

10

Bar Mitzva

A JEWISH boy becomes *Bar Mitzva,* a son of the commandment, the day he reaches his thirteenth birthday according to the Jewish calendar. (To determine a Jewish birthday, consult the Jewish calendar in appendix II.)

It is often said that on this day he becomes a man, but this is not so and has never been. It is, however, felt that he is a man in the religious sense that, having reached thirteen, he is aware of the meanings of the commandments and is able to observe them under his own responsibility without being told to do so by his father, who, up until this time, has been responsible for his conduct as a Jew. In addition he is considered an adult in one important respect: he is now able to form part of the *minyan,* or quorum, of ten adult males required for the recitation of many prayers, public reading from the Torah, etc. It is also at this time that he begins to put on *t'fillin* (phylacteries) (chapter 26).

Although the boy becomes bar mitzva on his Jewish thirteenth birthday, this event is usually celebrated the preceding Sabbath. Many Orthodox Jews, however, celebrate it on either the Monday or Thursday following his birthday. On all three days, Monday, Thursday and Shabbat, the Torah is read publicly in the synagogue and the bar mitzva may be called up to the reading of the scroll. The fact is that no special ceremony is needed; on his thirteenth birthday a Jewish boy is automatically bar mitzva and calling him up to the Torah is simply public recognition of this fact. In those cases, in the United States the great majority, when the bar mitzva is called up to the Torah on the Shabbat (Sabbath) preceding his birthday, he is given the last *aliya*, called *maftir*, and after this the *haftara* (chapter 28). The reason for this is interesting: the *maftir* is in reality only a repetition of the last verse of the weekly portion and thus is not a legal obligation on the congregation, although it is always read. Accordingly, it can be given to a boy who has not yet reached his legal majority. When he concludes the blessing closing the maftir, his father says the brief blessing, *Baruch Sheptarani*, in which he gives thanks for being relieved of the responsibility for the child. This is a strange blessing in that it reads literally, "Blessed be He who has freed me from the chastisement of this [child]." God's name and kingdom are not mentioned in the blessing which makes it all the more curious.

All commentators are agreed that it is not an expression of relief on the part of the father, but an expression of joy that the boy has entered into the community and is able to stand on his own feet in observance of the commandments. The fact is that this blessing is not mandatory and many religious Jews do not say it. To their way of thinking it is a senseless blessing because they are in no way relieved of the responsibility for their son. It is explained that this is why the usual formula, "Blessed art Thou, O Lord our God, King of the universe," is omitted: that because the blessing cannot be said with full intention, it is not said in full form.

While the boy is reciting the final blessings of the haftara, it is a widespread custom for the women and children to throw candy over him, and candy is distributed to the children in the synagogue.

Following the haftara reading, it is customary for the bar mitzva to give a short speech. Often this speech is given first in

Hebrew, then in English or Spanish, and, in some congregations, also in Yiddish, Ladino, German or Arabic. Among more traditional Jews, the speech is given during the kiddush which follows the service or during the afternoon at the *Seuda Ha-sh'lishit*, or third meal of the Sabbath, which is eaten in the synagogue.

The kiddush, or celebration, which follows the morning services, can be as simple as cake and wine (or more likely, lekach and bronfen—honeycake and schnapps) or as elaborate as a full meal. It is always given in the synagogue itself or the synagogue building. In the United States, and to a certain extent in other countries, it has become the custom to hold a reception in a hotel or other catering establishment on the Saturday night or the next day—Sunday. These receptions, which are often of a nonreligious nature, not uncommonly feature, as the Jewish humorists put it, "lots of bar and very little mitzva." While it is natural for parents to wish to celebrate such an important event as their son's entering the community, it should be remembered that this is done adequately with the kiddush offered in the synagogue. While there is certainly nothing wrong with the bar mitzva reception on Saturday night or Sunday, it is not a necessary part of the boy's reaching his religious majority. Where the reception is not Jewish in nature, and, in particular, where the dietary laws are not observed, the entire business is a betrayal of all that the bar mitzva has studied and prepared for to reach this important day in his life.

In the United States there has grown up in some non-Orthodox congregations the custom of celebrating in a similar fashion for a girl who has reached her twelfth birthday. This ceremony, called *Bat Mitzva*, or daughter of the commandment, is one which makes no sense in any Jewish context and is, for that reason, beyond the scope of this book to discuss. As we noted above, the bar mitzva ceremony is simply a public recognition of the fact that a boy can now form part of a minyan and must observe the mitzva of t'fillin. Since women are excused from all commandments depending on fixed times of the day, such as praying with a minyan and putting on t'fillin, public recognition, as in the case of the male, is pointless, since there is nothing to recognize. It is the Orthodox view that a celebration of this sort may properly be held in the home if the parents feel it is necessary, but that there is no place for it in the synagogue.

Even further removed from Jewish practice is the "confirmation" ceremony for teenage boys and girls, usually celebrated on Shavuot. This is, despite denials, a frank and open borrowing from the Christians (albeit in form alone—it has, of course, no Christian content) and every congregation that observes it seems able to establish its own rules, so discussion of it from a factual standpoint is really not possible. Most Jews the world over have never even heard of either the bat mitzva or confirmation ceremony, although the term *bat mitzva* to designate an unmarried girl who has passed her twelfth birthday is common and accepted.

REACHING PUBERTY—GIRLS

With the onset of maturity, signalized by the beginning of menstruation, the status of a girl changes in Jewish life. There is no ceremony to mark this natural change, but the girl is to some degree conscious of having entered womanhood. The most immediately noticeable change is in the synagogue. In all Orthodox congregations, men and women are separated in the synagogue and among the Sephardim even the tiniest girls are not permitted in the men's section. Among the Ashkenazim, however, small girls are allowed to visit the men's section and sit with their fathers and brothers during the services. When a girl reaches puberty she must henceforth remain with her mother in the women's section.

Among the very Orthodox, a girl on reaching puberty is treated as a woman in that it is forbidden to shake hands with her (because of menstrual impurity), and among the extreme Orthodox, she is taught not to sing in the hearing of men. (The laws concerning menstrual uncleanness are discussed in chapter 14.)

11

Engagement and Marriage

ENGAGEMENT

THE pre-marriage engagement of a couple is effected through a document called *Tenaim*. Basically this document sets forth the terms of the dowry and is binding upon both parties. Available in printed form, it is signed by the bride and groom and by two witnesses. It is ratified by the ceremony known as "taking *kinyan*," in which the contracting parties grasp a handkerchief or some other article of clothing to signify that an exchange has taken place and the agreement is binding. After the tenaim has been signed and kinyan taken, it is the custom to break a pot or dish, and often many dishes are broken, particularly by the women present, as a sign of the celebration of this important event.

Where in previous years the tenaim was signed well in advance of the wedding (and this is still the custom among the very Orthodox), today the tenaim is often omitted or signed, more as a formality than anything else, immediately before the wedding ceremony.

The custom of breaking dishes at the announcement of a couple's intention to marry is still very widely observed, accompanied by much merriment and enthusiastic shouts of "mazzeltov!" In our times this takes place when the couple makes the formal announcement, even though the tenaim may not be signed, as explained above, until just before the wedding itself, if at all.

The Sephardim do not write tenaim.

MARRIAGE

According to Jewish law, marriage is obligatory for men. A man is duty bound to marry and have children. A rabbi must be married as must a teacher of children, and among the Ashkenazim only a married man, or one who has been married, may wear the large prayer shawl, or *tallit*, at ordinary prayer.

Women, while not under the same obligation to marry, expect to, and it is expected that the community will help find husbands for unmarried women. One of the most important of all mitzvas is that of *Hachnasot Kala*: making possible, through providing a dowry, the marriage of orphaned or other poor girls.

A great many laws and customs surround marriage and its preliminaries, but the following is a basic outline.

Who May Marry and When?

Not all marriages are permitted. Including the obvious forbidden categories such as brother-sister, etc., the Torah and the later enactments of the rabbis give a total of forty-two prohibited degrees of relationship, such as aunt-nephew, father-in-law-daughter-in-law, and so forth. Most of these forbidden liaisons are academic in that there is little likelihood of anyone ever wanting to enter into such marriages, but there is one which should be noted: it is forbidden for a man who has divorced his wife to marry her sister while his divorced wife is still alive. Also, as we will see in the chapter on divorce, it is forbidden for a couple who have had an adulterous relationship to marry after divorce has freed them. In addition to marriages forbidden because of a specific degree of relationship, these other grounds exist.

1. ALREADY BEING MARRIED. In the case of women this is an absolute prohibition, and in the case of men it applies to all Ashkenazim. To explain this more fully, there is no permanent law against a man having two wives, but all Ashkenazim are bound by the *cherem* (ban) of Rabbenu Gershom, a French rabbi who, almost one thousand years ago, promulgated an official ban against three things: polygamy, divorcing a wife without her consent and opening someone else's mail without his or her consent. This cherem was signed by the thousand most prominent Ashkenazic rabbis of that generation and stated to be in effect for one thousand years.

The Sephardim, however, were not and are not bound by it and accordingly are able to have more than one wife at a time. At present the Yemenite Jews and some Arabic-speaking North African Jews are the only major communities to practice polygamy. The fact is that the entire Yemenite community and most of the North Africans have moved to Israel, where polygamy is forbidden by the law of the land, and as a result, may not marry a second wife if their first wife is still alive. In the case of those who had more than one wife when they emigrated, Israeli law did not oblige them to divorce all but one, as would, for example, United States law; and so, in Israel there are Jews with two or even—in rare cases—three wives, but fewer and fewer as the older generations pass on. In addition, even in those lands where polygamy is permitted by both the law of the land and religious law, Jewish custom has always been against having more than one wife, even where Jewish law permits it.

2. LACK OF A PROPER DIVORCE. Jewish marriages must be dissolved by Jewish divorce. A civil divorce is not enough, even where the couple had only a civil marriage. Until a Jewish divorce has been given, the couple is still married by Jewish law and neither partner may contract

marriage until such a divorce has been written and executed. In the case of a woman, remarriage without a Jewish divorce would make her an adulteress and her husband an adulterer. Worse still, any children born to such a marriage would be *mamzerim*, the product of a forbidden union, and forever disqualified from marrying Jews themselves. (For details concerning Jewish divorce see chapter 13.)

3. LACK OF CHALITZA. The Torah states that if a man dies without having children, his eldest brother (or, if he refuses, any other brother) must marry the widow. If the brother does not wish to do so, he must publicly refuse the widow and she must publicly accept this refusal in a ceremony called *chalitza* (see chapter 13), after which she is free to remarry. There are certain circumstances under which the chalitza is not necessary, but where it is, the widow cannot marry without it.

4. MAMZERUT. The child of a married woman by a man not her husband, and this includes the child born after the remarriage of a woman who has received a civil divorce but not a religious one, or of a widow who remarried without performing the chalitza ceremony when this was required, is a *mamzer*. This term also applies to a child of one of the forbidden degrees of marriage, such as brother-sister. Such a person, while himself a Jew, is not eligible to marry another Jew and all Jews not themselves mamzerim are forbidden to marry him or her. It should be noted that the child of a mixed marriage is not a mamzer, nor is the child of the marriage between a Cohen and a divorced woman, although both these marriages are forbidden. Mamzer is usually translated as "bastard" and the condition of being a mamzer, or *mamzerut*, as "bastardy." As can be seen, this translation is inaccurate.

5. LACK OF CONSENT. Although marriages are frequently arranged, particularly in Oriental and extreme Orthodox communities, no woman or man may be married without

freely given consent, nor may he or she in any way be coerced to give such consent. Accordingly, an arranged marriage is, in the end, dependent on both bride and groom accepting it.

6. MIXED MARRIAGES. Marriage between Jew and non-Jew is forbidden and no rabbi will perform it. There are no exceptions. The same applies to such schismatic groups as the Karaim. Once such a marriage has taken place, however, it is recognized as legitimate even if only performed under civil law. In other words, the children of such a marriage are not considered illegitimate in any sense nor is the couple considered to be "living in sin."

It should be noted that in very recent times, people calling themselves rabbis have appeared who will perform a ceremony uniting a Jew to an unconverted Gentile and there are even reports of such anomalous rites being carried out *mano a mano* with a Christian minister. Such nuptials are devoid of any Jewish significance; their only legitimacy resides in the fact that in the United States, people recognized as rabbis or ministers by the State are empowered to conclude a marriage once a marriage license has been issued to the couple by the State authorities.

7. MENTAL OR PHYSICAL INCAPACITY. A mentally deranged person may not marry because he or she will be unable to grasp the significance of the marriage vows. A person able to understand the marriage vows, even if quite feeble-minded, may marry. A eunuch or an impotent man may not marry.

8. A COHEN MAY NOT MARRY A DIVORCED WOMAN, A CHALUTZA OR A CHALALA. A *chalutza* is a woman who has performed the *chalitza* ceremony to free herself from the obligation of marrying the brother of her deceased husband. A *chalala* is the daughter of a Cohen who has married a divorced woman or a *chalutza*. A Cohen may not marry a convert to Judaism.

9. UNCERTAINTY ON THE PART OF THE RABBI PERFORMING THE MARRIAGE. Jewish law requires absolute certainty, attested to by witnesses, that both parties are free to marry. These witnesses must testify that neither bride nor groom is married, and, in the case of divorced people, a properly executed copy of the *gett* or Jewish divorce document must be produced (see chapter 13).

In the case of a woman whose husband has disappeared and is presumed dead, reliable witnesses must be found or reliable documents brought forward to prove that the man is, in fact, dead. If no such satisfactory testimony can be obtained, the unfortunate woman may not remarry and becomes an *aguna*, or woman whose husband has abandoned her but is not known to be dead. Despite the seeming rigidity of this law, its value has been proven over the centuries in which the Jewish family has remained the strongest social unit the world has ever known.

Following World War II and the wholesale annihilation of European Jewry by the Germans there were thousands of cases of *agunot*, and the importance of marriage to the Jew can be seen in the fact that many of the world's most famous and prominent rabbis dedicated most of their time to finding legal ways through which such women could be freed for marriage again.

10. LACK OF A CIVIL DIVORCE. The Talmud states, *Dina d'malchuta dina*: the law of the land is the law. Accordingly no rabbi will perform a marriage which is counter to the law of the land, which would be the case if one or both of the parties had been previously married and a civil divorce not obtained.

11. TEMPORARY GROUNDS. There are certain days and times of the year when, by Jewish law, it is forbidden to get married. These are Sabbaths and holidays—including the intermediate days—or *chol ha-moed*, fast days, the seven weeks between Passover and Shavuot (with the exception of Lag B'Omer and, in Israel, Yom Ha-atzmaut) and the period from the seventeenth of Tammuz to and

including the ninth of Av, Tisha B'Av. In all these cases the law forbidding the celebration of marriages can be set aside if a real emergency can be proven, but this is by no means a common practice. In addition, a Jew is not permitted to marry within seven days of the death of a parent nor is a widow or divorced woman permitted to marry within ninety days of the death of her husband or the divorce. All these laws can be set aside in case of emergency. As will be seen in a later chapter, two sisters or two brothers may not marry on the same day.

In general it can be said that any marriage not specifically forbidden is permitted.

Oifrifung

On the Sabbath before the wedding is to be performed, the Orthodox call the groom to the Torah. Actually, the bridegroom-to-be takes precedence over all others except the bar mitzva. In other words, the bridegroom must be called up, even if it means leaving out someone who would ordinarily be called up, such as a man with *yohrtzeit* (the death anniversary of a parent). This calling up of the groom is known among the Ashkenazim as *Oifrifung* (Yiddish) or, in German, Aufrüfung. The phrase "Ha-bachur ha-chatan" (bachelor and bridegroom) is used preceding his name when he is called up.

In traditional Orthodox synagogues it is the custom to throw nuts and dried fruits over the groom while he is saying the blessings for the Torah. The younger boys in the synagogue quickly dispose of the nuts that fall, sometimes by stowing them in their pockets for later enjoyment, but usually by shying them at the bridegroom's head.

Mikva

Jewish law states that a woman is made unclean by her menstrual flow in the sense that she may not have sexual intercourse with her husband until she has, after counting seven "clean" days, regained her purity by immersing herself in a *mikva*, or ritual bath, built according to certain specifications. Rules concerning menstrual uncleanness and the mikva will be found in chapter 14. It is the law that the bride must immerse herself in a mikva prior to the wedding, for obvious reasons, and even girls who might otherwise not be particular about the observance of the commandment will wish to observe it before marriage so as to enter into the state of matrimony in accordance with Jewish law.

The Day Preceding the Ceremony

It is customary that the bride and groom not see each other for at least one day before the ceremony, so that their joy at meeting under the *chuppa*, or marriage canopy, will be even greater. In addition, there is a law that both bride and groom must fast on the day of the ceremony, breaking their fast only after the marriage has been solemnized. If the marriage takes place on *Rosh Chodesh* (the first day of a Jewish month, with the exception of the month of Nisan) or on some other minor holiday, no fast is required.

12

The Marriage Ceremony and the Jewish Concept of Marriage

THE MARRIAGE CEREMONY

THE marriage ceremony itself is surrounded with literally hundreds of different customs. It is not our purpose to go into these to any great extent, particularly since they vary so widely from community to community. The essentials of the ceremony, however, have been constant and relatively unchanged for many centuries both for Sephardim and Ashkenazim, and there are certain customs which are found among all Jews of traditional background. We will discuss these in the order of their occurrence after a brief examination of the meaning of the marriage service.

The marriage ceremony is primarily a legal act which takes place in a religious setting; what we must remember is that there is no separation between law and religion in Jewish thought. Jewish "religious" law encompasses what other peoples tend to consider secular or civil matters, including both contracts and torts. In the case of marriage, we are talking about a contract.

Accordingly, although the ceremony itself centers around the giving of an object of value, usually a ring, by the groom to the bride, signifying actual monetary compensation, and by the reading of a marriage contract with legal binding force, the ceremony itself is called *kiddushin*, which means "sanctification."

So, what is materially a business transaction with compensation paid and a contract agreement entered into in the presence of witnesses, is in a more important sense a religious act in which bride and groom are sanctified to each other and both are sanctified to the Jewish people, whom their union will serve to increase. Finally, they are sanctified to the Creator Himself, who gave as the first of His commandments, "Be fruitful, multiply and replenish the earth."

The ceremony itself is performed in a synagogue or, these days, often in a hotel or reception hall, and starts with the bride and groom being escorted by their parents and brought under the *chuppa*. In some congregations this is a fixed canopy, while in others it is portable, being held usually by four friends of the groom by its four corner-posts. Among the more religious, particularly among the Chasidim, it is considered best to have the chuppa outside, under the open sky, for the ceremony. In the absence of a chuppa, one can be improvised by having four men (four tall men, obviously) hold up a *tallit* by its corners.

The bride, if she has not been married before, wears white, and has a veil which is placed over her head by the groom immediately before the ceremony. In many communities, if the bride is an orphan, and particularly if her marriage has been made possible by the community, the veil is placed on her by the rabbi, who at the same time blesses her with the words, "Our sister, be thou the mother of many thousands." Among the very Orthodox, the groom wears a white robe called a *kittel* (Yiddish) similar to the one worn on Yom Kippur.

Once the couple are standing under the chuppa, it is the custom for the bride to walk three, four or seven times around the groom, depending on local custom. There are at least two reasons given for this: one is that the bride shows in this fashion that her husband will be the center of her existence. Another and more commonly accepted explanation is that this symbolizes the fact that now the groom will be surrounded by the light and virtue that only marriage brings. The *Schulchan Aruch* (see chapter 25) says that it is only for the wife's sake that a man's house is blessed.

After the bride has walked around the groom, the rabbi or other person conducting the ceremony recites a portion of Psalm 118 and a short blessing. It should be noted that, technically, any knowledgeable Jew may conduct the marriage ceremony; such a person is called a *m'sader kiddushin.* In the United States this is always a rabbi, since the rabbi is authorized by state law to solemnize marriages, thus making a civil ceremony unnecessary. In most of Latin America, a civil ceremony is legally necessary before a religious wedding can take place and the person conducting the religious service is often not an ordained rabbi.

After the above-mentioned short blessing, the rabbi will often pronounce a short sermon, directed at the bride and groom. This in turn is followed by the blessing of the first of the two cups of wine which must be drunk during the ceremony. Both bride and groom drink from the same cup on both occasions.

At this point, the marriage itself is brought about. First the groom gives to the bride a purchase price in the form of a ring made of some precious metal. If no ring is available, a coin will do. He places this ring on the index finger of the bride's right hand, since this is the finger one uses to acquire an object with, indicating that the ring is not simply an adornment but a monetary compensation for the bride herself. The bride accepts the ring, thereby indicating her consent to the transaction.

What has happened here is that the groom has *acquired* the bride from herself and with her consent in exchange for the ring. The ring must be made of precious metal, with no stones, and must be the personal property of the groom. The reason why it must not have stones is that the bride might not be able to judge its true worth if it is too ornate. It must be the groom's personal property; otherwise the ceremony might be invalid, since the acquisition would be effected with an object which did not belong to the acquirer.

Immediately after this act, the rabbi or m'sader kiddushin recites the marriage vow and the groom repeats it after him, word for word, so there can be no possibility of error. The actual wording of the vow is: "Behold, thou art sanctified to me by this ring according to the laws of Moses and of Israel."

This declaration, following the purely legal act of acquisition, places the transaction in its proper religious setting since it makes it clear that the legal transaction just gone through is in obedience to the law of Moses—the written Torah—and of Israel: the enactments of the rabbinical courts in the Talmud and later literature.

Thus the marriage is actually performed by the groom, who acquires the bride by both word and deed in the presence of two witnesses who sign the marriage contract. The function of the rabbi or m'sader kiddushin is simply to see that everything is done correctly, "according to the laws of Moses and of Israel."

The second part of the ceremony now follows: the reading of the marriage contract, called the ketuba. This legal document, which is usually printed, is filled in before the ceremony in the presence of the bride and groom, but is signed afterward only by the two witnesses to the ceremony. It sets forth the obligations of the husband to the wife in terms of money paid in compensation for her virginity, when this is the case, and states clearly that he will live with her in marital relation as is the custom of the world. This is, in the words of a noted modern rabbi, Dr. Immanuel Jakobovits, a unilateral contract, since nothing is stated regarding any obligations of the wife toward her husband.

The ketuba becomes the personal property of the bride and is handed to her as soon as it is read. According to Jewish law, a married couple should not spend as much as one hour beneath the same roof without their ketuba, and Orthodox couples take the ketuba with them whenever they go on a trip together. This contract, obligating the husband for the support and cherishing of his wife, is a binding legal document in every sense of the word and stands until death or divorce ends the marriage.

After the ketuba is read, a second cup is blessed from which both bride and groom drink. The blessing on the wine in this second cup is the first of the "seven blessings" recited at the wedding. It is followed by the six other blessings and it is customary to repeat these seven blessings at the end of the wedding feast. Among the very Orthodox, the wedding is celebrated with a feast every night of the six succeeding nights and the seven blessings are repeated each time.

After the recitation of the seven blessings, a glass (not the one the couple has drunk from) is placed on the floor and the groom breaks it by stamping on it with his foot. Those present cry out, "mazzeltov!" It is generally stated that this glass is broken in remembrance of the destruction of the Temple, so that even at the most joyous of times we Jews might not forget that part of the Jewish people is still in exile. Dr. Jakobovits, above cited, states this to be the case and further says: "No other meaning attaches to this custom; the popular notion that this practice is meant to 'bring luck' offends against the rational character of Judaism, which knows no superstitions."

We may, nevertheless, be permitted to differ with even so eminent a scholar as Rabbi Jakobovits. Judaism, meaning the total experience of the Jewish people, is loaded with what must, in all truth, be called superstitions, many of them peculiar to the Jews. The fact is that the Jews, in common with most of the peoples of the world, believe that weddings and engagements are particularly attractive to what other people would call evil spirits, and what the Jews refer to as the *ayin hara*, the evil eye. The practice of making noise at a wedding or engagement by shooting off firecrackers, rattling tin pans, tooting horns, etc., is almost universal. It is apparently felt that these sudden and unusual noises will frighten off the evil influences. The breaking of dishes which always accompanies a Jewish engagement announcement is done in an atmosphere of great rejoicing and may have had its origin in some such belief, although other reasons are given for it.

The breaking of the glass at the marriage ceremony may very well have the meaning which Dr. Jakobovits and other famous rabbis have assigned it, but whether that is the original meaning or an acquired rationalization is impossible to say with certainty.

In any event, to say that Judaism "knows no superstitions" is to invite incredulity regarding other assessments of the Jewish experience, since every Jew is perfectly well aware of innumerable practices and beliefs, either peculiar to the Jews or shared with other peoples, whose superstitious nature can hardly be denied. To return to the breaking of the glass, if its sole purpose is to remind us of the destruction of the Temple, it is difficult to explain the happy cries of "mazzeltov!" when the act is performed.

After breaking the glass, the *birchat cohanim*, or priestly blessing, is given and those present remain in the synagogue until the bride and groom have left. The reason for this is most important: the ceremony is not valid until the newly wed couple have gone together into a room where they can be alone for a few minutes. This meeting must take place behind closed doors and their entrance into the room must be witnessed by the two men who sign the ketuba.

Jewish law and custom strongly object to two people of the opposite sex being alone in the same room unless they are married. This symbolic retirement of the couple indicates their married status and that their seclusion is not only not frowned upon, but approved by the community. The meeting usually lasts only a few minutes; long enough to give the couple a chance to talk to each other without others being present and customarily to break their wedding day fast with a little wine and cake—their first meal together as man and wife.

The presence of witnesses is a recurring theme in the entire treatment of Jewish marriage. This is, of course, due to its primarily legal character, but we must not forget that there is no separation between law and religion to the Jew. The religious character of the legal proceeding is shown by the fact that it is necessary to have a minyan of at least ten adult males present, of which the bridegroom and m'sader kiddushin may count as members. The minyan are not legal witnesses, but represent the entire Jewish people, in the presence of which many religious acts and functions must take place; another proof of the intimate connection between God and His chosen people.

This, in sum, is the course of engagement and wedding among the Jews. The customs which have grown up around marriage, many of them of great beauty and impressiveness, would require several books this size to describe, so we will mention only a few. Chief among these, and of great importance, is the celebration which follows the ceremony. Among the Jews the bride and groom do not leave for their honeymoon immediately following the ceremony (their symbolic seclusion, above described, is in a sense a substitution for this), but join with their family and friends in rejoicing and celebration. For example, it is common for the bride and the groom to be placed on two chairs in the middle of the floor—like a king and queen enthroned—and for the young men to dance around them in a circle. Finally the groom's chair is lifted up high and the young men carry him around the room, still seated. All of this gaiety and carefree celebration indicates that, however great the personal significance of marriage may be to the bride and groom, it is of equal communal importance since it perpetuates the Jewish people as a whole. The Talmud tells of a famous rabbi whose entire life was dedicated to the study of the Torah, from which he allowed nothing to distract him. On hearing the sound of wedding music, however, he would lay aside his books and go to where the wedding was being held in order to perform the great mitzva of dancing before the bride, to enliven her heart.

Among the Ashkenazim it is the custom for the bride to give a special wedding present to the groom: a tallit, or prayer shawl, of the best quality the bride can afford. It is a significant gift since, until he marries, a man may not wear a tallit for ordinary prayer and the use of the tallit is an announcement to any community in which he may find himself that he is married; a fact the bride certainly wishes to be known! This custom obtains only among the Ashkenazim since among the Sephardim, all men, married or not, wear the tallit. It is the custom, however, in all Sephardic and a few Ashkenazic communities, to place a tallit over the heads of the couple as they stand under the chuppa.

Another custom, mentioned earlier, must be noted here. It is forbidden for two brothers or two sisters to marry on the same day. The reason given by the rabbis is that one joy should not be allowed to interfere with another, but nine out of ten Jews familiar with this law, if asked its reason, will answer that it is for fear of the evil eye. Whatever the reason, the Shulchan Aruch, the standard code of Jewish law, definitely *forbids* that two sisters be married on the same day on the grounds that one joy must not be made to interfere with another.

THE JEWISH CONCEPT OF MARRIAGE

A final word regarding the entire concept of marriage among the Jews. In the Jewish view, the *refusal* to marry, under normal circumstances, is a sin. Marriage is the natural condition of human beings and God Himself has told us so; to advocate celibacy is to deny God and His commandments. Marriage is an opportunity to turn to holy ends a fundamental drive possessed by all normal human beings. The Jew who practices celibacy, far from being respected, would be considered by the rest of the community to be a miserly and despicable sinner who took a morbid pride in rebelling not only against his God-given instincts, but against God's revealed commandments.

And it should not be thought that in the Jewish view the sex drive is important only in men. On the contrary, in all Jewish writing on the subject, particularly in the Talmud, the husband is exhorted to be ever aware of his wife's desire and under no circumstances to deny her the comfort of a normal married sex life.

The recognition of woman's need for marriage as against man's obligation to marry is familiar to all Jews. An "old bachelor" is a sinner who has no one but himself to blame for his guilt, but an old maid is a stain on the reputation not only of her family, but of the entire community in which she lives. It is their responsibility to find her a husband or become the target of criticism by other communities and families more attentive to their obligations as Jews.

It may be asked, what if a woman doesn't want to get married; should she be forced to? Of course the answer to this is no. It would be foolish to deny that there are women, although they are exceedingly rare among the Jews, who do not want marriage. Such a woman is not considered a sinner nor a disgrace; it is simply felt that something is missing in her personality and she is considered, in fact if not by admission, as in some sense defective.

CIVIL MARRIAGE

Civil marriage alone is not by any means condoned in Jewish practice, but a couple married by a government functionary under civil law is considered married under Jewish law as well. If such a couple decides to separate, a Jewish divorce, or *gett*, must be given the woman by her husband if she is to remarry. Children of a couple married only by state law are legitimate.

This illustrates an important concept in Jewish law which, in many cases, recognizes a significant difference between *l'chatchila* (to start with) and *b'diavad* (after the fact). Civil marriage is forbidden to start with, but after it has taken place, it is recognized as effective.

Actually, Jewish law goes even further. If a Jewish couple has been living together as a married couple in the sight of the community in which they reside, whatever sort of a community it is, and particularly if the woman wears a ring given her by her common-law husband, the couple is considered married if their common-law liaison has lasted longer than thirty days. Their children are considered legitimate Jewish children and a Jewish divorce is necessary in the case that the "marriage" breaks up.

Casual sexual intercourse does not constitute marriage under Jewish law, but if such relations take place with the specific intention of marriage and a couple considers itself united in marriage by this relationship, they are married. If the intention is not there, if the relationship is simply one of "swinging," there is no marriage.

Lest there be any confusion, the above laws apply only to unmarried people. For a married woman, sexual relationship outside her marriage is adultery, and while the man in the case is considered primarily responsible, the woman is equally guilty and the sin is one of horrifying gravity.

If a couple has been living together in an informal unmarried relationship and then wishes to marry by Jewish law and custom, the law may technically be against it, but in practice the interpretation is liberal and an Orthodox rabbi must be consulted as to what steps should be taken. In the case of a Jew who has been living with a non-Jew who then converts to Judaism, the law states quite clearly that they may not marry, but once again, practice is invariably more permissive. In the case that the couple are married by civil law and the non-Jewish spouse converts, a Jewish religious wedding is considered necessary since the "informal" types of marriage described above, while technically legal and permanent, are not considered to be so "in our times."

No single book can give all the laws concerning marriage, and the laws and customs described in this chapter are simply an outline. There are innumerable cases in which decision must be made by a competent rabbi or rabbinical court.

13

Divorce and Chalitza

DIVORCE

UNDER Jewish law, marriage is ended only by the death of one of the spouses or by a Jewish divorce, called a *gett*. As we saw in the preceding chapter, although a civil marriage is recognized as valid to a certain extent, a civil divorce is not. The laws concerning the preparation of a gett are far from simple and this book does not pretend to indicate the course to be followed in the case of divorce. In practice, however, the nature of Jewish divorce is not hard to explain.

In the first place, divorce is given by the husband to the wife. The wife does not have the power to divorce her husband. If, however, a woman has a reason for wanting a divorce, she may go to a Jewish court of law (a *bet din*) or a rabbi and demand that her husband divorce her. If the bet din agrees that the reason is a legitimate one, and in this respect no favor is shown the husband by law, custom or tradition, the bet din may order the husband to concede the divorce, if necessary on pain of excommunication. By excommunication we mean the proclaiming of a *cherem* or ban on him and the denial to him of all contact with the community and its services. This step is very rarely taken; the pressures exercised by the community itself are usually sufficient.

Secondly, all Jewish divorces are by mutual consent. No man may divorce his wife without her consent except in the rarely occurring case of adultery on her part. For this reason, a married woman who goes insane cannot be divorced by her husband since she is unable to give her consent. Nevertheless, there is a way in which a man married to a hopelessly and incurably insane woman may remarry during her lifetime: he is given an "exemption" by a rabbinical court to the cherem of Rabbenu Gershom prohibiting polygamy and may take a second wife. Technically he will then have two wives, but may live only with the second.

The phrase "grounds for divorce" as a requisite for separation has little meaning in Jewish law. If both parties agree, a divorce can be legally forthcoming. It is an established fact, nevertheless, that the divorce rate among observant Jews is among the lowest of any national or ethnic group in the United States—far lower than that of Roman Catholics, for example, to whom divorce is actually forbidden by their religion.

The procedure for obtaining a gett is as follows. The couple must go to an Orthodox rabbi to arrange for the divorce. It is the rabbi's duty to attempt to effect a reconciliation, but if this proves impossible, the couple is cited to appear before a bet din, composed of the abovementioned rabbi, and two witnesses, both observant Jews and neither related to each other or to either member of the married couple.

The rabbi asks the husband if he is still determined to give his wife a divorce as he has stated previously, and the husband must reply in the affirmative, being questioned by each of the members of the court in turn. The rabbi then orders a scribe, or himself undertakes, to write the gett. This document must be written by hand, and special attention is paid to such details as the names of the couple; the *kinui,* or names by which they are commonly known; the name of the city and the country in which the divorce is given, including the names of any rivers that flow through the town, etc. In actual practice, because of its complexity, the gett is usually prepared in advance and the last few words may remain unwritten, to be filled in by the rabbi in the presence of the bet din in order to complete the document at the time the divorce is given.

When the document is completed it is examined by the members of the bet din and then handed to the husband. He holds the gett over his head and then drops it into his wife's hands, at the same time repeating a formula freeing her from him and their marriage so that she may marry again. The wife thereupon returns the document to the rabbi, who makes a tear in it, signifying that it has been executed and so that it may not be used again. A certificate, called a *sh'tar*, is then issued to the wife, attesting to the fact that the divorce was indeed given her on that day and she must be able to produce this sh'tar in order to remarry.

Divorce can also be given by proxy or even, in certain circumstances, by mail. The laws concerning these procedures are beyond the scope of this book, and in this, as in all matters pertaining to divorce, an Orthodox rabbi must be consulted. Jewish law and the law of the State of Israel do not recognize as legal a divorce written by any but an Orthodox rabbi who should, ideally, be a *m'sader gittin*: a rabbi specially versed in the laws of *gittin*—divorce.

Once a couple is divorced, they may remarry only if neither has gotten married (and divorced) in the meantime and if both have led respectable lives.

An important feature of the Jewish laws of divorce and remarriage must be mentioned here. If a married woman has an adulterous relationship with a man, whether he is married or not, she is forbidden to marry him after obtaining a divorce from her husband. If such a marriage does take place, through ignorance of the facts, that marriage must be dissolved. So important is this law that the adulterer's name is mentioned in the gett and in the sh'tar given the woman, to prevent any possibility of their marrying later. This law, incidentally, has come under fire recently in Israel where all matters of marriage and divorce are under religious law. Mention of the guilty man's name in the gett itself was not objected to, but mention in the sh'tar was, since it was said that this would harm his reputation. So far the religious authorities and the Knesset (legislature) have ignored the protest.

Any property, including dowry, brought by a woman to the marriage, must be returned to her on getting divorced, except in the case of infidelity on the woman's part. As noted above, a printed gett is not valid; it must be handwritten by an Orthodox rabbi.

CHALITZA

In accordance with the Torah (Deut. 25:5-10), if a man dies without having children, it is the obligation of his brother to marry his widow. The male child born of this *levirate marriage* would then be considered the legal heir of the deceased brother.

In our times this in many cases becomes impossible. Often the surviving brother is already married, for example. In any event, as early as Talmudic times, the rabbis decided that in every case where levirate marriage is indicated, the *chalitza* procedure should be resorted to. This procedure is found in the same chapter of Deuteronomy and recognizes the fact that there can be no marriage without consent of both parties. It gives the brother-in-law the option of refusing to marry his brother's widow. The widow then signifies her consent and is free to remarry whom she pleases.

Among observant Jews the chalitza ceremony is always carried out when indicated, since without it the widow may not remarry. In practice, the widow and her brother-in-law appear before a bet din composed of three observant Jews. The widow accuses her brother-in-law of refusing to marry her. The brother-in-law acknowledges this fact and the widow, following the procedure outlined in the Torah, takes off her brother-in-law's shoe (actually a special shoe provided by the bet din for that purpose) and spits on the ground in front of him. All the formulas of rejection and acceptance are in Hebrew, but must be translated into whatever language both can understand if they do not understand Hebrew. The widow is then given a document called a *gett chalitza*, and with this document she may remarry. The eldest brother must undertake the chalitza ceremony, but if he refuses, any of the other surviving brothers may do so.

No chalitza is needed if: the dead husband has a child by a former marriage; the dead husband was sterile or impotent; the surviving brother-in-law is married to a sister of the widow, or the surviving brothers-in-law are minors or mentally or physically unfit for marriage.

Among the Ashkenazim, levirate marriage is forbidden and chalitza required. Among the Sephardim, levirate marriage is permitted but chalitza is far more common. A widow who requires chalitza and does not undergo the ceremony is considered an adulteress if she marries again (since legally she should be her brother-in-law's wife) and her children will be *mamzerim* and not eligible to marry Jews.

Both the United States and the Soviet Union, well known for their strict laws governing the entrance of aliens, will give temporary visas to women who have come to perform the chalitza ceremony with a brother-in-law.

14

Menstrual Uncleanness and the Mikva

ACCORDING to the Torah, any appearance of blood from the vagina makes a woman ritually unclean. What this means is that she may not have sexual relations with her husband. By extension, her husband may not even touch her because this might lead to the violation of an important commandment (Lev. 15:19 and 18:19).

An immense amount has been written about ritual uncleanness and the conduct of married people during this period of impurity, but we cannot go into such detail here. Basically the law is this:

1. The moment a woman notices any appearance of blood from her vagina, even if it is only a spot on her underthings, she becomes a *nidda*, ritually unclean, and must abstain from sexual relations with her husband. In addition, she becomes generally unclean and communicates ritual impurity by her touch. For this reason, very observant Jews will not shake hands with a woman be-

cause it is assumed that all women are in a state of ritual impurity because we have no way of knowing otherwise, modesty forbidding our asking.

2. If the flow of blood is not due to normal menstruation—say from an injury—she is still a *nidda,* just as if she were menstruating. This also applies to the blood resulting from the loss of virginity on the wedding night. The couple must abstain from further sexual relations until (in this case) eleven "clean" days have passed in which no further blood is seen.

3. When bleeding is caused by normal menstruation, it is assumed that the period will last five days. At the end of these five days, the woman must count seven days in which no sign of blood appears. Then she must purify herself in a *mikva* (see below). Even if her period ends one day after it begins, she may not start counting the seven clean days until five days, including the day blood first appeared, have gone by.

Actually, customs differ here, and among some Sephardim, the minimum period before starting to count the seven clean days is not five but three days. In any event, all Jewish couples abstain from sexual relations during ten to twelve consecutive days out of every month. This may have something to do with the low divorce rate among Orthodox Jews, since experts tell us that sexual difficulties are at the bottom of almost all divorces. Perhaps this enforced twelve-day period of abstinence makes the couple appreciate each other more when they are free completely to express their love for each other.

4. If a woman's period goes on beyond five days, she must count the seven clean days from the day on which no blood appears.

5. When the seven clean days are counted, the woman must take a bath of total immersion in a specially constructed ritual purification bath called a *mikva.* All sizeable Jewish communities possess such a bath and it is considered so important that the Jewish law states that when a new community is being formed in a place, the

mikva must be the first construction undertaken. Only
then is a synagogue built. Immersion must be complete
and there must be nothing between her and the water. In
addition she must be accompanied by another woman,
over the age of twelve, who makes sure she is completely
covered by the water, even including the hair of her head,
which may not remain floating on the surface.

Since the Jewish day ends at sundown, the wife finishes
counting the seven clean days at this hour. The law is
that she must immerse herself in the mikva as soon after
this as the stars are clearly visible, so as not to delay the
performance of this important mitzva and to make possible the equally important mitzva of conjugal relations
with her husband. Accordingly, dusk is the usual hour for
women to visit the mikva and they are rarely seen there
during the daytime. This extends even to Shabbat and a
woman whose seven clean days end at sundown on Friday
will go to the mikva at that time.

6. The blood accompanying childbirth also makes a
woman ritually unclean. If the child born is a boy, she is
considered unclean for seven days as a result of the birth,
after which she must count seven clean days and then go to the
mikva. If she gives birth to a girl, the unclean period is fourteen days, after which the seven clean days are counted. This
is the law (Lev. 12:2-5) but custom in most communities,
based on the same verses, dictates a period of forty days for a
boy and eighty days for a girl. Use of the mikva has the special
name of *taharat mishpacha*, or family purity, and those families in which taharat mishpacha is observed will know what
the prevailing practice is. In any event, the above laws specify
a minimum period of abstinence from sexual relations after
giving birth. Since all cases are different, the attending physician's advice to his patient, in this case the mother, must be
followed.

The law regarding uncleanness as a result of childbirth applies
even if no blood issues from the vagina during the birth process,
as, for example, in the case of Caesarian section.

If no mikva exists in the place where a couple lives, the wife may take the bath of ritual purification in a river. In such cases it is customary to wear a very loose bathing costume so that her entire body is covered by water. If no useable river is available, a lake or the ocean will do.

The importance of taharat mishpacha to the observant Jew is based on the fact that the sexual relations of man and wife constitute one of the greatest and most important mitzvas; without the purification of the mikva it cannot, or should not, take place.

To the Jew, the idea of having intercourse with a woman during her menstrual period is revolting; so much so that it is difficult for most Jews to believe that there are people to whom it makes no difference. Yet physicians tell us that married couples who pay no attention to "the time of the month" are far more common than is supposed, although not among the Jews. This fear of, perhaps unwittingly, having intercourse at the time of the wife's uncleanness is so strong that it has led observant couples wishing to practice birth control to avoid the use of the "pill," because of the very high incidence of breakthrough bleeding (bleeding or spotting between normal menstrual periods) that occurs due to its use. In other words, evidence of blood might be discovered after having intercourse and this is a risk Jews simply do not wish to take. In addition, if even the slightest spotting occurs, the woman is ritually unclean for twelve days thereafter, and the number of days a month on which a couple could have sexual relations might be reduced to very few or even none.

Men also use the mikva, but for different reasons, obviously. Among the very Orthodox, and particularly among the Chasidim and students of the *Kabbala* (chapter 42), it is customary for men to visit the mikva on Friday afternoon, before the start of the Sabbath. Many men go to the mikva just once a year, before Yom Kippur, while others never go because it is not in their tradition to do so. Mikva in its strictest sense is an obligation only upon married women.

PART
IV

Illness, Medicine, Death, Burial and Mourning

15

Illness, Contraception, Abortion, Euthanasia and Suicide

ILLNESS

IT might seem odd to find laws concerning illness, but such laws, as well as a wide range of customs, exist among the Jews.

To begin with, visiting the ill, called *bikkur cholim* in Hebrew, is an important mitzva, and Jews look for opportunities to practice it. Bikkur cholim societies exist in most traditional Jewish communities and from simple visits to the ill, they have gradually taken responsibility for caring for indigent patients as well. They provide kosher meals for poor Jews in both Jewish and non-Jewish hospitals and pay hospital and doctor bills for patients unable to afford them. The large Jewish hospitals the world over are a logical outgrowth of the bikkur cholim societies, and the fact that non-Jewish patients are very much in evidence in all Jewish hospitals is a direct result of the rabbinical laws stating that the ill of the Gentiles must also be visited.

In addition to the positive command to visit the ailing, there are numerous laws concerning those situations in which the care of the ill comes into conflict with other laws, such as those prohibiting work and travel on the Sabbath, the dietary laws, the prohibition of any contact between husband and wife during the wife's menstrual uncleanness, fast days, and similar restrictions.

What all these laws boil down to is that preservation of human life takes precedence over all commandments except those forbidding murder, incest and the worship of idols. Accordingly it is not only permissible to violate the Sabbath for the sake of the dangerously ill, it is mandatory to do so and such an act is considered a positive mitzva.

In ordinary circumstances, when the Sabbath must be broken in an emergency, it is considered best to ask a non-Jew, for whom there is nothing improper about Sabbath work, to perform the necessary labor. But in the case of illness, for instance that of a sick man in a cold room who requires heat on the Sabbath, a fire must be lit for him and in such a case it is not permitted to ask a Goy to do it. The Jew—any Jew—must do it himself, so as to teach other Jews how important it is to remove sick people from danger. In the Talmud it states that if there is a town in which there is the slightest hesitation about violating the Sabbath for a dangerously ill person, the rabbi of that town should be considered a great sinner, because he has not taught his people proper reverence for human life.

As to what constitutes danger, the law is that if the patient says he is in danger and the physician says he is not, the patient is to be believed. If the physician says there is danger and the patient says there is not, the physician is to be believed. In the case that both the patient and the physician agree that there is no danger, but a second doctor says there is, it is considered that there is no danger. But if two doctors agree that there is danger, their opinion outweighs that of even "one hundred doctors" who say the contrary.

As noted earlier, a woman in childbirth and for seven days thereafter is automatically considered dangerously ill. In this particular case, however, it is permissible to ask a non-Jew to perform necessary work on Shabbat instead of doing it oneself. If, however, finding a non-Jew to do the work will cause delay, the Jew must not hesitate, but must do whatever is necessary. It is permissible to travel, light fire, handle money or do anything on the Sabbath or holidays which one does on weekdays if a dangerous illness is in evidence.

The suspension of fasting on Yom Kippur and other fast days is also indicated where there is a possibility that fasting may harm the observant person. Pregnant women are not obliged to fast if they feel discomfort, since during pregnancy all women are considered ill and their "cravings" for special foods must be catered to. The Talmud states that if a pregnant woman demands to be given pork on Yom Kippur, her wishes must be complied with.

By the same token, the dietary laws do not apply to medicaments if no substitute can be found for them. It is not uncommon, for example, to find children (or even grownups) whose particular nutritional needs require certain amounts of ingestible fat which is most easily available to their systems in the form of pork. In such cases if a doctor prescribes pork for a child, it is the duty of his parents to make sure that he gets it. Often this is done by having him eat the ordinarily forbidden meat at the house of a non-Jewish neighbor or friend, for whom the eating of pork is not improper.

In the case of a grownup, if the doctor prescribes pork and the patient is an observant Jew, it is to be assumed that he will reject it and probably vomit it up—a not uncommon occurrence—if he does force himself to eat it. In such cases it is the duty of those who attend him to lie to him and tell him that it is veal or some other kosher meat.

Customs and Rituals of Illness

The customs—as opposed to laws—surrounding illness are many and widely varied, but among them the three most important are the reciting of psalms, the adding of a name and the giving of charity.

When a person is dangerously ill, it is the custom to have psalms recited on his behalf by pious men. Similarly, in cases of dangerous illness, the very Orthodox will call in a learned man who, in a ceremony involving a short prayer, will add to the ill person's name a new one, in the hope of averting further illness.

This name is chosen by opening the Bible at random; the first suitable name that appears on the page is given to the ill person. It is also a widespread custom to use the name Chaim for a man or Chaya for a woman, instead of one chosen at random. (Both of these names have the general meaning of "life.") After the new name has been added, a prayer for the ill (the *Mi-sheberach*) is said in which the patient's new name is mentioned before his old one, although the old one is not abandoned.

There is sanction for this practice in the Talmud, but it is by no means mandatory. The fact is that Jews are not the only ones who have recourse to it, other peoples doing so in the hope that Death will not recognize the person under his new name. We have no evidence that this was the case among the Talmudic rabbis who recommended it, but if the custom were to be called superstitious, it could with difficulty be defended from the charge.

The third measure taken by the pious is the giving of money to charity in the name of the sick person in hope of averting more serious developments.

There are two other prayers and a further custom which should be mentioned. When a friend or relative of a sick person is called to the Torah (chapter 28), after his portion has been read he will often request that a special form of the prayer *Mi-sheberach* be recited in which the name of the sick person is mentioned and God's blessing for a full recovery, or *refuah shelemah,* is asked. This prayer may also be said on other occasions in the presence of a minyan.

After a man has passed through a serious illness, has escaped death or injury from violence or accident, or has returned from a voyage in which the ocean was crossed, he should go to the synagogue at the first opportunity, and, on being called up to the Torah, after his portion is read, say the blessing called *Gomel* in which God is thanked for having delivered him from danger. The text of all these prayers and blessings will be found in any *siddur.*

Finally, it is the custom that after a near-relative has been ill and has recovered, and particularly after he or she has had an operation, one gives a kiddush for the congregation following the Shabbat services, on the first possible opportunity.

CONTRACEPTION

The attitude of the Jewish law toward contraception is also based on the principle of the sanctity of human life. The Orthodox prohibit the husband from practicing contraception in any form, but allow his wife to do so if her life will be endangered by pregnancy, or even if she simply does not wish to have more children because pregnancy or birth is difficult or painful. She may practice contraception in such cases even over her husband's objections, but if the only reason is to stop having children, she should have her husband's agreement as common sense indicates she should, marriage being a partnership whose most important initial purpose is the establishment of a family.

Sterilization is also permitted with no limitations to speak of but only in the case of women. Jewish law is unequivocally against castration or sterilization of males, even including animals, unless its purpose is to preserve life. Castration is the accepted procedure in control of certain cancers, for example.

As noted earlier, the Orthodox forbid the use of oral contraceptives, but only because of the incidence of breakthrough bleeding. The use of the diaphragm is not prohibited nor is the use of post-coital spermicides or intrauterine devices, as long as no breakthrough bleeding results from use of the I.U.D.s. The extreme Orthodox tend to forbid contraception in any form except, of course, if there is danger in the wife's becoming pregnant. Coitus interruptus, withdrawal of the penis and deposition of semen outside the vagina, is totally forbidden to all Jews under all circumstances.

The desire to limit the size of the family is objected to mostly by the very Orthodox, that is to say, those among whom the men dress only in black. A great many Orthodox couples are believers in planned parenthood.

ABORTION

Jewish law is that therapeutic abortion for the purpose of removing the pregnant woman from danger to life is not only permissible but mandatory, if, in the opinion of competent physicians, it is necessary. Such an abortion is permissible even over the woman's objections.

In exact terms, this is taken to mean that until labor starts, the fetus has no independent life outside its mother; if its mother dies, it will die too. Once labor has started, the child's life is still considered less important than that of the mother since we know that the mother is alive and will live whereas we do not know that concerning the child. Therefore, in extremely difficult deliveries, it is permitted to dismember the child within the womb or the birth canal and remove it a limb at a time in order to save the mother's life. Once the child's head has appeared outside the birth canal, however, birth should not be interfered with, unless it is evident that the child would not survive the possible death of the mother, in which case it is permissible to do whatever is necessary to save the mother's life. Abortion for non-therapeutic purposes, for example to prevent the birth of a mamzer, conceived in adultery, is by general agreement not permitted. Abortion to prevent the birth of a deformed child in the case that the mother contracted German measles (Rubella) in the first three months of pregnancy, is permitted, according to most authorities.

Basic to the Jewish attitude regarding abortion is the Jewish belief that the soul of a human being enters the body at the moment of birth, not at the moment of conception, as is held by some other religions. Really, it is difficult to say with exactness just *what* the "Jewish belief" is regarding matters not covered by the laws of the Torah. A hint is contained in the law that a child who dies before he is thirty days old is not mourned for.

EUTHANASIA AND SUICIDE

Euthanasia, or "mercy killing," is absolutely prohibited by Jewish law and is considered equivalent to murder. At the same time it is understood that if a Jew is dying in pain and there is no hope for his recovery, we are not required artificially to prolong his agony, if this would be against his wish. On the contrary, he should be permitted to die as quickly as possible and obstacles to his dying should be removed.

To make this point quite clear, Jewish law forbids speeding up the dying process artificially: the Shulchan Aruch (chapter 25) says that it is forbidden to move a dying man in order to hasten his departure, even to the extent of removing the pillow from beneath his head. But if there is an outside hindrance to his dying such as "a knocking sound near the house, that is, a wood chopper, or if there is salt on his tongue and these impede the exit of his soul, it is permitted to remove it therefrom since no positive act is involved, but only the removal of the hindrance."

That this is open to broader interpretation is immediately obvious when we consider that most of the modern devices used to prolong life artificially can be nullified by the simple turning off of an electric switch or, if even this is felt to be interference, the failure to replace an empty glucose or plasma bottle or oxygen tank. Naturally such a decision is hardly one for a layman to undertake: a particularly competent Orthodox rabbi will be able in most cases to find a recent legal decision to guide him in his answer when consulted. And, of course, the law of the land must be our first consideration.

Once again, hastening the death of a human being by positive action is forbidden and this includes allowing the patient to have access to poison which he may use to that end, since suicide and its abetment are also forbidden. Suicide is, however, permitted if a Jew is faced with unbearable torture at the hands of heathens, particularly if he is being tortured to elicit information harmful to his people or his country, or to force him to commit idol worship, incest, or murder. Occurrences of this sort have, sadly, been far from uncommon in Jewish history.

16

Death and the Care of the Dead

THE laws concerning death, care of the Jewish dead, burial and mourning, are voluminous, and the subject of countless books and legal decisions. It is interesting to note that the single most authoritative book on the laws of mourning, the *Kol Bo,* was written in Columbus, Ohio. Its author, Rabbi Leopold Greenwald, came to the United States from Hungary and his book is the standard guide to the subject in Orthodox communities the world over.

Despite the great number of laws and customs, the essential rules governing the conduct of Jews at this saddest and most significant of times can be given in brief form.

WHEN A JEW IS ABOUT TO DIE

When an Orthodox Jew fears that the end may be approaching, he recites the *viddui,* a confession to God, followed by the Shema Israel and a starkly simple declaration of the Jews' belief that God is not only the dispenser of mercy and justice, but both are the same. The words of the Jew's final statement on earth are *Adonai Hu Ha-Elohim:* the Lord is God.

To understand this we must be aware that, according to all interpretations of the Bible, the two most commonly used names of God are meant to describe the two essential aspects of God that human beings are capable of understanding—mercy and rigor. In every instance that the Name spelled with the four Hebrew letters yud, he, vav and he—which Jews commonly pronounce Adonai, because it is forbidden to pronounce God's Name as it is actually spelled—is used in the Bible, it refers to the quality of God which we understand as mercy: the forgiving of sin and toleration of human weakness. When the name Elohim is used, reference is to the quality of rigor or justice, meaning the punishment of transgression. In our final declaration at the time of death we declare that Adonai (mercy) and Elohim (rigor) are one and the same thing as they pertain to God. It is these words, incidentally, which close the service for Yom Kippur in the Sephardic rite.

No Jew is to die alone. When it is evident that death is approaching, guardians are present at the bedside to make sure the dying man receives any comfort it is possible to give in his last hours. If he wishes help in the recitation of the viddui, this is given him.

It is a law that a Cohen may not enter the house of a dying person since if he is within the house when the death occurs, he will be defiled by the presence of the corpse. This law is disregarded in many communities and if the attending physician is a Cohen it is, of course, perfectly permissible. A Cohen is also permitted to attend a close relative who is dying, since he is not prohibited from contact with the corpse of such a relative.

It is a widely observed custom that when death occurs in a house, all water standing in glasses, vases, pots, etc., is emptied out into the street. The purpose of this is to let people know that someone has died so that neighbors may come to comfort the mourners and Cohanim will know that they may not enter.

CARE OF THE DEAD

A mitzva that takes precedence over almost all other mitzvas is that of seeing that a Jewish corpse receives proper burial. In the case of indigent Jews, it is the duty of the community to see to this and that duty is not shirked. I have, at two different times, lived in cities of the American Southwest when indigent Jewish hitchhikers have been killed in automobile accidents nearby. In one case—the city was Denver—the hitchhiker was a homeless wanderer who had no known relatives. He was buried with all respect by the Jewish community. In the other case, in Albuquerque, the victim was a student and his body was flown back to the East Coast so that it might be buried in his native city. The entire expense was paid by the small Albuquerque community since the lad's mother was a widow, without means.

BURIAL SOCIETIES AND PREPARATION OF THE BODY

Almost all communities have a burial society, called in Hebrew the *Chevra Kadisha*, or Holy Brotherhood. In some places it is known as the *Chevra shel Emet,* or Brotherhood of Truth. The members of the society are almost always unpaid volunteers who dedicate themselves to making sure that all Jews in their community receive proper burial. In cities with both a Sephardic and an Ashkenazic community, each group will usually have its own chevra kadisha. Among the Orthodox in the United States and all Jews in Latin America, preparation of the body and burial are handled by the chevra kadisha, and morticians and funeral parlors are not resorted to. No Cohen may belong to a chevra kadisha nor may a Cohen enter a cemetery, except for the burial of a near relative.

When death occurs, the chevra kadisha must be informed and the body taken care of by them. Everything should be left in their hands. The washing and preparation of the corpse is handled by them and is usually done by women. In the case of female corpses this is mandatory in most communities. There are occasions when complete care of the body is not possible—victims of fire and certain accidents—but wherever it is possible, the body should be washed in a special way and dressed in a shroud, called *tachri-chim.*

After the corpse has been prepared for burial, it is placed on the floor with straw under it (or sometimes on a special low platform) and covered with a cloth. A candle is lit at the head and the body is placed with the feet pointing toward the door, either in the home or in a special place maintained by the chevra kadisha, depending on local law and custom. If the body has been placed in a coffin, the coffin is placed on the floor in the same position. It then remains there until it is taken to the cemetery. The chevra kadisha usually administers the cemetery and keeps a stock of tachrichim ready. It also has an arrangement with a carpenter, usually a non-Jew, who will make a coffin for the deceased person on very short notice. This is simple since the coffin consists of six boards and the minimum number of nails necessary to hold them together.

The body must not be left alone. A *shomer,* or guardian, must be present at all times until the body is buried.

In actual fact, the preparation of the corpse and care of the dead is a complex subject and has been barely touched on here. Also, from the Jewish point of view, since the chevra kadisha, who are familiar with all the laws, takes over once death occurs, there is little point in going into more detail.

AUTOPSY AND DONATION OF ORGANS

The use of Jewish corpses and indeed of human bodies of any sort for teaching purposes in medical schools is violently opposed by certain extremely Orthodox Jews. Controversy regarding use of Jewish corpses in particular has been especially acute in Israel where many bequeath their bodies to medical schools for just this purpose. The purchase of non-Jewish corpses—with full consent of those responsible and within the law—for teaching purposes has been encouraged by some prominent Orthodox rabbis, including the late Rabbi Kook. The famous Sephardic Chief Rabbi, Benzion Uziel, even approved of dissection of Jewish corpses as long as proper respect and care were observed.

Other Orthodox rabbis, however, state flatly that no benefit may be derived from a corpse (this is indeed the law), Jewish or otherwise, and that dissection for teaching purposes is totally forbidden, particularly in the Holy Land. Obedience to this ruling would mean that medical education in Israel would come to a standstill and that, in fact, no observant Jew could aspire to being a physician anywhere in the world. Since there are many Orthodox physicians, it is obvious that a more liberal view has prevailed.

Autopsy to determine cause of death for purposes of protecting the living is viewed more leniently but even here there are certain extreme Orthodox elements who inveigh against it. Their opinions are rarely taken into account, and if there is any evidence of communicable disease or environmental factors having caused death, the law of the land in most countries makes autopsy mandatory and Jewish law cannot object to it.

Regarding the donation of organs such as kidneys, eyes, etc., for use in the living, this now has the approval of rabbis of the most unimpeachable orthodoxy. The reasoning is that, in the words of a Canadian rabbi, Rabbi N. I. Rabinovitch, "there is no greater merit even in death than contributing to saving a life." Donation of organs for strictly cosmetic purposes does not, in the opinion of most rabbis, justify mutilation of the dead.

17

Burial

THE body must be buried on the same day death occurs if this is possible; if not, on the day after, unless it is Shabbat. If a Jew dies on a holiday, it is permitted to have him buried by non-Jews on the first day of the holiday, with Jews supervising the work. On the second day, it is permissible for Jews to do everything, even though the holiday is still in force. On Shabbat or Yom Kippur no burials can take place, but the body may be buried in the evening, immediately following the end of Shabbat.

A Jew must be buried in a specially consecrated cemetery. The coffin should be made of the cheapest materials possible, usually pine boards, and often gaps are left in the bottom of it so that the body may be in contact with the ground. Where the law of the land allows, it is considered best to be buried directly in the ground, without a coffin of any sort, and in Israel all burials are effected in this fashion. In the Jewish view, man came from the earth and must return to the earth and the quicker the better.

In most communities, particularly in the Americas, no flowers are allowed at a Jewish funeral and no stone is raised over the grave until a year has gone by, although Sephardic custom allows a stone to be raised after thirty days. In general it may be said that Jewish law forbids excessive show at a burial: the coffin must be made of plain boards, no new clothes may be put on the corpse, with the exception of the shroud, and men are buried in the prayer shawl worn while alive. It is forbidden to bury precious objects with a corpse, except a wedding ring.

Viewing the body is forbidden. The coffin must be closed as soon as the body is placed in it and may not be reopened except for legal reasons, if there be any. The reason for all the above regulations is to assure that all Jews are equal in death. This is even the reason for prohibiting the viewing of the body; it is stated that a man who dies of poverty and starvation will show this on his face, so no one should be allowed to look at him and make comparisons with the appearance of a more fortunate man. Millionaire and pauper are buried in exactly the same conditions.

Embalming is not permitted except where the law of the land requires it. Such would be the case, for example, of a Jew who died overseas and his family wished the body returned to the United States for burial. United States law demands that the body be embalmed (or preserved with lime and wrapped in a special winding sheet) before it can be shipped into the country, and Jewish law has no objection to this because the law requires it. Cremation is prohibited by Jewish law except in special cases of plague, epidemic or natural disaster where it is necessary for the well-being of the living.

Burial itself is simple. The coffin is carried to the grave by people designated by the next of kin and the funeral service is said by the rabbi. Eulogies are delivered either at the graveside or in the small building maintained by the chevra kadisha in the cemetery. It is considered a mitzva for the friends of the family to cast the first shovelfuls of dirt onto the coffin, thus participating in the actual burial in accordance with the commandment.

After the grave is filled, the husband, father, son or brother of the deceased says *kaddish* at the graveside in the presence of a minyan, and this is the first time kaddish is said for the dead person. After washing their hands, those present leave the cemetery and the family returns to the home. It is only then that formal mourning begins.

It should be noted that while, among the Ashkenazim, women also accompany the body to the cemetery, among the Sephardim only men do so, even the wife, sister or daughter of the deceased being forbidden to leave the house or other place where the body has been kept.

18

Mourning, Shiva, Kaddish, Yohrtzeit and Yizkor

ON learning of the death of a father, mother, sister, brother, spouse or child it is necessary immediately to cover the head and say the following blessing: *"Baruch Ata Adonai, Elohenu Melech ha-olam, Dayan ha-emet"* (Blessed art Thou, O Lord our God, King of the universe, the True Judge).

On saying this blessing, which must be recited standing, the mourner must perform the act called *k'riah*, the tearing of his clothing. Formerly a cut was made in the outer garment or coat but today it is customary to tear one's shirt. The way it is usually done is that another person present makes a small cut in the garment of the mourner and the mourner then tears it lengthwise, not crosswise, from the cut to the length of three inches or so. Women must also perform the k'riah, but in such a way as to be consonant with modesty. The tear is made over the heart for a mother or father and on the right side for other relatives, husband, wife, etc.

In some places it is the custom to perform k'riah not on hearing the news of the death, but in the cemetery, following the burial.

This is not in accord with Jewish law, and even where it is the common practice, should not be done by observant Jews. The time to perform k'riah is on finding out about the death and certainly before the coffin is closed.

If death occurs or news concerning it is received on a Sabbath or holiday, the k'riah must be put off until after sundown. K'riah is an essential duty and an obligation on all Jews since it is a visible and physical sign of mourning, respect and grief for the departed relative.

Neither k'riah nor any of the other rites of mourning are observed for an infant less than thirty days old. K'riah is not performed for a suicide (but see below for definition) or for a *m'shumad*, one who has abandoned Judaism and adopted another faith. The question is often asked, what if one does not learn of the death of a parent until months, or even years, after it happened? The answer is that no matter when one hears of it, one is obliged to perform k'riah at once, unless it is a Sabbath or holiday. These days it is common to find the custom of using a necktie for k'riah, but this is not really acceptable.

THE PERIOD OF MOURNING: SHIVA AND SH'LOSHIM

On returning home from the cemetery, the family starts "sitting *shiva*." This means that they must remain in mourning for seven days, inside the house, after the burial. During this time they may not leave the house, except in emergencies, must not shave, cut the hair, put on new clothes, sit on chairs or wear shoes. Usually small stools or boxes are provided for them to sit on. Since the family cannot go to the synagogue to say kaddish, the congregation arranges to have a minyan pray at the house of the mourners during this seven-day period. If it is impossible to get a minyan to come to the house, those that say kaddish—the men—are permitted to pray in the synagogue so that the prayer will not be omitted. On Shabbat it is permitted to leave the house and pray in the synagogue.

Immediately on returning home from the cemetery and before starting to sit shiva, the family eats a meal, usually consisting of a hard-boiled egg, a pinch of ash and lentils. This meal must not be prepared in the home, but brought in by friends or neighbors.

Shiva, the seven-day mourning period, is observed no matter where one is on hearing the news of death and burial of a relative for whom mourning is obligatory, as long as the notification arrives within thirty days of the death. If it arrives after that, shiva is not observed.

If a Jewish holiday comes during the seven days of shiva, it is permitted to celebrate it and shiva ends at that point. If, for example, a family starts sitting shiva and an hour later the sun goes down and a holiday commences, shiva is over for them. This is true even if the time elapsed is less than one hour.

If the death occurs on a holiday or on one of the intermediate days of Sukkot or Passover, the mourners do not start formal mourning or sitting shiva until after the conclusion of the holiday. The last day of the holiday, however, counts as one of the seven days of the shiva period. This holds for both Sephardim and Ashkenazim.

After seven days of mourning are completed, the mourners may take up normal living again, but with restrictions. The twenty-three days following shiva are a semi-mourning period as well and the entire thirty days are called *sh'loshim*. It is forbidden during this time to shave, cut the hair or put on new clothes. It is also forbidden to attend parties and similar festivities during this period and many Jews extend this restriction to the entire year following the death of a parent. Such festivities as weddings, circumcision feasts, etc., to celebrate a mitzva, are not included in this proscription.

In many communities it is customary to say special memorial prayers in the synagogue on the thirtieth day after death and burial. In other places this is done at the cemetery.

A candle or other light is often kept burning in the home during the entire sh'loshim period and in many communities, particularly among the Sephardim, a lamp is kept burning in the synagogue for a full year and is discontinued only after the death anniversary.

As indicated, among the Orthodox mourning continues in a very modified form for a full twelve months after the death of a parent, in that mourners do not go to movies, theater or celebration of non-Jewish events. The *Yohrtzeit* (see below) signals the end of all mourning.

The Jewish law concerning excessive mourning is specific: it is not allowed. There are seven days of intense mourning and after that it is prohibited except in a very relative way since mourning after the shiva period is considered unhealthy for the living. The wearing of black clothes, a black tie or armband is prohibited if black is not the color a person uses at all times. In some Catholic countries, Jews will occasionally adopt local custom and wear mourning but this is against Jewish practice and should not be done.

KADDISH AND YOHRTZEIT

The kaddish prayer, an essential part of all prayer services, is said by male mourners for a period of eleven months following the burial. This prayer, which makes no mention of death, is a hymn of sanctification of God's Name and cannot be said except in the presence of a minyan. If less than ten men are present, kaddish cannot be recited and accordingly male mourners make a point of attending daily synagogue services since the kaddish must be said every day during the eleven-month period.

If mourning lasts for twelve months, why is kaddish said only for eleven? The answer usually given is that kaddish is said to mitigate the punishment in *Gehinnom* (the Jewish equivalent of hell) of dead relatives. Jewish tradition has it that no Jewish sinner is punished for more than a year in Gehinnom, so if the sons of a deceased person were to say kaddish for the entire year, this would lead people to think that the dead parent must have been a great sinner. Accordingly, kaddish ceases at eleven months so as not to provoke disrespectful thoughts concerning the dead. In most Sephardic communities, kaddish ends after eleven months for one week, and is then resumed for the remaining three weeks completing the full year to the death anniversary.

It should be noted that the above explanation of why kaddish is said for only eleven months is *aggada* (speculation), and must not be taken as Jewish dogma. (For a discussion of the Jewish attitudes toward the afterlife, see chapter 41.)

A final word about the kaddish: it is written not in Hebrew but in Aramaic, except for the first two words, *Yitgadal v'yitkadash,* "Magnified and sanctified." The explanation is that in Talmudic times, from which it dates, it was recited at the end of a sermon or lecture and many of the people who had gathered to hear were ignorant of Hebrew. Accordingly the prayer was recited in Aramaic, a language they all understood. But the first two words were in Hebrew because, according to Abudraham (Spain, 12th century), these exalted words of praise cannot be adequately expressed in any other language.

Yohrtzeit, a Yiddish word, is the death anniversary, according to the Jewish, not the civil, calendar. On that day it is required that close male relatives say kaddish, and among both Ashkenazim and Sephardim a twenty-four-hour candle or lamp is lit in the home. The Sephardim light a special lamp in the synagogue as well. The Yohrtzeit is celebrated every year on the anniversary date by all Jews: the Sephardim refer to it as the *Nachala.*

The forms of observing the anniversary vary greatly. The non-Chasidic Ashkenazim, or *Mitnagdim,* fast on the Yohrtzeit of a parent. Among the Chasidim, the Yohrtzeit is the occasion for a feast or kiddush following the morning services. Among the Sephardim, special memorial prayers called *Hashkabot* are said at the request of the mourner in the synagogue on the Sabbath preceding the anniversary. It is also common among the Sephardim to celebrate the anniversary with a feast held in the home at which prayers are recited and food and drink provided for those present. This feast is usually called a *Meldado,* or reading, among Ladino-speaking Jews. Arabic-speaking Jews call it a *Nachala,* the word for the anniversary itself.

It is common in many modern synagogues to find "memorial tablets" with the name and both the Jewish and civil date of the death of former members of the congregation and deceased relatives of living members. In our days, each name has an electric socket opposite it into which a small lightbulb is placed on the Yohrtzeit, remaining lit for twenty-four hours. This electric light is a perfectly kosher substitute for a *Yohrtzeit licht, hilula* (death commemoration) lamp or other memorial light, and, while not traditional, quite acceptable.

The death anniversary of a prominent rabbi is the occasion for special ceremonies in many congregations, depending on the connection of the congregation with the deceased. The Chasidim observe the Yohrtzeits of famous rabbis of their own particular group and the Sephardim will celebrate the nachala of a famous rabbi from the town or locality which was the point of origin of the founders of the congregation. All Sephardim celebrate the death anniversary of Simeon Bar Yochai with a meldado in the synagogue during which sections of the Zohar are read. The celebration of Lag B'Omer as the nachala of Rabbi Simeon Bar Yochai is more fully described in chapter 32.

UNVEILING THE GRAVESTONE

On the first anniversary of the death it is customary in some countries to go to the Bet Olam, or cemetery, and there unveil the gravestone, called in Hebrew, *Matseva*, which has been prepared in the meantime and placed on the tomb shortly before this date. There are special ceremonies accompanying this unveiling, but it should be noted that outside the Americas they are quite uncommon. Sephardic custom permits the unveiling of the stone on the thirtieth day after the burial, but Ashkenazi law or custom in most communities prohibits it until one year has gone by.

It is the custom of all Jews to visit the graves of their loved ones during the days between Rosh Hashana and Yom Kippur as well as on other dates, but there is no obligation to do so. When Jews visit a grave, on leaving they place a pebble on the gravestone. This is simply to indicate that someone has been there and paid respects to the memory of the departed Jew.

COMFORTING THE MOURNERS

It is a positive and important mitzva to comfort mourners. Nevertheless, the Jewish way of doing so is simply to appear in the house of the mourner, either immediately or during the shiva period and to sit here, keeping the mourner company. It is not permitted to greet the mourner, nor must the mourner greet those visiting him until the third day of shiva. It is really not even permitted to offer words of comfort to the mourner until the third day, because it is felt that the grief he feels will make it impossible for him to understand them and may even deepen his feelings of sadness.

Boys under thirteen and girls under twelve are exempt from sitting shiva but are expected to perform k'riah.

The above laws concerning mourning, burial and care of the dead cover only the basic points. In the event of circumstances not covered here, or about which there may be doubt, any Orthodox rabbi will indicate the course to follow.

YIZKOR

The Ashkenazim remember the dead four times a year with a special memorial prayer called *Yizkor* or *Hazkarat Neshama*, remembrance of the soul. It is recited in the synagogue after the Haftara is read, on Yom Kippur, Sh'mini Atzeret, the last day of Passover and the second day of Shavuot. A twenty-four-hour *yohrtzeit licht* is burned in the home on these four days. It is the custom in all Orthodox synagogues that people whose parents are still alive leave the synagogue during the recitation of the prayer. The reason usually given is that many people are moved to tears during the prayer and to see them crying would be upsetting, particularly for children present.

The Sephardim do not say Yizkor.

BURIAL AND MOURNING FOR A SUICIDE, AN APOSTATE OR AN INFORMER

As mentioned earlier, a person who commits suicide is not mourned for in any way nor are funeral services recited at his grave. He is, however, buried in a Jewish cemetery. This is the law, but its interpretation is such that it is almost never applied. The reason is that according to Jewish law, no matter how much like suicide a death may look, unless there is absolute proof from eyewitnesses who warned the person against what he was about to do and then saw him do it in spite of their warnings, any person's death is assumed to be the result of other causes, usually accident or murder. If there is any reason to suppose mental unbalance before death, even of a temporary nature, it is not considered suicide no matter what the circumstances. The same is true of suicide in the face of unbearable torture at the hands of heathens.

The case of an apostate is different. As explained in chapter 46, an apostate, in Hebrew, *m'shumad*, is in our times defined as a person who not only abandons the practice of Judaism, but actually and publicly enters the ranks of another religion, usually Christianity, by way of baptism. Such a person, no matter how "sincere" his motives, is an outcast. He is not to be buried in a Jewish cemetery and is not to be mourned for. On the contrary, the law is that his brothers are to dress in white and hold a celebration on the day he dies, to rejoice in the death of an enemy of Israel. It is assumed that his parents, no matter what his transgressions, will mourn his death because he is, after all, their child. This custom is not observed in our times.

What is still observed, as it has been in the past, is the custom of the family's mourning for a m'shumad at the time of his apostasy. Among Orthodox Jews, if a member of the family adopts another religion, his relatives sit shiva for him as if he were dead. As soon as the seven-day shiva period is over, all remembrances of the apostate, pictures, etc., are destroyed and he is never mentioned again; it is as if he had never existed.

There are certain circumstances in which even a m'shumad may be buried in a Jewish cemetery. Such would be the case of a minor child who converted together with his parents, since it is assumed that he did so under parental pressure. A Jew who converted under unbearable pressure—to save the lives of his wife and children for example—and had no opportunity to return to Judaism before death, would be a borderline case, subject to the decision of a Jewish court.

In the case of an informer, or *mosser*, the same rule applies regarding burial as that of a m'shumad. A mosser is a Jew who turns against his people, for money or whatever reason, and gives information leading to the death or disgrace of other Jews. Quite obviously this does not apply to informing the police regarding criminals, but to the providing of information to the authorities of lands in which the persecution of Jews and Judaism is an official, or unofficial but pervasive, policy: the USSR, for example. Such a person is considered the lowest and most despicable sort of criminal and denied recognition as a Jew at the end of his days, even though he maintained that he was Jewish during his life.

PART
V

Daily
Jewish Life

19

Morning, Afternoon and Evening

On awaking in the morning, Orthodox Jews, both men and women, even before opening their eyes, say the short prayer, *Modeh ani*, thanking God for having restored their souls to them.

On rising from bed, it is incumbent upon men to wash their hands before reciting blessings, dressing or anything else. For this reason, the very Orthodox keep a jug of water and a basin on a small table at the bedside, so that they may wash immediately on arising. This water is referred to as negelvasser [Y.], "fingernail water." Less Orthodox Jews will walk to the bathroom or kitchen to wash. The reason for the zeal of the ultra-Orthodox will be found in their next action, putting on the *tallit katan* or *arba kanfot*. This small garment, worn by all observant Jewish males, is not put on unless a blessing is said first. Since the blessing may not be said without washing the hands, and since the Orthodox do not wish to take as many as two steps without the garment on, they wash their hands, say the blessing and put on the arba kanfot at the bedside itself. Women also wash, since there is a general proscription of walking more than four paces in the morning until one has done so.

The arba kanfot, which in Hebrew means "four corners," is an oblong or square rectangle of cotton or wool with a hole cut into the middle of it so that it may be put on over the head and worn under the ordinary daytime clothing. On each of the four corners is a tassel or "fringe," made of four specially woven woolen cords or thick threads. They are wound and knotted together in a pre-scribed fashion so that each fringe terminates with eight thread-ends. This garment is worn in obedience to a specific command-ment found in Num. 15:37-41. Here God tells Moses to com-mand the Jewish people to make ". . . throughout their genera-tions *tsitsit* [fringes] in the corners of their garments. . . . And it shall be unto you for a fringe that ye may look upon it and remember all the commandments of the Lord to do them."

Nowhere in the entire Torah is there a more specific reminder to the Jews that they are God's chosen people and that obedience to His commandments is what He has chosen them for. Here we have a commandment, incumbent only upon Jews, without any possible physical benefit, whose only purpose is to remind us that God has elected us as those who will obey His law. The arba kanfot has often been compared to the uniform of a soldier. The purpose of the uniform is to identify him in his own eyes and those of others as a servant of his country, his people or his king.

The arba kanfot, or small prayer shawl, is worn only by men and is incumbent only between dawn and sunset, although by custom it is worn at all times except when bathing or sleeping. The fringes, as indicated, are called *tsitsit*, and readers who have taken the trouble to look up the entire commandment in Num. 15:38 will have found that a blue thread is specified as one of the four, and may wonder why this is not the case today, when all threads are white. The answer is that the dye used to color the blue thread was in Biblical and Talmudic times made from a mollusk called *chilazon* and only that mollusk could be used. We no longer know the identity of the chilazon.

However, there is an exception. The Chasidim of Bratzlav, dis-ciples of Rabbi Nachman of Bratzlav, a great-grandson of the

Baal Shem Tov (chapter 44), use the *p'til t'chelet* in the manufacture of their tsitsit. The p'til t'chelet is the blue thread. Rabbi
Nachman, on a voyage to Israel some hundred and fifty years
ago, found in the Bay of Naples a mollusk which he alleged is the
chilazon. His followers (they are unique among the Chasidim in
not having a living *Rebbe*, but in adhering to the memory of a
dead *Tzaddik*) use this small marine animal to make the dye and
wear the blue thread on both the arba kanfot under their clothing
and on the large tallit over their clothing when they pray. The
Bratzlaver Chasidim are few, but I bring this up to point out the
flexibility of custom and usage even among the most Orthodox
Jews.

The Chasidim usually wear the arba kanfot under the shirt,
but with the tsitsit outside the clothing, tucked into the pockets.
Some oriental Jews, such as the Yemenites, wear it over their
shirts but under their coats. Most Jews wear the entire garment
under the shirt and it is not visible at all. The arba kanfot can
ordinarily be bought at any Jewish bookstore.

After putting on the arba kanfot, the next step is getting
dressed and there is an important law regarding clothing that is
overlooked by many otherwise observant Jews. This is the law of
shaatnez, found in Lev. 19:19, which forbids the Jew to wear
clothing made of any cloth in which wool and linen are mixed.
This has been extended in the Oral Torah to include any garment
in which both wool and linen are used, for example a wool suit
whose buttons have been sewn on with linen thread or in which
linen buckram is used to stiffen the lapels. Such a suit would be
shaatnez, a forbidden mixture, and not kosher for wear by Jews.
This is another commandment whose reason for being is not discernible and whose underlying reason is to remind us of who we
are by giving us commandments which the rest of the peoples of
the world have not been given and which only we have the privilege of obeying.

It should be noted that Maimonides (Rabbi Moshe ben Mai-
mon, Spain, 12th century), in his *Guide for the Perplexed*, does
give reasons for many of the commandments known as *chukim*
(sing. *chok*): commandments for which no reason can be imagined. It is Maimonides' contention that most of these command-

ments were given to counteract the pagan practices of a religion—that of the Nabateans—which is no longer remembered,
but which was at least a matter of record in Maimonides' time.
He cites, in most cases, the specific practices these chukim were
supposedly designed to put a stop to. Suffice it to say that Maimonides' analyses of the meanings of the chukim have never been
taken seriously by the Jews, who believe that the Torah in its
present form was created by God before He created the universe
and was given to His chosen people when He saw fit.

After dressing, men must pray the morning prayer (called
Shachrit by the Ashkenazim, after the Temple sacrifice that it
replaces). The Sephardim call this prayer quite simply *t'filla*—
prayer. On weekdays the *t'fillin*, or phylacteries, are put on, but
not on Shabbat or holidays including, among the Sephardim, the
intermediate days of the holidays as well. A more complete
description of this prayer and of the others mentioned in this
chapter will be found in Part VI.

After praying Shachrit, breakfast is eaten. It is forbidden to
eat before praying in the morning, but tea or coffee without sugar
can be taken. The serving and eating of food in the Jewish home
is governed by the dietary laws, which are discussed in detail in
chapter 21. The blessings to be said before eating or drinking and
the grace after meals are discussed in chapter 26. Many of the
blessings are found in transliteration in appendix IV.

In the afternoon, usually just before sundown, the afternoon
prayer, called *Mincha*, is said. It is followed, right after sundown,
by the evening prayer, called *Maariv* by the Ashkenazim and
Arbit by the Sephardim. Before going to bed the *K'riat Sh'ma al
ha-Mitta*, or bedtime prayer, is said.

In all cases, except of course for the bedtime prayer, it is considered preferable to pray with a minyan, usually in the synagogue. However, where this cannot be done or where it is incon-
venient, prayers may be said at home and alone, with the omis-
sion of those prayers which require a minyan for their recitation—the kaddish, for example. Women ordinarily pray in the
synagogue only on Sabbaths and holidays; otherwise they pray at
home, often in an abbreviated form, and in whatever language

they prefer, if they pray at all. Men are required to pray and to pray in Hebrew. This is explained in chapter 26.

We have now seen some of the ways in which the life of a religious Jew differs from that of his neighbors. In addition it should be noted that religious Jewish males keep their heads covered at all times, since the head must be covered in order to pray, eat, or say any blessing. Most Jews cannot, of course, wear a hat at all times during the day since their work is among Goyim, and to wear a hat would subject them to ridicule. These Jews will, however, wear a hat at home and, of course, in the synagogue, which it is forbidden to enter with an uncovered head. Most Jews use a skullcap, called *yarmulka*, *keppala* or *kipa*, simply because it is more convenient, but any sort of head covering will do. The reason for covering the head will be discussed in chapter 26.

20

The Jewish Home—
the Mezuza

THE Jewish home is distinguished from the dwelling of a non-Jew before one even enters it, by the *mezuza* on the doorpost. The mezuza is a small piece of parchment made from the inner skin of an animal belonging to a species which Jews are permitted to eat, upon which are written the verses from the Torah, Deut. 6:4-9 and 11:13-21. On the obverse side, near the top, is written the name Shaddai, one of the names by which God is known in Hebrew. Interpreters of the Jewish tradition have said that the three Hebrew letters, *shin, daled* and *yud*, are actually an acronym formed of the first letters of the phrase, "Shomer Delet Israel" (guardian of the door of Israel). This name, Shaddai, is seen through a small hole in the mezuza case when the mezuza itself is rolled up and inserted in the case so that it may be affixed to the doorpost. If the case has no such opening, as most *mezuzot* do not these days, the word Shaddai is usually engraved or written on the case opposite where the name is when the mezuza is within it.

The reason why we Jews place a mezuza on our doorpost is found in the verse written upon the mezuza itself: "And thou shalt write them upon the doorposts of thy house and upon thy gates" (Deut. 6:9). Once again, this is a commandment we have been given to remind us that we are God's chosen people.

Mezuzas should be placed not only on the entrance doors to the house or apartment, but on every room door inside the house, with the exception of the bathrooms. A temporary building such as a *sukka* (chapter 30) does not require a mezuza nor does a building used only for dressing and undressing, such as a beach cabaña, bathhouse, etc. A detached garage also requires no mezuza because it is not a dwelling place. A house occupied jointly by Jews and Goyim does not require a mezuza.

When a Jew moves from a house or apartment, he should leave the mezuzas in place and the person moving in should pay him for them. If the person moving out does not know who will be moving in, or if he knows that it will be a Goy, he should remove the mezuzas because there is a possibility that they might be desecrated; he may then use them in his next dwelling. In places where it is feared that the mezuza at the entrance may be stolen or desecrated, it is the custom to put the mezuza inside the house on the inner doorpost instead of outside.

The laws concerning the mezuza are simple. First, it should be bought from a reliable person or store so that the buyer is sure it is properly written. Before placing it on the doorpost, the head must be covered and the following blessing said:

"*Baruch Ata Adonai, Elohenu Melech ha-olam, asher kid'shanu b'mitzvotav, v'tzivanu likboa mezuzot*" (Blessed art Thou, O Lord, our God, King of the universe, who has sanctified us in His commandments and commanded us to affix mezuzas).

The mezuza must be placed on the doorpost on the right hand side as one enters the house. It must be placed more than two thirds of the way up the doorpost from the floor and must be at least one handbreadth from the top of the doorpost. It should be placed at a forty-five degree angle, with the top, where the name Shaddai appears, pointed inward and upward. If the doorpost is too narrow to permit this, the end with the name Shaddai must always be at the top, even if the mezuza is straight up and down.

On entering or leaving the house, it is customary to touch the mezuza case with the fingertips, then kiss the fingertips as a sign of love, thankfulness and respect, that God has given us this commandment.

The mezuza is usually nailed up, if there are small holes in the end of the mezuza case for that purpose. It can also be put up with glue, solder or cement, if necessary, and every apartment in a building requires a separate mezuza. There is a story about the man who was looking over an apartment in a building in a Jewish part of town. The real estate agent saw him examining the front door, and, on asking the prospective buyer what he was looking for, was told that the customer was trying to figure out how he could put a mezuza on the doorpost. "Oh, don't worry about that," said the agent, "all the apartments are plugged in to a master mezuza on the roof!"

Twice in every seven years the mezuzas should be taken out of their cases and examined to make sure that damp or mold has not made them *pasul*, the opposite of kosher, which means that they cannot be used.

There are other things as well which visually distinguish the Jewish home once one is in it: such things as the kiddush cup, challa cover, havdala plate, etc. (All of these ceremonial objects will be described in the sections covering their use.) One thing often found, particularly in the houses of German Jews, is the *Mizrach Bild*, a framed picture or calligraphic collection of verses in Hebrew, which is hung on the eastern wall of the house. The purpose of this picture is to illustrate and identify the wall standing in the direction in which the *Amida* prayer (chapter 27) must be recited: facing Jerusalem.

21

Kashrut—the Dietary Laws

THE entire subject of what foods may be eaten by observant Jews is called *kashrut*, or "kosherness." The word *kosher* (S. *kasher*) means fit, acceptable or ritually useable. When applied to food, its opposite is *tref* or *trefa*, meaning literally, "torn by wild beasts," but in our times, meaning not edible by Jews. The word kosher applies to other things besides food; for example, a properly prepared mezuza is kosher. When applied to anything but food or wine, the opposite of kosher is *pasul*, meaning disqualified.

An integral part of what makes the Jewish home different is the observance of kashrut—the dietary laws. Before examining the basis of these laws, we should know what the laws themselves are. In essence, the Jewish dietary regulations fall into four categories:

- Laws concerning meat, fowl and fish.
- Laws concerning the mixture of meat and milk.
- Laws concerning wine and grape juice products.
- Laws concerning food on Passover.

131

To start with, all food is divided into three classifications. These are meat and meat-containing foods, milk and milk-containing foods, and foods which contain neither meat nor milk. Meat foods are commonly called *fleishig*, a Yiddish word; milk foods are called *milchig* and neutral foods are called *pareveh*. Milchig and fleishig may not be eaten together; pareveh may be eaten with either.

The laws concerning the three above-mentioned categories break down as follows.

MEAT (FLEISHIG)

Jews may eat the flesh of warmblooded animals that have a cloven hoof and chew the cud; none other. These include cows, goats and sheep among the more commonly available animals. Deer, elk, moose, buffalo, etc., are also kosher animals but since they must be slaughtered in accordance with Jewish law (see below) for their meat to be kosher, it would be most uncommon to find their meat on sale in kosher butcher shops. Pigs, although they have a cloven hoof, do not chew the cud and so are tref. The camel, which does chew the cud, does not have a cloven hoof and is also tref. Obviously all such animals as rabbit, possum, lapa (the *paca* or *tepezcuintle—Coelogenys paca*—commonly eaten in Latin America) are forbidden.

Birds are also considered fleishig and Jews may eat all commonly domesticated fowls such as duck, chicken, turkey, etc. All parts of fowls may be eaten. Forbidden are birds of prey such as the eagle and the hawk which, in any event, are eaten only by primitive peoples.

Now, the fact that the above-mentioned animals and birds are acceptable does not mean that their flesh is automatically kosher. Jews may eat their flesh only if the animals have been slaughtered by an authorized Jewish slaughterer, called a *shochet*. The shochet must have been licensed by the local rabbinical authorities to perform ritual slaughter, called *sh'chita*, which consists in killing birds and animals with a highly honed knife across the main veins and arteries of the throat so that the blood drains out and the animal loses consciousness immediately, feeling no pain.

The knife used by the shochet must be, literally, razorsharp and the tiniest nick makes it pasul. The blood must be drained out of the carcass onto the ground and covered.

The animal is then opened and its lungs and entrails examined by the shochet. If abnormalities, excrescences or adhesions of any kind are found, the animal is declared tref. This applies to four-legged animals; birds are killed the same way but not opened and "searched" in the way large animals are.

Even after the animal has been slaughtered and searched in accordance with the laws of kashrut, the meat is not ready to be called kosher. It must have removed from it certain parts which are, by Jewish law, not edible. This is the work not of the shochet, but of the butcher, so only meat purchased from a licensed kosher butcher is kosher. The parts removed are mainly the fat around the kidneys and other organs and the sciatic nerve and connected tendons in the hindquarter.

The fact is that in the United States only the forequarter is sold, the hindquarter going to non-Jewish butchers. This general-ly follows Ashkenazic custom. The Sephardim in Latin America and elsewhere and most of the butchers in Israel remove the sciatic nerve and tendons from the hindquarter, so its meat is also kosher. The process of removing these parts from the hindquarter is called in Yiddish *treibering* (in Hebrew *niker*), but it is almost never done in the United States.

After the meat has been brought home, it must undergo two additional processes before it is edible. First it must be soaked in cold water, in a special vessel used only for that purpose, for half an hour. Then it must be placed on a specially grooved board, sprinkled thickly with coarse salt and left to stand for one hour to draw all possible blood out of it. The salt must be washed off and the meat can be cooked and eaten. This soaking and salting pro-cess is called *kashering*.

The reason for the form of slaughter, the draining out of the blood and the kashering of the meat in the home is in compliance with one of the most important of the dietary laws: the absolute prohibition against eating blood in any form. The reason for this prohibition will be discussed a little further on, but the purging of meat of all possible blood is basic to kashrut. Meat broiled on an open flame need not be kashered since the broiling draws out the blood. Liver contains so much blood that it must be broiled first and only then may be prepared in other ways. Fowls must be soaked and salted both outside and inside. Ground meat is kashered by the butcher before grinding it and in many butcher shops the butcher will kasher all meat sold by him, but this is often done only at the request of the customer. In the case of prepared foods containing meat, such as sausage, canned soup, etc., kosher products are identified as such on their labels or wrappings. Products not so identified are tref.

MILK (MILCHIG)

All foods made of or based on milk are kosher by nature. There is some difference of opinion regarding certain cheeses, but Orthodox Jews will usually eat them. The objection of the Orthodox is that they are coagulated with rennet, which is made from the lining of an animal's stomach and thus is fleishig and not to be mixed with milk. The answer given by many rabbis is that in the first place, rennet passes through a stage in which a dog would not eat it thus losing its original characteristics and can no longer be considered fleishig. In the second place, even if it were fleishig, it would be considered null and void because it constitutes less than one part in sixty of the entire substance. This rule applies only to forbidden mixtures, such as meat and milk, and certainly does not apply to substances, such as pork, for example, which are forbidden in themselves. Even the tiniest amount of such a substance would make the entire product tref.

It is true that the extreme Orthodox will not drink milk unless the cows were milked by Jews and the milk processed under Jewish religious supervision, called *Hashgacha*. Such milk is called *chalev Israel* and is available only in a few large cities. Usually even the most observant Jew will drink any commercially marketed milk that is government inspected. Only the ultra-pious demand chalev Israel.

All foods containing milk are classified as milchig and thus forbidden to be eaten with meat. This includes bread, cake etc.

baked from dough that has milk in it, margarine containing milk solids and so on. Milk from non-kosher animals is forbidden.

PAREVEH

All foods that are neither fleishig nor milchig are *pareveh*. This includes fish, eggs, all vegetables, grains and fruits, liquors and beverages such as coffee, tea, soft drinks, beer, wine, etc.

All pareveh foods are kosher by nature. In practice there are Jews who will not eat cauliflower because they feel it is impossible to rid it of the tiny insects usually found in it and these insects are not kosher. Most Jews eat cauliflower, however.

Fish are an important pareveh food. Jews are permitted to eat only those fish which have fins and easily detachable scales. In reality the law is liberal and the fish need have only rudimentary fins and three or four scales, but these must be detachable by hand. Fish without scales such as shark, catfish, eels, etc., are not kosher. It appears that both swordfish and sturgeon have been declared kosher by some Conservative authorities, but most Orthodox Jews will not eat them. Also forbidden are any of the other animals that live in the water such as shrimp, crab, lobster, crayfish, oysters, etc.

Fish need not be bought from a kosher dealer and may be eaten with either milk or meat. Nevertheless, there is a strong custom against having fish and meat on the table at the same time since it is believed to be unhealthy to eat them together. Usually the fish is served first, the dishes cleared away and the meat brought on. The blood of fish may be eaten but no one does.

Eggs are pareveh and the eggs of any kosher bird may be eaten. If on breaking an egg, a blood spot is found, it is considered permissible, even by the very Orthodox, to remove the spot and if the yoke is not broken in the process, the egg may be eaten. If, however, the yolk is broken, the egg must be thrown away. Hardboiled eggs need not be worried about since it is assumed that normally no blood spots are present. When making a cake or pudding, for example, it is considered best to examine each egg as you break it, but even if you don't the cake will be kosher.

So much for the categories of food. As for its preparation and serving, Jewish law rests on one basic prohibition: it is forbidden to mix milchig and fleishig. What does this mean in practice?

Meat and milk, or anything containing meat and milk, may not be eaten together, used together in the preparation of food, put on the table at the same time, be cooked in or eaten off the same dishes. This means that all kosher homes have separate sets of dishes, silverware, cooking utensils, pots and pans for the preparation and serving of milchig and fleishig foods. This extends to glasses, tablecloths and napkins as well. Separate sections of the refrigerator are set aside for the two types of food, and in electric dishwashers, separate removable racks are used for milchig and fleishig dishes and other utensils.

It is permissible to eat meat immediately after drinking milk or eating milchig food. In the case of hard cheeses, the mouth should be washed out first. After eating meat, however, it is forbidden to eat milchig foods for six hours, among Eastern European Jews, and this rule is generally observed in the Americas. German Jews wait three hours as do most Sephardim, while Dutch Jews traditionally consider seventy-two minutes to be sufficient.

Packaged and prepared foods containing meat or meat by-products (canned soups, shortening, etc.) are not kosher unless the meat used in them is kosher and the products are so identified on the label or package. Gelatine and glycerine are both derived from animal products and are not considered kosher although there is a kosher gelatine made from seaweed. The fact is that gelatine made from bones which have dried out completely would be kosher, in the opinion of Orthodox rabbis, because it passes through a stage in which a dog would not eat it and becomes edible once again. The trouble is that no commercially available gelatine meets those specifications; it is made from fresh bones of tref animals to which meat is still clinging.

Kosher products can be identified by examining the list of ingredients which United States law requires on every package. If it is quite obvious that nothing but milchig or pareveh ingredients are found in the product, it can be considered kosher as far as the ingredients themselves go. Doubt may arise as to whether the product was prepared in vessels or machinery which had previously been used for the manufacture of non-kosher products without proper cleaning in steam. If doubt exists, the product should be considered non-kosher and a kosher substitute sought.

It is felt, and rightly, that a business that does not keep the Sabbath cannot be trusted to keep the laws of kashrut. A "kosher" butcher shop that stayed open on Saturday would have its license taken away by Monday. But what about buying manufactured products with a *hechsher* in a non-Sabbath-observing store? The answer here is that most states have laws making the sale of a non-kosher product as kosher a very expensive proposition if the seller is caught—and there is constant inspection. It is accepted that in any case where it costs more to deceive the purchaser than to tell him the truth about food, we need not fear. Accordingly it is perfectly all right to buy kosher hot dogs from your supermarket, if you can find them.

Products that are certified as kosher by rabbinical inspection of both ingredients and manufacturing process are marked with the Hebrew word כשר . According to strict Jewish law, they should also have the signature of the rabbi who attests to their kashrut. Since the labeling laws in the United States make it illegal to label a product kosher if it is not, usually the Hebrew word "kosher" is enough. Another kosher identification which can be relied on without question and which requires no signature is that of the Union of Orthodox Congregations, a "u" within a circle Ⓤ. Any food with this mark is guaranteed kosher.

WINE AND LIQUOR

In order for a Jew to drink it, all wine made of grapes must be certified as kosher on the seal which holds the cork or cap of the bottle in place. Without this certification, grape wine, grapejuice, brandy or any other liquor made from grape alcohol is not kosher. This also includes grape jelly.

Wine that is not kosher is not called tref, but *nesech*, and is prohibited for a different reason than other foods. In brief, wine that is kosher is manufactured entirely by Jews, without the presence of any non-Jew. The reason for this is that grape wine plays an important part in the ceremonies of many religions and care must be taken to avoid wine that might have been used in or dedicated to idol-worship or similar practices. As indicated above, this also includes liquor distilled from wine or grapes. The Ashkenazim are strict about this but Sephardim tend to be more liberal. In part this is due to the fact that today most Sephardim come from Moslem countries and the Moslem religion prohibits the use of alcoholic beverages in all forms and in addition does not involve idol-worship of any sort whatsoever.

Does this mean that non-Jews in countries where Ashkenazim live or lived are to be considered idol-worshipers? Technically and legally they are not and this will be discussed in chapter 48, but let us say that as far as the laws concerning wine go, they are.

All other liquors, soft drinks, beer, cider, whiskey, vodka, etc., are considered kosher by nature although the very Orthodox will not drink blended whiskey because it may contain glycerine. Straight (bottled in bond) whiskey, Scotch, rum, slivovitz, aquavit, tequila, etc., are all acceptable to all Jews. Other liquors such as arrack, anise, etc., must be checked to see if the alcohol used in them is grape alcohol. If it is, they are not kosher, unless so labeled.

As a final observation on which animals may be eaten and which not, some years ago I was sitting in shul on Shabbat, listening to the Torah being read while following the *baal koreh* from a book in front of me. Suddenly I became aware that the text being declaimed was *"kol sheretz ha-of asher lo arba raglaim"* (Lev. 11:23). My Hebrew left much to be desired in those days and to me, anyway, it looked like the words meant "all birds with four legs."

I later discovered that while *of* certainly means bird, it also means any animal with wings and that *sheretz ha-of* means any creature with wings that swarms—insects, to be exact. At the moment, however, I was unaware of that interesting fact and turned to the fellow sitting next to me and said, "Hey, Moishe . . ."

"Unch," grunted my neighbor, whose Hebrew—or so I thought—was much better than mine, and I went on, "What does this mean?"

He looked at it and answered, "It means all kind of birds what they got four legs."

"Ah, come on, Moishe," I said, "Birds . . . four legs . . . What kind of bird has four legs?" Moishe looked at me sternly and said:

"You've seen every bird there is?"

PASSOVER

The laws concerning food eaten on Passover will be discussed in chapter 32.

22

The Reasons Behind the Dietary Laws

Now that we know what the dietary laws are, it is appropriate that we have an understanding of *why* they are. The question might be asked, wouldn't it be more logical to explain why the laws exist and why we should observe them and *then* explain how?

In the first place, the purpose of this book is not to preach but to teach; its main effort is directed at telling Jews what Judaism is, not exhorting them to its observance. In the second place, we quoted from th Torah in chapter 5 the answer given Moses by the Jewish people when he gave them the Law that God had revealed to him: "All that the Lord has said, we will do and obey." A more accurate translation would be, "we will do and listen to." This is rather puzzling; in actual fact the words "listen to" are usually taken in this context to mean something like understand.

What is important in their answer is the order in which the words appear: first we will do and only then will we listen or understand. This is the key to the Jewish attitude toward the commandments: first we observe them, perform them, and then we look into them, examine them and try to figure out their meaning.

And finally, as we have said earlier, the reasons for customs can be given, but the reasons for the commandments we cannot give because we do not know them for certain. Nonetheless, in the specific case of the dietary laws, God has given us very definite indications regarding them and it is important to outline their significance, if only because so much nonsense is said and written about them and their meaning for Jews now and in earlier times.

To start with, the dietary laws are not hygienic in nature but ethical or religious. The purpose of the dietary laws is not healthiness but holiness, and this is indicated in the Torah itself where in almost every instance that the dietary laws are set forth, we are told, "... keep yourselves holy for I the Lord am holy." To understand what this means, we must first understand the Jewish concept of the physical world. Perhaps the easiest way is to compare our view of life with that of the Gentiles.

The pagans—and some of them, like the Greeks and Romans, reached high degrees of civilization—glorify and deify physical life. Hunger, sex, the craving for power, vengeance, strength and finally torture and death, are raised to an end in themselves and the pagans build their religious life around them.

Historically, Christianity has done the exact opposite. Man's natural drives such as sex, hunger, the gratification of the senses and the desire for power, identification and affection were regarded as unholy and sinful. They were considered stumbling blocks on the path to salvation. Such now rarely encountered phenomena as self-torture, mutilation and the practice of hermitry were the natural expression of this way of looking at life.

The Jewish view is entirely different from either. The Jews say that sex, hunger, the "ego drive," physical beauty, even bloodthirstiness, are essentially neutral; that man can turn them to any use, holy, unholy or neither, *and that it is the function of the Torah and the commandments to direct these natural urges of man to holiness.*

In a sense the drives man is born with or acquires can be compared to electric current. Plug it into a stove and it produces heat, into a refrigerator and it produces cold; but it is the same undefined energy that does both. That describes man's urges; there is nothing either good or bad about them, it is simply the use to which we put them.

To give an example: the rabbis say that the man whose nature it is to wish to shed blood may turn this to a good end and indeed to holiness and observance of the commandments by training to become a shochet, or ritual slaughterer, thus making sure that animals are killed painlessly and in accordance with God's law. It is also said that a man with an inborn desire to shed blood may ennoble that urge by becoming a surgeon.

The meaning of this for the dietary laws is that hunger can also be made an instrument for the fulfilling of God's commandments. When the food we Jews eat is prepared and eaten in the manner which God Himself has prescribed for us in His Torah, we are serving Him through the satisfaction of our hunger. There is nothing more basic to life than eating and drinking. We must do both every day if we are to live till the next day. What God has done in giving us the dietary laws is to show us a way to make those essential needs function as an important part of our service to Him in keeping ourselves holy, as befits a chosen people.

The laws concerning meat are particularly significant. Some Jewish commentators on the dietary laws say that the eating of meat is a concession to human weakness; in other words, we eat meat because we are not morally strong enough to keep from doing so. The ideal would be not to eat meat at all. I am not able to agree with that line of thought because it is obvious that the eating of meat is a commandment, if not by law then at least by custom which amounts to law. For example, if we do not eat meat during the week, perhaps because of poverty, we are enjoined to do everything possible to have meat on the table on Shabbat because by enjoying it we honor the Sabbath and the commandment of God to honor the Sabbath day and keep it holy.

But, and it is here that the dietary laws show their meaning, there is more than one way to make use of meat. It is possible to be bestial and cruel in so doing, by killing the animals painfully, by cutting limbs off a living animal or by cooking or eating animals alive. And it is quite true that many peoples do exactly that today. In the Jewish view, these are unholy actions, unbefitting a holy people. You are what you eat, morally and psychologically as well as physically, or even more so. If you commit a cruel act in regard to the animal you eat, such as cooking it alive, it is thought that it could result in you yourself becoming bestial and cruel in your relations with other human beings. For that reason, while the Jews are allowed and even encouraged to eat meat, they want to be sure that the animal is dead when they do so; so that no cruelty is involved in the eating, as well as that the meat they eat contains no life whatsoever.

How do we do this? The Torah tells us that "the blood is the life," and, to our eyes at least, the life of a living being is visible in its blood. If it has no blood it has no life. For that reason the laws of kashrut demand that all meat we eat be purged of every possible bit of blood so that we will be conscious that our eating is an act not of cruelty but of sanctification.

And sanctification is not too strong a word. As we Jews know, our original religious services were based on sacrifices of animals at the Temple in Jerusalem. There is no longer a Temple in Jerusalem and no sacrifices are offered up to God on its altar. So, in the absence of a Temple, we are taught that the table of each individual Jew takes the place of the altar and the food eaten there takes the place of the sacrifices. It is for this reason that bread, symbolizing all food, is always eaten with salt by Jews, because the Torah states (Lev. 2:13) that all sacrifices must be eaten with salt. Meat is an important part of our diet and when we prepare it and eat it as God has instructed us to, we are performing an act of sanctification.

And what about the laws concerning separation of meat and milk? Are they also to make us holy? The answer is yes. These laws are based on a commandment so important that it is repeated at three separate times and places in the Torah (Exod. 23:19, Exod. 34:26 and Deut. 14:21): "you shall not cook a kid in its mother's milk."

Is this law hygienic in nature? Apparently not. It is simply that cooking a baby animal in the milk of its mother is a revolting act, disgusting in its purposeful cruelty and brutalizing to those who perform it. We are forbidden to do this and because of the commandment's threefold repetition and the rabbinical principle that bids us "build a fence around the Torah," we are prohibited from cooking any meat in any milk, and finally, from eating meat and milk at the same time or even using the same pots, plates or utensils to prepare and serve them.

A good example of the mistakenness of the notion that the dietary laws have hygiene as their basis is the law concerning the eating of pork. My friend Elie Shneour, in his book, *The Malnourished Mind*, says:

> "We rationalize our taboos by giving them an aura of logic, when in fact there is none. A good example of this is the belief that Moses' injunction against the eating of pork by Jews is based on the susceptibility of pork to trichinosis. . . . As far as trichinosis is concerned the argument is . . . doubtful. The observation of trichinae in muscle requires a high-powered optical microscope for identification, and the pathological symptoms of trichinosis are otherwise so varied that no diagnosis of it is possible without this advanced tool."

Professor Shneour looks at it from a scientific point of view; from a religious point of view, the law against eating pork has always been cited as the typical example of a *chok*, a law whose reason for being we cannot begin to imagine.

A second important aspect of kashrut concerns the role of the dietary laws in the preservation of the Jewish people. These laws set us apart from the *umot ha-olam*, the peoples of the world, and they are clearly intended by God to do so, as the Torah states. It is said that the problem of intermarriage would hardly exist if the dietary laws were observed generally. Certainly, if you can't eat at a man's table, you are not likely to marry his daughter!

As we have stated earlier, the purpose of this book is to tell what the laws and customs of Judaism are, and, to the extent possible, why they are. It is not intended to tell the reader what he should do, only how to do it if he wants to, and why, if he is interested in knowing. Without departing from that principle, it is appropriate to bring to the reader's attention one particular aspect of the dietary laws.

There are Jews who do not observe any of the dietary laws, nor those of the Sabbath, and who explain their attitude by saying that Judaism is an all or nothing proposition. To observe some of the commandments and not the rest, they say, is not only improper, but hypocritical—usually their favorite word. They do not wish, they assert, to be "hypocrites." However, although many of these Jews may well believe what they are saying to be true, the reader should understand that this is simply not so. Every single mitzva has its own value. To give a concrete example, the mitzva of putting on *t'fillin* for men. As you know there are separate t'fillin for the head and the hand (chapter 26) and they are always put on together. If, however, it is not possible to put the t'fillin on the head, perhaps because of a wound or bandage, the t'fillin should still be put on the hand because *t'fillin shel yad* (hand) and *t'fillin shel rosh* (head) are separate mitzvas. (Of course the same rule applies if it is the t'fillin of the hand that cannot be put on.)

In the same way, it might seem difficult for those unaccustomed to observance to take the plunge and immediately become 100 percent kosher. But one thing is certain: if someone feels it is impossible to observe all the mitzvas, each one that is observed increases his or her net worth as a Jew. There is no hypocrisy involved in observing only some mitzvas if you are, or think you are, unable to find a way to observe them all.

23

Sabbath

WORDS enough to fill hundreds of volumes have been written on the Sabbath, its observance, its meaning to the Jew and its historical development. In a reversal of our usual procedure, before examining how the Sabbath is observed, we will attempt to understand *why* it is observed.

The wording is known to every reader. The fourth commandment of the Ten Commandments (which in reality contains two of the 613 commandments of the Torah) tells us two things: "Remember the Sabbath day to keep it holy," and "You shall not do any manner of work." This means that we are required to do something special on the Sabbath to honor it, and that we are prohibited from working on that day.

As for the reason, the Torah states that God created the world in six days and rested on the seventh, thereby ordering us to rest as well. We are quite aware that God does not get tired and need rest, but "the Torah speaks in the language of men" and all commentators agree that God did indeed "rest" from His labor of creation solely and simply to give us Jews, His chosen people, the example and basis for this commandment.

First, let us define exactly what the Sabbath is. It is the seventh day of the week, the day we call Saturday. It begins at sundown on Friday night and ends at sundown on Saturday night. By both custom and law, we are obliged to observe the Sabbath from eighteen minutes before sundown on Friday night until about forty-two minutes after sundown on Saturday night, when three stars of major magnitude are visible in the sky. The reason why the Sabbath, as well as all other days, is figured from sundown of the "previous" day, is found in the opening verses of the Torah, where the creation of the world is described: "And there was evening and there was morning, one day" (Gen. 1:5). Evening comes before morning in reckoning the day.

As for the way Sabbath is observed, there are two aspects: a positive one, "Remember the Sabbath day to keep it holy," and a negative one, "Do no manner of work." Let us start with the positive side of *sh'mirat Shabbat*: "guarding the Sabbath."

Preparations for Sabbath begin on Friday when the housewife cooks enough food for both Friday night and Saturday. This is because the cooking and preparation of food is among the things that are considered "work" and forbidden on the Sabbath. However, food prepared before Shabbat may be reheated on the Sabbath as we will see. It is customary to set the table before Shabbat starts at sundown, if this is possible, and families that can afford to have a special tablecloth or other decoration to set the Sabbath meal above the meals eaten the rest of the week. It is, in fact, the principal meal of the week; as I used to explain to non-Jewish friends, "Jews have their Sunday dinner on Friday night."

In many homes one of the dishes prepared on Friday afternoon is destined to be eaten the next day at noon. This is the dish called *Tcholent* in Yiddish, *Schalet* or *Sholet* by German-speaking Jews, *Adafina* in Ladino and Jaquetía and *Chamin* in Hebrew and Judeo-Arabic. It usually consists of meat (an essential ingredient) and beans, barley, potatoes, chickpeas or whole wheat, depending on the family and its origin. These ingredients are seasoned and put into a heavy iron pot with more or less water, depending on whether you like the tcholent soupy or "stiff," placed in the oven before the start of Shabbat and left to cook all night long and the next morning at low heat. On Saturday at noon it is taken out of the oven and eaten for lunch. It is justly celebrated as one of the most delicious dishes in the world. Since the oven is lit before the Sabbath starts, tcholent does not violate the prohibition against lighting a fire on the Sabbath.

Of all the different dishes known collectively as "Jewish food," it is probably the only one, with the possible exception of the Passover matzos, actually invented by the Jews. It is also the only dish that Jews the world over have in common because it was created to permit them to eat hot food on the Sabbath without breaking the Sabbath laws, which are the same for Jews everywhere.

Appendix V contains complete instructions on the preparation and cooking of tcholent with an additional recipe for *oriza,* an adjunct to the *adafina* eaten by Moroccan and Tunisian Jews.

INAUGURATION OF THE SABBATH

The Sabbath is inaugurated in the home by the lighting of candles eighteen minutes before sundown. Since the sundown time in a Jewish *luach*, or calendar, may not apply to the place where an observer lives, it is easy to find out the proper time by looking in a local newspaper. In the case of Jews who live in Alaska, northern Scandinavia or other places in the far north where the "midnight sun" shines, observant Jews use as their guide to the beginning of Sabbaths and holidays, the time in a designated place to the south of them. Thus the Jews in Alaska start eighteen minutes before the sun sets in Seattle, and the Jews in Northern Sweden, Norway and Finland base themselves on the time in Hamburg, Germany, by long custom.

The candles are lit by the woman of the house, and in her absence, by one of her daughters or any other woman who happens to be present. If no women at all are there, the candles are lit by a man. Two candles must be lit, although it is the custom for unmarried women to light only one candle, in many homes, in addition to the two candles lit by the mother. The candles must be of sufficient size to burn until the Friday night meal is over. In other homes, all women over the age of twelve light two candles. Among the Sephardim it is customary to place a special floating wick in a vessel partially filled with olive oil and to use that in preference to a candle; usually two such lights are lit. It is also technically permissible to say the blessings over two electric light bulbs, specially turned on for that purpose and left burning all through Shabbat till Saturday night.

The woman who says the blessing must cover her head, usually with a kerchief, light the candles and *after* lighting them say the following blessing:

"Baruch Ata Adonai, Elohenu Melech ha-olam, asher kid'shanu b'mitzvotav v'tzivanu l'hadlik ner shel Shabbat" (Blessed art Thou, O Lord, our God, King of the universe, who has sanctified us in His commandments and commended us to light the Sabbath light).

During the first part of the blessing, the woman moves her hands around or in front of the candles in a waving motion. For the second part of the blessing, she covers her eyes with her hands, uncovering them and gazing at the candles after she says "amen."

The reason she does this is to hide the light from her eyes; the waving motion at the beginning is simply a matter of centuries of custom. Her reason for hiding the light from her eyes is so that she will not see or enjoy it until after the blessing has been said. This is because in almost every other case, the blessing is said *before* we perform the mitzva. It cannot be in this case for two reasons. One, the candles may not light and the blessing will have been said in vain; two, the Sabbath is considered to have begun in each individual house the moment the housewife has pronounced the blessing. If she were to say the blessing first, it would already be Shabbat and she would be unable to light the candles because the lighting of fire is prohibited on the Sabbath.

I confess that I find it difficult to accept that the mere saying of a blessing without the physical act of lighting the candles would start the Sabbath off, before sundown, but this is the reason commonly given. It is a fact, in addition, that if the housewife knows she has some last-minute work to do before sunset she may make a spoken or even a mental reservation to the effect that her blessing does not mean Shabbat has begun and go ahead and finish her work before that time.

What must be understood, however, is that the minute the sun is down, Shabbat has started and no candles may be lit. If, for example, one forgets to light the candles and suddenly realizes that the sun has set, one must celebrate the Sabbath without candles, because to light them would be a flagrant dishonoring of the very holiday, the Sabbath, that one is intending to honor.

To make this important point clearer, I recall a time, some years ago, when I was living in a South American city that had a good number of English-speaking Jews, mostly North Americans. They decided to form an English-speaking congregation and hold their own Sabbath services. The organization was duly formed and they started having "late Sabbath services" at a Jewish club in a suburban part of the city. These services were held on Friday night, around nine o'clock: the latest the sun sets in that part of the world is 6:54 P.M.

The President of the group, a good friend, invited me to come. I explained that it would be difficult for me to get to the place the services were being held without traveling, which is forbidden on Shabbat, but that in addition, I had been told that one of the women in the congregation lit candles at the commencement of the services, which started a good two hours after sunset. Was this true, I asked.

My friend answered that it was, and that while he understood my objections, they felt that what was important was the "spirit" of honoring the Sabbath by lighting candles, and it didn't much matter at what hour they were lit. My answer to him went something like this: "Imagine," I said, "that in a small city in Latin America the North American residents got together and formed an American Club, where they could meet once a week, socialize, celebrate the national holidays and honor their native land. On the night of each meeting, an American flag was placed on the ground in front of the door and every member as he came in wiped his feet on the flag. Well," I told him, "that would be exactly the same as you are doing when you attempt to 'honor' the Sabbath by lighting candles after Shabbat has already started."

I guess what I said must have made sense, because from that

time on, the candles were lit by the Jewish caretaker's wife before sunset and were already burning when the late Sabbath services started.

In countries where it doesn't get dark until very late during the summer, such as the Northern United States on daylight saving time, it is customary not to delay the Friday night meal, but to inaugurate the Sabbath at any time one wishes to in the evening before sundown. Jewish law states that in such cases, as soon as the candles are lit and the blessings said, Shabbat has started in that home and members of the family observe it accordingly. Although it is permitted to start Shabbat early, it is not permitted to end it before its appointed time.

In Orthodox families, the father and, often, the children, go to the synagogue on Friday evening before sundown for the *Kabbalat Shabbat* and *Maariv* services (see chapter 28). Since women are excused from the fixed hours of prayer, the wife usually waits at home and welcomes the husband on his return from the synagogue. It is, of course, permissible for women to attend evening services in the synagogue, but in Orthodox congregations it is not commonly done. In many families it is the custom for the father to bless the children on his return from *shul*. (The blessings are found in appendix IV.)

If the synagogue is some distance from the house, the father will often forgo the Friday evening service and will pray at home. After the prayers, whether in shul or in the home, the family has Shabbat dinner. It starts with the father reciting the verses 10 to 31 from the thirty-first chapter of Proverbs. This section, called *Eshet Chayil* (A Woman of Valor), is recited by the husband in praise of his wife. This is followed by the *Kiddush*, or prayer of sanctification, of the Sabbath.

Kiddush, the text of which will be found in appendix IV, is recited by the father, standing, with a cup of wine or other liquor in his hand. It is customary that all present stand for the kiddush, although in some families the women remain seated. The first part of the kiddush is a repetition of the verses from Genesis describing the origin of the Sabbath. Then the blessing is said for the wine or liquor, and the second part of the kiddush, which is the actual sanctification, is said.

After the kiddush is said, the father sips from the wine cup and

passes it to his wife, who also drinks from it. In many families, all
the children drink from the kiddush cup as well. Usually, every
man at the table has his own kiddush cup, whose wine or liquor he
blesses and from which he drinks. After the kiddush, all wash
their hands and the blessing for bread is said over the two Sabbath loaves, or *challot*. The bread is distributed to all and the
Sabbath meal is eaten.

If no wine or other liquor (beer will also do) is available, the
kiddush may be said over the challot. These braided loaves, called
barches by German-speaking Jews, are baked specially on Friday
for Sabbath eve use and in almost every town with a Jewish community of any size there is at least one bakery that makes them.
Most Sephardim do not use any special type of bread such as the
challa, but they do put two loaves on the table as do the Ashkenazim. Both Sephardim and Ashkenazim cover the loaves with a
napkin or a special challa cover until the kiddush is over, if wine
is used.

The reason for the two loaves is to indicate that the Sabbath
meal is especially abundant, since ordinarily only one loaf is on
the table at a meal, and to the Jews, as to other people, bread
symbolizes food in general. Also given as a reason is that the
double-the-ordinary amount of bread reminds us of the double
portion of manna which fell on the eve of the Sabbath when the
Jewish people were in the desert on their way to the Promised
Land. The challot are covered because wheat was mentioned
before grapes in the list of seven things with which the Holy Land
is blessed (Deut. 8:8), and if they were uncovered, the blessing for
bread would take precedence. There is another and what might
seem a fanciful reason, but Jews understand its purely symbolic
meaning: both bread and wine are of great importance, so when
wine is held up, the bread is covered so that it will not be "in-
sulted."

And there is even an explanation for why food served on the
Sabbath tastes better than ordinary food—a "fact" known to all
observant Jews. According to our teachings, all five senses are a
function of the soul, the *n'shama*. On Shabbat every Jew receives
a *n'shama yetera*, an extra soul, and since he has, on this day, two

souls instead of one, all his senses are doubly acute and he is able to appreciate the *taam Shabbat*, the Sabbath taste. This belief comes to us through the mystic tradition, the *Kabbala*.

During and after the meal, special songs in Hebrew and Aramaic are sung. These are called *z'mirot* (sing. *zemer*) and each one has an enormous variety of different tunes, depending on where and by whom they are sung. There are z'mirot for Friday night, for Saturday noon and for the close of the Sabbath; there is no special order in which they are sung and no special number—in some houses only one zemer will be heard while in others four or five may be. The Chasidim sing melodies without words called *nigunim*, some of which are slow and minor in key while others are so lively and gay they practically invite one to leave the table and dance—and this is precisely what many Chasidim do.

At the end of the meal the *birchat ha-mazon*, or grace after bread, is said, with the addition of a few short paragraphs and prefaced by the singing of the 126th psalm.

On the following day the entire family goes to the synagogue. Among the Ashkenazim it is customary to start the services around nine o'clock and end between eleven o'clock and noon. The Sephardim usually start much earlier—at eight o'clock or so—because it is their custom to be finished by ten o'clock or ten-thirty so they can spend the rest of the morning before lunch enjoying a drink or a visit with friends.

On returning home a different kiddush is said by the father, and in many families this kiddush is recited sitting down. Z'mirot are sung and in many houses *tcholent* (S. *adafina* or *chamin*) is the only thing eaten, aside from the challa and dessert. If tcholent was not made, it is possible to reheat food cooked the previous day on a flame or electric stove burner which was lit or turned on before Shabbat and left burning. Such food, however, cannot have been allowed to cool off to room temperature, but must be kept partially warm from the time it is cooked until it is reheated and it may not be heated to a point at which it is hotter than one's hand can stand. Any water used in reheating food or in making tea from previously prepared tea concentrates must have been boiled before the start of the Sabbath and kept warm until it is needed. The pot or other vessel containing the food may not be placed directly on the flame; another "vessel" must be placed between it and the flame, and this is usually an asbestos or metal plaque called a "blech" in Yiddish.

It is considered a mitzva to increase the enjoyment of the Sabbath by eating hot food, but the Sabbath may not be broken in order to procure it.

The third meal of the Sabbath is called the *shalosh seuda* (S. *seuda ha-sh'lishit*) and is eaten by the men in the synagogue. It is eaten between the *mincha* (afternoon) and *maariv* (S. *arbit*) or evening prayers, and usually only fish is eaten in addition to the bread over which the blessing is said. This is the Ashkenazi custom; the Sephardim usually serve salad vegetables with olive oil. Wine or liquor is also drunk, but sparingly, and some of the Sabbath z'mirot are sung. The most learned man present will usually speak on some subject related to the Torah, most often the portion which was read that morning.

After the Sabbath has ended, the *Havdala* is said in the synagogue and repeated in the home. The word *havdala* means "separation" and the ceremony serves to mark the division between the Sabbath and the rest of the week; it is a pleasant and colorful ritual. A cup is set on a plate and filled with wine or other liquor until it overflows. It is then picked up and the prayer "Behold, God is my salvation" is said, after which the blessing for the wine or liquor is recited and the cup set down. A spicebox, usually in the form of a tower or a fish, is then picked up. This spicebox is called a *Hadas* (Y., *B'somim Bicksel*) and is filled with aromatic and pleasant spices which are appreciatively sniffed after saying the appropriate blessing. It is also permitted to use sweet-smelling flowers instead of spices and Moroccan Jews commonly use fresh mint leaves. The spices are a sort of compensation for the fact that the *n'shama yetera*, the "extra soul" leaves us at the end of Shabbat and we supplement our weekday soul with the extra fragrance.

After the blessing on the *b'samim*, or spices, a special candle which was lit before the ceremony started is held up. It is made of six separate wicks braided together, each wick symbolizing a day of the week. The hands are held out to the candle while the blessing is being said and the fingernails examined so that the light will be used and the blessing not said in vain. The cup is taken up again and the *Hamavdil* blessing is recited, after which the wine is drunk and the candle doused in the wine which has overflowed onto the plate. It is customary at this point for the men present to wet their fingertips with the wine on the plate and then touch them to their eyes and their pockets so that the coming week will bring both good vision and good business. Women do not drink from the havdala cup.

In many homes and congregations the song "Hamavdil Ben Kodesh L'chol" (He who separates the holy from the everyday) is sung as is the famous song dedicated to Elijah, the Prophet: *Eliyahu Ha-Navi*. Saturday night is associated with Elijah since Jewish tradition has it that he will be the one to announce the arrival of the Messiah (chapter 41) and that this will take place at the close of the Sabbath. The Sephardim are particularly fond of post-Sabbath songs which they call *pizmonim* and of which they have a large number.

The Chasidim have a special feast after havdala. It is called *M'laveh Malka*, or "Ushering out the Queen." The queen is, of course, the Sabbath, and this feast often goes on until well after midnight with singing and dancing among the men.

This is a brief and basic picture of the positive commandment to "remember the Sabbath day." Jews consider that the Sabbath is one of the greatest of God's gifts to them and the historians of the Jewish people have repeatedly stated that, "As much as Israel has kept the Sabbath, the Sabbath has kept Israel." Shabbat has been, without a doubt, one of the most powerful forces in preserving the Jews as a people over centuries of exile and persecution.

SABBATH RESTRICTIONS

Now we must consider the negative commandment which tells us what we may *not* do on the Sabbath.

This commandment, "Thou shalt not do any manner of work,"

is the origin of what often appears to be an endless list of prohibitions; nonetheless, the laws of what constitutes forbidden activity on the Sabbath are really quite simple for the average Jew:

1. No work is permitted. This means not only work done for pay, but anything that causes exertion—washing the car, mowing the lawn, hammering, painting, cutting, etc. As part of this rule, objects with which the Sabbath can be violated are classified as *muktzeh*, which means that they may not be touched on Shabbat. All tools, writing instruments, money, matches, cigarettes, etc., are muktzeh. Permitted objects are called *muter*. A chisel would be muktzeh, because cutting wood is prohibited on the Sabbath, but a table knife would be muter because cutting food is permitted.

2. Writing or making permanent marks on anything is forbidden.

3. Business is forbidden. Jews may not touch money, buy, sell, talk business or arrange business deals.

4. Lighting a fire is forbidden and, by extension, putting out a fire, except where danger is involved, stoking a fire, making a fire burn brighter or causing a metal object to glow are all prohibited. For this reason the use of electricity on the Sabbath is forbidden since a spark is produced or metal caused to glow whenever it is used.

This prohibition on the use of electricity applies only to putting it into use on the Sabbath. It does not apply to benefiting from electricity (or fire either) which has been lit or put into use before the Sabbath starts. Accordingly, Orthodox Jews will not turn on or off an electric light, use the telephone, ring a doorbell, play a radio, record player or TV on the Sabbath although they may certainly make use of a light turned on before Shabbat. Observant Jews will unscrew the bulb in the refrigerator so that it will not light up when the door is opened. Concerning the use of a refrigerator, when the door of the refrigerator is opened enough times, the entrance of warm air will cause the automatic thermostat to start the refrigerator's mechanism operating, thus using electricity. This secondary putting into operation of the appliance is not forbidden and no one need worry about violating the Sabbath no matter how many times he opens the refrigerator door.

Smoking is obviously one of the things forbidden as lighting or keeping a fire going.

5. Cooking and the preparing of cooked food is prohibited.

6. Tearing, cutting and altering the shape of anything is forbidden and this includes paper. Accordingly, letters and telegrams which arrive on the Sabbath are left unopened until after sundown.

7. Travel is forbidden on any sort of vehicle or animal and the distance it is permitted to walk outside the limits of the town or city in which one lives is about a mile. The use of the elevator is forbidden because one must start and stop it. In Orthodox neighborhoods, and in Israel, many apartment buildings are equipped with "Shabbat elevators" which are set before Shabbat to operate continuously, stopping at every floor of the building automatically. Use of these elevators is no violation of the Sabbath.

8. Playing of musical instruments is forbidden as is the playing of games such as baseball and football because of the exertion involved. Actually this is a strict interpretation and many Orthodox authorities say that there is nothing wrong with adults playing ball games as long as the sport is non-professional and money is not charged for watching it. For children, it is unquestionably acceptable.

9. Bathing is not really forbidden, but the regulations surrounding it are so complex that it has become the custom in most countries not to bathe at all on Shabbat. The exception to this is the use of the *mikva* for women whose period of menstrual uncleanness has ended. Bathing is also permitted for health and hygienic reasons and after having sexual intercourse. Jewish law states that drying oneself is an essential part of bathing, so those who do bathe on the Sabbath do not dry themselves with a towel, but allow the air to dry them and thus avoid the possibility of *chilul Shabbat*—violating the Sabbath.

10. Cutting is forbidden, as mentioned above, with the exception of food. Circumcision is permitted and indeed obligatory on Shabbat under normal circumstances.

11. Carrying anything outside one's house is forbidden. This extends to even something as small as a handkerchief (which can, however, be worn around one's neck as a scarf, thus becoming a "garment"). Since a key may not be carried, the solution has been to have a copy of one's house key made and then gold plated and made into a tieclasp or a brooch (for women). This is then considered an ornament worn on the clothing and is acceptable.

Lest there be any misunderstanding, freedom to carry applies not only to one's own house, but to any house or building in which one happens to be: what is forbidden is carrying from one house to another or from a building into the public domain such as the street or sidewalk, or even a garden attached to one's house if it has no wall around it.

12. Burying the dead is forbidden on Shabbat.

These are the main prohibitions and what they all add up to is that Shabbat is a day of rest, relaxation and the enjoyment of life. Reading, eating, drinking, prayer, visiting friends (if no travel is involved), playing with the children—these are Shabbat's chief diversions and rest is Shabbat's chief aim.

Of course there are occasions on which the Sabbath may and must be broken. These include danger to life and attendance upon the ill (chapter 15), national emergencies and military service. On the last day of the Six Day War—a Sabbath—one of the most revered Chasidic rabbis in the entire world, dressed in his best Sabbath clothes and accompanied by his Chasidim, dug trenches with a pick and shovel to demonstrate publicly that defense of one's country, in this case Israel, is no violation of the Sabbath.

The entire Torah, and this includes the laws of the Sabbath, is to live by, not to die by. With the exception of the laws forbidding murder, incest and the worship of idols, all laws may be broken to preserve human life.

Of course, not all laws and regulations of the Shabbat have been covered in this short chapter, but the basic concepts underlying them have.

24

Jewish Clothing and Personal Appearance

In the Americas, in our times, there is little or nothing in the appearance of the Jew to distinguish him from the rest of the population. There are, however, certain articles of clothing and distinguishing marks, some of them visible, others not, and others seen solely in the synagogue that deserve mention, however brief:

CLOTHING

ARBA KANFOT. The arba kanfot, a four-cornered garment, ordinarily worn under the shirt, is described in chapter 19.

TALLIT. The tallit is the large prayer shawl, worn during morning prayers. It is described in chapter 26, as is the *gartel*, a woven sash worn about the waist by all Chasidim at prayer.

KITTEL. The kittel is a white robe, usually with lace down the front and at the cuffs. It is worn by men on Rosh Hashana and Yom Kippur, by the *sheliach tzibbur*, or reader, on certain other holidays and by the leader of the Passover *seder*. It is also worn by bridegrooms under the wedding canopy among the very Orthodox. Its white color signifies purity and rejoicing, but it also resembles the *tachrichim*, or burial shroud, and serves to remind us of our relatively few days on earth.

SHAATNEZ. Shaatnez is the law forbidding the mixture of linen and wool in clothing. It is discussed in chapter 19.

CHASIDIC CLOTHES. Most Chasidim, particularly the rabbis, maintain their traditional style of clothing, which is of Eastern European origin. The round fur hat worn by the *Rebbes* is called a *shtreimel*. The high fur or velvet hat worn by some rabbis, particularly during the week, is called a *spodek*. The black, overcoat-like robe worn by many Chasidim is called a *kaftan*, while the more elaborate robe for festive occasions is called a *zhupetzeh* or *pekesheh*. A simpler robe, worn in the house, is called a *chalat*. Chasidim of some parts of Europe, particularly Galicia and the Ukraine, wear a sort of plus-fours pants which end at the knee. From the knee down their legs are covered with long white stockings, called in Yiddish, *weisse zekelach*. The Lubavitcher Chasidim, including even the Rebbe, wear ordinary snapbrim black felt hats and most of them wear regular western clothing as well; usually black, doublebreasted suits.

WOMEN'S CLOTHING. Among the very Orthodox, it is considered immodest for women to wear slacks, shorts, skirts above the knee or short sleeves. Little girls are, of course, excepted. Orthodox married women who do not wear the *sheitel* (see below) keep their hair covered at all times in observance of a Talmudic ruling that it is immodest for a married woman to expose her hair freely. Some very fashionable hats have been designed to help women comply with this law and they are often seen in Israel, but many women, particularly the older ones, cover their hair with a kerchief, called in Yiddish a *tuch*.

PERSONAL APPEARANCE

Beards

In the Torah we are told not to "destroy the corners of your beards" (Lev. 19:27). The very Orthodox take this to mean that the beard should not be touched at all, but allowed to grow. This commandment actually applies only to the use of a razor and most Orthodox Jews today shave with a depilatory powder or wax or, most often, with an electric shaver which is a sort of clipper, rather than a razor.

Payes (S. Payot)

In the same chapter and verse of Leviticus we are commanded not to "cut round the corners of the head." This phrase, "corners of the head," refers to the temples and the area adjacent to them. While most Orthodox Jews, including some Chasidim, interpret this to mean that one must not clip this area completely, there are others who believe it to mean that the hair growing there must not be cut at all, so they let it grow into long *payes*. Some payes are curled and hang down the sides of the face (the Yemenites, for example), others are tucked behind the ears while others are wound around the finger and tucked up into a sort of lump at the temple.

SHEITEL. As noted above, married women among the more Orthodox do not expose their hair. Among the Ashkenazim the practice exists of married women cutting the hair short immediately before marriage and thereafter wearing a wig, called in Yiddish a *sheitel*. This practice is today restricted mostly to the very Orthodox. Sephardic women do not wear a wig, but cover their hair carefully with a kerchief.

25

The Books of the Jews

THE Jews are known as the People of the Book, a name given them by Mohammed. Really, they should be called the People of the *Books,* because there are several books which, when taken together, contain much of the raw material of Judaism.

It should come as no surprise that, without exception, these books are in Hebrew or Aramaic, the languages understood by all learned Jews from Lodz to London and from Brooklyn to Bombay. The books on which Jewish living is based must be accessible to Jews the world over, whose spoken languages number in the scores.

THE BIBLE

This book, "The Old Testament," is the foundation of everything Jewish since it contains the Torah, on which Jewish law is based; the Prophets, who, with the Torah as their inspiration, laid down the patterns of Jewish life and morality; and the Writings, which put the experience of the Jews' relationship with God into poetry and legend of a literary and spiritual sublimity which has never been equaled.

Jews know The Old Testament as the "TANACH," an acronym made up of the first letters of the three divisions of the Bible: *Torah* (Law), *N'viim* (Prophets) and *K'tuvim* (Writings).

The first division of the Bible (the Torah) we have already discussed in the chapters on the Jewish religion. It consists of the five books—Genesis, Exodus, Leviticus, Numbers and Deuteronomy—and is otherwise known in English as the Pentateuch. In Hebrew it is called either the Torah or the *Chumash*, a word meaning something like "five-fold," for the number of books making it up.

Beyond its division into five books, the Torah is marked off into fifty-four weekly portions called *sidrot* (S. *parashiot)*, one of which is read on each Sabbath of the year, starting on the Sabbath after Simchat Torah. After the public reading of the *sedra* in the synagogue on the Sabbath, a short portion selected from the Prophets and relating to the sedra is read. This supplementary portion is called the *haftara* (pl. *haftarot*) and in the case of several of the sidrot is different in Ashkenazi and Sephardi tradition. The sidrot themselves are exactly the same in both rituals. Most standard Jewish editions of the Bible, in whatever language, indicate the division of the text of the Pentateuch into the sidrot and list the haftarot as well.

The second division of the Bible (the N'viim) is in turn divided into two parts—the *N'viim Rishonim*, or First Prophets, and the *N'viim Achronim,* or Latter Prophets. In the N'viim Rishonim we find Joshua, Judges, First and Second Samuel, First and Second Kings, Isaiah, Jeremiah and Ezekiel. The N'viim Achronim are Hosea, Joel, Amos, Obadia, Jonah, Micah, Nahum, Habakkuk, Zephaniah, Haggai, Zechariah and Malachai.

The third section of the Tanach is the K'tuvim. The first three books are Psalms, Proverbs and Job. Jewish tradition has it that King David wrote the Psalms while King Solomon wrote Proverbs. Job is considered by many students to be the most deeply philosophical book of the entire Bible and is, perhaps, more widely studied by Gentiles than by Jews who have a tendency to shy away from it and leave its analysis to men of great learning.

The next five books are referred to as the five *M'gillot*, or scrolls. They are the Song of Songs, which is read, particularly by the Sephardim, before the Friday night service; Ruth, read on *Shavuot* in many congregations; Lamentations which is read in all synagogues on the fast day of *Tisha B'Av;* Ecclesiastes which is read on *Sh'mini Atzeret* by the Ashkenazim in the synagogue, and the book of Esther, which is read in scroll form in the synagogue on Purim. It is interesting to note that the *M'gillat Esther* is the only book of the Bible in which the name of God does not appear. The reason will be found in chapter 35.

The last books of The Old Testament are Daniel, Ezra, Nehemiah and Chronicles. (Part of the book of Daniel, incidentally, is written in Aramaic.)

THE TALMUD

Next in importance to the Bible is the huge collection of closely connected books called in English, the *Talmud*. In Hebrew it is usually referred to as the *Shass*, an acronym formed from the first letters of the words *Shisha Sedarim*, meaning "six sections" or "six orders," into which this enormous repository of wisdom and law is divided. To the Jewish scholar, Talmud means only the *Gemara* (see below), but we will use it to mean the entire *Shass*, since it is the accepted English term.

The Talmud contains the Oral Torah, or *Torah Sheb'al Peh*, which was discussed in chapter 6. As we noted there, it is divided into the *Mishna* and its completion, the *Gemara*, and in its entirety contains the laws by which Jews live and have lived for millennia. The Mishna and the Gemara both contain two types of material, *Halacha* and *Aggada*. Halacha means law, which we are required to observe. Aggada, on the other hand, means something like "legend," and includes speculation on the afterlife, stories about the rabbis, and to some degree about figures in the Bible, advice, counsel, medical lore and observations, demonology, theories concerning the nature of sin, etc.

While we must accept Halacha as law which is binding upon us, we are not obliged to accept as either law or dogma anything contained in the Aggada and this includes the aggada in the

Midrash. In the words of Rabbi Samson Raphael Hirsch (Germany, 19th century), one of the greatest modern defenders of the Oral Torah, ". . . it is absolutely impossible to derive Halacha from Aggadic statements."

We cannot begin to analyze the intricacies of the Talmud, its authorities or its component parts in this book. Suffice it to say that there are *two* Talmuds: the Jerusalem Talmud and the Babylonian Talmud. The Mishna in both is the same, it is only the Gemara that differs. The *Yerushalmi*, or Jerusalem Talmud, was written down in Palestine by those who remained there after the destruction of the Second Temple. The *Bavli*, or Babylonian Talmud, was compiled in the Torah academies of Babylonia or present-day Iraq, by the rabbis of that land and its communities that had been forced to leave their homeland. Although the Jerusalem Talmud is studied by especially learned men, it is the Babylonian Talmud that is the basis of most Jewish law.

THE MIDRASH

The Midrash is a collection of very early rabbinical commentaries on the text of the Bible. Its contents are largely homiletic, which is to say that it draws moral lessons from the Bible text by means of stories and legends which illustrate its meaning and which reflect the ancient Jewish traditions concerning its figures. For example, in chapter 5 we noted that Abraham's father was a worshiper and "according to Jewish tradition also a manufacturer" of idols. The phrase in quotes refers to material found not in the Torah, but in the Midrash. There are several *Midrashim* and four of them in particular (*Mekilta, Sifra, Sifre debe Rab*, and *Sifre Zuta*) contain important Halacha material as well as Aggada and homiletics. Here again, it is important to distinguish between them because, while the *Aggadot* of both the Midrash and the Talmud are great sources of moral guidance, we are not expected to take many of their statements literally. In a great many cases they are obvious parables or allegories.

The Midrash is composed of a large number of books, but their analysis is not possible here.

THE SHULCHAN ARUCH

The *Shulchan Aruch*, divided into four sections, is a codification in orderly form and progression of all the *Halachot* (laws) of practical application contained in the Talmud and the *Mikra,* or Written Torah. It is the day-to-day text used by rabbis and congregations in answering questions of Jewish law. The Shulchan Aruch was compiled by the Sephardic rabbi Joseph Karo (Turkey, 16th century) as a condensation of an even more voluminous work and its success was immediate. It was adopted by all Sephardic communities as their basic guide to law and conduct. Its adoption by the Ashkenazim followed the inclusion in its text of a gloss by Rabbi Moses Isserles (Poland, 16th century), which indicated the laws and customs of the Ashkenazim where they differed from those of the Sephardim. Since the name "Shulchan Aruch" means "a set table"—in the sense of a table set with dishes—Rabbi Isserles's gloss was given the name Mappah, which means "a tablecloth." For quick reference on simple questions of Jewish law and ceremony, there is a condensation of the Shulchan Aruch oriented to Ashkenazi usage, called the *Kitzur Shulchan Aruch*, and an English translation of this valuable book is available in several editions.

THE ZOHAR

The *Sefer Ha-Zohar,* or "Book of Splendor," is the most important document of the Jewish mystical tradition, the *Kabbala.* (For an idea of its contents, see chapter 42.)

THE SIDDUR

The *Siddur* is the daily prayerbook. In it are usually found prayers for the entire week, blessings for special occasions and, depending on its size, all sorts of other prayers, services, ceremonies and formulae for use during the year. There are thousands of different editions of the siddur, some containing only the bare three daily prayers, while others contain extensive commentaries on these prayers, as well as services for everything from circumcision to burial, psalms, devotional readings from the Kabbala and rabbinic literature and folktales illustrating the text and translations into many different languages ranging from English to Tatar. The three main types of *nusach*, or prayer service—as found in the siddur—are *Ashkenaz,* used today mostly by German, Lithuanian and White Russian Jews; *S'phard,* which is a modified form of the Spanish ritual, used by almost all Chasidim; and *Sephardi*, the "oriental" Sephardic ritual used by Ladino and Arabic-speaking Jews. There are variations of many sorts in the order of prayers and even the prayers themselves as found in the siddur, depending on regional tradition; the nusach of Aleppo is slightly different from that of Damascus, for example, and every congregation seems to have some slight departure from the order in which the prayers appear in the book. Thus it always takes a few weeks to get accustomed to the way the daily and Sabbath services are recited in any new congregation.

THE MACHZOR

The *Machzor* is similar to the siddur, except that it contains only the service for the holidays—the *Yomim Tovim.* The most commonly found *machzorim* are those for Rosh Hashana and Yom Kippur, but there are also machzorim for Passover, Shavuot and Sukkot. The main and almost only use of the machzor is in the synagogue, whereas the siddur is also used in the home.

THE PASSOVER HAGGADA

The Passover Haggada, a small book, contains the entire service for the two first nights of Passover as it is celebrated in the home at the seder, described in chapter 32.

These are the basic books of the Jews, to be found in every Jewish congregation and, in the case of the Bible, Siddur and Passover Haggada, in most Jewish homes as well. To be sure there are many other books which are essential to the deciding of questions in Jewish law; special attention is given to the decisions of earlier rabbis in similar cases. These decisions are to be found in the hundreds of printed volumes of *responsa.*

THE RESPONSA

The word *responsa* means in Latin, "answers." In Hebrew the answers together with the questions that prompted them are called *Shaalot u-T'shuvot:* questions and answers. They are letters from one rabbi to another, and more eminent, rabbi, asking for opinion on legal and often on moral questions. The opinion in answer is printed together with the questioning letter in collections of the "answers" given by a particular rabbi. It would by no means be unusual for a rabbi in the United States to consult the opinions of rabbis from Spain, Turkey, Poland, France, Egypt, Tunisia and Germany, as well as American contemporaries, in reaching a decision on a current case in Jewish law. The span of time covered by these earlier decisions could be well over a thousand or even two thousand years, counting the rabbinical decisions in the Talmud. The fact that all these *poskim*, or respondents, wrote their opinions in Hebrew makes this enormous body of case-law literature available to Jews everywhere in the world at all times.

THE COMMENTARIES

In addition to the several books of the Jews listed above, there are many commentaries without which it is simply not possible to study them adequately or to make use of them in determining proper conduct as Jew. These commentaries, particularly the basic observations on the Torah and the Talmud, are the work of men of great genius, who were able to assimilate immense amounts of text, tradition and history and then to coordinate it all, making the statements and grammatical constructions of one part available for the clarification of the meaning of other parts. These men—Rashi, Maimonides, Ibn Ezra, Kimchi, Nachmanides, Elijah of Wilno and their like—operated at an intellectual level easily comparable to that of Newton and Einstein in completely different fields. And just as Newton and Einstein's "commentaries" on the nature of the physical world are necessary for the understanding of that world, so are the commentaries of the great rabbis essential to the clear understanding of the Torah, both written and oral.

This is an important point and one which should not be overlooked. The Bible, far from being a simple document, is a text of great sophistication and intricacy, and the same is true to an even greater degree, if only because of its greater volume, of the Talmud. It is not enough to "read" the Torah to understand its meaning for Judaism, particularly if it is being read in translation by a person with little knowledge of the original Hebrew. For those readers who wish to obtain a more profound comprehension of the Torah without having recourse to study with a scholar, perhaps the most convenient way is through study of the *Chumash* in an edition which has both the English text, the original Hebrew, and an English translation of one or more of the standard commentaries. In my opinion, the best edition for this purpose is the widely available *Soncino Chumash*, which incorporates most of the commentaries of Rashi as well as several classic medieval commentators, all in an excellent and reliable English translation. For those with less time to dedicate to study, the edition of the Torah with the commentaries of the late Rabbi Joseph H. Hertz is also excellent and perhaps even more suited to the nonscholarly modern reader. The *Hertz Chumash* is also widely available and can be found in almost all Jewish bookstores.

PART VI

Prayer: Private and Communal

26

Private Prayer, Blessings and the Grace After Meals

PRIVATE PRAYER

As we have already noted in chapter 19, the Jewish male is obliged to pray four times daily on ordinary weekdays. Women are excused from these prayers since each of them has certain time limits. *Shachrit* (S. *T'filla*) cannot be prayed earlier than dawn when there is enough light to distinguish a light blue thread from a white thread; the latest one may pray it is noon. *Mincha* must be prayed between noon and sundown and *Maariv* (S. *Arbit*) must be prayed after sundown. *K'riat Shema al ha-Mitta* is prayed immediately before retiring.

According to Jewish law, any precept that depends in any way or is limited in any way by the time of day is not obligatory upon women. The reason for this is that the responsibilities of women are considered more important, in a religious sense, than these commandments, and they cannot be expected to interrupt their activities to observe them. The activities of men are less important and they must put them aside to pray.

As distasteful as it may be to the Women's Liberation Movement, Jewish tradition assigns to men and women quite different roles and responsibilities. And as unseemly as it may appear to the "male chauvinists," women's responsibilities are considered as important as those of men or even more so, and the position of women in Jewish life is one of respect, not only for her superior moral and spiritual qualities, but for the job she does in preserving not only the family but the entire Jewish people.

As we have pointed out elsewhere, abuse of women and wife-beating, so common among other peoples, is "not done in Israel," and the rights of women are protected both by law and by custom to an extent unknown in any other society. It is safe to say that in no other culture or religious system is the respect accorded women greater than in Judaism. The Talmud tells us repeatedly that a man should realize that any blessing he may have comes to him by virtue of his wife; an unmarried man or one away from his wife, says the Talmud, is only half a man.

Further, women are in no sense excluded from prominence in public life: Miriam and Deborah in the Bible need no commentary any more than does Golda Meir. In Israel today, one of the most learned teachers and commentators of the Torah is Nechama Leibowitz; most of the courses she teaches are open only to rabbis who already possess a high degree of learning.

To return to the subject of prayer, women certainly may, if they wish, pray the same prayers as men, but if they prefer, may use shortened versions of those prayers (in any language they wish), make up their own prayers or not pray at all. Men ideally should pray in Hebrew and follow the order of prayer of their particular tradition. Since any good siddur will tell the reader all he may want to know about the prayers themselves, there is little point in describing them here, but some commentary on them might help to place them within the daily life of the Jew.

In the first place, the prayers themselves technically are substitutes for the sacrificial services which were held at the Temple. The exception is the Maariv, or evening prayer, which was instituted after the Temple was destroyed. Nevertheless, even during the Temple period, prayers were said regularly both within and outside the Holy Land.

Shachrit

Shachrit, called by the Sephardim simply *T'filla*, or prayer, is the morning service. Among the Ashkenazim, married men or men who have been married wear the *tallit*, or prayer shawl. At least this used to be the general custom but these days it is quite common in Orthodox Ashkenazi congregations for boys after the age of bar mitzva to start wearing the tallit. There are several explanations for restricting the tallit to married men, but the simplest one is that the commandment "Make for yourself *g'dilim* (the woolen cords of the *tsitsit*" (Lev. 22:12) is immediately followed (Lev. 22:13) by the words "If any man take a wife." This is interpreted to mean that a man should not wear the tallit with its tsitsit until he has married. One's best course is to follow the custom of one's congregation.

Among the Sephardim, all men old enough to pray wear it. Most observant Jews wear a tallit made of wool with tsitsit, or fringes (see chapter 19), of the same material. There is no prescribed size, but it is felt that the tallit should be large enough to cover the entire upper body. In practice this means that it is about seventy inches in width by fifty inches in length although these measurements may vary widely. It is unquestionably permitted to say the proper blessing before putting on such a tallit. On a rayon or silk tallit of very small size such as is found in many modern non-Orthodox synagogues, there is a question as to whether the blessing may be said although it is certainly permitted to wear one without saying the blessing. According to one opinion, if the tallit and tsitsit are of the same material the blessing may be said, but not if they are of different materials. It is a fact, however, that today any tallit with properly made wool tsitsit is considered kosher in most places.

In the case of the *arba kanfot* (chapter 19), the small four-cornered garment worn under the shirt, this is usually made of cotton, particularly in hot countries, and the tsitsit of wool. The blessing for the arba kanfot is different from that of the large tallit.

All men over the age of thirteen put on *t'fillin* during the weekly Shachrit service. The t'fillin, or as they are called in English, phylacteries, are small leather boxes containing the Biblical verses Exod. 13:1-10, and 13:11-16, and Deut. 6:4-9 and 11:13-21. They are mounted on leather straps, one of which is placed on the head so that the box rests high on the forehead. This is the *t'fillin shel rosh*, and it contains four separate compartments in which the four selections mentioned above are kept, on four separate strips of parchment. The *t'fillin shel yad* is placed on the upper arm, opposite the heart, and contains only one compartment with the four selections on one piece of parchment. The verses must be written by hand by a qualified *sofer*, or scribe.

These "ornaments of prayer" are used in obedience to the commandments of the Torah. The t'fillin shel yad is placed on the biceps, facing inward toward the heart, and the strap is wound seven times around the arm and tied on the hand. This is in response to the commandments, "It shall be for a sign upon thy hand" (Exod. 13:16), and "Therefore ye shall lay up these words upon thy heart" (Deut. 11:18). There are differences in the way the t'fillin are put on, the basic one being that the non-Chasidic Ashkenazim wind the strap on their arm toward the body while the Chasidim and Sephardim wind it the opposite way. When the strap reaches the hand, there are three main ways of tying it corresponding to the customs of Mitnagdim, Chasidim and "oriental" (Ladino and Arabic-speaking) Sephardim. Left-handed men wear the t'fillin shel yad on the right arm.

The t'fillin shel rosh is placed on the head with the box on the upper part of the forehead in obedience to the commandment, "and they shall be as frontlets between thy eyes" (Deut. 6:8).

The Chasidim wear, in addition, a sort of sash, commonly woven of black silk, which is wound around the waist and tied or tucked in at the sides. This sash is called a *gartel* (girdle) and its use is rooted in the kabbala as forming a sort of barrier between the "ignoble" lower part of the body and the upper part.

It is not permitted to eat before praying Shachrit, but tea or coffee without sugar may be taken. On Shabbat, when the service starts late and lasts for over two hours, many people will pray the first few prayers of the service at home and then eat breakfast before leaving for the synagogue.

Mincha and Maariv

The afternoon prayer, *Mincha*, is usually started just before sundown so that the evening prayer may be said immediately following it.

The evening prayer, called by the Ashkenazim *Maariv* and by the Sephardim *Arbit*, is ordinarily said very fast, and the *Sh'moneh Essreh* (S. *Amida*)—repeated in both Shachrit and Mincha by the reader—is not repeated in Maariv. The reason for praying this service at a high speed comes to us through tradition. We are told that during the many times Jews were forbidden to pray, first by the Romans and Greeks, then by the Catholic Church and finally, in our times, by the Communists in many lands, they would take their prayerbooks and pray in the fields and the woods where no one could see them. Since Maariv is prayed after sundown, they would pray as quickly as possible so that they could read the prayers by the remaining light and return home before darkness set in.

K'riat Shema al ha-Mitta is said at the bedside and the *Shema Israel* is repeated before going to sleep. Children are taught to say the Shema in Hebrew and in whatever language is spoken in the home.

Other Private Prayers

Most of the prayers which are said in the home, or at any rate outside the synagogue, are described in other parts of the book as they come under discussion. One which might be mentioned here is the *T'fillat ha-Derech*, a prayer recited before setting out on a journey. It really should be said before leaving the house but I confess that at one time in my life when I traveled a great deal, I usually used to remember to say it either in the airport or as I was fastening my seatbelt, although I always managed to recite it before the plane took off. There is one phrase in the prayer, at least in the version I recite, which asks for protection from wild animals on the road. I once asked a rabbi I know if that was really germane these days and without hesitating a second he said, "Yes indeed; the way some people drive. . . ."

BLESSINGS

The blessings are an important part of private prayer. It is taken as a rule by observant Jews that every man should say one hundred blessings every day and in fact these blessings are contained in the weekday prayers. An ingenious explanation of why this should be so is that they counteract the ninety-eight curses contained in Deut. 28:15-58 plus the two in Deut. 28:61.

In addition to the blessings in the liturgy, the Jew is used to giving thanks to God during the day for all manner of favors which others take for granted. The observant Jew, for example, thanks God with a blessing every time he takes a drink of water. On this subject, there are separate blessings for different sorts of food and a list of them with an indication of their application is given in appendix IV.

But the blessings for the food we eat and the drink we enjoy are not the only ones the observant Jew has on his lips. The purchase and wearing of new clothes, for example, have their blessings as do seeing lightning or hearing thunder. But most interesting of all are the *B'rachot* (A. *Brochos*), or blessings which thank God for having given us the commandment to do a certain thing. Here we are not thanking God for having given us something concrete such as food or for having created the world so that we may enjoy it; we thank God for having commanded us to go out of our way and take the trouble to do something no one else does, such as putting up a mezuza, wearing tsitsit, sitting in the sukka or lighting the Sabbath candles. Why we do this explains the essence of Judaism better than a lengthy essay: when we light the Sabbath candles the blessing is, "Blessed art Thou, O Lord our God, King of the Universe, Who has sanctified us with His commandments and commanded us to light the Sabbath light." We are saying, in effect, "Thank You, God, for having commanded us to do this. You didn't tell the Gentiles to do it, only *us* did You favor with Your commands." In other words, we are thanking God for having chosen us as His people, which is what Judaism is, in the end, all about.

WASHING THE HANDS AND COVERING THE HEAD

Both prayer and blessings are subject to definite rules and laws. Certain prayers, such as the Amida, or Sh'moneh Essreh, are said standing, while others, such as the Shema Israel, are said sitting down. These will be commented on in their turn, but there are two rules which are general: one's hands must be clean before starting to pray and, in the case of males, one's head must be covered.

The washing of the hands is most important on arising in the morning, before saying the first blessings, and the reasons given for it are many. The main one, however, is the general statement that "evil spirits" rest on one's hands at that time. This is further emphasized in the law that water used for rinsing the hands must be thrown out and not used for anything since the "evil spirits" will remain in the water. This indicates what we know perfectly well to be the case: that the "evil spirits" are pathogenic organisms—microbes and fungi. There is no reason to believe that the rabbis from earliest times were unaware of this; the contagious nature of disease is made clear in the pages of the Torah in the regulations concerning leprosy and gonorrhea (the "issue from the flesh"). Since there was no other way to describe what they knew to be the case, the term "evil spirits" was borrowed from popular folklore because all understood it.

The covering of the head is another matter entirely. There are dozens of explanations for this custom but none of them are convincing and most authorities and rabbis who have issued opinions on this subject agree that it was not originally obligatory by law, but is a custom which has been observed with such fidelity over the centuries that it now has the force of law. This is because *Minhag Israel, Torah hi*; the customs of Israel are Law. This is stated in different words in the phrase, *minhag oker din* (A custom can abolish a law), so strong is the force of custom in Jewish life.

As a result it has become law, at least in our times, that to say any prayer or blessing, the head must be covered; and since observant Jews say blessings throughout the day, the head is kept covered at all times. This has acquired in addition the connotation of respect for God in general and the covered head and observance of the Torah have become synonymous. I seem to recall reading a letter from Groucho Marx to a newspaper columnist in which he says something to the effect that "I read your column religiously. This means I read it with my hat on." A great deal can be learned about a people by the wisecracks of its wittier members.

BREAD AND THE GRACE AFTER MEALS

One of the most important blessings (in reality a collection of blessings) is the *Birchat ha-Mazon,* or grace after meals, the text of which is found in all siddurim. Recited in compliance with the commandment contained in Deut. 8:10, "And you shall eat and be satisfied and bless the Lord your God," it is said only if bread in a piece the size of an olive is eaten. If bread is not eaten at the meal, a much shorter form of the grace is said.

Regarding the eating of bread itself, the Jewish law is that the hands must be washed first. This is done by cleansing the hands carefully and then ritually washing them by pouring water over them from a glass or other container; not water direct from a faucet. This is to make sure there is no contaminating substance in the water, which could be seen in the container and the water consequently would not be used. After washing, the hands must be dried and the following blessing said:

"Baruch Ata Adonai, Elohenu Melech ha-olam, asher
kid'shanu b'mitzvotav, v'tzivanu al netilat yadaim"
(Blessed art Thou, O Lord our God, King of the universe,
Who has sanctified us in His commandments and commanded us to lift up our hands).

"Lift up" in Jewish application here refers to the action of lifting up the hands after washing to remove the water.

After saying this blessing it is forbidden to speak until we have said the blessing for bread, otherwise we would have to wash again. The bread is taken, dipped in salt (or salt sprinkled on it) and the following blessing said:

"Baruch Ata Adonai, Elohenu Melech ha-olam, ha-motzi lechem min ha-aretz" (Blessed art Thou, O Lord our God, King of the universe, Who brings bread out from the earth).

The bread is eaten immediately after saying this blessing. Why do we eat bread with salt? As we noted earlier, since the destruction of the Temple in Jerusalem, the table of every Jew is a substitute for the altar, and the food—symbolized here by bread—is a substitute for the sacrifices. The Torah states (Lev. 2:13) that all sacrifices must be eaten with salt.

And why does the blessing say, ". . . who brings bread out from the earth"? If it were potatoes we could understand this phrasing, but bread? The answer is that in the case of potatoes, the blessing says, "who creates the fruit of the earth"; that is to say God creates the fruits of the earth and leaves them there for men to dig up and use just as they are. In the case of bread, however, God himself takes a hand in bringing it forth from the earth for man's use, because it is only through the direct blessing of God that man can make bread. Animals, even the most intelligent of them, eat grass or eat each other; only man can take the grain from the earth, store it and make bread out of it when he needs it, because God has given man the ability to do so. For this reason, the verse (Gen. 3:19) in which God told Adam (representing all mankind), "In the sweat of your face you shall eat bread," has always been understood by the Jews as a blessing. It should be noted that the actual wording of the *b'racha* is based on Psalm 104:14.

After saying *hamotzi*, the blessing for bread, no other blessings need be said for any other food during the meal unless wine is brought to the table in which case it must also be blessed.

After bread has been eaten and the meal terminated, the Birchat ha-Mazon is said. The grace said on Shabbat contains extra material as does the grace recited on holidays or at a wedding or a *briss.* On Shabbat and Yom Tov, grace is prefaced by the singing of Psalm 126. In our times this psalm is often sung to the tune of *Hatikva*, the Israeli national anthem.

Before the grace is recited, all knives should be removed from the table. The reason is that, as we have already seen, the table of the Jew replaces, in a sense, the altar of our holy Temple and the commandment regarding the construction of the altar is that no iron be lifted upon it (Deut. 27:5).

If three to nine adult males eat together, this is known as a *M'zumen* and a special introduction to the grace is recited. It is interesting to note that this invitation to say grace which is pronounced by the leader of the grace is the only instance of Yiddish entering the formal prayers. The leader starts off by saying, *"Raboisai, mir vellen benshen"* (Gentlemen, let us say grace). It is also possible to say it in Hebrew, *"Rabotai nevarech,"* and this is the way it appears in many siddurim, but among Ashkenazim, even when they customarily do not speak the language, the Yiddish invocation is more common. Those present respond in Hebrew and if a *minyan* of ten or more men eat together, the response is slightly different.

In the case of a m'zumen or a minyan saying grace, it is necessary to wash the hands (by custom only the fingertips) with a small amount of water passed around the table in a glass or other container. This water is called *mayim achronim*, "final water."

While in its essentials the same prayer, the grace recited by Sephardim is different throughout in many details from the Ashkenazic grace.

As for the bread itself, to be considered genuine bread, over which the blessing hamotzi can be said and after which the Birchat ha-Mazon can be recited, it must be made of one or more of the "five species" of grain: wheat, barley, rye, oats or spelt, a kind of red wheat. Bread made from any other sort of grain, such as corn (maize), ground legumes, etc., does not have the hamotzi blessing.

Although at one time there was considerable difference of opinion, in past centuries Orthodox authorities came to agree that bread made by Goyim may be eaten, even if bread made by Jews is available.

If Jews make bread, it is the law that from each batch of dough a small amount, the size of an olive, must be taken and burned after saying the following blessing:

"Baruch Ata Adonai, Elohenu Melech ha-olam, asher kid'shanu b'mitzotav v'tzivanu l'hafrish challa" (Blessed art Thou, O Lord our God, King of the universe, Who has sanctified us in His commandments and commanded us to separate dough).

Women baking bread at home should remember to do this; otherwise the bread will not be kosher. Bread baked by a Goy is kosher even if no dough is separated.

This commandment applies if the dough is kneaded with water and if a minimum of 1,680 grams (3⅔ lbs.) of flour is used in it. If more than 1,248 grams (2¾ lbs.) but less than 1,680 grams of flour is used, or if the dough is kneaded with eggs, fruit juice, etc., instead of water, dough is separated but no blessing is said. If less than 1,248 grams of flour is used, no dough need be separated.

27

Communal Prayer:
the Synagogue,
the Congregation and
the Weekday Prayers

SINCE almost all Communal Prayer takes place in the synagogue, we will start with a description of what an Orthodox synagogue is likely to look like. Then we can examine the organization of a typical congregation. After that, we will discuss the religious services as they are celebrated on weekdays and on the Sabbath. Holiday services will be discussed under the holidays themselves.

THE SYNAGOGUE: ITS PHYSICAL PLAN

Most synagogues are laid out on a rectangular plan with the longest part running from West to East. On the east wall of this oblong room is a closet-like sliding double-door, usually some three or four feet above floor level. In front of this door in Ashkenzai synagogues hangs a velvet curtain called a *parochet*. In Sephardic synagogues it usually hangs behind the closed door. When the door is open and the curtain pulled aside, we see that there is a recess in the wall and that in this recess are kept the

Sifrei Torah, or scrolls of the Torah. This cabinet in which the scrolls are kept is called by Ashkenazim the *Aron Kodesh*, and by Sephardim the *Heichal*. In English it is called the Ark.

Under and in front of the Ark is a platform, usually around a yard deep and three or four yards long, a foot or two off the floor, reached by a step. One must ascend this platform to open the doors of the Ark and it is from this platform, called a *duchan*, that the Cohanim give the priestly blessing.

In many synagogues there are one or two chairs on either side of the Ark, on the platform, and the President and any distinguished guests sit on them during the service.

Above the Ark, suspended from the ceiling, hangs a lamp that is always lit, day and night, called in Hebrew the *ner tamid*, or eternal light.

Why is the Ark on the east wall? Because prayers are said facing Jerusalem and also facing the Ark; thus the Ark must be in the direction of Jerusalem, which in Europe and the Americas is East. In such places as Hong Kong and Bombay, the Ark will be on the west wall.

Facing the Ark, and usually about half way down the synagogue toward the west wall, is a table or desk, often on a raised platform, but which must never be as high as the Ark. It is here that the Torah is read. This platform, with its table, is called the *Bima* by most Ashkenazim, although the Germans call it the *Almemor*. The Sephardim commonly call it the *Teba*.

Among the Sephardim, the *Sheliach Tzibbur*, or reader, stands on the Bima while leading the prayer service. Among the Ashkenazim, the reader usually stands before a small lectern in the forward part of the synagogue, almost always to the right of the Ark. This lectern is called the *Omed*.

In Ashkenazic synagogues, the seats or benches on which the male worshipers sit usually run crosswise in the *shul*, that is to say, from north to south, and are located behind and most often also in front of the Bima, between it and the Ark. In Sephardic synagogues only the seats behind the Bima run crosswise; the seats at the sides of the Bima are parallel to it and run from West to East almost down to the Ark. The space between the Bima and the Ark is empty and quite often covered with oriental rugs.

In synagogues built specifically as synagogues, i.e. not adapted from a house or apartment, the women are seated in a gallery one floor above the men's section. This gallery is called the *Ezrat Nashim* and is reached by a staircase. In many Sephardic synagogues this section is open and the women look down upon the men, who can avoid seeing the women by simply not looking up. In Orthodox Ashkenazic synagogues, however, the women's section is separated from that of the men by a screen or curtain through which the women can see but through which they cannot be seen. This screen is called a *mechitza* and observant Ashkenazim will not pray in a synagogue which does not have one. Many Sephardic congregations hold that the railing fronting the women's gallery is a mechitza in the legal sense and that no curtain is required.

In the case of a synagogue which has been converted from a house or even an apartment, the women's section is to one side or behind the men's section and separated by a curtained partition which constitutes a legal mechitza.

Reform and Conservative synagogues have no separate section for men and women, who sit together during services, but separation of the sexes is an absolute law in Orthodox practice. The reasons given for it vary, but they all come down to the idea that women are a distracting element and that it is not possible to concentrate on prayers if the sexes are mixed. It is said that even the presence of one's mother at prayers is disturbing since at this particular time we wish to remember first of all that we are children of God.

The fact is that separation of men and women at religious services is common to a great many peoples, apparently as a result of thousands of years of experience which has shown that both are more at ease that way. Among the Ashkenazim, as noted earlier, it is common for pre-pubescent girls to move freely in and out of the men's section or to sit with their fathers and brothers if they wish. After their first menstruation, however, they must sit in the women's section. In Sephardic synagogues, even the tiniest girls are not allowed in the men's section.

All Orthodox synagogues have a place for the men to wash their hands before praying and most have at least one other room in which kiddush can be offered after the services, and in which the third meal of the Sabbath, the *Shalosh Seuda* (S. *Seuda ha-Sh'lishit*) is eaten toward evening.

The above description of the arrangement of the synagogue does not hold true for every Jewish house of worship. Many are improvised in one or two rooms and lack everything but the Ark, which is a simple cabinet on legs with a curtain hung in front of its doors and a table on which the *Sefer Torah* is read. Worshipers in such synagogues often sit on benches around tables.

The technical Hebrew name for a synagogue is either *Bet ha-Knesset*, house of assembly, or *Bet ha-Midrash* (A. *Besmedrash*), which means house of study. Although the expression *Bet T'filla*, or house of prayer, exists as a generic term for the synagogue, it is interesting to note that no actual synagogue is ever referred to by that term; another indication that Jews see themselves first and foremost as a people rather than as a sect. The fact is that there is no word for religion in the Hebrew language.

Ashkenazim usually call their synagogue a *shul*, a Yiddish word, while Ladino-speaking Sephardim call theirs a *snoga* or *esnoga*. Reform Jews refer to the synagogue as a temple and Conservative Jews formally use the word synagogue, but informally tend to call it a shul, just as do their more orthodox brethren.

THE CONGREGATION

The congregation is called in Hebrew the *Kehilla* or, among the Sephardim, the *Kal*. The meaning of both these words is, more or less, the collectivity.

Since there is no human central authority in Judaism—the Torah takes the place of a church hierarchy—any group of Jews may form a congregation, whose purpose, in addition to having a minyan for collective prayers, may be the study of Torah, mutual aid, support of community institutions such as the mikva, schools, care of the ill, etc., or simply the provision of a place where Jews with similar backgrounds and traditions can meet.

The organization of congregations is pretty much the same

everywhere. The members elect a president, called a *Parnass*, and one or more *Gabbaim*, or trustees. The function of the Gabbaim is the proper conducting of the religious services, apportioning the different honors to members of the kehilla and enforcement of the *takkanot*, or special regulations, that the congregation may have adopted. Many congregations, for example, have a *takkana* that no one not a Sabbath-observer may serve as reader. In some congregations, Parnass and Gabbai are synonymous. Another functionary of the congregation is the *shamash* (A. *shammos*), or beadle, whose responsibility is the care of the synagogue and also some details of the service. He is usually a paid employee of the congregation. Of course there is also a treasurer and the usual officials of any organization.

There may be different brotherhoods within the congregation. We have already discussed one in chapter 16; the *Chevra Kadisha* or burial society. Others may be a *Chevra Shass*, a group dedicated to the study of the Talmud at specific hours or on certain days, or a *Chevra T'hillim*, which recites psalms at certain times.

Reform and Conservative congregations have all sorts of "committees," ranging from the "Pulpit Committee" to the "Kitchen Committee." In Orthodox congregations certain men seem eventually to drift into accepting responsibility for different functions of the congregation and function as committees on a less formal basis.

THE PLACE OF THE RABBI

If we have not mentioned the rabbi so far, it is because it is by no means necessary for a congregation to have a rabbi, although most congregations want one when they can afford one. Really, the only things for which it is absolutely necessary to have a rabbi are the writing and supervision of divorces and the proper supervision of conversions. Both these responsibilities can be taken care of outside the congregation through the rabbi of another congregation or community institution, either at home or in another city. Even marriages may be performed by a *m'sader kiddushin* who is not a rabbi, if a legal civil marriage has already been performed. In many places outside the United States, the m'sader kiddushin is not an ordained rabbi. The rabbi's role is essentially that of a judge, to whom questions of Jewish law are referred. If no rabbi is available, an outside rabbi can be consulted. (For a more detailed analysis of the rabbinical function, see chapter 43.)

Often a foreign observer sees through to the meaning of a phenomenon more clearly than those who have always lived with it. The "convert" Aimé Pallière says: "In effect, in the synagogue service all the Jews are equal, all are ministers, all can participate in the holy offices and even officiate, in the name of the entire community, if they have the necessary capacity. The dignity which distinguishes the *Chacham*, the Rabbi, the sage, is not a matter of rank in the clergy, it is in the field of learning, of piety emphasized by knowledge."

Nevertheless, most congregations, when they reach the size and position where they can afford a rabbi, want to have one. This is true even if one or more members have *s'micha*, meaning that they have been ordained rabbis by a rabbinical court. It is quite common to find men with s'micha who do not exercise as rabbis, preferring to earn their living as businessmen, professionals or employees.

This attitude marks one of the great differences between Jews and non-Jews. In essence, the congregation wants a rabbi not because it needs him, but because a rabbi is an *adornment* to the congregation. The more learned the rabbi is and the more time he spends in the study of the Torah, the greater is their pride in having him. Christians will take great pride in having a beautiful church or an impressive stained-glass window in their cathedral; Orthodox synagogues are usually not very impressive inside or outside—their edifice is a human one, themselves. Their chief adornment is not a stained-glass window but a man whose needs and those of his wife and family are taken care of so that he can dedicate himself to the study of the Holy Law and share his knowledge, as he sees fit, with the members of the congregation.

This, at least, is the traditional attitude. Jews who allow themselves to be overly influenced by their non-Jewish neighbors will too often choose architecture over more human values and it is possible and not uncommon to find "building campaigns" being run for the expansion of a synagogue that is empty on all but two or three days of the year.

Of course in some congregations the rabbi is a spiritual and worldly leader and a man whose directives guide every phase of the lives of his followers. This is particularly true of many Chasidic groups. In other cases the influence of a rabbi may extend far beyond the limits of the congregation to which he ministers, and in some countries such a man is dignified by being officially recognized as the "Chief Rabbi" of the land. In other countries certain rabbis have in the course of time come to be recognized by the Jewish community as spiritual leaders and authorities to which questions of Jewish law are submitted in the knowledge that their decisions will be universally accepted. This was the case of the *"Chafetz Chaim"* (Rabbi Israel Meir Ha-Kohen, 1838-1933), head of a yeshiva in the Polish-Lithuanian village of Radun, who during his lifetime was considered the greatest rabbi in Europe. In the United States, the late Rabbi Aaron Cotler was referred to as the "Gaon," or Eminence, of the American Jews.

WEEKDAY SERVICES

The purpose of going to a synagogue is to pray with a minyan. A minyan is a quorum of ten males, aged thirteen or over, whose presence is necessary for the saying of many prayers and for the public reading of the Torah. In contrast with such religions as Catholicism in which services (the Mass) may not be conducted in the absence of a priest, no one man is ever necessary, but ten men often are. The difference is that their rank means nothing: all that counts is that they be Jews. The fundamental religious democracy of Judaism is expressed in a well-known Yiddish proverb: "Nine rabbis can't constitute a minyan, but ten cobblers can."

Among the prayers that cannot be said with less than ten men present is the kaddish (see chapter 18) which is said for the eleven months following the death of a parent and other close relatives. For this reason it is not uncommon to find that in some synagogues the majority of the men at weekday services are mourners. The Sh'moneh Essreh (S. *Amida*) prayer is said in silence by all worshipers and then repeated with certain additions in the morning and afternoon services by the reader. This repetition of the Amida requires a minyan. Finally the Torah is read on Monday and Thursday as well as the Sabbath, and this too requires ten men for the public reading from the scroll, or Sefer Torah.

Among the Ashkenazim the services are prayed aloud, although not in unison, by the entire congregation, led by the reader who stands at the front of the synagogue and faces the Ark with his back to the worshipers. This reader is sometimes the rabbi, but more often is someone requested to perform this duty—considered an honor—by the gabbaim of the congregation. Certain worshipers have precedence over the others in being given this honor: a mourner or one who is observing yohrtzeit, for example. A bridegroom on the day before his marriage goes before all others.

Among the Sephardim, the reader leads the prayers in a loud voice and the other worshipers pray more or less silently except for certain portions which are sung, or, as in the case of the kaddish, recited in unison.

Shachrit is prayed early enough in the morning so that the worshiper will have time to get to his work after the service. In New York City this means that it is prayed at seven or seven-thirty, giving the members time to return home and eat breakfast and be at work by nine. In the suburbs, it is prayed earlier—six or six-thirty—because most of the worshipers commute.

Mincha, during the winter months, is prayed as late as possible before sundown so that as many people as possible can get to the synagogue on the way home from work. By custom, at all times of the year, Maariv is prayed directly after Mincha, although it can be prayed at any time up to midnight. During the summer months, when daylight saving time is in effect, Maariv is often prayed even before sundown. Although the times for prayer are fixed, the limits can be stretched and often are. The Chasidim long maintained that if one's concentration was not strong enough, prayer should be put off until it was and they would often pray Shachrit at the time when most people were praying Mincha.

After morning prayers it is the custom in many communities for those who have prayed together to eat a piece of cake and take a drink of whiskey or some other liquor. This is particularly true if one of the worshipers has yohrtzeit. He will usually bring a modest kiddush with him and those present are invited to partake. A blessing is said over the liquor and cake and the worshipers drink to each other's health with the toast, *"l'chaim!"*—"to life!" Despite all the talk about the dangers of drinking on an empty stomach, ulcers are seldom found among observant Jews and as for morning drinking leading to alcoholism, that post-Shachrit snort has never produced a *shikker* (alcoholic) yet, to my knowledge.

The order of prayers, incidentally, will be found in any siddur.

Because they are excused from formal prayer (chapter 26), women are almost never seen in the synagogue on weekdays.

28

Sabbath Services in the Synagogue and the Priestly Blessing

SABBATH SERVICES IN THE SYNAGOGUE

SABBATH services in the synagogue really start a little before Shabbat when the weekday Mincha service is said with a few additional prayers for the coming Sabbath.

Mincha is followed by a special service called *Kabbalat Shabbat*, or welcoming the Sabbath. It is a series of prayers and psalms ending with the song, "L'cha Dodi" (Come, my friend, let us greet the bride), written by the Kabbalist Solomon Alkabetz, a disciple of Isaac Luria (see chapter 42). It is the custom among all Jews that when the final verse is sung, all stand and face the door, as if the Sabbath herself, in the form of a bride, were entering. Chasidim and most Sephardim bow in welcome at the last words, "Come, O bride, Queen Sabbath."

Kabbalat Shabbat is followed by Maariv which has additional Sabbath prayers. In some congregations the song "Shalom Alei-chem" (Peace be with you, ministering angels) is sung, whereas in others it is the custom to sing the song in the home before the kiddush. In most congregations, kiddush is said in the synagogue by the rabbi or reader, and then, of course, repeated in the home. The reason for saying kiddush in the synagogue—for it is basically a home ceremony on Friday night—may be traced to the days when there was little wine available and not every family could afford or even obtain it. Thus the kiddush said in the synagogue served for all. A second reason is that in former times, poor travelers slept in the synagogue and the kiddush was said for their benefit. Prior to the evening service, the Sephardim recite the entire Song of Songs. Following the service, in the home, they sing the cryptic kabbalistic hymn dedicated to Simeon Bar Yochai, alleged author of the Zohar.

Morning Services

As noted earlier, services on the Sabbath usually begin around 9 A.M. among the Ashkenazim and an hour or so earlier among the Sephardim. Any siddur will show the contents of the service so we will restrict our comments to the way it is carried out in most synagogues.

To start with, it is customary on arriving at the synagogue to greet the other members with the words "Good Shabbos." Sephardim say, "Shabbat Shalom"— peaceful Sabbath—to which the answer is, "Shabbat shalom u-m'vorach"—peaceful and blessed Sabbath. The greetings are used at the end of the service as well and when greeting other Jews at any time during the Sabbath, starting with Friday night.

On Shabbat no t'fillin are worn, since the Shabbat itself is considered adornment enough. The tallit is worn by married men, or men who have been married, among the Ashkenazim, and by all males among the Sephardim.

By long custom, the first part of the service, up until the words "Shochen Ad" (He inhabits eternity, exalted and holy is His name) are prayed by one man as reader, who at that point turns the rest of the Shachrit service over to a second man who is called the *Baal-Shachrit*. The gabbaim, or directors of the congregation, decide who will have the honor of leading the prayers for each part of the service.

Beginning with Shochen Ad, several important prayers lead up to the central part of any Jewish religious service, the *Shema Israel*: "Hear, O Israel: the Lord our God, the Lord is One." Three customs attached to the recitation of the Shema should be noted here: first, the tsitsit of the tallit are kissed; second, the eyes are covered; and third, the Shema is recited sitting down.

The tsitsit are kissed because the commandment concerning the wearing of tsitsit follows the Shema (and the tsitsit are kissed again at that time). The eyes are covered to shut out all distractions. It is the sitting down for the most important prayer of all that puzzles many people. The reason is this: if it were necessary to stand during the *k'riat shema*, the recitation of the Shema, people who otherwise would say it at its proper time during the weekday prayers might not be able to do so and would end up not praying at all. The example is given of the man who is picking fruit in a tree when the time for prayer comes. Since it is impossible for him to stand, he would not pray because he would not be able to say the Shema, the central part of the prayer. But since he can say the Shema sitting down, he goes ahead and prays. A similar example is given of a man who is sitting on a scaffold painting a house: he prays with his paintbrush in his hand.

Shortly after the Shema Israel, the second major event of the service takes place. This is the praying, in silence, of the *Amida* (A. *Sh'moneh Essreh*). This must always be prayed facing Jerusalem, standing, and with the feet together. (Many Jews cover the head with the tallit during the silent recitation of this prayer.) As for why the feet must be kept together, one explanation is given in the famous book, *Taamei Ha-Minhagim*: this shows that we do not wish to "lift up our feet" and go elsewhere but wish to remain where we are and dedicate ourselves to God. A second explanation was given me by a friend who said that it is to guard against the possibility that a mouse or some other non-kosher animal might run between our feet as we recite this holy prayer. I must confess that both these explanations sound a little far-fetched to me, but they are the only ones I have ever heard.

At the end of the prayer, when the words *"Hu yasseh shalom alenu"* (May He make peace for us) are said, the worshiper should take three short steps backward to indicate that he has finished, since otherwise it would be impossible for the others to know, since it is prayed in silence. This, incidentally, has given rise to a joke: when one Jew asks another, "How's business?," if it is slow he is likely to answer, "Like Hu yaaseh shalom alenu" (going back instead of forward).

The reader then repeats the Amida aloud with the addition of the *kedusha*, after the Shema, the most important prayer of the service. In many Sephardic congregations, the custom is to recite the kedusha first aloud and then to pray the rest of the Amida in silence. After the reader's repetition of the Amida, the third central feature of the service occurs: the *k'riat ha-Torah*, or public reading of the weekly portion from the Torah scroll, or *Sefer Torah*.

The Sefer Torah is a parchment scroll, rolled on two wooden axles. On this parchment is written, by hand, the entire text of the Torah. If as little as one letter is incorrect or illegible, the entire scroll is *pasul*—ritually unuseable.

Among the Ashkenazim and some North African and Ladino-speaking congregations, the Sefer Torah is covered with a velvet mantle with holes in the top through which project the top handles of the two wooden axles. On top of these handles are often placed crownlike decorations made of silver which are removed before the mantle is taken off the scroll. These adornments are called *rimmonim*, which means pomegranates. The mantle is open at the bottom so that it may be easily removed. The scroll itself is kept from rolling open by a girdle which is untied and removed so that the scroll may be opened for reading.

The *Sifrei Torah* of Arabic-speaking congregations are quite different in appearance. The scroll is contained in a cylindrical wooden or metal container, hinged at the back, opening in front. The scroll is not removable but is read while still inside its case. The base of the case is flat, permitting it to be stood upright on a table or desk, opened and read from in that position.

The reading of the weekly *sedra* (S. *parasha*), or portion of the Torah, is surrounded by traditional customs. In most congregations, one man is called on by the gabbai to draw aside the *parochet*, or curtain covering the Ark, and to open the doors. This same man then removes the Sefer Torah from the Ark and hands it to a second man whose privilege it is to carry it to the *bima* where it will be read. The carrying of the Torah to the bima is in itself a ceremony, since the scroll is carried very slowly so that all may have an opportunity to kiss the mantle-covered Sefer Torah as it is carried by. This is usually done by touching the mantle with one's tallit and kissing the tallit.

At all times when the Sefer Torah is upright and not resting on something all must rise and remain standing until it is lowered again.

When it reaches the bima, the Sefer Torah is turned over to the gabbaim who remove the mantle, untie the girdle keeping it from rolling open, lay it on the reading table and re-cover it by laying the mantle upon it or by laying on it a special covering cloth. Usually the Sefer Torah is exposed only when it is actually being read. The gabbaim then call the first man—always a Cohen if there is one present—to the honor of saying the blessings over the first of the eight sections into which the weekly portion is divided.

The above description of the taking out and preparing for reading of the Sefer Torah applies to Ashkenazic congregations. In Arabic-speaking synagogues the metal cylinder encasing the scroll is brought to the edge of the open Ark. The case is then opened and invocations recited. The man who opened the Ark and then the Sefer Torah hands it to a second man who raises it and carries it, still open, to the *teba* (A. *bima*). There he lifts it high and turns it in all directions so that those present may see the scroll, opened to the portion of the week. It is customary for the men to lift up the fringes of the tallit toward the open scroll and then kiss the fringes. Women hold out their hands to the scroll, then kiss their fingertips. This lifting up and exhibiting of the Torah is called *Hagba*, and all Sephardim perform it prior to reading the portion. (Ashkenazim, as we shall see, perform it after.) After Hagba, the Sefer Torah is placed upright on the reading desk, the scroll itself within covered by a special cloth, usually tied to the container, and the Cohen called up to say the blessings for the first portion.

The honor of being "called up" to the Torah is called an *aliya*; the third aliya, by long custom, is usually given to the rabbi if he is called up. We say called *up*, because any move in the direction of the Torah is up, just as is a move in the direction of the Holy Land. To "go on aliya" means to emigrate to Israel.

In Ashkenazi synagogues, one of the gabbaim calls out the Hebrew name of the man honored—that is his name and his father's name—and the portion he is being called for. Each portion is called a *parasha* (Sephardim use the word to mean the entire *sedra*). There are eight men called, but in reality there are only seven *parashot*; the last man called up reads a repetition of the last paragraph of the preceding parasha, called the *maftir*. Among the Ashkenazim, this last aliya—maftir—is considered the greatest honor of all and is usually given to a man with a special reason for being called up, such as the fact that he is observing a yohrtzeit, that he is to be married the next day, or that the "man" in question is turning thirteen and is celebrating becoming a bar mitzva.

The man called up, on hearing his name, goes to the bima by the shortest possible route to indicate his wish to reach the Torah quickly. On arriving he stands in front of the scroll and the reader, called the *Baal Koreh*, removes the cover from the Torah and opens it, indicating with a pointer the first verse of the section to be read. The man called up touches the letters with the fringes of his tallit and kisses the fringes, after which he recites the blessings for reading from the Torah. At this point the Baal Koreh takes over and reads, in a clear voice, often in one of the traditional modes, the text to be declaimed. When he finishes, the man called up says the concluding blessings, and steps aside to allow the next man called up to approach.

If the man whose portion has just been read has recently escaped from danger, recovered from a serious illness or returned from a long journey, he says the blessing called *Gomel*, thanking God for having dealt kindly with him. All those present reply in a ritual Hebrew phrase asking God to continue to deal kindly with him.

At this point the gabbai, or one of the two men who must stand at the bima with the Baal-Koreh, recites the *mi-sheberach* prayer in which blessings are called down upon the man, his family, and anyone else he wishes to have included, by name. A special mi-sheberach for the ill, asking for a complete recovery, may also be said on request, and there are several other special forms of the prayer for a bar mitzva, a bride or bridegroom, etc. If a man's wife has given birth in the week preceding the Sabbath, a special prayer is said for her since she is considered dangerously ill, as are all women in childbed. If a daughter was born to her, the prayer also asks for a blessing on the child and the phrase *"Vaykareh sh'ma b'Yisrael"* (Let her name in Israel be called) is pronounced, followed by the Jewish name to be given her. This is the ceremony by which girls are given a name in Judaism.

Toward the end of the prayer, in all its forms, it is customary for the man at whose request it is being said to pledge money as a donation to the congregation. This can be as little or as much as he wants and the sum is called out in Hebrew, as part of the blessing. Since the phrase recited uses the man's name, plus the word (in the Ashkenazi pronunciation) *shenudar* (who pledges), the action of making a donation at this time is called "shnuddering." The donation itself is called a *nedar*.

Some congregations, those of Young Israel, for example, have an internal regulation or *takkana* prohibiting shnuddering, and the form of the blessing makes no allowance for a donation at that time.

It is the custom for the man who has had his portion read to wait until the man following him has finished his portion and said the concluding blessing before returning to his seat. He tries to return by a longer route than he took coming up to the bima, to indicate his reluctance to leave the Torah. An unmarried man who, among the Ashkenazim, does not ordinarily wear a tallit, will borrow the tallit of the person nearest him if he is called up, since the tallit must be worn when approaching or in contact with the Torah.

As indicated above, the last man to be called up says the blessings for the maftir, concluding the *sedra* of the week. After saying the final blessing he immediately recites an abbreviated form of the kaddish. A mi-sheberach is said for the entire congregation and two men are called up for *hagba* and *gelila*. Hagba, which, as explained earlier, is the elevation of the Torah, is accomplished by grasping the scroll by its two bottom handles, opening it and raising it high so that all may see. All present rise. The man honored with hagba then sits down and the second man called up performs the ceremony called gelila, which is the closing of the scroll, tying it together with its girdle and replacing the mantle and rimmonim on it.

While all this is going on, the man called for maftir is saying the preliminary blessings for the *haftara*, a short portion from one of the prophets which is in some way related to the sedra of the week. In most congregations he then reads the haftara himself (the reader does not read it for him) and says the concluding blessings. While the haftara is being read the man who performed hagba holds the Sefer Torah.

After the haftara is read, in many congregations the gabbai takes the Sefer Torah and holding it, recites the prayer for the well-being of the government. This is particularly common in the United States, and their version of the prayer is particularly beautiful and evocative. Since the Yom Kippur war in Israel (and in many cases before it) numerous congregations have adopted the practice of saying a special prayer for the soldiers and sailors of the armed forces of Israel.

On the Sabbath preceding *Rosh Chodesh*, the first day of the Jewish month, the blessing of the month is said. This is a prayer in which the coming month is named, and the day, hour, minute and second that it starts is proclaimed to the congregation, both in Hebrew and whatever language is spoken by the members.

This, with other prayers which can be found in the siddur, concludes the ceremony of *k'riat ha-Torah*, and the Sefer Torah is returned to the Ark by the same man who brought it to the bima. There it is handed to the same man who took it out and he replaces it within the Ark, shutting the doors and drawing the parochet. A concluding prayer is said and the Shachrit service is over, to be followed immediately by *Musaph*, the additional service for the Sabbath and holidays.

K'riat ha-Torah, as practiced by the Sephardim, is somewhat different. As noted earlier, hagba is performed before the first man is called up. The calling up itself is also different in that instead of the man's name and his father's name, his name and family name are used, followed by the phrase *"likro baTorah"* (to read in the Torah). The initial and concluding blessings are slightly different as well.

After the concluding blessing is said, the mi-sheberach is recited, and in Moroccan and Arabic-speaking congregations, if the man called up is observing or is approaching the death anniversary of a parent or close relative, special memorial prayers called *Hashkabot* are said at his request.

In most Sephardic congregations, when a man is called up to the Torah, his children and his wife (and sometimes other relatives) rise and remain standing while he is saying the blessings both before and after the reading. In many places, his sons remain standing all the time he is on the bima (S. *teba*). Ashkenazim do not have this custom.

Contrary to the custom of the Ashkenazim, when the concluding blessings have been said, the man returns directly to his seat without waiting for the next man called up to have his portion read. In both Ashkenazi and Sephardi congregations, when a man who has been given an aliya returns to his seat, those near him shake his hand and congratulate him. Ashkenazim use the phrase *"Yasher Koach!"* (May your strength increase), while Sephardim say, *"Chazak Ubaruch!"* (Be strong and blessed).

After the Sefer Torah has been returned to the Ark, the man who was called to the concluding portion, maftir, has the privilege, among the Ashkenazim, of being the reader for the additional Musaph prayer service.

As a final commentary on the k'riat ha-Torah, the function of the Baal-Koreh should be explained. It might be asked why we need a Baal-Koreh at all: why can't the man called up read his portion himself?

In the first place, the Hebrew in which the Sefer Torah is written is unpointed; that is, no vowel signs are indicated, and not everyone can read unpointed Hebrew. Outside Israel most Jews cannot. In the second place, not everyone has a pleasing or even an audible voice and the Baal-Koreh is supposed to make himself heard by all present. Finally, in those congregations in which the Torah is read to a traditional cantillation mode, there are few men able to read the entire portion in this fashion, since learning the mode requires long and arduous training.

All of this being the case, the custom has grown up that no matter how learned a man may be, or even how good a Baal-Koreh he may be, his portion is read by whoever is acting as Baal-Koreh. This avoids embarrassing those unable to read unpointed Hebrew or, in some cases, unable to read Hebrew at all. As long as the Baal-Koreh reads the entire sedra, everyone is on the same level.

Musaph

The Musaph is an additional service that is said on Shabbat and holidays, including Rosh Chodesh (chapter 36). The prayers vary somewhat in Ashkenazic and Sephardic rituals and can be found in any siddur. One of the most important differences is that the Sephardim, after repeating the *Amida* prayer, call upon the Cohanim in the synagogue to bless the congregation with the *Birchat Cohanim*. The exact wording of this priestly blessing is found in Numbers 6:24-27: "The Lord bless you and keep you. The Lord make His face to shine upon you and be gracious unto you. The Lord turn His face unto you and give you peace."

THE PRIESTLY BLESSING

Birchat Cohanim (the priestly blessing) is given the same way in all congregations. After the Cohanim have been called upon in a loud voice by the reader, they retire to the rear of the synagogue where they remove their shoes (since they may not give the blessing with shoes on) and then wash their hands, assisted by the Leviim. They then go up to the front of the synagogue where they stand on the platform which is in front of the Ark.

Then they cover their heads and faces completely with the tallit and hold their hands up before their faces in a special prescribed fashion. Some Cohanim hold their hands up under the tallit, but others keep their hands outside the tallit which covers their face. This is done facing the Ark. They then turn, and, facing the congregation, give the blessing. This is done by having the reader recite the blessing one word at a time and the Cohanim recite them after him. It is customary that the rest of the congregation bow their heads and cover their eyes, usually with the tallit, so that they may not, even by accident, catch a glimpse of the Cohen's face while he is saying the blessing. This is because we are told that the *Shechina*, the Divine Presence, rests on the face of the Cohen at this time. In reality this commonly heard explanation is not accurate. The Talmud says that during the time of the Temple it was true but that now we do it to prevent distraction.

As noted, the Sephardim call upon the priests to give the blessing every Shabbat during Musaph, although in many Sephardic congregations the blessing is given after the *amida* in the Shachrit service as well. In others it is given only during Sachrit. In Israel, among both Sephardim and Ashkenazim, and in some parts of the Orient, Iran for example, the blessing is given every day during the Shachrit service.

Outside Israel the Ashkenazic custom is quite different: the Birchat Cohanim is given only on Sukkot, Passover and Shavuot, and on Rosh Hashana and Yom Kippur, but only if the festivals fall on a weekday. With the exception of Yom Kippur, if any of these holidays falls on a Sabbath, the Birchat Cohanim is not given. It is given on all these holidays during Musaph and on Yom Kippur during Mincha as well.

Thus we see that while the Sephardim make a point of giving the blessing every Sabbath, the Ashkenazim make an equally strong point of not giving it on that day, with the exception of Yom Kippur. The reason given by most Ashkenazi sources for this custom is that the blessing should be given only by those who are joyous at heart and such joy can be found in its fullest form on a festival which falls on a weekday alone. On Yom Kippur joy is greatest because we are forgiven our sins on that day so even if it does fall on Shabbat the blessing is given.

The platform on which the Cohanim stand is called a *duchan*, and for that reason the giving of the priestly blessing is called *duchening* by Ashkenazim, from the Yiddish verb *duchenen*. The blessing is also referred to in the siddur by the Hebrew term *nesiat kappayim*, raising the hands.

After the services are over, in many congregations a kiddush of some sort is often given after which the worshipers return home for Sabbath lunch, kiddush and z'mirot (chapter 23).

The Mincha, or afternoon service, is different from the week-day Mincha in that the first three portions of the next week's sedra are read from the Sefer Torah, followed by the Sabbath Amida. After Mincha the men of the congregation sit at a table and eat the third meal of the Sabbath, called *Shalosh Seuda* (S. *Seuda Ha-shelishit*). At this meal some of the z'mirot that were sung at the Sabbath table are repeated, certain psalms are recited and *divrei Torah*, words of Torah, are spoken by the rabbi or another learned man present. Aside from bread, fish is about the only thing eaten at this meal by the Ashkenazim, for reasons found in the Kabbala. Among the Sephardim, cucumbers and other salad vegetables are usually on the table. Wine and liquor are drunk, but sparingly, and the full grace after meals is said. Prior to the grace, the Kabbalistic hymn *"B'nei Heichala"* (Sons of the Palace) is sung to a tune traditional among almost all Ash-kenazi communities. The Sephardim recite it but usually do not sing it.

Following this meal, the Maariv, or evening service, is prayed, Havdala is said and those present leave the synagogue, wishing each other in Yiddish, "A gut voch," or in Ladino, "Semanada buena." In Hebrew the phrase is "Shevua tov!" and they all mean the same thing: "A good week!"

Sometimes before, but usually after, Mincha, the Sephardim recite a long collection of psalms and prayers called *Alfa Beta*. At the time Havdala is said they are fond of singing songs called *Pizmonim l'motzei Shabbat*, songs for the conclusion of the Sab-bath.

After Shabbat is over there are two more "services" which should be mentioned. One is the *Kiddush Levana*, or Sanctifica-tion of the (new) Moon. This prayer is said by the entire congre-gation of males present after the concluding service, once every month between the third and sixteenth days of the Jewish month. Although it is said to thank God for renewing the months, every month, it is not said at the beginning of the month but toward the middle, when the moon is full. It is necessary that the moon be visible when the prayer is said, so worshipers usually pray outside where it can be seen. For this reason the Kiddush Levana prayer is always printed in large letters in the siddur, so that it can be read by the scarce light outside the synagogue.

The second "service" is that of *M'laveh Malka*, the Farewell to the Queen, as the Sabbath is commonly called. This feast is celebrated by the Chasidim at night after Shabbat has ended, often in the rabbi's house or some other location, rather than in the synagogue. Special prayers are said and Kabbalistic hymns are sung; there is great joy at this feast and the Chasidim often sing and dance, accompanied by their *Rebbe*, until late at night to prolong the joy of the Sabbath until the last possible moment.

PART
VII

The Holidays

Introduction:
Holidays, Major and Minor

THE Jewish holidays are divided into major and minor feasts. The major holidays are called *Yomim Tovim*, or "Good Days," and everything prohibited on the Sabbath is also prohibited on a *Yom Tov*, except for carrying and for cooking and preparing food. Because using fire and carrying is permitted for essential things, it is also permitted for non-essentials, and we may use electricity, smoke, carry things to the synagogue, etc. It is necessary nevertheless, to avoid actually lighting a fire; instead we light it from one already lit. Those who smoke, for example, light their cigarettes from a candle.

On minor holidays all is permitted that is permitted on any weekday; specifically work.

The major holidays are *Sukkot*, including *Shemini Atzeret* and *Simchat Torah*; *Passover*, the first two and last two days; *Shavuot*, two days; *Rosh Hashana*, two days; and *Yom Kippur*. On Yom Kippur, all things prohibited on the Sabbath are forbidden.

The minor holidays are *Rosh Chodesh* (the first day of the

Jewish month), *Chanuka, Chamisha Assar B'Shvat* and *Purim*.

In the prayer service additional prayers are said on all the holidays and some note is taken of them in the section on each holiday; not all the extra prayers are listed, however. One which does deserve mention is the *Hallel*.

Hallel is a special collection of psalms (113-118) which is recited during the Shachrit service of all holidays except Rosh Hashana, Yom Kippur and Purim. It is recited on the intermediate days of Passover and Sukkot. On the last two days of Passover and on Rosh Chodesh, a shorter version is said. This "Half Hallel" is also recited on Israel Independence Day. Hallel can only be said in the presence of a minyan. In the synagogue it is recited standing and in a loud voice, the worshippers following the reader. Among the Sephardim, certain parts are sung.

Among the major holidays, Rosh Hashana and Yom Kippur are referred to as the "High Holidays" and in Hebrew as the *Yomim Noraim*, or "Days of Awe." The three holidays of Sukkot, Passover (in Hebrew, *Pesach*), and Shavuot are called "Pilgrim Holidays" or simply the "Three Festivals." In Hebrew they are called the *Shalosh Regalim* (the "Three Pilgrimages"), because on these days Jews made a pilgrimage from all over Palestine to the Temple in Jerusalem. All of these holidays are based on specific commandments in the Torah.

As noted earlier, the priestly blessing is given on all holidays except Simchat Torah in the Musaph service. Ashkenazim omit it if the holiday falls on a Sabbath, except for Yom Kippur when it is given even if the holiday coincides with Shabbat. The Sephardim in many congregations also give the Birchat Cohanim during the Shachrit service of holidays, particularly Rosh Hashana, and repeat it during Musaph.

The
High
Holidays

29

Rosh Hashana and Yom Kippur

ROSH HASHANA

ROSH HASHANA is, of course, the Jewish New Year. It is a joyous but at the same time a solemn festival and is celebrated for two days both in Israel and outside the Holy Land.

In addition to marking the beginning of the Jewish calendar year, Rosh Hashana is the beginning of a ten-day period of repentance called the *Aseret Y'mei T'shuva*, or ten days of "turning," which ends on Yom Kippur. We Jews are taught that it is decided on Rosh Hashana what the fate of every Jew will be during the coming year, but that the decision made on high is not sealed until Yom Kippur, and may be changed for the better in the intervening ten days. Accordingly, these are days of soul-searching and repentance, which in Hebrew is literally, "turning." In other words, the emphasis is not so much on feeling guilt for whatever one may have done or not done, as it is on deciding to turn from one's earlier course and act differently in the future.

Selichot

Prior to the High Holidays and between Rosh Hashana and Yom Kippur it is the custom of Jews everywhere to say *Selichot*, or penitential prayers, either at midnight or in the early morning hours, before the morning service. These prayers, many of them of great beauty and poignancy, are recited by Sephardim starting on the first day of the month of Ellul—one month before Rosh Hashana. They are said up to Rosh Hashana and during the days between Rosh Hashana and Yom Kippur. Often the congregation, or those among them who wish to say Selichot, will meet at the house of one of the members (often a different one every night) and at midnight recite the appropriate selichot. The penitential prayers can also be recited in the synagogue at midnight. As is the case with many of the meetings of the Sephardim for religious purposes, this is called a *meldado*, a word derived from the Ladino *meldar,* meaning to read Hebrew. When held in a private house, food and drink are always served.

Ashkenazim start to say Selichot on the Sunday before Rosh Hashana, unless the holiday falls on a Monday or Tuesday, in which case they start on the Sunday of the preceding week. It is common for Ashkenazim to meet in the synagogue at five or even earlier in the morning, and to say Selichot until it is time to pray Shachrit. Ashkenazim also say Selichot between Rosh Hashana and Yom Kippur. Sephardim and Ashkenazim have many selichot that are peculiar to their own traditions.

The Synagogue Service

The prayer service has the same elements as the Sabbath: Shachrit, Musaph, Mincha and Maariv, with which the holiday starts at sundown. It is distinguished from all other holidays, however, by the blowing of the *shofar*, a ram's horn, which is done during Musaph. The shofar is blown for several reasons, among which are the announcement of the ten days of repentance, the call to prayer of the entire Jewish people, and the remembrance of several historical events which have had a signal importance in their development as a people, including the giving of the Torah on Mount Sinai. When the first day of Rosh Hashana falls on a Sabbath, the shofar is not blown, but is blown on the second day only. Otherwise it is blown both days.

The service is much longer than the Shabbat prayers and contains extra Torah readings as well as special hymns and prayers. Whereas the regular weekday and Shabbat services differ but little between Ashkenazi and Sephardi *nusach*, or rite, the holiday services are quite distinct and the special holiday prayerbooks, called *machzorim*, vary in length as well as in content. Nonetheless, the services are very similar in their basic elements and conception.

While the entire liturgy can be found in any *machzor*, we may still take note of two exceptional prayers, one recited by the Ashkenazim and the other sung by the Sephardim.

In Ashkenazic congregations, during the repetition of the Musaph Amida (A. Sh'moneh Essreh), the awesome prayer *U-netaneh Tokef* is heard. It is difficult to imagine a more impressive example of liturgical prose in the tradition of any religion. It is short, a bare two paragraphs, but it states in terms of great emotional intensity the events that are taking place in God's eternal vigilance over His chosen people. For it is on this day that the fate of Israel is decided: who shall live and who shall die. This terrifying description of the awe-stricken hosts of heaven and the trembling people of Israel ends with words of hope: "But repentance, prayer and charity avert the severe decree."

Perhaps I may be pardoned a personal reminiscence here. I once spent Rosh Hashana in an unfamiliar synagogue in Sydney, Australia. At this time my oldest son was a combat Marine in Viet Nam and we had no way of knowing, at any given moment, whether he was alive or dead (as so many of his closest comrades were before the end of their thirteen-month tour of duty). The U-netaneh Tokef was recited and when I heard the words, "Who will live and who will die, who at his time and who before his time, who by fire and who by water, who by the sword and who by wild beasts," I was so overcome by emotion that I had to leave the synagogue before the prayer ended and was only able to return after I had composed myself. At no time during my son's long absence in Viet Nam was it so forcefully impressed on me that whether we ever saw him again depended entirely on God's decision on that fateful day.

U-netaneh Tokef is not said by Sephardim but can be found in most Sephardic machzorim as a sort of index in the back for meditation on solemn days. Although they lack this prayer in their liturgy, they have an exceptionally beautiful song, unknown to the Ashkenazim, called *"Et Shaarei Ratzon."* It describes in poetic form the binding of Isaac for sacrifice by Abraham as it is related in the Midrash. Considered one of the most important holiday prayers, it is sung after the Torah reading during Shachrit on Rosh Hashana.

In Ashkenazic congregations, the men, particularly the older men, wear a white robe called a *kittel* during both the Rosh Hashana and Yom Kippur services. The robe represents both purity and repentance and is a reminder of the shortness of life, since the kittel is also a shroud.

The traditions of Rosh Hashana vary greatly from one community to another. Common to them all, however, is the custom of wishing one another a good year at the conclusion of the services and during the days following the holiday. In Yiddish the greeting is "A gut yohr" and in Ladino, "Muchos años y saludozos." In Hebrew the Ashkenazim use the phrase, "L'shono toivo tikosevu" (in the Ashkenazi pronunciation) meaning, "May you be inscribed for a good year," or simply "Shana Tova"—a good year. The Sephardim also say Shana Tova, and commonly use the phrase "Tizku L'shanim Rabot"—May you be worthy of many years.

The service on the eve of Rosh Hashana is followed in the home by kiddush and a feast. Among the Ashkenazim the challa is not braided as it is the rest of the year, but round, symbolizing the year which has just begun. It is customary that instead of dipping the bread in salt as is usually done (chapter 26), one dips it in honey to indicate the hope that the coming year will be a sweet one. In many families this is done up to Yom Kippur and in others through the end of Sukkot. Traditional families eat the head of a fish on this night since the word *rosh* actually means the *head* of the year. All Ashkenazim eat an apple dipped in honey with a special request to God for a "good and sweet year."

Sephardim have the custom of eating pumpkin, leeks, beets

and dates on the occasion of the Rosh Hashana feast and accompany them with special blessings remarking on the symbolism of their names. These blessings have been ingeniously translated into English by Rabbi David De Sola Poole, in his edition of the Sephardic machzor for Rosh Hashana.

The first day of Rosh Hashana can fall only on Monday, Tuesday, Thursday, or Shabbat.

The second night of Rosh Hashana is also the occasion for a feast and kiddush is said but without the *shehecheyanu* blessing said the first night. This blessing, as explained in Appendix IV, is a particularly important one since it thanks God for having "kept us alive, preserved us and enabled us to reach this time." Actually, the blessing is said over any "new thing," such as eating a fruit you have never eaten before or a fruit you have not tasted in over a year. Since everyone wants an excuse to recite the *shehecheyanu* on this occasion, the custom has arisen of having a new sort of fruit on the table on the second night of Rosh Hashana.

Not long ago, on our way to Israel, my wife and I spent Rosh Hashana with an old friend, (Rabbi) Mayer "Mike" Rich in New York. Mike's children bought mangoes, which they had never eaten, for the *shehecheyanu* blessing, but knowing that we had just come from South America where mangoes are hardly a novelty, bought New Zealand Kiwi fruit for us. *Yidishe kop*! (Jewish brains): we had had two huge mango trees in our back garden.

Tashlich

On the first day of Rosh Hashana (the second, if the first day is Saturday), it is customary to go to the banks of a lake, stream, ocean or any body of water in which fish live and there say a prayer called *Tashlich*, stating that we cast our sins into the water. This is accompanied, among the traditional Jews, by shaking one's pantscuffs and often turning one's pockets inside out to get rid of crumbs, representing sins. If no body of water is available, Tashlich can be performed in front of any running water which is outside, even a faucet or fountain. The custom apparently dates only from medieval times, but it is widely observed by both Ashkenazim and Sephardim. In at least one community I know of, Tashlich is traditionally an opportunity for the ladies to show off their latest dresses and the walk to a nearby lake is a real fashion parade.

YOM KIPPUR

Yom Kippur is called in English, the Day of Atonement, and in Spanish, *Día de Perdón* (Day of Pardon). Both these definitions are correct, yet the words "atonement" and "pardon" do not mean the same thing. The word "kippur" contains within it both those meanings: atonement, which means the expiation of sin on the part of the sinner, and pardon, which means the forgiveness of sin by God.

Both the origin and significance of this day are found in the Torah (Lev. 16:30-31): "For on this day shall atonement be made for you to cleanse you; from your sins you shall be clean before the Lord. It is a Sabbath of Sabbaths unto you and you shall afflict your souls; it is a law forever."

The literal meaning of "atonement shall be made for you" in the context of the Torah is that while the Temple stood, the High Priest, or *Cohen Gadol,* made atonement for all Israel on that day as a representative of the Jewish people. The words "it is a law forever" clearly show us that even if there is no Temple and no High Priest, atonement will continue to be made for us; we make atonement for ourselves through our fasting, our prayer and the great confession that we recite in the name of all Israel. What is evident from the plain meaning of the text is that pardon for our sins is always given us directly by God; it should not be thought that during the Temple service the High Priest gave absolution. The words "ye shall be clean before the Lord" indicate that the High Priest only officiated as *our* representative: pardon came and comes from God alone.

And what are the sins that God forgives us on this day? Jewish doctrine is clear on the point: on Yom Kippur only those sins committed by man against God are forgiven. Sins committed by man against his fellow man are not forgiven by God until they have been forgiven by the person against whom they were committed.

We ask pardon on this day for the sins we have committed in violating the commandments of the Torah, but typically we do not ask for ourselves alone, but for all Israel. The *Viddui*, or confession, that forms such an important part of the service, lists all manner of sins, many of which we might personally never dream of committing, yet we still ask God to pardon us those sins, since we speak in the name of all Jewry, not just ourselves.

Now the question may be asked, does God forgive the sins of all mankind on this day? Quite obviously He does not: only those of the Jews, His chosen people. We know this from the very content of the Torah's words which were directed only to the Jews, but in addition we find that many of the sins listed in the Viddui can be committed only by Jews—such as violations of the dietary laws—since for a Goy there would be no sin involved.

Accordingly, the observance of Yom Kippur makes no sense at all unless we accept that we are God's chosen people. If we were not, there would be no point in it and the same applies to every one of the Jewish holidays.

The words "It is a Sabbath of Sabbaths unto you and you shall afflict your souls" show us that all the laws which apply to the Sabbath concerning work, etc. also apply to Yom Kippur and that we should afflict our souls by fasting to heighten repentance. It is necessary that this be clearly stated, because ordinarily we are forbidden to fast on Shabbat. This explains why the fast of Yom Kippur is kept even when the holiday falls on the Sabbath, whereas all other fast days, if they fall on Shabbat, are postponed to the next day, Sunday.

The Day Before Yom Kippur: Kapparot

On the day before Yom Kippur many people perform the ceremony known as *Kapparot* (A. *Kapores*). In this ceremony a chicken is taken in the hand and circled around the head of each member of the family, a hen for the women and a cock for the men, while reciting a formula which states: "This is my change, this is my redemption, this is my substitute. This chicken is going to be killed while I shall enter into a long, happy and peaceful life." It is customary to have the *shochet*, or ritual slaughterer, come to the house and slaughter the fowls immediately after the invocations have been said. The fowls themselves are always given to the poor or to charitable institutions such as hospitals, orphanages, etc.

Many rabbis have inveighed against this custom, and although the words of the ceremony appear in all siddurim, many Ashkenazim do not perform it and most of those that do use money instead of chickens, giving the money to charity afterward. Almost all Sephardim, however, consider it of great importance and make every effort to observe it.

It is considered a great mitzva to eat well before Yom Kippur.

The Holiday Itself: Fasting

Although Yom Kippur is a holiday, it is also a twenty-four-hour fast day. The purpose of fasting on Yom Kippur is not as a sign of mourning as on *Tisha B'Av* (chapter 37), but for the purpose of purifying our thoughts and increasing the intensity of our repentance. It is an essential part of the atonement we make for the sins which God forgives us and all Israel on this day.

The Yom Kippur fast commences shortly before sundown on the day before the holiday and ends after the concluding service. During this time nothing can be eaten or drunk, including water. It is forbidden to wash one's mouth out, to brush one's teeth or to bathe one's body. Only the face and hands may be washed in the morning, before prayers. All the prohibitions of the Sabbath also apply to Yom Kippur so we may not carry, light fire, smoke or use electricity as we may on other Yomim Tovim. Snuff may be taken on Yom Kippur when sniffed up the nose.

Children less than nine years old are not allowed to fast, even if they wish to. Between nine and twelve they may fast a part of the day and from twelve on should try to fast the entire day, the same as adults. A person dangerously ill, a pregnant woman or one in the first thirty days after childbirth is not required to fast. As previously stated, if a pregnant woman gets a craving for a certain food on Yom Kippur it must be given her, even if it is a forbidden food such as pork, and even if the holiday must be violated (such as by handling money) in order to obtain it.

Some people simply cannot fast. If such a person who has been fasting starts to complain of dizziness and it is seen that his eyes are growing dim—that is, that he looks as if he were about to faint—he must be given food until he has recovered. If there is danger in fasting because of a plague or epidemic, and the physicians of the town advise that it is necessary to eat in order to keep up resistance to the disease, everyone in the community is required to eat: no one is at liberty to fast. Perhaps the most famous instance of this obligatory breaking of the Yom Kippur fast occurred in 1848 when Rabbi Israel Salanter, one of the most revered figures in Judaism, mounted the bima in the Great Synagogue in Vilno and publicly ate before the assembled congregations on Yom Kippur to impress upon them the need for keeping up their strength during a cholera epidemic which was decimating the city.

There are other prohibitions in addition to those against work and eating or drinking. Marital intercourse is forbidden as is the use of perfumes or ointments, except for medical purposes. In addition no shoes or other clothing made of leather may be worn on Yom Kippur. Observant Jews usually wear tennis shoes on this day and use a cloth belt. If not wearing shoes will subject Jews to ridicule on the part of the Goyim, it is permitted to wear them to the synagogue, removing them on arrival and wearing cloth slippers or other non-leather footwear during the service. The two main reasons given for this prohibition are that we do not wish to remind ourselves of our forefather's sin of worshiping a (golden) calf and that we do not wish to utilize any material for which it was necessary to kill an animal. A further reason is that it is a sign of mourning, since mourners too are forbidden to wear leather shoes.

The Synagogue Service

The Mincha service preceding the holiday has special additions to it, and when it has finished, just before sunset, Yom Kippur begins with the *Kol Nidrei*. All the men present put on the tallit and many wear the white *kittel* as well. This is the only time during the year that the tallit is worn for the evening service.

The Kol Nidrei, or "All Vows"—whose complete text may be found in any Yom Kippur machzor—is an unusual prayer which asks God not to take into account any vows we make. The Ashkenazi version of the prayer states, "From this Yom Kippur to next Yom Kippur," but the Sephardic machzor says, "From last Yom Kippur to this Yom Kippur." Although it dates from Talmudic times (Nedarim 23b), its present form and wording were set by Rabbenu Tam in the 12th century C.E., when he gave it the status of a prayer to be included in all services on the eve of Yom Kippur. It took on great and tragic significance during the Spanish Inquisition (as well as other organized persecutions of the Jews in Europe, starting with the Crusades), when Jews were forced into accepting baptism and the taking of vows that only the immediate certainty of death for their wives and children as well as themselves made them accept. As mentioned earlier, many Spanish Jews, faced with the choice between baptism and death, chose to live. To the north, in the Rhineland, the Jews, when faced with the same alternative, chose martyrdom unhesitatingly. Of course many Spanish Jews also died for the "sanctification of the Name," and a great many more fled to the east, where their descendants live to this day. The reference to vows already taken in the Sephardic version is usually understood to refer to forced conversion to Christianity. It should be remembered that this prayer too is said in the name of all Israel, not just that of the man who is reciting it.

After sundown the Maariv prayer is said with numerous additions, including the viddui, or communal confession of sins.

The prayers for Yom Kippur day, starting with the morning Shachrit, are so voluminous, at least among the Ashkenazim, that they occupy the entire day, from eight in the morning until sundown. In many congregations, however, there is a short recess of an hour or so between Musaph and Mincha. The Sephardic service is somewhat shorter, but still manages to take up most of the day. At the Mincha service, the entire book of Jonah is read as a haftara to the Torah reading, which on this day is short, as it is at the Sabbath Mincha.

After Mincha the Yom Kippur services conclude with an additional service called *Neila*, said only on this day. In Sephardic synagogues it begins with a hymn called *"El Nora Alila"* (God of Awesome Actions), sung to a cheerful traditional melody. It is so attractive that some Ashkenazic congregations have adopted it and sing it at the beginning of the Neila Amida. When the sun is down, the holiday is over and the Neila service ends with a single blast of the shofar among the Ashkenazim and four blasts among the Sephardim.

On rising and leaving the synagogue, all Jews are accustomed to call to one another, "L'shana ha-baa b'Yerushalaim!" (Next year in Jerusalem), to which the person so greeted answers, "Amen!" The Sephardim also say, "Tizku l'shanim rabot."

Religious Jews, on returning home, are accustomed to drive the first nail in the construction of the *sukka* (see next chapter) so as not to delay the performance of a mitzva.

After Yom Kippur we are expected to feast and rejoice. We should not lose sight of the fact that Yom Kippur is a holiday of rejoicing and a Yom Tov—a good day—in its most literal sense.

The
Three
Festivals

30

Sukkot

THE first of the Three Festivals, or *Shalosh Regalim,* is *Sukkot,* which comes just five days after Yom Kippur. Historically it celebrates the bringing of the fruits of the harvest to the Temple in Jerusalem and follows the commandment of the Torah (Lev. 23:42-43) to "dwell in sukkot (temporary dwellings) for seven days so that your generations may know that I (the Lord) made the children of Israel dwell in sukkot when I brought them out of Egypt."

Observance of this holiday involves each family building a *sukka* and eating at least one meal a day in it for the eight days that the holiday lasts outside Israel.

The sukka is a temporary shelter, and by custom it is built along the side of the house so that the outer wall of the house constitutes one wall of the sukka, supporting the roof and the other three walls. Of course it can and preferably should be built so that all four walls are independent, but this is often impossible or impractical. The walls of the sukka may be made of wood, composition board, latticework or even cloth, hung from the rods or beams that support the roof. The roof itself must, however, be covered with *s'chach*—green branches or some other vegetable matter such as green straw, leaves, etc. Actually, bamboo is kosher for the roof of the sukka, but when used it is usually overlaid with greenery of some sort.

The roof must be made so that stars can be seen through the gaps in it, but not so loosely constructed that a light rain can wet everyone inside. The material used for the roof must be detached, that is to say it cannot be rooted in the ground, so a living vine cannot be used unless it is cut off first. A sukka cannot be built under a tree. Finally, and this is most important, a sukka cannot be built with stolen materials. This is interpreted to mean that any green branches or other covering for the sukka or its walls must be bought and paid for. It is possible to gather s'chach from someone's land if permission is obtained from the owner, but even here, some symbolic payment should be made.

The Sephardim have somewhat more complicated rules concerning the sukka and its construction, requiring two *amudim,* or posts, but a sukka built according to the indications in the preceding paragraphs is kosher. The sukka, since it is temporary and will be pulled down after the holiday, requires no mezuza.

The sukka should be big enough so that people can sit in it and eat. The observant sleep in the sukka when weather permits. It is customary to decorate the walls of the sukka with pictures, often drawn by the children, of the *lulav* and *etrog*, the Temple in Jerusalem, the Temple menora (lamp), and other Jewish themes. Sephardim usually hang oriental rugs on the sukka walls. Fruits and vegetables, hung from the ceiling by strings or threads, are the commonest form of adornment.

The sukka is built between Yom Kippur and the beginning of the holiday, and, as noted earlier, it is the custom of the observant to drive the first nail on returning home from the synagogue on Yom Kippur, so as not to delay the performance of the mitzva. It should be completed and ready for use before the holiday starts, but if it is not, it may be completed or even built on the intermediate days of the festival, but not on the first two days when work is forbidden.

If a family is unable to build its own sukka, perhaps for lack of space, it may observe the mitzva of dwelling in the sukka by sitting in a communal sukka, built by the congregation, or in the sukka of another family or friend. Almost all congregations build a sukka next to the synagogue, and during the holiday, kiddush is said in the sukka, rather than the synagogue itself. To observe the commandment properly, at least one meal a day should be eaten in the sukka, but if this is not possible, something requiring a blessing should be eaten or drunk.

Many Jews have the custom of saying special Aramaic prayers of welcome every night at the door of the sukka. They invite Abraham, Isaac, Jacob, Joseph, Moses, Aaron and David to enter and join them in celebrating the holiday. These guests are known by the Aramaic name of *Ushpizin*. The custom is of Kabbalistic origin and is attributed to the "Holy Lion," Rabbi Isaac Luria (see chapter 42).

The obligation of sitting in the sukka and eating meals there does not apply to women and children, but they invariably participate, and, in the case of the children, enjoy the sukka more than the grownups.

The second important mitzva of Sukkot is that of taking the *lulav* and the *etrog*. This is done in obedience to the Torah (Lev. 23:40), where we are told, "And you shall take on the first day the fruit of the noble tree, branches of palm trees, boughs of thick trees and willows of the brook and you shall rejoice before the Lord your God seven days." These four plants have been determined to be the citron, or in Hebrew, *etrog* (A. *essrog*), the palm branch or *lulav,* the myrtle or *hadassim*, and the willow or *aravot*.

The commandment is observed in the following fashion. The hadassim are placed on the right side of the bottom of the palm branch (seen from behind by the person holding it) and the aravot on the left. They are bound to the lulav with a piece of woven palm leaf called an *aguda*, and are placed a few inches from the base of the lulav so that all three may be grasped at the same time in the right hand. The *aguaa* must be made of palm leaf since if we used another material t'iere would be five "species" of plants involved, instead of the foi.r we have been commanded to take.

The etrog is then taken in the left hand with the *pitam*, the small, button-like protuberance on the blossom end, pointing down, and held, side by side with, and touching, the lulav. The blessings are said and the etrog reversed so that the pitam points up. The etrog and lulav, held together as indicated, are then shaken in the direction of the six cardinal points: east, south, west, north, toward the heavens and toward the earth. Chasidim shake them south, north, east, heavenward, earthward and west in that order. The taking and waving of the lulav and etrog may be done at any time in observance of the mitzva, and it is usually done in the sukka in the morning. During the holiday prayer service, however, it is done just preceding the recitation of the Hallel during Shachrit and repeated during the Hallel itself. It is taught that we wave the lulav pointing to the six cardinal points to testify that God rules over creation in all directions.

After the Musaph for the holiday is said, one or more Sifrei Torah are taken out of the Ark and placed on the bima. Every man present who has a lulav and etrog takes them and carries them around the bima and the inside of the synagogue, while singing the special prayers called *Hoshanot*. On Shabbat the lulav is not taken nor are the circuits (called *Hakafot*) made, because it is feared that if this were permitted, the lulav would be carried from the home to the synagogue in violation of the Sabbath laws against carrying.

If no sukka is available, the mitzva of taking the lulav and etrog can and should be observed, just as the mitzva of sitting in the sukka should be observed even if no lulav is to be had. There is an interesting law in this regard. If there is a town in which there is a sukka but no lulav and etrog, and another town in which there is a lulav and etrog but no sukka, if traveling, we are obliged to go to the town with the lulav and etr   because there are more mitzvot involved in taking them than in sitting in the sukka.

In the siddur you will notice that there are blessings for entering and for sitting in the sukka, but no blessings to be recited before undertaking the work of building a sukka. This is because the commandment is to *dwell* in the sukka and this can be accomplished by sitting in a sukka one has not built oneself. It is even permitted to have a non-Jew build a sukka. Nevertheless, each

Jew derives great satisfaction from building his own sukka and every family takes pride in having a sukka even if there is a communal sukka for the entire congregation.

The holiday of Sukkot is often spoken of as having eight or even nine days. These are the first two days, of which only the first is observed as a holiday in Israel; the four (in Israel, five) intermediate days or *chol ha-moed*; Hoshana Rabba, Shemini Atzeret and Simchat Torah. Actually, the obligation to sit in the sukka and eat at least one meal a day there extends through Hoshana Rabba, which indicates that Shemini Atzeret and Simchat Torah are separate holidays. This will be discussed below.

First, however, we might ask why we celebrate *two* days of the major holidays of Sukkot, Passover and Shavuot outside Israel, but only one day in the Holy Land. The answer usually given is that in earlier times outside Israel, there was often doubt about the precise day on which any given holiday came, and so as to make sure we celebrated it at the right time, two days were, and still are, observed. To my mind there is a weakness in this explanation: both days could have been wrong. A better explanation is that given by a Chasidic rabbi: we are given the extra day of rejoicing to compensate us for the fact that we are not in Israel.

31

Hoshana Rabba, Shemini Atzeret and Simchat Torah

HOSHANA RABBA

THE seventh day of Sukkot is called Hoshana Rabba and is a half-holiday. This means that special services are said on this day but we are permitted to work when the services are over. Three things distinguish this rather unusual festival.

First, those present take the lulav and etrog and make seven circuits, or *Hakafot*, around the synagogue, while chanting special Hoshanot prayers. Secondly, after the seven hakafot are completed, additional Hoshanot prayers are said and all take willow branches (called *hoshanot* in Hebrew) and beat them on the floor of the synagogue until the leaves are beaten off. This is a symbol of joy and at the same time reminds us that a tree, after losing its leaves, comes to life again through the rain that God sends. So also can man, with God's help, return to life after misfortune. The third distinguishing feature is that the reader, or *sheliach tzibbur,* wears a white kittel just as on Yom Kippur. The fact is that this half-holiday is celebrated with a solemnity reminiscent of Yom Kippur, and tradition has it that it is also a *yom ha-din*: a day of judgment.

In many congregations, particularly among the Sephardim, it is the custom to stay awake the entire night of the eve of Hoshana Rabba and to gather in the synagogue, where a special collection of readings and meditations is recited. This collection is called the *Tikkun Leyl Hoshana Rabba,* and, among the Sephardim, contains many selections from the Zohar.

SHEMINI ATZERET

Strangely enough, there is some doubt as to whether Shemini Atzeret is separate from Sukkot or is the eighth day of the festival. As noted above, the obligation to sit in the sukka extends through Hoshana Rabba in the fullest sense. We must say the blessing thanking God for having commanded us to dwell in the sukka, and those who welcome the *Ushpizin* do so on that night. On the eve of Shemini Atzeret and the following morning of the holiday, we are also required to sit in the sukka, but without saying the blessings. In that fashion we attempt to serve the holiday from both points of view.

There is no special ritual, such as that of lulav and etrog, and even the sukka is sat in in a half-hearted way. The holiday is a happy one, but the most colorless of the major feasts. One special prayer, called *Geshem,* is said for rain. We are told that on this day God judges the world regarding water: this means that in Heaven it is decided how much rain the world will get and when, who will die by drowning, who by thirst, etc. For this reason, the prayer is recited in a solemn and plaintive melody and the reader wears a white kittel as on the great day of judgment, Yom Kippur. Among the Ashkenazim, Yizkor is said and the book of Ecclesiastes is read. It is a full holiday and work is forbidden.

SIMCHAT TORAH

In Israel, Shemini Atzeret and Simchat Torah are celebrated as one holiday, on the same day, but in the diaspora we are given two holidays to compensate us for not being fortunate enough to live in our Holy Land. And of all the holidays in the year, Sim-chat Torah, or the Rejoicing in the Torah, is the happiest and most exuberant.

Like all holidays, Simchat Torah begins at sundown, but the atmosphere in the synagogue is unlike any other festival of the entire year. The Maariv prayer is said normally enough and after the Shemoneh Essreh the special prayer *Ata Hareyta L'daat* is said. This prayer is composed of verses from several psalms and books of the Bible, and in many traditional synagogues the cus-tom exists of auctioning off the honor of reciting it. The highest bidder wins and usually proceeds to call on a different man to recite each verse, favoring as many of his friends as the number of verses allows.

During the Ata Hareyta prayer the Ark is opened. At the end of it, all the Sifrei Torah are taken out and carried around the synagogue seven times: a process that can take several hours to complete.

Each circuit, called a *Hakafa,* starts at the bima. The Gabbai, or President, calls out the name of a different person to carry each Sefer Torah during each hakafa. If seven hakafot are not enough to give everyone a chance to carry a Sefer Torah, usually more hakafot are added until all have had the honor. During the hakafot the *Hoshiana* prayers are sung in a loud and cheerful voice to a traditional melody. The small children, boys and girls alike, follow the men around during the hakafot, each child car-rying a small paper flag on a stick. In traditional shuls, an apple is stuck on top of the flag and a candle on the apple.

At the end of each hakafa, the Sifrei Torah are brought back to the bima and at this time special Simchat Torah melodies and songs are sung in Hebrew and other languages—Yiddish, Ladino or Arabic, depending on the congregation. While these songs are sung, the men dance with the Sifrei Torah and without them, in a circle, until they are tired out and the next hakafa begins. The singing, rejoicing and dancing follow each hakafa, and it is not unusual for the service to end after midnight. The gaiety and high spirits of the celebrants cannot be imagined by one who has never seen them.

In heavily Orthodox parts of some cities, and of course in all of

Israel, the street in front of the synagogue is blocked off by the police by prior request, and the men of the congregation take the Sifrei Torah out into the street and dance with them for hours, urging passersby and spectators to join them in their rejoicing. Anyone recognized as a Jew is likely to be pulled into the dancing circle, finally sharing the happiness of the worshipers whether he had intended to or not.

After the final hakafa, the Sifrei Torah are returned to the Ark with the exception of one, from which the first three sections of the last sedra of the Torah, *V'zot Ha-b'racha* (Deut. 33) are read.

A strange and touching Simchat Torah custom should be noted here. In Moscow, thousands of Jewish youths gather every year on the eve of Simchat Torah in the streets surrounding the last large synagogue left open in the Russian capital. They defy the police and the government in so doing and risk arrest and persecution, but on the eve of Simchat Torah, there they are. They dance and sing the pitifully few Hebrew songs they may know and all efforts of the Communist government to prevent them from gathering on that night have failed. These young people may never go near a synagogue otherwise; most of them know not a word of Hebrew nor a single prayer, but they know they are Jews and that in Moscow they must "keep the faith" by rejoicing on Simchat Torah. Why Simchat Torah alone of all the holidays? No one knows.

On the morning of the festival the Shachrit is prayed and the seven hakafot are made, to the accompaniment of singing, dancing and general merriment. After the hakafot have ended, the Torah reading, or *k'riat ha-Torah*, takes place.

In this connection it should be pointed out that Simchat Torah marks the end of the cycle of Torah readings for the year because the last sedra, *V'zot Ha-b'racha*, is read and finished at this point in the service. The man honored with reading the maftir, the last portion of the scroll, is called the *Chatan Torah*: the Bridegroom of the Torah. This is one of the most important honors of the year. Simchat Torah also marks the commencement of the Torah reading cycle, since as soon as the last part of the last sedra has been read by the Bridegroom of the Torah, the cycle is recommenced with the reading of the first three sections of Genesis, the first sedra. The man called to read this first portion is called the *Chatan B'reshit,* or Bridegroom of Genesis, also a great honor. The full sedra is read on the following Sabbath, called Shabbat B'reshit (Genesis Sabbath).

While the last sedra is being read, it is the custom that every man over thirteen be given an aliya. This means that many of the verses have to be repeated so as to get everyone in, but it is also customary to take more than one Sefer Torah out and to read this same sedra at different places in the synagogue at the same time. This means that more men can be called up more quickly since aliyot are given at the reading of each of the scrolls. Toward the end of the reading of the main scroll on the bima, a large tallit is held up over the bima by four men forming a sort of roof. All boys under the age of thirteen in the synagogue are called up and recite the blessings together, after which a portion is read together with a blessing from the Torah itself, Gen. 48:16: "The angel who has redeemed me from all evil, bless the lads . . ." This collective aliya is called *Kol Ha-neorim* (All the Lads).

In Orthodox Ashkenazic synagogues, every man, after he has been given an aliya, immediately celebrates the holiday by downing a healthy shot or two of booze, which is always awaiting the worshipers in a corner of the shul. The drink cannot be taken until one has been called up to the Torah, however, so there is always a lot of good-natured protesting and begging to be called up so the whistle can be properly wet.

After Shachrit has concluded, Musaph is prayed and this is always the occasion for great merriment. Traditionally, the Baal-Musaph, or reader for this service, is the victim of the pranksters in the congregation. I have seen one Baal Musaph, himself a rabbi and an extremely learned man, tied up with a couple of gartels, the Chasidic sash, while standing in front of the omed, and, technically unable to interrupt his praying, taken and carried horizontally, face up, above the heads of the worshippers all around the synagogue, holding the siddur up in front of his face and continuing to pray while those who carried him danced their way back to the omed.

Simchat Torah is the one major holiday on which the Birchat

Cohanim, the priestly blessing, is not given, because it is assumed that a certain degree of drunkenness may prevail. In one congregation of which I was for many years a member, there was a special Simchat Torah tradition. At that point in the Musaph service where the Cohanim would ordinarily give the blessing, the most learned man in the congregation—himself not a Cohen—would ascend the platform, put his tallit over his head and raise his hands as if about to pronounce the blessing. Instead of doing so, he would produce a glass full of whiskey, over which he would say the blessing *shehacol* (see appendix IV) and pour the *mashke* down with obvious relish.

Although the reason given above for omitting the priestly blessing certainly makes sense, a more accurate explanation might be that the Holiday itself, at least under the name Simchat Torah, is only about a thousand years old. The hakafot apparently did not become a general practice until the 16th century C.E.

Among the Sephardim the festival is joyous, but not nearly as exuberant as among the Ashkenazim, particularly the Chasidim.

Simchat Torah brings to a riotous conclusion the cycle of holidays of the month of Tishri which began with the solemn observance of Rosh Hashana on the first day of the month.

32

Passover, Sefirat Ha-omer and Lag B'omer

PASSOVER

THE second of the Three Festivals in order during the Jewish year is Passover, in Hebrew, *Pesach*. Everyone knows that this holiday celebrates the most important event in the history of the Jewish people, their rescue from slavery in Egypt and their deliverance from that land. What many people do not realize is that in many ways it is more important than either Rosh Hashana, which commemorates the creation of the world, or Yom Kippur, which celebrates God's pardoning us our sins.

A quick examination of the Ten Commandments will give us a clue. When God wanted to give a definition and a description of Himself to His chosen people, He did not say, "I am the Lord who created the world," or "I am the Lord who forgives your sins." What He said was, "I am the Lord, your God who brought you out of the land of Egypt and the house of slavery." God's words to us show us how important is the event we celebrate on Passover.

Quite obviously then, Passover is worthy of the closest attention and observance. Since it is particularly significant for children, as we will see, Jewish parents make sure that their children are kept out of school on the holiday so that they will remember and appreciate it as a genuine departure from everyday life. The commandments regarding Pesach are found in the twelfth chapter of Exodus. There we are told when it must be celebrated—the fourteenth of Nisan—and how it must be celebrated: by a feast, the eating of matzot, and the clearing of all leaven, or *chametz*, from the house. Further commandments defining even more exactly the observance of Passover are found in Lev. 23 and Deut. 16.

Shabbat Ha-gadol

The Sabbath preceding Passover is called *Shabbat Ha-gadol*, or the Great Sabbath. A variety of explanations is offered for this name. Among them is the fact that it occurred on the tenth of Nisan, four days before the first Passover, and on that day the Jews sacrificed a lamb in defiance of the Egyptians, who worshiped this animal. By showing their faith in God's protection in taking this action, the Sabbath on which they did so is commemorated as "great." Although sermons are seldom heard in Orthodox congregations, it is customary for the rabbi to preach on this Sabbath.

Taanit B'chorim

The day before Passover, i.e., the day that ends with the first *seder* in the evening, is a fast day for firstborn sons and is called *Taanit B'chorim* (the Fast of the Firstborn). The reason is obvious: it was on this day that the firstborn sons of the Egyptians (who, after all, were also human beings and God's creatures) were struck down while the firstborn of Israel were spared. In theory, the firstborn sons must fast from sunup until the seder starts, but in practice this fast is avoided by attending a *siyyum*, which is a small ceremony celebrating the finishing of the study of a *masechet*, or tractate, of the Talmud. Orthodox and many Conservative congregations arrange to bring to a close the study of a certain tractate on that morning. The rabbi, after the last paragraph is expounded, recites appropriate blessings and eats and drinks, joined by those present. Once the fast has been broken by this *seudat mitzva*, or feast celebrating the performance of a commandment, those present, even if they are firstborn sons, need fast no longer.

Actually, any seudat mitzva would do, such as the feast attending a circumcision or *pidyon ha-ben* (redemption of the firstborn sons) (chapter 9), but since we cannot count on such an occasion, the siyyum has been universally adopted. If you are a firstborn son and there is no synagogue near you where a siyyum is being held, too bad! You will have to fast, but with the compensation that the seder meal will taste better because of your hunger.

Ma'ot Chittim

One other pre-Pesach custom, *Ma'ot Chittim*, deserves mention: the collection of money to buy matzos, wine and other food for the poor on Passover. In most congregations, ma'ot chittim campaigns are run for indigent Jews in North Africa and similar poverty-stricken areas, as well as for yeshivas and hospitals. All observant Jews are anxious to observe this charitable action before the holiday.

The Observance of Passover

Passover starts at sundown on the fourteenth day of Nisan. In Israel only one day is observed at the beginning of the holiday, but in the diaspora two days and two *seders* (see below) are held: on the nights of the fourteenth and fifteenth of Nisan. There are four intermediate days, or *chol ha-moed*, and the last two days are full holidays on which work is forbidden. In Israel only the seventh day is a holiday.

There are three essential things which distinguish the Passover. The first is the prohibition against eating, drinking or having in one's possession any food made of leavened or fermented grain during the full eight days of the holiday. The second is the obligation to eat matza during at least the first day of the Yom Tov, and the third is the celebration of the seder in the home, at which time the entire story of Passover is recited for the benefit of the children in the family.

The Passover Dietary Laws

The laws concerning eating and drinking on the eight days of Pesach are simple in concept but not so simple in application. Reduced to their essentials, on Passover it is forbidden to eat or possess any sort of food prepared from the five species of grain— wheat, oats, barley, rye or spelt (a sort of red wheat)—unless the grains in question have been carefully controlled so that there is no possibility of their having fermented at any point. What this means in practice is that we may not eat any of the above grains in any form except that of matza or matza products.

Thus on Pesach we are forbidden the use or possession of flour, spaghetti, cold cereals, hot cereals, beer, whiskey, malt vinegar, monosodium glutamate (MSG) or any food or seasoning containing MSG (which is prepared from wheat), flavorings such as vanilla which contain grain alcohol, ketchup, prepared mustard, perfumes containing grain alcohol and, of course, bread, cakes and pastries of any sort.

What it comes down to is that we are forbidden all foods except those into which it is obvious that no chametz or anything containing chametz can have entered: grains, flour, anything made of grain or yeast. In the case of foods with more than one ingredient, one of which might be chametz, such foods must be certified as being *pesadik* or *kasher l'Pesach* (kosher for Passover) by a label affixed to them stating this to be the case. Vessels, pots, utensils and machinery can become chametz by contact with chametz-containing substances, and for that reason the machinery used to process food or drink products must be thoroughly cleaned with steam and certified pesadik by an Orthodox rabbi before the products can be used on Passover. This explains the "kosher for Passover" label on such things as soft drinks, bottled milk, etc. It simply shows that the premises where these products are made have been inspected and found free of chametz.

Observant Jews will keep away from such things as chewing gum or hard candy on Pesach on the chance that they might have some mixture of chametz unknown to the purchaser. As noted above, ordinary flour is prohibited, but potato flour is permitted as is the so-called "Passover-cake flour" which is made by grinding matzot very fine. In Latin America, the bread made from the *yuca* or *cassava*, known in Brazil as *bijú* and in the Caribbean as *casabe*, is permitted, as is the cassava flour called *farinha de mandioca* in Brazil.

Permitted foods are: matzot, dishes prepared from matzot, matza meal or matza flour, if, of course, no baking powder, soda or yeast is used to raise the dough; all fresh vegetables except peas and beans (permitted by most Sephardim); meats, soft drinks, fruit and foods and drinks made from fruit; liquors such as slivovitz, brandy (kosher), wishniak, rum (but excluding whiskey, gin, vodka and most liqueurs, which are made with a grain alcohol base), coffee, if nothing is mixed with it; tea, sugar, salt, pepper, sodawater, dairy dishes and fish. Vinegar made of apple cider or sugarcane is permitted.

There is a major difference in the observance of the Passover dietary laws between Ashkenazim and Sephardim. Ashkenazim prohibit the eating of *kitniot*, or lesser grains, such as corn (maize), rice, lentils, dried peas and beans, fresh peas and beans (although stringbeans are permitted). Most Sephardim permit all the kitniot on Passover with the exception of the chickpea, or garbanzo. The reason for this prohibition is interesting: in Arabic the chickpea is called *chommos*— which sounds too much like *chametz*, hence the prohibition!

Passover Dishes and Tableware

A separate set of dishes must be kept for Passover use, since anything made of ceramic, porcelain, clay or plastic which has been in contact with chametz, cannot be *kashered*, or purged, and made useable on the holiday. Theoretically, glass vessels may be freed of chametz by filling them with water and allowing them to stand for seventy-two hours, changing the water every twenty-four hours. In practice, glass vessels used during the year are not used on Pesach; drinking glasses, etc., form part of the Passover set of dishes.

Silverware and metal pots and pans without handles of wood or plastic may be kashered by thoroughly cleaning them and then dipping them in actively boiling water, rinsing with cold water afterward. Metal pans used for baking bread or cake cannot be kashered, nor can enamelware or stoneware cooking vessels.

The stove must be prepared by thoroughly cleaning it and then turning up the flame in the oven, the broiler and all the grates, until the grates are red hot. A dishwashing machine can continue to be used, but it must be washed carefully with boiling water and another set of trays substituted for those used during the year. When Passover ends, these trays are stored with the Passover dishes and kept for next Pesach.

Tablecloths, napkins, etc., in use during the year cannot be used on Passover. The special dishes, glasses, napery, etc., used on Passover must be sealed away during the rest of the year. It is common to keep them in special boxes which are taped shut. They are taken out only when the house has been prepared for Pesach as shown in the next section.

Preparing the House for Passover

All food and cooking utensils, dishes or other objects which contain chametz or which have been in contact with chametz must be removed from our possession before Passover. Items containing chametz which have never been edible are permitted to be kept. This includes such things as shoe polish and rubbing alcohol, which is poisonous. Medicaments required for the preservation of life or health may be kept even if they contain chametz, if no non-chametz substitute can be found.

Now it is obvious that removal of all these things from our possession is impossible if we are not to suffer serious monetary loss. Accordingly, we have two ways of taking care of this situation. In the case of non-food things such as dishes, pots, electric mixers, etc., we place them in a box or set them aside in a room or a section of a room and then seal them off by taping paper over the shelves. If we have a garage or other building outside the house, this is even better. In the case of *chametzdik* food or drink, we put it in the same place and then sell it to a Gentile. In this way, even if it is on our premises, it does not belong to us.

This sale is made through the rabbi of the congregation, who draws up a special contract with a certain Gentile, who buys from him the chametz of the entire congregation. To sell chametz, you must go to your rabbi and he will note on the contract the amount and approximate value of your chametz and where it is located. The deal is closed by "taking *kinyan*"; both you and the rabbi grasp a piece of clothing such as a handkerchief, or even a pen will do, to signify that the transaction has been made. If your own rabbi is absent or is not accustomed to making such a contract, you may go to any other rabbi in your town or locality and he will add your name to the *sh'tar*, or document. Of course one does not need to be a rabbi to make such a transaction with a Gentile, but in practice the rabbi usually does it since he is acquainted with all the laws for drawing up the contract, and it is easier for members of the congregation to comply with the commandment in that fashion.

After the holiday the chametz is bought back from the Gentile by the rabbi for a sum which gives the non-Jew a profit on the transaction.

Bedikat Chametz—Searching for Leaven

Once all chametz has been removed from the house or sold to a Gentile, the utensils which need to be purged or *kashered* for Passover use are cleaned, dipped in boiling water and set aside. The refrigerator is carefully cleaned and either special shelves are put in it or the existing shelves, after having been removed and purged with boiling water, are covered with fresh paper, aluminum foil or plastic wrap. (Holes should be made in these coverings to allow the air to circulate; not a Jewish law— just a practical point.) The stove is prepared as indicated and then we are ready for the final ritual which will free the house of chametz.

This ceremony is called *bedikat chametz*, or searching for leaven, and is carried out by the father of the house on the night before the first seder night. In this rite, the mother or daughters put several small pieces of bread at different places in the house. Some are accustomed to put ten pieces while others use five or seven. The bread is placed in different rooms before evening falls. When it is dark, all lights are extinguished and the father takes a candle, a wooden spoon or piece of shingle and a feather, and, after saying a blessing to be found in any Passover *haggada*, goes through the house accompanied by the rest of the family, searching for chametz by the light of the candle. The search is carried out in silence.

As he finds each piece of chametz that has been placed earlier, he sweeps it onto the shingle or wooden spoon with the feather. When all the pieces have been gathered up, he makes a special statement in Aramaic and then repeats it in whatever language is understood by all the family, to the effect that all chametz in his possession which he has not seen, is annulled and of no value. The chametz is then wrapped or put in a paper bag, together with the feather and the wooden spoon or shingle, and laid aside. The next morning, before ten o'clock, it is taken and all three—chametz, feather and spoon—are burned, after the statement is made that all chametz in the house, seen or unseen, is annulled and regarded as "the dust of the earth."

If the first seder is on a Saturday night, the bedikat chametz is done on Thursday night and the chametz burned on Friday. The above-mentioned statement, however, is not made until Saturday morning, before ten o'clock or thereabouts.

The Day Before Passover

It is now the day before Passover, which starts that evening. Final preparations can be carried out, vessels purged, etc., and all must be done before noon. It is permitted to eat chametz only until about ten o'clock on this morning and matza may not be eaten at all, so as not to diminish the pleasure of eating it at the seder table that night. The rest of the day is occupied in preparing food for the seder dinner, setting the table and in general getting ready for the seder celebration. As explained, this is a fast day for firstborn sons.

The reason for the extensive "spring cleaning" of the entire house and the painstaking search for and removal of chametz is compliance with a specific commandment: "the first day you shall put away chametz out of your houses" (Exod. 12:15). The importance of this commandment is that it makes us conscious to a profound degree of the difference between the feast of our liberation and the rest of the year, and between our Jewish way of life and that of the Gentiles. After all, what is more common to our everyday life than bread? We eat it at every meal. The absolute prohibition against even having bread in the house over these eight days serves as a constant reminder during this entire period that our total life-style is changed, just as it was changed from slavery to freedom—the most radical change there can be in the human condition—at the time of the Exodus from Egypt.

Eruv Tavshilin

If the first seder is on a Wednesday night, an *eruv tavshilin* must be made. This is done by taking, on the Wednesday, a cooked egg and a piece of matza (the law is, something cooked and something baked), and setting them aside, wrapped together. A blessing is said which can be found in any siddur or haggada. The day after the second day of Pesach, which is Saturday, the food is taken out and eaten. The reason for this is that while the law permits us to cook on a holiday, it is only permitted to cook enough food for the holiday itself. If, however, Shabbat immediately follows the holiday, it is obviously necessary to prepare enough food for the Sabbath as well. Thus the food set aside represents the food which will be prepared for the Sabbath since the law states that if the preparation of the food is commenced before the holiday, it may continue into the holiday itself. On Shabbat, of course, cooking is forbidden.

The Matza .

As mentioned above, the second distinguishing feature of Passover is that in addition to having no chametz in the house, we are commanded (Exod. 12:18 and 13:7) to eat matza. In actual fact, the commandment applies only to the first night; during the rest of the holiday the eating of matza is optional. The amount that must be eaten on the first night is a *k'zait*: a piece the size of an olive.

The many laws concerning the preparation and baking of matzot need not be gone into here since perfectly kosher matzot are available commercially to Jews everywhere, with the exception of the Soviet Union, which more often than not makes the baking of matzot a crime.

Care must be taken, however, to make sure that the words "kosher for Passover" appear on the package, since in the United States it is possible to buy matzot that are not pesadik, simply because there are people who like to eat them all year round. The basic law for ordinary matzot is that they must have only two ingredients: wheat flour, and water which has been allowed to stand for twenty-four hours to make sure no yeasts are in it. As soon as the dough is kneaded, the matzot must be baked and then kept from exposure to humidity so that they may not ferment from a combination of moisture and airborne yeasts.

Specially made matzot, such as the "egg matzos" made by some firms for Passover, are kosher if properly certified. There is also a very special matza called *matza sh'mura*, or "guarded matza," made in the following fashion:

The wheat from which the flour is to be made is supervised by Orthodox rabbis from the time it is ripe and ready for harvesting until it is actually cut and threshed. This means that while it is still standing in the field awaiting reaping it is observed to see that no rain falls on it which could cause it to swell. Of course while it is green and still growing, no fermentation is possible.

Once the wheat has been cut, it is observed through the threshing process and the unground wheat is stored in conditions which make exposure to moisture impossible.

The grinding of the wheat into flour and its storage is carefully observed. The flour cannot be ground at too high a speed, for example, because that might cause it to heat up and be susceptible to fermentation.

The matzot are prepared by hand, the dough kneaded with water and the shortest possible interval—usually less than a minute—allowed to pass before the matzot are put in the oven.

The resulting matzot are called *sh'mura mishaat k'tsira*, which means guarded from the time the grain is cut. Somewhat less rigidly supervised is the *matza sh'mura mishaat t'china*, observed from the time the grain was milled into flour.

Although most matza sh'mura is made by hand, there does exist a machine-made matza sh'mura with a *hechsher*, or kosher certification, issued by a well-known Orthodox rabbi. These are quite acceptable as matza sh'mura, due to the absolute trustworthiness of the rabbi whose signature appears on the hechsher. (Does this mean that there are rabbis whose certification of a product as kosher is in doubt or not to be trusted? Unfortunately this is just what it does mean. The same problems exist among Jews as among any people.) Matza sh'mura are not eaten by most Jews all throughout the holiday, but observant Jews do their best to have them for the seder plate (see below) on the first two nights.

There are many Passover dishes which can be prepared with matzot or matzo meal (ground matzot). These include puddings, cakes and of course, the famous matzo balls. It may surprise you to know that the very religious—all Chasidim for example—do not make or use matzo balls in the soup served at the seder or during all of Pesach, because it is feared that the ground matza may have some speck of chametz which the hot water will cause to swell and ferment. Chasidim make a special noodle out of potato flour which they serve in the soup. Any Jewish cookbook will have dozens of recipes for matza-based Passover dishes.

The Seder

The third thing that distinguishes the Passover is the celebration of the *seder* in the home of every Jew. This feast, accompanied by the reading aloud of the *Haggada*, is in observance of the commandment contained in Ex. 13:8: "And you shall tell your son on that day, saying, 'It is because of what the Lord did for me when I came out of Egypt.'"

While on other holidays the feast celebrating the day may be started at any time after sundown, even quite late at night, the Passover seder should be started as soon as it is dark so that the children will not get tired and fall asleep before the seder is over. The entire seder is really for the benefit of the children, so they must sit at the same table with the adults. To have the children sit at a separate table as is sometimes done at other celebrations is forbidden on Passover.

The long, interesting ritual followed during the seder is described in all good *Haggadot*, so we will not go into it here. If doubts exist regarding any point, a complete Hebrew-English haggada should indicate the proper procedure. The following observations are intended to explain the meaning of some of the most notable features of this most joyous of family feasts.

The Passover table must be set with a special tablecloth and the most beautiful silverware the family possesses. Nothing should be placed on the table, with the exception of silverware and crystal, but those things needed to celebrate the seder itself. All other food and drink is to be brought in later.

If at all possible, pillows should be placed on the chairs of all the men present, but especially that of the *baal-haggada*, the leader of the ceremony, who sits at the head of the table. This is so that they may recline while drinking the four cups of wine to show their freedom from slavery. Women need not recline, but may if they wish.

Every place must have a wine cup, usually on a small plate, for the drinking of the *arba kosot*, the four cups one is required to drink on Pesach. Special, kosher-for-Passover grapejuice is now generally available and can be used in place of wine for the younger children who may become drowsy from real wine. Every place must also have a copy of the haggada so that all can join in or follow its recitation.

In many families, the baal-haggada—usually the father or grandfather—wears a white kittel, both as a sign of rejoicing and as a reminder of life's shortness. In front of the baal-haggada is the seder plate. Specially made plates, some of them very beautiful, can be purchased for the seder, but any large plate from the set of Passover dishes will do. On this plate the following five foods are placed (the order of their arrangement on the plate varies from family to family):

BETSA: an egg which has been hard-boiled and then roasted in the oven. This commemorates the offering made by the pilgrims who went to the Temple in Jerusalem for the holiday.

ZERO'A: a roasted bone with a little meat on it. This symbolizes the Passover lamb, sacrificed at the time of the
Exodus and also during the period of the Temple.

MAROR: bitter vegetable. Among the Ashkenazim this is
usually fresh sliced horseradish. If none is available, ro-
maine lettuce is permissible, and according to some authorities, even preferable. If neither is available, any bitter vegetable such as ordinary radish or even onion will
do. The maror reminds us how bitter our life was in
Egypt as slaves.

CHAROSET: a thick paste made of grated apples, ground-
up or pounded almonds, walnuts or other nuts, honey or
sugar for sweetening, and a little wine to moisten it. This
symbolizes the mortar out of which our forefathers made
bricks in Egypt, and for this reason it is considered best
to use slivers of stick cinnamon for flavoring because they
look like the straw in the original mud-and-straw mixture.
Ordinary ground cinnamon will do if the other sort is not
available. Many Sephardim make their charoset out of
dates. Among Moroccan Jews, the charoset is commonly
made by the Chevra Kadisha and distributed to the community.

KARPAS: any green vegetable over which the blessing *boreh pri ha-adama* is said. Ashkenazi families usually use
parsley, and Sephardim, particularly Moroccans, use cele-
ry tops, but many Ashkenazim use boiled potato. Karpas
is eaten by indication of the Talmud (Mishna, Pesachim
10:3) mostly to excite the curiosity of the children.

In addition to the seder plate and its contents, a small dish or
glass of salt-water or vinegar must be on the table or even on the
seder plate itself. Into it is dipped the karpas at the proper time
during the ceremony.

Three matzot are needed for the ceremony and observant Jews
try to obtain sh'mura matza. In any event, the matzot used must
be free from cracks or breaks. They are usually put on a plate,
separated from each other by three napkins or three folds of a

large napkin; special matza covers with three compartments can usually be bought in Jewish bookstores. They are called the *matzot shel mitzva* and are referred to as *Cohen, Levi* and Israel. Matzot shel mitzva means matzos (used in the observance) of the commandment.

When the table is set and ready, the seder can begin once it is dark outside. The seder may not be celebrated during daylight hours as explained in the haggada itself. The haggada is read right through, from beginning to end, its directions followed, the blessings recited, the Passover meal eaten, grace said and the songs sung to the tunes traditional in the family.

While it is customary to recite the haggada in Hebrew, it is perfectly permissible to read it in any language one wishes. In fact there is one section, the one starting "Rabban Gamaliel used to say . . ." that *must* be read in whatever language those at the table understand. It explains the essentials of the seder and it is important that everyone appreciate what they are.

It is the custom in many families to read the text of the haggada in Hebrew and stop every paragraph or so to give a translation or paraphrase in the language spoken in the home. Generally not all the haggada is translated but the most important and unfamiliar parts are, particularly the first part, before the meal is served. Anyone who happens to know of an explanation or interpretation of any part of the text is encouraged to interrupt and give it, and anyone with a question is encouraged to ask it.

I know of families where the haggada is read in Hebrew and translated at the same time into French and Arabic. In my own home, when our older children, now grown up, were small, they spoke only Spanish, so we became accustomed to translating parts of the haggada into that language, with explanations. Later on our younger children forgot Spanish and spoke only English, so we recited the vital parts in English. But since we had been accustomed to reciting these parts in Spanish, we continue to do so, and today our seder is conducted, at least in part, in three languages. It appears to be a fact that one of the most famous of the Chasidic rabbis, Rabbi Yitzchak Eisik of Kalev (Nagy-Kallo), recited the entire haggada in Hungarian alone. Many of the songs toward the end of the haggada, particularly "Echad Mi Yodea" (Who Knows One?), are more often than not sung in the language of the country or in Yiddish or Ladino.

The Passover meal itself starts, at least among the Ashkenazim, with an unusual dish: a hard-boiled egg in a plate of salt-water. It is said that the salt-water represents the Red Sea over which the Jews crossed on their way to freedom, and the egg represents the Jewish people, since it is the only food that gets tougher the longer it is in hot water! The salt-water is also said to represent the tears we shed in slavery in Egypt.

The second dish is usually *gefillte fish*, which most people think of as a strictly Jewish invention. Actually the Chinese know it too and the Japanese have a version of it called *kamaboko*, but in Europe it is typically Jewish, and is known to the Goyim in Slavic countries as "Jewish fish." The third course is soup with either matzo balls, or, among the more observant, potato flour noodles. Then the main meal is served. Nothing roasted on an open flame should be eaten since this would be an imitation of the Passover lamb which was so roasted and which we can no longer eat since our Temple has been destroyed. Meat roasted in the oven can be eaten.

There are, of course, hundreds of different customs observed by members of different communities. The North African Sephardim, for example, at one point in the seder have the baal-haggada get up and march around the table three times with the plate containing the matzot on his shoulder. He stops at every place on his way, circling the head of the person sitting there three times with the plate. The *Shomronim*, or Samaritans (see chapter 3), celebrate the seder collectively on Mount Gerizim on the West Bank Territory of Israel. They sacrifice a lamb, roast it on an open fire, eat all its meat before sunup and observe the seder with a staff in their hands and traveling shoes on their feet, just as our forefathers did in Egypt, the night the Exodus commenced.

To return to more contemporary Jews, after the meal, the grace is said, the rest of the haggada recited and the songs sung, ending with *"Chad Gadya"* ("One kid, that my father bought for two *zuzim* . . .").

One universally observed custom should be noted here. At the beginning of the seder a large silver cup (if there is one; if not, any goblet) is placed on the table and left empty until the third of the four cups of wine is drunk, after the meal. It is then filled for Elijah the Prophet and the baal-haggada leaves the table and goes to the front door, which he opens, and recites a supplication to God to destroy His enemies and those of His people, Israel. The door is opened to allow Elijah to enter, since it is he who will announce the coming of the Messiah (chapter 41). In some families Elijah's cup is filled at the beginning of the seder.

Another and more unpleasant reason is sometimes given for the custom of opening the front door during the seder. It is so that any Gentile passing by may look in and see for himself that nothing sinister is taking place in the house. Many people are probably familiar with the *bilbul dam*, or blood libel, in which the insane accusation is made that Jews employ the blood of non-Jewish children in the manufacture of the Passover wine or matzot. Opening the door is one means of dispelling this macabre belief.

And it would be a mistake to think that the blood libel went out with the Middle Ages. In late 1945 and early 1946, blood libel accusations brought about pogroms or attempted pogroms in the Polish cities of Rzeszow, Krakow and Czestochow, culminating in a pogrom on July 4, 1946, in the city of Kielce, in which sixty to seventy Jews were killed, including women and children, and over one hundred injured, most of them seriously. This pogrom was caused directly by a blood libel accusation, and after it was over, Cardinal Hlond, the chief spokesman for the Catholic Church in Poland, made a public declaration to the effect that the Jews had brought it on themselves, although he did not impute the use of Christian blood to them.

The pogrom in Kielce brought about the exodus from Poland of almost all the Jews remaining there after the Second World War, finally convinced that neither the Polish people nor the Roman Catholic Church had abandoned the criminal anti-Semitism that has always been one of their sorriest distinguishing features. When the blood libel will crop up again, no one knows, but it is premature to hope that we have seen the last of it. In just fairness it should be noted that the Catholic Church, through the Popes, has always condemned the blood libel as false.

The Synagogue Service for Passover

The festival prayers for Passover are essentially the same as those for the other three holidays, with the exception of the prayer *Tal*, a supplication for dew, which is recited on the first day of Passover during Musaph.

As explained above, Passover lasts eight days outside Israel and seven within the Holy Land. A tourist or visitor to Israel who does not intend to remain is obliged to observe the holiday for eight days and to celebrate two seders, although it is customary to observe the second day in private so as not to arouse comment. If an Israeli is visiting outside Israel and intends to return within a year, he need observe only one seder and the seven days of the holiday. This applies to personnel of the Israeli diplomatic corps, for example. The same law applies to all other holidays with the exception of Rosh Hashana, which is observed for two days in Israel as well as in the diaspora.

All Moroccan Jews have the custom of celebrating the last night of Passover as a special feast called *Noche de Mimona*. Each family sets a table with an enormous variety of sweet foods and confections and plays host to anyone wishing to call on them. This custom is not seen to any degree in the United States, but in Latin America it is very widely practiced in cities with large Moroccan Jewish communities, such as Mexico City, Caracas, Buenos Aires, Belém (Pará) and Rio de Janeiro.

Sefirat Ha-Omer: The Seven Weeks after Passover

The second night of Passover marks the start of a seven-week period called *Sefirat Ha-Omer*, or counting the *omer*. An omer is a sheaf of grain, brought to the Temple for the Shavuot holiday. Why we count the omer, that is to say, count each day during this seven-week period between Pesach and Shavuot—which commemorates the giving of the Torah on Mount Sinai—is the subject of much explaining. Perhaps the best explanation is found in the Gemara of the tractate on Passover in the Talmud. Here it explains that God told Moses (Exod. 3:12), "When you have brought the people out of Egypt you shall serve God upon this mountain." Moses told the people this at the time of the Exodus and they asked him, "When will we begin to serve?" He answered, "In fifty days," and the people began counting each day in anticipation.

Orthodox Jews are accustomed to observe this period between the two holidays as one of semi-mourning. They do not listen to music, cut their hair, go to parties, etc. In addition, no weddings are celebrated during these seven weeks except in case of emergency. The reason for this semi-mourning is that a plague carried off thousands of the students of Rabbi Akiba, one of the outstanding figures of the Talmud, and we mourn to commemorate that fact. In some communities it is customary to begin the semi-mourning period not after the second night of Passover, but after Rosh Chodesh Iyyar, sixteen days after the first day of Pesach.

Lag B'Omer

There is, however, a break in this mourning period. It comes on the thirty-third day and is called *Lag B'Omer*. *Lag* is an artificial word made up out of the letter lamed, which has a numerical value of thirty, and gimel, with a numerical value of three. Lag B'Omer means "thirty-three in the Omer." On this day, we are told, the plague stopped and we celebrate this happening. A second and commonly heard explanation is that Simeon Bar Yochai, the alleged author of the Zohar, died on this day and left instructions that his death anniversary was to be celebrated as a holiday, not a day of mourning.

Weddings can be performed on this day and thousands are. Hair can be cut, music played and in general all *Sefira* (another name for the Sefirat Ha-Omer period) prohibitions are suspended. Lag B'Omer never falls on Monday, Wednesday or Shabbat. If it happens to fall on Sunday when the barbershops are closed, it is permitted to get a haircut on Friday. Lag B'Omer is a minor holiday which means we are permitted to work as on any other weekday.

In Israel, the small village of Meiron is the site of a huge celebration on Lag B'Omer because it is there that Simeon Bar Yochai is buried. Literally scores of thousands of people come from all over the country on that day to Meiron, pitching tents in which they live. Many dance the entire night through, particularly around Bar Yochai's tomb. Boys having their hair cut for the first time have this done on Lag B'Omer at Meiron, and the hair is thrown into a huge bonfire which is kept burning near the saint's tomb.

In the neighboring and ancient town of Safed (Tsefat), a centuries-old Sefer Torah is taken from the house of the Abú family, its owners, to Meiron and the people dance down the streets after it in a joyous celebration. This custom has been observed yearly for the last 155 years. Along the route taken by the dancers, people stand at the doors of their houses with bottles of *arrack*, a powerful anise-flavored grape brandy, and glasses in their hands, offering a drink to whoever happens to be passing by. It is easy to get downright *shikker* if you don't know how to turn down the invitations after the first couple of shots.

Lag B'Omer is also a holiday for schoolchildren and yeshiva students, everywhere in the world.

In Israel there is one further interruption of the Sefira period of semi-mourning and that is the fifth day of Iyyar, *Yom Ha-atzma'ut*, or Israel Independence Day. This holiday is discussed in chapter 36.

33

Shavuot

SHAVUOT is the last of the three Pilgrim Festivals in order of celebration during the Jewish year. It commemorates two different events: the bringing of the first fruits of the grain harvest to the Temple and the giving of the Torah on Mount Sinai, which occurred fifty days after the Exodus from Egypt. Its name means "weeks," because it comes seven weeks after Passover, on the sixth and seventh days of Sivan. In Israel it is celebrated only on the sixth.

In the Torah the commandment to celebrate the feast of the first-fruits appears in Exod. 23:16, but is not clearly defined as to time until later in Deut. 16:10: "And you shall keep the feast of weeks unto the Lord." Although we no longer have a Temple in Jerusalem, we continue to celebrate this feast because the Torah instructs us to do so, and our faith in the restoration of the Temple has never flagged.

It is customary to decorate the synagogue with green branches and flowers on Shavuot and it is also customary among both Ashkenazim and Sephardim to eat dairy dishes and foods sweetened with honey. The Ashkenazim eat *blintzes* and *kreplach*, while the Sephardim eat *borekes*, a baked pastry filled with cheese. Of all the explanations for this custom, a Chasidic one has always seemed to me the most attractive: we Jews eat milk dishes to show that as far as the Torah is concerned, even the most learned of us is like a little child in the extent of his understanding.

The reason for eating honey is obvious: the Torah was given us on this day and its sweetness knows no comparison.

The synagogue service is that of the Three Festivals, with the addition, among the Ashkenazim, of the prayer *Akdamot*, which is sung to a traditional melody before the Torah is read. The Sephardim recite *Azharot*, or "warnings" which urge worshipers to observe the commandments of the Torah. In some Sephardic congregations a special *ketuba*, or wedding contract, is read in both Hebrew and Ladino, which celebrates the marriage of Israel to the Torah. This unusual document is not found in Sephardic siddurs, at least none I have ever seen, but the congregations have copies of it. In one such synagogue, in New York, it is, or was, mimeographed and distributed to the worshipers so that they would be able to follow the reading in both languages.

In many Ashkenazi congregations the book of Ruth is read after the morning Shachrit service. The reason given is that King David was born and died on Shavuot and since he was descended from Ruth, the reading of this *megilla* is appropriate. In Israel an actual scroll is used, but outside the Holy Land it is read from a copy of the *Tanach*—the Bible.

In Israel the custom has arisen of bringing first-fruits of the harvest to the villages and towns in a sort of festival which is, we are told, more folkloric than religious. This is debatable, since the very folklore of our Holy Land acquires religious significance, particularly when related to a holiday such as Shavuot.

The Reformed and some Conservative Jews have instituted the custom of Confirmation for whole groups of teenagers on Shavuot.

Having discussed the High Holidays and the Three Festivals, we can now go on to a brief consideration of the minor holidays—days that are celebrated, but on which work is permitted.

The
Minor
Holidays

34

Chanuka

CHANUKA means dedication, in the sense of dedicating a building or place of worship. It commemorates the rededication of the Temple in Jerusalem by Judah Maccabee, his brothers and their troops, the Hasmoneans. These courageous rebels vanquished and drove out of the Holy Land the vastly superior Syrian armies of Antiochus, who represented the Roman Empire. On the twenty-fifth day of Kislev, 165 B.C.E., they rededicated the Temple, which had been defiled by the Syrians in a vain attempt to stamp out the Jewish religion from among the Jewish people.

It is told that when they cleaned out the Temple and put it into shape for worship, they wished to light the *Menorah*, or Temple lamp, but found consecrated oil enough for one day only. It took a week to prepare the oil under ordinary circumstances, but they went ahead and lit the Menorah with the oil they had on hand and by a miracle it burned for eight days, giving them time to prepare enough oil to keep it burning after that time. For this reason we celebrate the holiday for eight days and light the eight-branched Chanuka lamp, or *Chanukiya*.

The Chanukiya can be either an oil lamp, in which it is considered best to use olive oil, or a candelabrum. In either case the lamp must be big enough so that the lights remain lit for at least thirty minutes, otherwise the lamp is not kosher.

There are eight lights on the lamp, plus one extra one called the *shamash*, or servant, which is used to light the other lights. On the first night, one light is lit—the farthest to the right—using the shamash to light it, after saying the appropriate blessings. The song *"Ha-nerot Hallalu"* is sung or recited, followed by the Chanuka hymn, *"Ma'oz Tzur"* (Rock of Ages), which is sung to a traditional melody known the world over. On the second night the second light from the right is lit, followed by the lighting of the first light, making two lights plus the shamash. On the third night three lights are lit in the same order, from left to right, and so on successively until the eighth day when all eight lights are shining. Blessings and songs will be found in any siddur. The order in which lights are lit may vary according to the custom of the family or the community.

The Chanuka lamp should be set next to a door or window so that it can be seen from outside. The lamp is entirely for adornment and its light may not be used to read by, examine things by or for any other practical purpose. In the United States one often sees electric Chanuka lamps in the windows of Jews and according to most rabbinical opinion, these lamps are kosher.

Gambling, which is frowned upon the rest of the year, is permitted and even encouraged on Chanuka, with a sort of "put and take" top called a *dredel*, in Hebrew, *s'vivon*. This is a four-sided top with the Hebrew letters nun, gimel, heh and shin, one on each side. The players all bet the same amount (and nuts and candies are used more often than money) while one player spins the dredel. If nun comes up, this is understood to mean *nisht*, or "nothing," in Yiddish, and the bets remain while the dredel passes to the next player. Gimel stands for *gantz*, or "all," and the player who has spun the dredel takes everything in the pot: new bets are placed and the dredel passes to the next player. Heh means *halb* or "half," and the player takes half of what is in the pot, and shin stands for *shtell*, or "put," and the player must put an amount equal to his original bet in the pot and pass the dredel to the next player.

The custom originated, we are told, in Roman times, when the study of the Torah was forbidden, as it is in Russia today. Jewish children were given these tops and when Roman authorities came to inspect the schools, they found the children playing instead of studying. The letters really stand for *Nes Gadol Haya Sham* (A great miracle happened there). In Israel, the letters on the top are nun, gimel, he and pe and stand for *Nes Gadol Haya Po* (A great miracle happened here).

On the fifth night of Chanuka, after the fifth light is lit, it is customary to give the children *Chanuka gelt*, Yiddish for Chanuka money. The custom of giving other sorts of gifts really belongs to Passover and Purim, and its adoption in the United States at Chanuka is in imitation of the Christian custom of giving presents at Christmas, which comes at about the same time as Chanuka. I recall once witnessing a class at a "Jewish" kindergarten where the teachers, instructing their little charges about Chanuka, had trained them, when asked, "What is just as important as getting presents on Chanuka?" to answer: "Giving!"

This is nonsense. Children are not expected to give anything on Chanuka to their parents or friends; they are only supposed to receive. Chanuka is not a "Jewish Christmas" and no service is done to Judaism by attempting to turn it into one. Neither is it a major holiday on the same level of importance as Passover or Shavuot, for example, and to overemphasize it as a sort of antidote for Christmas has proven to be exactly the wrong direction to take. The right way to do it is to give the major holidays their deserved emphasis, and this includes keeping one's children out of school, so that they will enjoy and remember them. I make no apology for the intrusion of personal opinion here; what I have stated is fact, proven again and again, and the proof is visible in the way children of families who take this path adhere to Judaism.

The giving of gifts on Chanuka does have a long tradition in one sense: gifts to the poor, particularly gifts of food and money to yeshivas, hospitals, etc., are an important part of the observance of Chanuka and have been for centuries.

It is the custom of the Ashkenazim to eat *latkes*, or potato pancakes, on Chanuka. Where this custom originated is not known except that it was not among the Hasmoneans. The potato was unknown in the Old World before Columbus discovered the New. And while we are on the subject of Columbus, he may have been born in Italy, but his parents were Spaniards and his native language Spanish. All Spanish historians are in accord on one fact concerning Columbus: he was a Jew (Columbus Day is still not a Jewish holiday, however).

35

Purim

THE entire story of the holiday of Purim is found in the book of Esther in the Bible. The foolish King, Ahasuerus; the Heroine, Queen Esther; the Hero, her uncle Mordechai; and the Villain, wicked Haman, are familiar figures to all of us. Purim is a minor holiday in the sense that work is permitted on it, but in practice, many Jews do not work on Purim because it is considered a Yom Tov, by custom if not by law. A well-known Yiddish proverb says, *"Purim iz nisht kein yomtov un kadoches iz nisht kein krenk"*— Purim is no holiday and malaria is no illness. (And there are those who insist that the proverb is complete only when you add, *"Un kish mir in tochos iz nisht kein beleidigung"*—And *kish mir in tochos* is no insult!) A further Jewish proverb asserts that work done on Purim will bring no profit.

Purim is celebrated on the 14th of Adar and, in a Jewish leap year, in Adar Sheni. In cities which were walled at the time of Joshua, such as Jerusalem, Purim is celebrated on the 15th of Adar, a day after it is in most places. This day is called Shushan Purim, because the Jews of Shushan (Iran), scene of the events described in the book of Esther, were still fighting their enemies on the 14th and did not start to celebrate until the 15th. In cities in Israel where it is uncertain if they were walled at the time of Joshua, the Jews take no chances; they celebrate *both* days and they have a high old time doing it.

The religious service for Purim features the reading of the entire book of Esther from a special parchment scroll, the *Megillat Esther*, after the evening service and again at the morning service. The children are provided with a whirling noisemaker called a *grager*, and every time the name of the villain, Haman, is mentioned, the gragers are whirled and those present stamp their feet and hoot to drown out the hated name of this enemy of the Jews.

A special section is added to the grace after meals on Purim. Among the Ashkenazim (and in Israel among the Sephardim as well) a triangular cookie, filled either with *lekvar* (a sort of prune jam), or *mohn* (poppyseed), is eaten. In Yiddish, these pastries are called *Homentashen*, or Haman's pockets and in Israel they are called *Oznei Haman* (Haman's ears). Sephardim take dough and mold it around a hardboiled egg in the form of a man with arms and legs, bake it and eat it. This confection also represents the despised Haman.

It is customary among all Jews to send gifts of food to their friends and neighbors on Purim and, according to tradition, there should be at least two kinds of food (almost always pastry) on the plate. These days, paper plates, specially printed for *Shalach Manot* (A. Sh'lachmones), the sending of Purim gifts, are available at Jewish bookstores.

Purim is the one day in the year on which drunkenness is not only permitted but actually encouraged, at least in theory. There is a Jewish saying to the effect that only when one is so drunk that one cannot distinguish in the *Megilla* between *"baruch Mordechai"* (Blessed be Mordechai) and *"arur Haman* (Cursed be Haman) has one fulfilled the observance of Purim. Among Jews who observe Purim in its full sense, it is indeed an exuberant holiday and no one goes hungry or thirsty until long after the holiday is over, the following night. Orthodox Jews, and in particular the Chasidim, celebrate with a *Seudat Purim*, or Purim feast, at the close of the holiday and far into the night. This festivity features all sorts of clowning and merriment including the *Purim Shpiel* (Y.), or Purim play, in which Mordechai, Esther, Haman and the other figures of the drama described in the Book of Esther have parts.

In Orthodox communities the children still dress up in masquerade costumes and go from house to house begging for gifts and even money. Many Jewish readers will probably remember what they used to say (and perhaps still do): *"Haint iz Purim, morgen iz ois, git mir a penny un warf mich arois!"* (Today is Purim, tomorrow it's over; give me a penny and throw me out). The resemblance to Halloween is immediately noticeable, but the holidays have no connection whatsoever.

Traditionally, dressing up in disguise for Purim has never been restricted to children, and grownups in riotous costumes can be seen in some of the most Orthodox synagogues in Jerusalem. We do it to remind ourselves of Esther's adopting a false identity in order to save her people. In Tel Aviv a full-fledged carnival called the *Adloyada* used to be celebrated which has been favorably compared to the carnivals of Rio and New Orleans. It has been discontinued as an economic austerity measure but may be revived in a more favorable time.

It is strange that this nonholiday should be so important in Jewish life. Speculation as to why this is the case is not lacking and it is only fair to note that there are some peculiar features about the day. In the first place, the Megillat Esther is the only book of the Bible in which God's name is not mentioned. The explanation given is that the book was actually written not in Hebrew, into which it has been translated, but in the language of the Medes and the Persians, who were the book's authors. The custom of men dressing in women's clothes for the Purim *shpiel* is out of character and even violates a commandment of the Torah. Drunkenness, so atypical a phenomenon in Jewish life, is raised to the level of a mitzva. There are even scholars who point out that the names of Purim's two heroes, Esther and Mordechai, bear a suspicious resemblance to Ishtar and Marduk, the principal deities of the ancient Babylonians.

What is being hinted at here is that Purim may well have been a pagan holiday which their leaders found it impossible to keep the Jews from observing, so they converted it to a Jewish holiday. Nevertheless, recognizing its non-Jewish origin and its undeniably non-Jewish character, they refused to give it the status of a full holiday.

This is what certain scholars have claimed, but there appears to be solid archeological evidence that King Ahasuerus really did live and that the events described in the book of Esther really did take place. The holiday may have disguised pagan aspects which have kept it from being a full Yom Tov, but there can be no question that today and for centuries it has been a uniquely Jewish festival. There is a Jewish proverb that says that when Messiah comes all holidays will be abolished—with the exception of Purim.

36

T'u B'Shavat, Rosh Chodesh and the Special Sabbaths

T'U B'SHVAT

T'u B'Shvat is the name commonly used to designate *Chamisha Assar B'Shvat*, the fifteenth day of the month of Shvat. It is so called because the Hebrew letters tet and vov, T and U, have the numerical value of fifteen.

T'u B'Shvat is a minor holiday which is, nonetheless, observed with satisfaction by Jews everywhere. It is the New Year of the Trees, and we celebrate it by eating fruits from Israel or that grow in Israel, such as figs, dates, pomegranates and especially, the carob bean, called in English "Saint John's Bread," and in Yiddish, *Bokser*.

It is above all a children's holiday and is celebrated widely all over Israel, where it is the custom for schoolchildren to go out and plant saplings on this day. Every year enormous numbers of trees are planted in Israel on T'u B'Shvat. There is no special synagogue service, but part of the *Tachanun* (penitential prayers) is omitted and it is forbidden to fast because of the festive nature of the day.

YOM HA-ATZMA'UT

On the fifth day of the month of Iyyar, 5708 (May 14, 1948), the State of Israel was reborn, and that day, Yom Ha-atzma'ut—Israel Independence Day—is celebrated everywhere Jews live. In Israel itself, if Yom Ha-atzma'ut falls on a Friday or Saturday, it is celebrated on the preceding Thursday to avoid any possibility of violating the Sabbath.

Military parades and demonstrations are an important part of the Independence Day celebration, but besides its patriotic significance, the holiday has a distinctly religious cast in Israel, due to the undeniable miracles and the divine intervention that accompanied the rebirth of the Jewish state. An abbreviated form of Hallel is said and there are additional prayers, not only celebrating independence, but also remembering the Jewish heroes who gave up their lives in the War of Liberation and in the wars of defense which have succeeded it.

The Chief Rabbinate of Israel has decreed that Yom Ha-atzma'ut be considered a break in the *Sefira* period of mourning between Passover and Shavuot (chapter 32), similar to Lag B'Omer. Hair may be cut, new clothes put on and weddings performed. Outside Israel the religious nature of the holiday is not yet recognized to the same degree, but in some congregations, half-Hallel is said as in Israel, during the Shachrit service.

ROSH CHODESH

Rosh Chodesh is the first day of the Jewish month and a minor holiday in the sense that Hallel is said as well as the additional Musaph service after Shachrit. The festival prayer *Yaaleh v'yavo* is said both during the *Sh'moneh Essreh* (S. *Amida*) and the grace after meals.

Work is permitted on this day, but it is the custom among the very observant to consider it a half-holiday for women, during which certain types of work, particularly sewing, are prohibited. The day before Rosh Chodesh, except for the months of Tishri, Cheshvan, Tevet and Iyyar, is celebrated by the very religious as a fast day called *Yom Kippur Katan,* or little Yom Kippur. If

Rosh Chodesh falls on a Saturday or Sunday, Yom Kippur Katan is observed on the preceding Thursday. The special prayers for this fast day are found only in the most complete siddurim since it is observed by few Jews. The holiday is of Kabbalistic origin and dates, apparently, from about the 16th century C.E. It is a minor holiday in that work is permitted.

As noted in chapter 28, the exact date and time, to the second, of the commencement of each month are announced in the synagogue on the Sabbath preceding it. For further discussion and explanation, see chapter 38 (The Jewish Calendar).

SPECIAL SABBATHS

There are four Sabbaths during the year which are distinguished by having a special *maftir*, the last section of the Torah portion, or *sedra,* to be read. In practice, two Sifrei Torah are taken out, and, when the last section is reached, the first scroll is closed, bound and covered and the second scroll opened for the reading of the special maftir. A special Haftara also follows.

These Sabbaths are the following:

SHABBAT SHEKALIM. The Sabbath preceding Rosh Chodesh Adar, the first day of Adar, is called Shabbat Shekalim in remembrance of the half-shekel that every Jew over the age of twenty was required to contribute to the maintenance of the Temple. The maftir and haftara read on this Sabbath concern that contribution. In our times, in the United States, it is customary to make a donation of threehalf-dollars to charity or to the State of Israel on Purim, a day when everyone comes to the synagogue and money can be handled.

SHABBAT ZACHOR. Shabbat Zachor is the Sabbath before Purim and on it we are commanded to remember (*zachor*) what Amalek did to us when we came out of Egypt. Haman, the enemy of the Jews in the book of Esther, whose story is celebrated on the upcoming holiday, was a descendant of Amalek. In addition to the special maftir and haftara, the Sephardim have a great many special prayers and *piyyutim,* or hymns, which are sung on this day. The lesson of this Shabbat is that hatred of the enemies of the Jewish people is a mitzva and one we should not forget.

SHABBAT PARAH. This Sabbath, always called *Parashat Parah*, the weekly portion of *parah* (the red heifer), is celebrated on the Sabbath after Purim and its special maftir and haftara concern the purification ceremony of the red heifer (Num. 19:1-22). Among other things it is a reminder of the need to prepare for Passover, which will be coming along shortly.

SHABBAT HA-CHODESH. The "Sabbath of the Month," always called *Parashat Ha-chodesh,* is the Sabbath before the first day of the month of Nisan. The extra portion read is Exod. 12:1-20, which establishes Nisan as the first month in the calendar and gives instructions for preparing for and celebrating the Passover. It should be noted, to avoid confusion, that in our present Jewish calendar, Tishri is considered the first month.

On these four Sabbaths, a boy who has not yet reached the age of thirteen may not be called up to maftir, the last portion of the Torah to be read, because a special maftir is read which is not merely a repetition of the last short section as it is on ordinary Sabbaths (see chapter 10). Accordingly a boy whose thirteenth birthday is to be reached during the following week may not be called upon these Sabbaths in the usual fashion for the celebration of his bar mitzva. Instead he is called up, but an adult, usually his teacher or the rabbi, says the blessings. In some congregations the boy may then say the blessings for the Haftara and recite it, but in others, even this is done by another person over the age of thirteen.

To my mind, the best way around this is to follow the custom of the very Orthodox and wait until the boy's thirteenth birthday and call him up to the Torah on the first day thereafter, Monday, Thursday, or Saturday, on which the Torah is read publicly in the synagogue. The event can be celebrated with a party or reception at any time after that.

There are other Sabbaths which are distinguished as well. One of them is the Sabbath on which the sedra, *B'shallach* (Exod. 13:17 to 17:16) is read. This particular Sabbath is called *Shabbat Shira,* the Sabbath of Song, because on that day the song of Moses at the Red Sea (Exod. 15:1-18) is read. Sephardim have special melodies for this day and the Ashkenazim have always had the custom of throwing kasha out for the birds to eat.

In actuality, Idelsohn, in his book *Jewish Liturgy,* lists twenty-nine Sabbaths which have prayers or hymns not heard on ordinary Sabbaths. Included among them are the Sabbath on the intermediate days of Chanuka, *Shabbat T'shuva*, between Rosh Hashana and Yom Kippur, *Shabbat B'reshit,* on which the opening chapter of the Torah is read, and many others. By no means all congregations, even the most Orthodox, recite special prayers or hymns on all these Sabbaths.

When Rosh Chodesh falls on Shabbat, this is also a special Sabbath, and two Sifrei Torah are read from, to include the special Rosh Chodesh maftir.

37

Fasts

IT has been pointed out that fasting in Judaism can have quite different reasons, depending on the particular fast. One purpose is *t'shuva*, which means literally, "turning" or repentance. Another important reason for fasting is as a sign of mourning. A third reason is of a somewhat less well-defined nature, but can be described as an attempt to ward off an evil happening. For instance an evil dream is "propitiated" by fasting. If a Sefer Torah should accidentally be dropped on the floor in the synagogue, the entire congregation present at the time (excluding the women) is expected to fast between sunup and sunset for one month, always excepting the Sabbath. This is usually described as a penance for allowing such a terrible thing to happen, but its real purpose is to ward off the consequences of such an accident, which are believed to be disastrous.

YOM KIPPUR

Yom Kippur, a twenty-four-hour fast, is a day of "turning" and does not in any sense involve a feeling of mourning. On the contrary, it is a Yom Tov, a holiday. The same can be said of the fast observed by bride and groom on the day they are to be married: they fast so as to enter matrimony with pure hearts and minds. Other fasts do have mourning as their reason; such a fast is *Tisha B'Av*.

TISHA B'AV

Tisha B'Av which comes, as its name indicates, on the ninth day of the Jewish month of Av, commemorates the saddest date in Jewish history: the destruction of the *Bet Hamikdash*, our holy Temple in Jerusalem. There were, of course, two Temples, one of which was destroyed by Nebuchadnezzar in 586 B.C.E., and the second of which was destroyed by Titus in 70 C.E. Both Temples were destroyed on the same day, the ninth of Av. According to the Mishna, there were three other tragic events which also took place on this day, but it is the *churban Bet Hamikdash,* the destruction of the Temple, that we remember on Tisha B'Av.

As on Yom Kippur, the fast starts before sundown and ends after sundown on the following day. Nothing may be eaten or drunk, including water. In the synagogue the *parochet,* or curtain, in front of the Ark is removed. At the evening service, only enough candles are lit to read the service by and the worshipers do not sit on benches or chairs but on the floor or the underside of the benches which have been turned over. Wearing of leather shoes is prohibited, just as on Yom Kippur. On the eight days preceding Tisha B'Av, the observant abstain from drinking wine or eating meat, except on the Sabbath.

After the evening service, the book of Lamentations is read and this is followed by the reading of *kinnot,* mourning hymns and prayers which are published in a special booklet and kept in the synagogue for this day. Ashkenazim and Sephardim have many different kinnot, in part due to the fact that the expulsion of the Jews from Spain in 1492 also occurred on the ninth of Av. At the morning service neither tallit nor t'fillin are worn since they are considered adornments. They are, however, put on in the afternoon for the Mincha service so that the mitzva may be observed. Lamentations is read after the service, as are the kin-not. Work is permitted in Tisha B'Av but shaving is forbidden as is marital intercourse and even the study of the Torah, because this is a pleasurable occupation.

Now that all of Jerusalem is once again in the possession of the Jews, and the *Kotel Ha-maarabi,* or West Wall of the Temple, belongs to the State of Israel, there is talk about changing Tisha B'Av to a joyous holiday instead of a day of mourning. Whether this will ever be done is debatable, but two things are certain: the "Wailing Wall" is no longer the scene of weeping but of rejoic-ing, and the observance of Tisha B'Av lacks much of the tragic sadness it has had in the past.

If Tisha B'Av falls on a Sabbath, the fast is observed on the tenth of Av, the Sunday.

OTHER FAST DAYS

While there are several other fast days, few people if any observe all of them. Perhaps the most important one is *Shiva Assar B'Tammuz,* the seventeenth of Tammuz, which commem-orates the day the walls of Jerusalem fell (under the siege of Titus) as well as other tragic events. *Tzom Gedaliah,* the Fast of Gedaliah, on the third day of Tishri, the day after Rosh Hashana, remembers the murder of Gedaliah, Governor of the Jews under Nebuchadnezzar, which brought in its train great tragedy to the Jewish people. *Assara B'Tevet,* the tenth of Tevet, is the day on which Nebuchadnezzar's siege of Jerusalem began.

Taanit Esther, the Fast of Esther, is observed on the day before Purim in memory of the three-day fast held by the entire Jewish community of Shushan previous to Esther's going to King Ahasuerus to save the Jews of Persia. This lengthy fast is consid-ered a heroic deed which we cannot be expected to imitate today.

Taanit B'chorim, the fast of the firstborn, is described in chap-ter 32 where it is referred to as, in a sense, an act of sympathy for the firstborn of the Egyptians. It is also considered a fast of thanksgiving to God for having spared our sons while He slew those of the Egyptians.

The fast of the bride and groom, on the day of their wedding, is a fast of *t'shuva*, repentance and purification.

Asceticism for its own sake is not only not part of Jewish tradition and practice, it is considered a violation of Jewish law. We are told that he who denies himself a legitimate pleasure commits a sin, presumably because he spurns what God offers, and this is particularly true of fasting. The Hebrew phrase is concise and clear: *ha-yoshev b'taanit nikra choteh:* "Who fasts (for self-affliction) is called a sinner."

With the exception of Yom Kippur and Tisha B'Av, all fasts extend from sunup to sunset, and washing, study, work, etc., are all permitted. Fasts occurring on Shabbat, with the exception of Yom Kippur, are postponed to the following day, Sunday. If the first day of Passover falls on Sunday, which is to say that it starts on Saturday night, Taanit B'chorim, the fast of the firstborn, is observed on the preceding Thursday.

PART
VIII

Just for
Jews

38

The Jewish Calendar

As everyone knows, the earth revolves on its axis every twenty-four hours. The civil calendar has the 24-hour day as its basic unit, but calculation of the year on the basis of days alone is not possible, because the earth completes its circuit around the sun in 365 days, 5 hours, 48 minutes and 46 seconds. Those extra hours, minutes and seconds add up to a day every four years and so the civil calendar adds an extra day on leap year. Thus a month on our civil calendar can have 28, 29, 30 or 31 days, depending on the month and the year, and a year can have 365 or 366 days to make up the 12 months each year must have.

The Jewish calendar also operates on the basis of a 24-hour day and a 12-month year, but there the resemblance ends. The Jewish month is based on the moon and is either 29 or 30 days long, depending on the month, because it takes the moon 29 days, 12 hours, 44 minutes and 3 seconds to pass through all its phases and complete a Jewish lunar month.

If every month were exactly 29 days and 12 hours long, the months with 29 days and the months with 30 days could simply be alternated throughout the year, as they are in some years.

However, the 44 minutes and 3 seconds left over eventually add up to one day and this must be figured into the calendar. Accordingly, either or both of the second and third months, Cheshvan and Kislev, can have either 29 or 30 days, depending on a complicated "order" of the months and years. This gives us a Jewish year of either 353, 354, or 355 days and this is obviously much less than a full solar year. The discrepancy is taken care of by adding a full extra month, seven times in every nineteen years. This month is called *Adar Sheni* or *V'Adar*, both meaning "second Adar," and comes after the regular month of Adar in the third, sixth, eighth, eleventh, fourteenth, seventeenth and nineteenth years in the 19-year cycle. This extra month, Adar Sheni, has 29 days, but when it comes in any year, an extra day is added to the previous month, *Adar Rishon* (first Adar), to give it 30 days.

Thus a leap year with the added month can have 383, 384 or 385 days depending on the number of days in the preceding year. So we see that a Jewish year can be 353, 354, 355, 383, 384 or 385 days long.

If this sounds complicated, believe me, it is. You see, there is one additional factor in determining the length of the two changeable months which we have not yet mentioned: Rosh Hashana can never fall on a Sunday, Wednesday or Friday.

The reason for this is that if Rosh Hashana fell on a Wednesday or a Friday, Yom Kippur would fall on Friday or Sunday, that is to say, either preceding or following Shabbat. This would mean that we would not be able to prepare food, bury the dead or anything else of the sort for two full days, since all prohibitions applying to Shabbat also apply to Yom Kippur. If Rosh Hashana were to fall on Sunday, Hoshana Rabba would fall on Shabbat and we would not be able to have the Hoshana circuits in the synagogue (see chapter 31), nor would we be able to postpone Hoshana Rabba until the next day (because the next day is a full holiday, *Sh'mini Atzeret*, which in Israel includes *Simchat Torah* as well).

All adjustments to cover these exigencies are made in the first six months of the year so that the period between the first day of Nisan and the end of the year is always 177 days.

The fact is that the Jewish calendar is far more than a curiosity; it is a living reminder of our status as the chosen people. The Israeli journalist Moshe Kohn points out that "through the adjustments we must constantly make in our calendar so that, for example, Pesach always falls on the first full moon following the vernal equinox and Yom Kippur never falls on a Friday or a Sunday, we transform the "accidental" connection between us, the earth, the sun and the moon into a dynamic, creative relationship between all of us and between us and the Creator. . . . In Judaism, we the people control time, we fix the times."

He goes on to point out that the first commandment which was given to us to observe as a people is (Exod. 12:1-2), "This month is for you the first of the months," and quotes the Midrash to the effect that in this commandment, God handed over the ordering of time to man. Since this took place before the Jews left Egypt, he concludes, "our first step on the way to free, responsible peoplehood was the acquisition of control over time." And the instrument is the Jewish calendar.

The names of the Jewish months, in order, are:

Tishri: 30 days (September-October)
Cheshvan: 29 or 30 days (October-November). This
   month is also called *Marcheshvan.*
Kislev: 29 or 30 days (November-December)
Tevet: 29 days (December-January)
Shvat: 30 days (January-February)
Adar: 29 days except in leap year when it has 30
   (February-March)
Adar Sheni or *V'Adar*: 29 days (March-April)
Nisan: 30 days (March-April or April-May)
Iyyar: 29 days (April-May or May-June)
Sivan: 30 days (May-June or June-July)
Tammuz: 29 days (June-July)
Av: 30 days (July-August)
Elul: 29 days (August-September)

Equivalent months on the civil calendar can vary slightly. In other words Kislev on some years might cover December and the first day or so of January, and the same is true of the other months.

The date of the year on the Jewish calendar (at the time of writing 5738), marks the number of years since the creation of man on the sixth day of creation. This is gone into more fully in Chapter 54.

Appendix II is a section showing the Jewish calendar as it compares with the civil calendar for the years 1900 to 2000 C.E.

Appendix III is a chart showing the civil dates of the major holidays from 1975 to 1999 C.E.

Jewish writers, when giving non-Jewish dates, use the abbreviations B.C.E. (Before the Common Era) and C.E. (Common Era) where Christians use B.C. and A.D.

39

Eretz Israel

So much has been written about the Holy Land and its meaning to the Jewish people, both before and since the establishment of the State of Israel, that it would seem unnecessary to discuss the subject in a book such as this. Nonetheless, there are certain aspects of the *kibbutz galuyot*, the Ingathering of the Exiles, and the rebirth of the Jewish state that may benefit by clarification.

To begin with, in the view of Judaism, Eretz Israel is *our* land. We may welcome strangers to live in it as we were strangers in the lands that gave us shelter, but the Land belongs to us. How important this is is pointed out in the commentary of Rashi on the first verse of the Bible: "In the beginning, the Lord created the heaven and the earth." Rashi quotes earlier authorities to the effect that, since the purpose of the Torah is to teach us the commandments, the logical place to start it would be Exod. 12:1-2 which contains the first commandment that Israel, the chosen people, were expected to observe: "This month is for you the first of months." The reason the Torah begins instead with the words describing God's creation of the world is to justify the Jews' claim to the Holy Land. God created the world, they argue, and had the right to give any part of it to anyone He wished. Regarding the Holy Land, they say: "Of His own will He gave it to them and of His own will He took it from them and gave it to us."

In the "section of curses" God says: "I will bring the land into desolation" (Lev. 26:32). Two famous commentators, Rashi and the mystic Nachmanides (Rabbi Moshe ben Nachman, Spain, 13th century), observe that this is not a curse but a blessing. A contemporary saint, the late Rabbi Ahron Jeruchem, says: "This is a cheering message, a consoling prediction that no other nation will be able to reconstruct Eretz Israel." He points out that since the exile, a variety of different peoples were in possession of the Land and that all of them tried to inhabit it and cultivate it to no avail. "All their efforts to develop it failed, because strangers do not offer the proper climate for growing, for life in the land of Israel."

Secondly, taking up residence in the Land of Israel is a great mitzva. The actual wording of the commandment is found in Num. 33:53: "And you shall take possession of the land and dwell therein, for unto you have I given the land to possess it." The first part of the sentence appears to command us in positive terms to live in the Holy Land and the second part provides the reason for the views expressed above: that Israel is the Jews' and no one else's.

Nachmanides, the great Kabbalist and commentator, was the strongest advocate of considering these words a positive commandment. He backs up his views with an analysis of the famous incident of the spies, as told in the 13th and 14th chapters of Numbers and recalled by Moses in Deut. 1:21, where God tells the Jewish people: "Go up and possess it as the Lord has spoken to you." When they refused to go up as Moses reminded them, God said (Deut. 1:43), "you rebelled against the word of the Lord." This is a clear indication that what we are dealing with is a commandment.

I have gone into so much detail because two other famous commentators, Rashi and Maimonides, considered that what the text means is simply that if we want to dwell in the Land, we will have to go in and possess it. The words, according to them, are an admonition, not a commandment. As a result, residence in Israel does not figure on Maimonides' list of the 613 commandments. Modern Jewish thinking tends very much to favor Nachmanides' views. The mitzva of residence in Israel, *yishuv b'aretz*, is considered so important that its observance sometimes even seems to excuse transgressions of certain other commandments of the Torah. Much can be forgiven those who dedicate themselves to building the Land.

This explains the attitude of tolerance on the part of many or most religious people toward the irreligious and even antireligious *chalutzim*, or Pioneers. Modern Israel's first Chief Rabbi, Ha-Rav Kook, said, and quite accurately, that these young people were free of the idolatry, immorality and superstition which marked earlier rebels against the Torah. In his opinion, they suffer only a lack of perception which keeps them from seeing the truth of the Torah. He went further and said that their outward evil hides an inward holiness. The attitude of many religious Jews today is that we who live outside Israel have no right to find fault with the non-religious Israelis, because in the final analysis, they are there developing the Land and fighting in its defense, and we are not.

For the Jew who lives outside the Holy Land, there is no divided loyalty in his love for Israel. This is something which gave rise to confusion within Israel itself in the initial stages of its independence. Ben Gurion, against the advice of many of his fellow Zionists, issued an order in the first days of the War of Independence that all men in the fighting forces must take an oath of allegiance to the new state. Immediately, hundreds of Jewish volunteers from the United States made it clear that they would resign if forced to do so, since this would have meant abandoning American citizenship.

Americans have been accused of many things since 1776, but cowardice has never been one of them, and Ben Gurion, originally from Russia, which explains much, realized to his amazement that these men were perfectly willing to die for their Jewish motherland, but they were not willing to give up their American fatherland, in whose armed forces most of them had also served.

To a Jew from Tzarist Russia, who had never been allowed to consider himself a Russian, this attitude was totally unexpected. The decree was rescinded since the volunteers were desperately needed, but in succeeding military crises, Israel made it clear that no one who is not a citizen will carry a weapon.

Of course there are anti-Zionist and anti-Israel Jews. They are a tiny minority and represent completely opposed currents in Judaism. One such group is the American Council for Judaism, regarding whom Rabbi Leo Jung has observed that "they are un-American, un-Jewish and have no counsel of significance to offer." This minuscule coterie of extreme assimilationists is an unheard voice in Jewish life.

Quite different is the case of the opposite extreme in Judaism: the religious zealots who maintain that the establishment of a Jewish state in Palestine is a sin because we are obliged to wait until Messiah arrives for this to take place. These Jews, in their great majority Hungarian-speaking Chasidim from Transylvania, are headed by the Satmarer Rebbe, Rabbi Joel ("Yoilesh") Teitelbaum, who lives in the Williamsburg section of Brooklyn. In Israel these same Jews form an organization called the *Netorei Karta*, or Guardians of the City (Aramaic), mostly resident in the Mea Shearim quarter of Jerusalem. Among other things they refuse to recognize the State of Israel and refuse to speak Hebrew, claiming that it is a holy language which should be reserved only for prayer. Their daily speech is Yiddish, Hungarian or English. Small numbers of Jews with similar opinions who belong neither to the Satmar or Netorei Karta groups are to be found in Israel and other countries. Almost without exception they are Ashkenazim.

Religious Jews, although totally opposed to them on the issue of Israel, find themselves unable altogether to condemn them for the simple reason that, in their eyes, these people represent the hard core of Judaism. When everyone else forgets, *they* remember.

This fanatic and self-sacrificing dedication to the Torah as they interpret it, outweighs their aberrant refusal to recognize the State of Israel. It is felt that had it not been for Jews like them in past generations, Judaism as we know it would never have survived in Europe under the pressure that was exercised upon it. In a sense we honor our own forebears in them.

In their own way, say many religious Zionists, the Netorei Karta and the Satmarer Chasidim are as blind to reality as the leftist kibbutzniks who refuse to recognize the Torah. And, like those non-religious pioneers, they hide under their outward evil an inner holiness.

Pro- or anti-State of Israel, all observant Jews who live in Eretz Israel are obliged to observe an entire set of mitzvot that Jews outside the Land are aware of only academically. The principal one is that of taking *t'rumot* and *maaser,* the Priests' dues and Temple tithes, from all produce grown in the Land. This is done by taking from each species—fruit, vegetables, greens, and products made from them—a quantity amounting to a little over one one-hundredth and redeeming it against a coin set aside for that purpose. After the coin is used a certain number of times (depending on the value of the coin), it must be redeemed with a smaller coin and that coin destroyed and thrown away. The portion redeemed must be wrapped up and disposed of, not eaten.

In recent years this law has come to apply to people living outside Israel as well because of the large amount of food exported from Israel, which must have t'rumot and maaser taken from it, no matter where it is consumed. The genuinely observant Jew will make it a point to take maaser (as it is usually called) from any food that comes from Israel that does not have a hechsher on it stating that maaser has been taken. The number of times a coin may be used (and it must be local currency, not Israeli money) can be found out from any Orthodox rabbi. No blessing is said, since there is always the possibility that maaser has already been taken and the blessing would be said in vain, but a simple statement is made when the maaser is redeemed. It is perfectly acceptable to say it in English: "I herewith take maaser from each species in accordance with the Law."

No one need worry about Israeli wines, since all the major wineries that export their products are careful to take maaser from all their grapes.

Has the exile ended with the establishment of the State of Israel? In a sense it has, but in another and very important sense it has not. The general feeling is that as long as there is one Jew in the world who wants to come to Israel and cannot, the exile is not over. This explains why, even in Israel, at the Passover seder we say, "This year slaves, next year free; this year here, next year in the Land of Israel." As is the case with Jewish prayer, we speak not only for ourselves but for all Jews, including those in the U.S.S.R. and Syria.

40

Saints and Sinners

SAINTS, as the Catholic Church, for example, understands the term, are not really part of the Jewish experience. Nevertheless, among the Sephardim in particular, there are figures that come close to sainthood in the Roman Catholic sense, in that they are considered able to perform miracles after their death. I know of one Moroccan synagogue in Latin America in which there is a small room off to one side of the main men's section. In that room are several oil jars in which float burning wicks, placed there by people who have come to pray and ask certain favors. Behind each of the lamps, on a card, is written in Hebrew and Latin letters the name of a long-dead rabbi from Morocco, Spain or Palestine. The main difference between this scene and the lighting of candles for Catholic saints is the absence of idols or images; a great and fundamental difference to be sure, but the similarities are there as well.

Among both Ashkenazim and Sephardim there are still people who visit the graves of certain rabbis and leave messages written on paper there in the hope that the spirit or soul of the rabbi will come to their aid. By and large, however, when Jews speak of saints, they refer to living people.

Who are these living saints? Mostly they are Chasidic rabbis who are consulted by their followers in the hope that the rabbi, through his intercession, can procure for them a cure for illness, success in business or the resolution of family problems. Some of these "wonder rabbis" still have large followings, not only of Jews but even of Gentiles, who are convinced that their intercession will aid them.

Other Chasidic rabbis are quite genuine saints in the truest sense of the word, and are revered for their piety and learning. They have not permitted themselves to be turned into cult-objects by the credulous and superstitious. It is in no way inappropriate to refer to the Lubavitcher Rebbe, the Gerer Rebbe or the Bobover Rebbe, to name three, as saints. Their saintliness can be seen in their faces, and the miracle stories told of at least one of them by his followers are hardly necessary to convince even the casual acquaintance of the spirit of holiness that pervades even his simplest actions. There is nothing contradictory about the idea of living saints in Judaism, particularly when one remembers that the Hebrew word for saint is *tzaddik*, which means simply a man of justice.

The intercession of dead saints, however, is another matter, and there is a serious question as to whether the fundamental spirit of Judaism, which gives great value to the living and none to the dead in a spiritual sense, is not being violated. Although Ecclesiastes tells us that a live dog is better than a dead lion, and Jewish tradition firmly maintains that God values one live sinner more than a thousand dead saints; nevertheless, the pilgrimages made to the graves of dead saints, particularly in the Holy Land, cannot be condemned as a non-Jewish practice.

Of course the word saint as used here has little if anything in common with the Christian meaning of the word. Jewish saints are, without exception, men of great learning or at least men to whom great learning is ascribed, and their sainthood is based in large measure on this fact. Christian sainthood is based entirely on the fact that miracles are attributed to those who qualify as saints and that in every case the miracles must have taken place after the death of the person in question. Further, almost all saints of the Catholic Church, both men and women, were unmarried or, if married, had through widowhood or abandonment of their spouses ceased to live in marital relation with them, celibacy being seemingly almost an essential requisite for sainthood. An unmarried Jewish saint is an impossibility and none exists since an unmarried man is by definition a sinner.

As to sinners in general, the fundamental Jewish attitude is that no man is a complete sinner, without redeeming features, and that the possibility of *t'shuva*, repentance, is always present. The fact is that sin plays a relatively small part in Jewish religious thinking; the great emphasis is on mitzva. It is safe to say that for every one time the word *aveira*, sin, is heard in a Jewish lesson, discussion or sermon, the word *mitzva* is heard fifty times. The same applies to Jewish religious writing.

In a legal sense, sin and crime are fundamentally the same thing to the Jewish way of thinking, except that crime is a sin not only against God but against another man as well, and for that reason far more serious than a sin against God alone. As we read in the chapter on Yom Kippur, sins against one's fellow man are not pardoned by God on that day—until they are forgiven by the injured party.

The treatment of crime in Talmudic times by the Sanhedrin and the courts of the Jews has little place in this book since it has little practical application today, but it is worth noting that compensation, rather than retribution, was the basis of the law. In other words, where the Bible says "an eye for an eye," the Jewish law has always understood this to mean "the value of an eye for an eye." There was one exception and it is worth thinking about: the crime of murder was in no way subject to compensation, either in terms of money or penal servitude. The Jewish law states that no mercy must be shown to the murderer. Nonetheless it is a fact that while the Sanhedrin held the power of life and death over the Jews in the Babylonian exile and in Palestine for centuries, a Sanhedrin that passed more than one death sentence in a generation was known as a "murderous court." In modern Israel there is no death sentence except for the crime of participating in genocide and only one man, Adolf Eichmann, has received it.

As for the concept of original sin, that is that all men are born in a state of sinfulness, inherited, as it were, from Adam, this would seem so out of step with Jewish thinking as to be inconceivable. But the fact is that original sin *has* figured in Jewish thought and we see it, disguised, in the regulation that a stillborn male child or one who died shortly after birth, must be circumcised at the graveside before being buried; a custom rarely practiced these days. Original sin also appears in the writings and speculations of certain Kabbalists, who seem to have borrowed it from non-Jewish sources. In any event, most Jews have never heard of the concept and it has no importance.

Finally, to the Jew, sin consists entirely in overt action. The idea that it is possible to commit a sin in one's thoughts is foreign to Judaism. No matter what goes on in one's head, until one acts, no sin is committed. Of course the same applies to mitzvot as well; Jews place very little value on good thoughts or noble intentions—what counts is performance. As we noted in chapter 6, the Jew who says that the mitzvot don't count, all that really counts is having a "Jewish heart," has been influenced by Christianity. We call him a "Cardiac Jew" and, with his religion based on the "Jewish heart," he deserves no more serious a name.

41

The Afterlife,
the Messiah
and the Soul

ABOUT the only thing that can accurately be said about the Jewish concept of life after death is that Jews believe in it. But if you try to pin down just what form that belief takes, you are unlikely to meet with much that is universally applicable.

The fact is that when God gave us the Torah, He revealed to Moses how He wanted His commandments obeyed, but in the entire Torah there is not a single word which can literally be taken to refer to life beyond the grave or to a "world to come." In other words, God did not see fit to tell us anything at all about an afterlife, although many commentators have said that there is not a word in the Torah that does not contain a *remez*, or hint, about the world to come. Whether this is the case or not, the *p'shat*, or plain sense, of the Torah says nothing; everything said on the subject by commentators, rabbis, prophets, visionaries and mystics is *aggada*, speculation, and we are under no obligation to accept it, with the exception, according to most Orthodox authorities, of the doctrines concerning the Messiah and the resurrection of the dead, discussed below.

Rabbi Samson Raphael Hirsch expressed this in his usual forthright fashion and I have never seen his words improved on:

"... I have never found myself curious to inquire about *olam ha-ba,* the world after the resurrection of the dead, and related matters. For the reality of these matters ... is hidden from human vision. ... Whatever is said about them is no more than a guess, however close at what may be the truth, and there is no obligation upon Jews to know these and matters like them.

"... it is enough that we believe wholeheartedly in the words (Psalm 16:10), 'You will not leave my soul in perdition,' without enquiring into matters hidden from us and that no eye has ever seen."

The emphasis of Judaism is almost entirely on the observance of God's commandments in this world and living the way a Jew should live. What happens after death we leave in God's hands and He has revealed nothing concerning it.

We can set forth briefly those beliefs most widely held.

HEAVEN. This is usually called *Gan Eden*, or the Garden of Eden, and it is believed that the souls of the righteous have a place there. Actually, the Mishna, basing itself on Isaiah 60:21, says that "All Israel have a place in the world to come" (introduction to Abot) and the Talmud adds that the righteous of the Gentiles also have a place in the world to come.

HELL. In Hebrew, hell is called *Gehinnom*, from which comes our word, Gehenna. It is the general belief that no Jew is ever sentenced to more than a year there. After that, sin is purged and he goes on to Gan Eden. It is also a widely held belief that the Sabbath is so holy that Gehinnom is closed down on Shabbat and the souls suffering there are given a Sabbath respite.

JUDGMENT. It is believed that on dying, a Jew's soul ascends to a heavenly tribunal where an accusing angel and a defending angel weigh his sins and his mitzvot on a scale, deciding his destiny. To give an idea of the relative unimportance of sin compared to mitzva in the Jewish concept, there is a story about a great sinner who died and arrived at the heavenly tribunal to find the accusing angel piling sin after sin on the scales. When he had finished, the defending angel could find only one good deed: he had once saved a woman from drowning in a river, at the risk of his own life. The woman was put on the scales, but the sins still outweighed the mitzva. So the defending angel added the carriage the woman was riding in and even the horses that drew it, but the sins were still slightly heavier. Finally he threw in the mud on the carriage wheels and tipped the scales in favor of the petitioner.

REINCARNATION. In Hebrew, reincarnation is called *Gilgul Neshamot*, and a great many Orthodox Jews maintain that under certain circumstances, never very clearly defined, the soul of a Jew can return to life in the body of another person or even of an animal or a plant. It is not necessarily as a punishment that gilgul occurs, but often some good work that the soul was unable to accomplish while on earth is completed in that soul's reincarnation in another body.

Allied to this is the once common belief that the *ruach* (see below under soul) of a dead person can, for reasons of vengeance or other motives, take possession of the body of a living person. Such a malicious spirit is called a *dibbuk* and must be exorcised by a learned man. Judaism is by no means free of beliefs and legends picked up in its wanderings among the peoples of the world.

MESSIAH AND THE RESURRECTION OF THE DEAD. This is the most widely held belief of all and is considered by most Orthodox Jews to be an absolute article of faith. In brief, it is said that some day a Jew will appear who will announce the end of the world as we know it and the establishment of the kingdom of God, in which finally the lion will lay down with the lamb. This Jew, and he will be a person, not an incarnation of God, as if such a thing were possible, is called *Mashiach*, or Messiah. When he arrives there will be a resurrection of the dead, called in

Hebrew, *T'chiat Ha-metim*, and all the resurrected of the Jews will gather in Israel, there to live forever. Mashiach will be a descendant of the house of David and will be announced by Elijah the Prophet.

It is possible to hear it said that he who denies that the Torah makes direct reference to the world to come denies the Torah, and belief in the eventual arrival of Mashiach and the T'chiat Ha-metim is all but universal among religious Jews. Nevertheless, if one were to say, "While not denying what the sages have said, I have no belief concerning any aspect of the life after death or the world to come; all I believe is that my soul is in the hands of God and my faith is in Him," such a Jew would not be considered a heretic, even by the most pious. Much more important than speculation about the afterlife is the acceptance of the revelation of the Torah, which is entirely concerned with life and the living.

The Soul

Belief in the soul is not optional, it is *essential* to Judaism, as it is to every religious system known, even the most primitive. It is the soul, according to Jewish belief, that distinguishes man from the beasts, and the physical evidence of the soul is speech, possessed by all men and by no animals. This is more fully discussed in the last chapter of this book.

According to the belief of most reasonably well-educated Jews, the soul consists of three elements—*Nefesh*, *Ruach* and *N'shama:*

Nefesh. Nefesh is the spark that keeps human beings alive. When we speak of "preservation of life" for which almost all commandments may be disregarded, the Hebrew phrase is *pikuach nefesh*. By the same token, danger to life is called *sakanat n'fashot*. We must not think of the nefesh as simply a mechanical or animal life force; it also contains the personality of the human being, but seems to lack any purely spiritual quality, and the implication of the above phrases is that it dies with the body.

RUACH. Ruach is the spirit. The word actually means a wind or breath of air, and is used just as we use the word spirit in English. The Holy Spirit of prophecy, for example, is called the *Ruach Ha-kodesh*. As one of the components of the soul, it appears to survive the death of the body, but to what extent and for how long it is difficult to determine. The disembodied spirit that is believed to "possess" those afflicted with a dibbuk (see above) is the *ruach*.

N'SHAMA. N'shama is the "holy soul", that part of the human being which is eternal and which is possessed by all men but by no animals. The power of speech is centered in the n'shama as are the senses and the intellect. Jews agree that the eternity of the n'shama is a genuine eternity; that is to say, just as it will always exist, so has it always existed. This contrasts with the belief of the Christians that the soul comes into being at the moment of conception and is "eternal" from that point on. The Kabbalists in particular say that the souls of all men were present in the soul of Adam—clearly a being symbolic of mankind—by which is meant that the soul which man receives from God at the time of his birth has been waiting since eternity within God and will return to Him when physical life is ended.

This should not be understood to mean that the soul is a "piece" of God, in any sense. God, as we know, is indivisible; humans are humans, not God in any form, and there is no term in any language to describe the "gap" between God and man. Nevertheless, the soul that makes man human partakes of the divine.

This concept of the three-element soul we owe largely to the Kabbala and it explains so well those things that make us human as opposed to animal that it has achieved general acceptance. It remains, however, "aggada," and no Jew could possibly be called a heretic for not accepting it. What *is* basic to Judaism is the belief in an immortal soul given to us by God.

42

The Kabbala

THE literal meaning of the Hebrew word *kabbala* is "receiving" or "something received." In modern Hebrew it means any sort of receipt. We have already encountered it in the name of the Friday evening service, Kabbalat Shabbat. To the Jew it has the additional meaning of the mystic tradition in Israel, which for many centuries was indeed received by one adept from another and only a small fraction of which was written down.

By "mystic tradition" is meant, in broad terms, an attempt to understand the secret or hidden meanings of the Torah, speculation concerning the creation of the universe, comprehension of the way in which God manifests Himself in that creation, communication in as direct a form as possible with God through prayer, and finally, the regulation of the behavior and life of the mystic with the object of unifying the "upper worlds," through which God's creative force operates, and the "lower world" in which we live.

The Kabbala is by no means a unified doctrine or discipline, but an agglomeration of several mystic philosophies and methodologies, one of whose important objects is not the search for hidden worlds, but the understanding of the world we occupy right now.

To give an example: the question is asked, if God created the world out of nothing, where did the "nothing" come from, since before the Creation only God existed? Are we to understand that He created the universe out of His own "substance," as it were? The answer to this must obviously be no, but how do we explain the contradiction? The answer given us by the Kabbala is that when God decided to create the universe He "contracted" Himself and left a space occupied by nothing. From that void He created the universe. The Kabbalistic writers go on to prove that this contraction, or *tsimtsum*, as it is called in Hebrew, must not be understood in a literal or physical sense, but in a metaphoric sense. Many other contradictory puzzles such as the existence of evil in a world created by a "good" God are also the subject of Kabbalistic speculation.

For many centuries the book *Zohar* has been the most important document of the Kabbala and the most widely studied. It is written in Aramaic and first saw the light in Spain, around the year 1280 C.E. Although it was purportedly written by the Talmudic sage, Simeon Bar Yochai, a painstaking analysis of its language, style, vocabulary, grammar and contents by Professor Gershom Scholem would appear to indicate that its author was Rabbi Moses de León, who lived in Guadalajara, Castile. Whatever the case, the Zohar set forth in language of surpassing beauty and impressiveness the Kabbalistic ideas that were dominant at that time. The Zohar became so important that for centuries it took a place alongside the Bible and the Talmud as one of the three most important books in Judaism; fragments of it are today found scattered through the prayer rituals of both Ashkenazim and Sephardim.

After the expulsion of the Jews from Spain and about two hundred and fifty years after the Zohar first appeared, Rabbi Isaac Luria, an Ashkenazi who lived in Safed, Palestine, created a new doctrine of the Kabbala which is in many respects an extension of the Zohar but which takes a different direction. Today both the Zohar and the Lurian Kabbala, between which there is no conflict, form the basis of mystic thought among the Jews. A detailed examination of the ideas contained in either of these Kabbalistic systems is beyond the scope of this book and the capacity of its author, but the following observations may help place the Kabbala in general in the context of Judaism.

In the first place, the Kabbala is entirely Jewish. It is firmly based on the Torah and has as its underlying premise the fact that the Jews are the chosen people of God. There are no books of the Kabbala written by non-Jews, and no Kabbalist has ever been anything but a Jew, already learned in the Bible, Midrash and Talmud. Kabbala is, in a sense, the crown of a Jew's learning. After he has penetrated deeply into the Torah, then and only then may he undertake the study of the Kabbala.

Among the Ashkenazim there was, for centuries, a ruling that study of the Kabbala, particularly the writings of Luria's disciples, was forbidden to anyone under the age of forty, because it was considered dangerous before that grade of maturity and presumed knowledge of the Torah had been reached. The Sephardim permit the study of the Zohar at any age, but after the expulsion from Spain, Kabbala became to a fair degree the product of Ashkenazi thinkers. Sephardic or Ashkenazic, all Kabbalists are and always have been Jews; the idea of a non-Jewish Kabbalist is self-contradictory because the whole premise of the Kabbala is that Israel is the chosen instrument of God's will. Kabbala is a philosophy and a spiritual discipline in which Gentiles cannot participate in any meaningful sense.

Kabbala has never been the property of the Jewish masses, although many of its ideas have made profound impressions on everyday Jewish thought and life. Until recently, in fact, there was a generally accepted prohibition against translating works of the Kabbala out of Hebrew or Aramaic into current vernacular languages. This prohibition was recently lifted by the present Lubavitcher Rabbi, Menachem Mendel Schneersohn, who authorized English and other translations of the book *Tanya,* or *Likutei Amarim* (Collected Discourses), one of the most important modern Kabbalistic texts, written by Rabbi Schneor Zalman of Liadi, founder of the Lubavitch dynasty, and based to a large degree on Luria's Kabbala.

As this shows us, Kabbala is far from being a relic. No year passes that does not see the publication of new books, all of them in Hebrew, on the Kabbala. Rabbi Abraham Kook, who died in 1935, was at the same time Chief Rabbi of the Holy Land and one of Judaism's foremost Kabbalists, as well as a Zionist and a thinker of great practicality and liberalism.

The magical practices sometimes associated with the Kabbala have never been an important part of it. Kabbalistic amulets designed to ward off the evil eye and protect children from demons are still in vogue among some Sephardic communities, but by and large the Kabbala is and always has been the province of learned men who find in it a source of inspiration which strengthens their devotion to God and His chosen people and gives a greater meaning to their own lives.

There is a belief that Kabbala consists mostly of the search for hidden meanings in words by the calculation of their numerical value, and the discovery of words with a similar numerical value that explain the first words. This method is called *Gematria* (a Greek word) and is based on the fact that each Hebrew letter has a numerical equivalent. There is no question but that it is used to determine meanings which are otherwise obscure, even in the text of the Chumash, but the Kabbala is far more profound than that, and it is doubtful if any culture has produced a mystic philosophy of greater genuine depth although, as noted above, it is not a universal philosophy; it is restricted by its very nature to Jews and can have no meaning for Gentiles.

43

Education and Rabbinical Ordination

THE value Jews place on education requires no comment in a book written primarily for Jewish readers. What might be briefly examined is the traditional forms of Jewish education and their institutions.

CHEDER. Literally "a room," cheder in the United States usually means a Hebrew school in the larger cities to which children in the lower grades go in the afternoons when they get out of public school. Its curriculum consists mostly of the Hebrew language.

TALMUD-TORAH. A Talmud-Torah is a Jewish elementary school, in the United States often synonymous with cheder. Sometimes, however, it refers to a sort of Orthodox day-school where students study "English" courses in the morning and Hebrew in the afternoon. It contains only the elementary school grades.

YESHIVA. A yeshiva is often thought of as a sort of university or rabbinical academy. While it can be both, it is

more often neither. The immense majority of *yeshivot* are
Jewish secondary schools or high schools with perhaps one
or two years of college. In them the students, all males,
study the regular course required by the state Board of
Education, and dedicate the rest of their time to the study
of the Talmud. The language of religious instruction in
most Ashkenazi yeshivot continues to be Yiddish, even in
Israel. In Israel, North Africa and other places, Talmud
is the only subject taught in most yeshivot.

The usual age for entering a yeshiva is eleven or
twelve, by which time the student already knows Hebrew,
which he has studied in a Talmud-Torah. Most yeshiva
students in the United States receive a high school diplo-
ma from the yeshiva in which they study, but few of them
receive rabbinical ordination, called *s'micha* in Hebrew.
Actually s'micha is not the objective of yeshiva study, except in a few cases; most yeshiva students study the Torah, in this case the Talmud, for its own sake. Not all yeshivas even give s'micha, and a great many men who have
s'micha do not exercise as rabbis, but are simple businessmen, professionals or employees. I once belonged to a
Young Israel congregation in the United States in which
no less than fourteen members had s'micha! As a matter
of fact, it took the congregation several years to get a
man to come in as their official rabbi and it is not hard to
figure out why.

S'micha itself is, in a sense, the equivalent of a law degree in civil life except that it qualifies one to be not only
a lawyer, but a judge. It is given, after extensive examination, by a board of rabbis, and the subjects covered are all
in the realm of Jewish *law*; theology does not figure in a
s'micha examination. A man with s'micha should be able
to decide legal questions brought before him and should
have the inclination and ability to acquire further knowledge regarding the sources of Jewish law. In this regard,
Jews have an expression which non-Jews have great difficulty understanding: they will speak with admiration of a
man who "knows how to learn." It indicates that the man

in question is able to take difficult Talmudic texts and by dint of going to supplementary documents and the exercise of intelligence, reach a clear understanding of them; something not everyone is equipped to do. Of course, one of the reasons the phrase sounds strange is that in proper English it should be "knows how to study"; the word "learn," as used by Jews to mean the study of the Torah, is a direct borrowing from Yiddish, *lernen*, which means to study.

S'micha may also be given by a single rabbi to a student although this is not common today. Such documents as the *Sh'tar Gerut* (certificate of conversion to Judaism) and the *Gett* (Jewish divorce) must be executed by an Orthodox rabbi with the proper s'micha or they are not accepted by Orthodox communities nor by the State of Israel.

METIVTA. A metivta is an academy where higher studies in the Talmud, other religious literature and even the Kabbala, in some instances, are carried out. Students at a metivta already have s'micha and most of them are married. The most prestigious metivta in the United States is the famous Bet Medrash Gevoa in Lakeside, New Jersey.

RABBINICAL ACADEMIES. There are three institutions in the United States which can properly be called rabbinical academies, since their main function is to turn out men who will work as rabbis of congregations. These are the Yeshiva Yitzchak Elchanan, which is the rabbinical academy of Yeshiva University in New York and is Orthodox (albeit "modern" Orthodox); the Jewish Theological Seminary, also in New York, which is Conservative, and the Hebrew Union College in Cincinnati, which is Reformed.

Yeshiva Yitzchak Elchanan is called "modern" in that the language of instruction is English or Hebrew, and that, in addition to Talmudic studies, it gives courses which prepare the student for the task of acting as religious counselor, administrator, etc., of the congregation in which he will exercise. There are, to be sure, many students at Yitzchak Elchanan who study the Torah for its own sake as well.

The Jewish Theological Seminary, often referred to as The Schechter Seminary after its distinguished founder, Rabbi Solomon Schechter, is Conservative, but in former years gave its graduates an Orthodox s'micha. This appears to be the case no longer and neither a divorce nor a conversion prepared by a Conservative rabbi is acceptable to the Chief Rabbinate of Israel.

The Hebrew Union College does not give s'micha as such, but confers a rabbinical ordination which enables the possessor to officiate in Reformed congregations.

JEWISH DAY SCHOOLS. There is an increasing tendency in the United States to found schools in which the regular state board of education curriculum is taught together with a fairly intensive Jewish curriculum, emphasizing Hebrew, Jewish history and religion. These schools differ from the yeshivas in that Talmud is not studied, the language of instruction for all courses is English and the schools are co-educational. In Latin America these schools are even more common and a higher percentage of Jewish children attend them. They range in orientation from Orthodox to left-wing Socialist. While Yiddish is not taught in day schools in the U.S.A., it remains a required course for Ashkenazic children in most of the Latin American schools, since it is still an important language south of the border.

The real reason most parents insist that their children attend such schools is fear of intermarriage. How real and well founded this fear is need not be commented on to North Americans, except to mention that intermarriage is less common in Latin America than in the North, and much of the credit must go to the Jewish day schools.

BETH JACOB SCHOOLS. These are Orthodox schools, for girls only.

SUNDAY SCHOOLS. Reform and Conservative congregations will often have Sunday schools in addition to the weekly after-public-school Hebrew classes. Jewish history and the holidays form the main part of the curriculum, and in many congregations, the teachers are volunteers who not only are not professionally prepared to teach, but often are ignorant of most aspects of Judaism as well. Of course, there are Reform and Conservative congregations that make every effort to obtain highly qualified teachers for their Sunday schools.

44

Orthodox, Conservative and Reform

In the United States, Jews are divided into three main religious sectors: Orthodox, Conservative and Reform. There are divisions within these groups as well, but they are of little practical importance. In Latin America and the rest of the world, almost all Jews are Orthodox, in classification if not in practice, although the equivalent of Conservative and Reform congregations do exist, particularly in Canada and the U.K. and, increasingly—as regards Conservative congregations—in Latin America.

ORTHODOX

Orthodox Jews are also called Torah-true. They accept the revelation of the entire Torah, both written and oral, by God to Moses, and the obligation of Jews to observe the commandments contained in the Torah, as well as the enactments of the rabbinical courts of their own tradition. As noted above, the majority of Jews the world over are Orthodox although the degree of observance may vary. The strange term "non-observant Orthodox" has been coined in the United States to describe Jews who do not observe all the commandments but who are, nevertheless, married in and buried out of Orthodox congregations. As odd and self-contradictory as "non-observant Orthodox" may be, it does serve a useful descriptive purpose.

Among the Orthodox Ashkenazim there is a division into Chasidim and Mitnagdim. The Chasidim belong to a sect founded around the middle of the eighteenth century by a Polish-Ukrainian holy man named Israel Ben-Eliezer, called the Baal Shem Tov. *Baal Shem* means "master of the Name" and refers to a supposed ability to perform miracles by the invocation of a secret name of God, known only to the adept. *Baal Shem Tov* means "Good *Baal Shem*." The Baal Shem Tov's doctrine was one of joy in being a Jew, joy in observance of the commandments and joy in living a Jewish life. This is an extreme simplification of Chasidism, which has reached heights of religious experience unsurpassed in history, but it must serve us for the moment.

The Baal Shem Tov's immediate disciples came to be known as Tzaddikim, or saints, and founded dynasties which, in many cases, passed to their sons and sons-in-law after their deaths. Miracles were and still are attributed to these Tzaddikim, called *Rebbes*, who are invariably known by the name of the European town or village which was the center of their dynasty. Many if not most Chasidim would have difficulty in identifying Rabbi Samuel Taub, for example, but if the same man were referred to as the Modzhitzer Rebbe, recognition would be instantaneous, not only by Chasidim but by many Mitnagdim as well. The Modzhitzer Rebbe's melodies are famous all over the Jewish world.

Chasidism is by no means a movement of the past, but appears to be gaining strength after a long period of decline. In present day Orthodoxy, one of the most influential groups is that of the Lubavitcher Chasidim, under the leadership of the brilliant and scholarly Lubavitcher Rebbe, Menachem Mendel Schneersohn. Their methods are modern, their organization excellent and their "missionaries," schools and institutions are to be found in Jewish communities the world over from Zurich to Sydney. At one time there were fourteen Lubavitcher schools, mostly teaching a combination of a trade and the Torah, in North Africa alone. In the

Soviet Union, hidden Hebrew schools are being operated in small apartments and cellars in defiance of the government; it is the Lubavitcher organization that keeps them going.

In our days, the Chasidim are considered the most conservative and even reactionary element in Judaism. This is ironical, since at the time of their origin, they were considered dangerous radicals and heretics and were even placed under a ban by some of the prominent rabbis of their time. To these enemies of their movement they gave the name of Mitnagdim, or Opponents, and it is by this name that non-Chasidic Ashkenazim are known to this day. The enmity that at one time existed between Chasidim and Mitnagdim, however, is today a thing of the past.

With certain exceptions, the Chasidim tend to maintain their traditional forms of dress (see chapter 24) and to segregate themselves into close if not closed communities. They pray according to the so-called *Nusach S'phard*, a modified Sephardic order of prayer which is different from both the ritual of other Ashkenazim and that of the Sephardim of Spanish and Levantine extraction. The *Nusach Ashkenaz* is found today mostly in German, Lithuanian and White Russian congregations.

Sephardim are almost one hundred percent Orthodox and each Sephardic community has its own variations on their general customs and traditions.

CONSERVATIVE

Conservative Jews are those whose congregations belong to an organization called the United Synagogue. Thirty years ago (1948), Professor Boaz Cohen of the Jewish Theological Seminary could say: "As I understand it, Conservative Judaism is dedicated to the proposition that Jewish law as embodied in the sacred Scriptures, interpreted in the Talmud, and elaborated in the subsequent halachic writings is binding upon every Jew."

At that time, the most immediate difference between a Conservative and an Orthodox congregation was that men and women sat together and the sheliach tzibbur faced the congregation instead of the Ark and Jerusalem. Apparently worried about an already emerging tendency in the Conservative movement,

Professor Cohen made the forceful statement that ". . . we must not allow the Conservative movement to degenerate into a sect, party, or faction as far as Halacha is concerned. There must not be, e.g. a Conservative law on Kashrut, the Sabbath, or Gittin* in contrast to the Orthodox law on the same subject."

Since that time, what Professor Cohen inveighed against has, quite undeniably, come to pass. A Conservative law has come into existence which is directly opposed to Orthodox law and we find that women are being called up to the Torah in many if not most Conservative synagogues and that serious consideration is being given to the "ordaining" of women rabbis. More divergent still is the Conservative position on travel on the Sabbath. Orthodoxy prohibits it except where necessary to preserve life or aid a dangerously ill person or in defense of one's country. Conservatives, however, say that if one must drive to get to the synagogue on Shabbat, it is permissible to do so.

The Orthodox attitude is that you make a point of living in a house or apartment within walking distance of a synagogue. If it isn't within walking distance, you don't take the dwelling. This more or less sums up the difference between the two ways of looking at beng Jewish: the Orthodox adjust their lives to the demands of living like a Jew according to the Torah, while the Conservatives, to a certain degree only, seek to adjust the Torah to the demands of living among the Gentiles.

REFORM

The Reformed Jews take a radical approach in which they declare that revelation is not central to belief, and that even the commandments given in the Torah can be discarded if they conflict with the demands of modern living. To be more exact, Reformed Jews tend to believe that God may have revealed *Himself* to Moses, but deny that He revealed the Torah as an eternal covenant with His people. This has been supplemented with the assertion that, while we are obliged to observe those commandments whose nature is *ethical*, we are at liberty to disregard com-

*Divorce

mandments governing diet, Sabbath observance, ceremony, and the like.

The Reform desire to adjust themselves to the times in which they live has led to some strange and embarrassing conclusions. To give one example: all references to return to the Holy Land and the reestablishment of a Jewish state in Palestine were expunged many years ago from the Reform prayer book. The reason for this was that in the stated opinion of Abraham Geiger—an opinion fully endorsed by Reform Jewry—the hopes of restoration of a Jewish state in Palestine as well as the Ingathering of the Exiles in Israel are extinct in our consciousness. To express such hopes, said Geiger, compiler of the most widely accepted prayer book in use in the past century, would be a lie. Rabbi Kaufman Kohler, at the time Chairman of the Central Conference of American Rabbis (Reform), went even further when, in praise of David Einhorn, whose prayer book forms the basis for the Union Prayer Book used in almost all Reform congregations, he said: "Every lie uttered in prayer is blasphemy before God's throne, be it the antiquated belief in resurrection or the hope for a return to Jerusalem." How the members of congregations that pray from such books are adjusting to the reality of the State of Israel and the fact that they, who gave up all hope of seeing our Homeland restored to us, were wrong while millions of Jews who never gave up hope for a minute were right, I do not know. That they have managed to make such an adjustment is a matter of undeniable fact, however, because support of Israel in both money and activity by Reform Jews is in no way inferior to that of other Jews: a justifiable motive of pride.

In a more general sense it is difficult to say much about what Reform does stand for, because it appears that each congregation is able to make its own laws, regarding even the most fundamental things. A few years ago we were subjected to the spectacle of the "rabbi" of a Reform congregation in a large city who made a public declaration that he was an atheist and did not believe in the existence of God. He was defended in this ludicrous act by most of the members of his congregation. Of course such examples of extreme behavior cannot be taken as typical of Reform Judaism, but the fact that they are tolerated makes it hard to give any universally applicable definition of the Reform movement in strictly Jewish terms.

Nevertheless, it should not for a moment be thought that Reform Jews are any less Jewish in the basic sense than their more observant brethren. Some of them may have gotten close to the edge of giving up Judaism entirely (and as far as that goes, so have some Orthodox Jews), but until they do they are full-fledged Jews and the Orthodox would be the first to assert that fact.

45

Conversion to Judaism

THE Jews do not maintain, nor are they interested in, missionary activity except among themselves. Historically this has not always been so, but for over a thousand years it has. Behind this attitude is the belief that there is no reason why anyone should want to become Jewish who is not already Jewish.

A well-known case in point is that of Aimé Pallière. Pallière, who died in 1944, was a French Roman Catholic, originally trained for the priesthood, who became convinced through his studies that Judaism was the only way of life possible for him. He approached the great Sephardic rabbi, Elie Benamozegh of Leghorn (Livorno), and asked him to instruct him in Judaism with a view to converting. To his surprise, Rabbi Benamozegh discouraged him, telling him that if he wished to be a brother to the Jews, he could do so within his own tradition.

Pallière became a disciple of Rabbi Benamozegh and a learned scholar of Hebrew, Jewish law and Jewish philosophy. He was the editor of a Jewish magazine, a member of the Central Committee of the French Zionist Organization and the author of innumerable speeches, articles and books which preached the eternal truth and values of Judaism. Although usually thought of and referred to as a convert, the fact is that Aimé Pallière never underwent formal conversion, because his master, Elie Benamozegh, had convinced him that it was not necessary that he do so.

Aimé Pallière was a man of exceptional brilliance, guided by a rabbi of even greater intellectual capacity. Simpler people than Pallière have reached the conclusions he did, and their burning desire to share the peoplehood of Israel has not been quenched by the repeated refusals of the rabbis to whom they have gone. Such people are eventually accepted and undergo conversion. There is a Jewish tradition that their merit is even greater than those who were born Jews.

The process of conversion follows a well-established pattern; there is nothing spontaneous about it. A non-Jew wishing to convert to Judaism must, by Jewish law, be refused twice. The third time he petitions, if there is a third time, his sincere conviction is accepted. In such a case the rabbi to whom he has gone will give him instruction, assign reading matter and tell him to find a Hebrew teacher so that he may pray with the congregation.

In the case of a male, once he has satisfied the rabbi that he knows enough about Judaism to become a Jew, he must undergo circumcision. Since he is an adult, this is usually, in our times, done in a hospital with a three-man *bet din*, or rabbinical court, in attendance, to make sure the circumcision is carried out properly by the attending physician. On recovering from the operation, there remain only the final steps of immersion in a *mikva* (see chapter 14) and the simultaneous acceptance of the commandments, or *kabbalat mitzvot*, both in the presence of a bet din. If the man is already circumcised, which is quite common these days, a drop of blood called the *dam ha-brit*, or "blood of the covenant," is taken from the place where his foreskin was. This is done by a *mohel* on the instructions of a rabbi and no special blessings are said. It is at this time, however, that the convert-to-be indicates what Hebrew name he will take.

In the case of a woman, the procedure is the same except, of course, that there is no circumcision. She is rejected, finally accepted after the third time she petitions, is given instruction, taught some Hebrew, accepts the commandments and is immersed in the mikva. Since she must be completely naked for this immersion, it obviously cannot take place in the presence of a bet din. Accordingly, the bet din remains outside the mikva and the immersion is overseen by a reliable female witness within, who reports to the bet din that everything was done correctly. After the conversion ceremony has been completed, the rabbi writes a *sh'tar gerut*, or certificate of conversion, which is the proselyte's proof of his Jewish identity, and which he will require to get married, emigrate to Israel as a Jew, etc. The State of Israel will not accept a sh'tar gerut which was not written by an Orthodox rabbi and will not accept as a Jew any convert who cannot produce one.

Regarding those who wish to convert to Judaism for the purpose of marrying a Jew, technically this is not possible but in practice most conversions are made for this reason. It is not within the compass of this book to discuss when and under what circumstances such a conversion may be made, but it can be said that the inclination is to interpret the law liberally. One thing should be carefully noted, however: a Cohen may not marry a *gyoret*, or woman convert to Judaism, although the daughter of a Cohen may marry a *ger*, or male convert.

As far as the conversion of a child goes, this is usually deemed impossible, since Jewish law states that it is permissible to do someone a favor in his absence, but to do him a disfavor is not permitted. Since a minor child is considered absent in the sense that he is not able to decide complex questions on a rational basis, he may not be converted to Judaism, even at the request of one of his parents, since sad experience has shown that being a Jew is anything but favorable much of the time. The adoption of non-Jewish children by Jews is discouraged, but in these times there are almost no Jewish children and childless couples will take the course of adopting Gentile infants. Regarding the conversion of such children, a particularly learned Orthodox rabbi must be consulted, preferably before the adoption takes place.

By Jewish law we are not permitted to try to talk anyone into becoming Jewish. This applies even to one of the partners in a mixed marriage; the Jewish spouse is not allowed to attempt to convert the non-Jew to Judaism. If a desire for conversion is expressed by the non-Jewish spouse, however, we are by no means required to discourage it, as we would be in other circumstances. It is equally prohibited to try to convince a non-Jewish son-in-law or daughter-in-law to convert.

Once conversion is brought about, the convert is a Jew in every sense. This is made particularly clear in Maimonides' answer to the question of whether a ger could use the phrase "God of my fathers" in the prayers. The answer was that Abraham is the father of a ger, just as he is the father of a Jew. For this reason, *gerim*, in place of their non-Jewish father's name, use the name Abraham. A ger may take any Hebrew name he wishes, but women usually take the name Ruth, herself a convert.

Any children born to a gyoret, a female convert, are Jewish by birth and require no further conversion.

46

Apostasy

You will sometimes hear it said that a man's religion is no one's business but his own, and his opinions must be respected, even if he wishes to abandon his ancestral faith and adopt a new one. Whether this statement is true of others it is not the purpose of this book to examine: it has never been true of Jews.

A Jew's religion is not only his own business; up to a certain point it is every Jew's business and he has no more right to abandon it than a soldier has the right to abandon his comrades in the middle of a battle because of "sincere" conviction that the enemy is right. Such a man is considered a traitor and treated like one. Perhaps the best illustration of the Jewish attitude is found in a famous parable from the Talmud: A shipwreck occurred and the people saved themselves in a lifeboat. Suddenly, one of those aboard noticed that another man had an auger and was drilling a hole into the floor of the boat. He immediately cried out to him to stop what he was doing and the driller answered: "What are you yelling about? I'm only drilling under my own seat."

M'shumad, or apostate, is an ugly word in Jewish speech. As

319

we have seen in the laws on mourning, a m'shumad is not buried in a Jewish cemetery nor is he mourned by his family. On the contrary, his brothers are supposed to celebrate his death as the demise of an enemy of Israel.

As is the case with such laws in Judaism, the interpretations placed upon them are not always quite so rigid. A m'shumad is often buried in a Jewish cemetery, but in a special section apart from the rest of the graves; there is, however, no formal mourning for him. In former times a m'shumad was considered to be anyone who openly defied the commandments; anyone who publicly ate pork or violated the Sabbath, for instance. In our times, the word m'shumad has come to mean a person who formally abjures Judaism and adopts another religion, usually through baptism. If he does not do both these things, he is not a m'shumad and may be buried in a Jewish cemetery and mourned for, since it is felt that no matter how flagrant his violations of the Torah, he may have repented before he died and in addition, may have been a victim of mental imbalance. Once he is baptized and makes a public declaration that he is a member of another religion, however, he is an outcast, although legally in many respects he remains a Jew.

Marriage to a non-Jew is no longer considered to be a proof of *shmad*, or apostasy, since most such marriages take place under civil law and even those celebrated in a church do not usually require that the Jewish spouse adopt the religion of the non-Jew. This is true even of the Roman Catholic Church and has ever been so.

Actually, Jewish law recognizes more than one type of apostasy. Those who convert for reasons of money, prestige or passion are quite different from those who do so out of spite or hatred. The former are despised, but the latter are held to be enemies of Israel and we are not even permitted to help them in time of distress as we would an ordinary non-Jew.

In all laws concerning marriage, the rule is, "once a Jew, always a Jew." This means that if a woman becomes an apostate, any children born to her will still be Jewish, even if they are born after her apostasy. It also means that if a Jewish woman is married to an apostate, she must get a Jewish divorce from him in order to be free to remarry. If an apostate dies without children, his widow is obliged to go through the *Chalitza* ceremony (see chapter 13) with his brother in order to be able to marry again.

One of the basic laws of the State of Israel is the Law of Return, under which any Jew residing in the Land may claim Israeli citizenship. On March 18, 1979, the Supreme Court of the State of Israel handed down a ruling in the case of a woman member of the Jews for Jesus movement, that since she had converted to Christianity she can no longer be considered a Jew and is accordingly not eligible for Israeli citizenship under the Law of Return, despite having been born a Jew.

47

A Jewish Miscellany

THERE are a few subjects, some of importance, others perhaps less so, that do not seem to fit into the rest of this section. I have explained them here because they are uniquely Jewish and because Jews ask about them.

PRONUNCIATION OF GOD'S NAME

In chapter 16 it was mentioned that God's Name is never to be pronounced by Jews. This refers specifically to the Name spelled with the Hebrew letters yud, heh, vav and heh, and usually rendered into English as Jehovah or, by some scholars, Yahweh. Both of these pronunciations are forbidden and Jews must never say them aloud. In prayers the word *Adonai* (Lord) is substituted, but even this name may not be used except in prayer. In conversation or discussion, God is referred to, even when speaking English, as *Ha-Shem* (The Name). Of course other circumlocutions such as The Creator, The Lord, etc., are often heard.

The other Name of God which appears most commonly in the

Bible is *Elohim*, which is usually translated as The Lord. We may pronounce this Name as it is spelled, but only in prayer. In other contexts, such as when reading or quoting from the Bible, we distort it slightly by substituting *k* for *h* and saying "Elokim." The same is true of the name *El*, which we pronounce as *Kel*, when it is not included in a prayer. In writing, observant Jews spell any reference to God in incomplete form, namely G-d, or the L-rd. I have not done so in this book only because I felt it would distract the reader.

The reason for this avoidance of God's Name is dual. In the case of speech, we are commanded not to take the Name of the Lord in vain. To avoid any possibility of breaking this commandment, we never pronounce the Name of the Lord. In addition, the Name of God as it is written with the four letters is prohibited in speech by the Oral Torah: it was pronounced only once a year, by the Cohen Gadol, or High Priest, on Yom Kippur in the Temple in Jerusalem. As for writing it, we fear that the paper on which it is written might be put to undignified use and thus desecrate the Name. For this reason, all old and no longer useable books and documents on which the Name appears in Hebrew should be buried in a specially consecrated place, called a *geniza*. In most communities, the geniza is in the Jewish cemetery.

STATUARY AND IMAGES

Replicas of the statuary of the Greeks, many of them representing gods and goddesses such as Aphrodite, Mercury, etc., are widely available. May an observant Jew have them in his house as a decoration? The extremely observant reject them and any carved or molded figures of human beings, but many Jews feel there is nothing objectionable about them since the gods they represent are no longer worshiped by anyone. Nonetheless, there are strictures against possessing such images and a means of making them acceptable does exist. If the nose of the statue is broken—even a chip or scratch will do—it may remain in the possession of even an observant Jew.

HOUSEWARMING

The inauguration of a new house is called in Hebrew, *Chanukat Ha-bait*, and it is customary to celebrate it. Really, there is no fixed ritual or ceremony, but on purchasing the house or completing its construction, one must say the blessing, *Shehecheyanu* (appendix IV), even before making use of it. When it is ready to live in, a mezuza must be affixed to the doorpost. It is usually at this time that the celebration is held. The owner of the house should recite Psalms 15, 101, 121 and 30 in that order, unless his tradition is different, in which case he should do as his people have done in the past. If he does not handle Hebrew well, it is all right to say the Psalms in English. In many communities it is customary to invite the rabbi to the house for the chanukat ha-bait, since he will know the prayers and ceremonies locally used. It is also a universal custom that those invited bring bread and salt as symbolic gifts to ensure prosperity and happiness.

TATTOOING

Tattooing is forbidden in the Torah (Lev. 19:28). Commentators have said that the flesh should have no mark other than that of the covenant: circumcision. Those Jews who carry on themselves a number tattooed by the Germans should not attempt to have it removed, however.

WHISTLING

Whistling is considered "not Jewish" by traditionally oriented Jews and it is definitely improper to whistle inside the synagogue. The disfavor with which whistling outside the shul is looked upon by some Jews is usually attributed to the fact that the non-Jewish peasants in Russia and Poland were given to whistling and we do not imitate them because of the commandment forbidding us to follow the customs of the Gentiles (Lev. 20:23). The other explanation which I have been given is that the Temple in Jerusalem was destroyed because of *sinat chinam*, groundless hatred between Jews. After it was destroyed the Jewish sectarians whose hatred had brought it down walked over the ruins, whistling to show their happiness. There is no law against whistling; just a custom which, except inside the synagogue, and on Tisha B'av, need not be taken too seriously.

FINGERNAILS

The Jewish law is that when one cuts one's fingernails, the clippings must be kept and burned together with a piece of wood. Nevertheless, the custom in our day is simply to flush them down the toilet. There is a well-established custom that the nails should not be cut in sequence from thumb to little finger, but in a staggered order of some sort. In actual fact, burning the clipped fingernails is less a law than a legal precaution: in the case of a woman who is menstrually unclean, it is feared that her husband or another person might touch or (in the mikva) step on the clippings and become unclean in turn. In the case of the man, we have a Kabbalistic tradition that it is dangerous for a pregnant woman to step on fingernail clippings since they are impure. As for cutting them in a staggered order, I have never heard any sort of explanation. The very observant do tend to look on burning the clippings as a law.

MENTIONING STRANGE GODS

Jews have always been clear on the point that God is one and there are no other gods. Nevertheless, the first of the Ten Commandments says, "You shall have no other gods . . ." and to protect this commandment we seek to avoid even mentioning the names of false gods. For this reason, the very observant will not pronounce the name of the founder of Christianity. He is referred to in Hebrew as *oto-ha-ish*, meaning "that man." In Yiddish he is called Yashke, Yashke Bubik or Yoshke. The crucifix is called a *tzelem*, or image.

WARDING OFF EVIL

Jews, when mentioning the possibility of something evil, will automatically say, *"chas v'shalom!,"* *"cholila!"* (A.) or *"chas v'chalila!,"* all of which mean, "Heaven forbid!" When complimenting a child it is thought proper to say *"Imbeshreer"* (Y.: unbewitched), or *"kein ayin hora,"* (no evil eye)—which has become corrupted into *"k'naina hora"* or even *"kinnehora."* The same is true when asking about or mentioning someone's age. One will say, particularly of a child, "He is seven years old, kein ayin hora." In the case of an older person we often hear, "I am forty-five, *biz hindert un tzvantzig"* (Y.: until one hundred and twenty). It is assumed that everyone wants to live to that age, which was Moses' age when he died. These harmless superstitions are the verbal equivalent of knocking on wood.

OTHER COMMON PHRASES

The expressions "with God's help" or "if God wishes" are common when a Jew speaks about something yet to happen. The Hebrew ways of saying them, also commonly heard, are *"b'ezrat ha-Shem"* and *"im yirtzeh ha-Shem,"* the latter expression commonly being corrupted in Yiddish into *"mirtzeshem."* Observant Jews on making an appointment or promising something for a future time will say, *"b'li neder,"* meaning literally, "without vowing," to avoid the appearance of taking a vow. When mentioning an enemy of the Jewish people one utters the phrase *"y'mach sh'mo"* (May his name be blotted out) after his name. In the case of one dead, Hitler or Stalin, for example, the phrase is *"y'mach sh'mo v'zichrono"* (May his name and memory be blotted out). In the case of more than one person, we say *"y'mach sh'mom."* The idea of loving one's enemies is considered unrealistic by the Jews, just as it is by many Christians, with the difference that the Jews don't pretend to accept it.

COUNTING JEWS

It has always been considered improper and, by some authorities, forbidden, to count heads among Jews, even for the purpose of determining if there is a minyan present for the saying of Kaddish or other prayers. Accordingly, when counting the Jews in a room, it is customary to substitute for the numbers "one, two, three," etc., the words of the ninth verse of Psalm 28: *"Hoshia et amecha u-varech et nachalatecha u-r'em v'nasem ad ha-olam"* (Save thy people and bless thine inheritance and tend them and carry them forever). In Hebrew, of course, the verse has ten words. It is also common to hear, in Yiddish, "Not one, not two, not three," etc. (Nit ein, nit zvei, nit drei . . .). This rule, or very strong custom, applies only to counting Jews who are physically present. It is based on an interpretation of Exod. 30:12, "That there shall be no plague amongst them when you count them." This is taken to mean that counting will bring a plague among those who are counted.

PART
IX

Seen Through Jewish Eyes

48

The Gentiles

THE subject of a Jew's relations with non-Jews is an important one. There exist well-defined laws and regulations covering most aspects and perhaps it would be best to discuss them one at a time.

Business with Gentiles

Starting with the Torah (Deut. 24:17) which prohibits us from prejudicing the judgment of the stranger, there are innumerable laws obliging us to treat all men on an equal basis. The Talmud (Chullin 94a) says, "It is forbidden to deceive people and this includes Gentiles." The classical rabbinical commentaries go further and say that a Jew who steals from or cheats a Gentile commits a greater sin than if he cheated a Jew, because he also desecrates God's Name. Medieval and modern authorities have also repeated this command in many forms: Jew and Gentile must be treated alike in all business and personal dealings in which honesty is involved.

Marriage with Gentiles

Marrying a Gentile is totally forbidden. If it takes place, however, the couple are considered married and their children legitimate. As explained in chapter 1, only if the mother is Jewish is the child Jewish.

Eating with Gentiles

Observant Jews will not eat at the table of a Gentile because the food is not kosher, nor, for that matter, will they eat at the table of a nonobservant Jew, for the same reason. It is perfectly proper for a Gentile to eat at the table of a Jew, however.

Drinking with Gentiles

Very observant Jews will not drink in the company of Gentiles and in particular, will not share wine with a Gentile. This is due to the fact that wine is an important element in religious ceremonies, our own and those of the Gentiles who practice *avoda zara,* or idol worship (literally "strange worship"), and the Gentile might be pledging his gods as he drinks. This leads us to the next point, and quite a difficult one.

Are Modern Gentiles Idol Worshipers?

The answer to this question is full of contradictions. The great rabbinical judges and authorities in both medieval and modern times have stated clearly that in our day the Gentiles are *not* to be considered idol worshipers. What this means is that all the numerous Talmudic prohibitions against associating with idol worshipers, greeting them on their holidays, doing business with them under many circumstances, and a long series of restrictions of business and personal relationships with them do not apply to the Gentiles of today. This is accepted; we are obliged by Jewish law to visit their ill and help their poor, etc.

Once we get out of the area of friendship and business, however, it is obvious that to the Jewish way of thinking, many of today's Gentiles are still worshipers of idols. The use of devotional images in Christian churches is ingeniously explained away by orthodox Jewish thinkers, but Jews are still stringently prohibited from entering churches in which such images are displayed (Shulchan Aruch, Yoreh Deah 142:14). Certainly the practices of present day Hindus and Buddhists must be considered idol worship or the term has no meaning at all. In addition, the prohibition of *yayin nesech*, wine made by Gentiles (see chapter 21), is based entirely on avoidance of *avoda zara*. If some of the Gentiles are not idol worshipers, why does this prohibition continue to be obligatory for all observant Jews?

There is, however, an important reason for not making apparent our attitude in this respect and that is *darchei shalom*, keeping peace, between the Jews and the peoples of the world, among whom they live. A closely related reason is our natural wish to avoid offending others. It is also a fact that by no means all images are idols. There is nothing wrong with a Jew laying a wreath before a statue of George Washington on a national holiday, for example.

Observance of Christian Holidays

Jews are not permitted to observe Christian holidays. This does not include civic holidays such as Independence Day (July Fourth), nor does it include the civil-religious holiday of Thanksgiving, which Jews have as much or more reason to celebrate as non-Jews. There is an important commandment (Lev. 20:23) which orders us not to follow the customs of the Gentiles. This commandment is referred to as the *chukot ha-goy* and is sometimes used to reason that while we should observe Thanksgiving, we should not celebrate it with turkey and cranberry sauce, since this would be a violation of the chukot ha-goy prohibition. Rabbis of unquestionable Orthodoxy have stated that this would be a foolish extension of the commandment and that the Jew who refrains from eating kosher turkey on Thanksgiving for this reason denies himself and his family a legitimate pleasure, because the chukot ha-goy applies only to customs and laws related to idol worship and Thanksgiving is not even suspected of any such connection.

The case of Christmas, however, is entirely different. Jews whose children attend public schools are obliged to inform both the school authorities and their children's teachers that their children are not permitted to participate in Christmas activities of any sort, including singing Christmas carols.

During the years I lived in the Midwest in a small city and my children attended the local public schools, I took the above described course as did many other Jewish families, and I do not know of a single case of embarrassment or discomfort resulting from it.

Now does this mean that Jews should attempt to force the prohibition of Christmas activities in public schools? It is my personal opinion that they should not. Apart from the previously mentioned darchei shalom, the fact is that despite the separation of church and state, Christmas is part of the national folklore, and Christian children should not be deprived of their holiday, as long as no attempt is made to involve non-Christian children.

Of course the prohibitions for Jews regarding Christmas apply even more strongly to Easter, if this were possible, but the question is asked, may Jewish children observe Hallowe'en? Perhaps prohibiting them from participating in classroom activities might be considered unnecessary, since the holiday has long been devoid of religious significance in the United States, but observant Jews do not allow their children to go "trick or treating" because of the *chukot ha-goy*. It doesn't appear to be a very serious matter in any case.

To give a parallel, Carnival, as it is celebrated in Brazil, has lost any religious meaning it may once have had. Nevertheless, the only club in the entire city of Rio de Janeiro, a city of clubs, which does not have a carnival celebration, is the Hebraica, although it is in no sense a center of religious observance. On the other hand, the New Year's Eve (December 31) celebration at the Hebraica is known, even among the Goyim, as the most exuberant blowout in the city. The strictly observant will not celebrate New Year's Eve because of the chukot ha-goy, but this is one of those instances in which it is recognized that a prohibition is so widely and generally violated that Jews who do so are not to be considered unobservant.

Gentile Violations of Jewish Law

In most communities in the Americas, it is forbidden to send flowers to a Jewish funeral. What should we do if a Gentile sends flowers? The answer here is that while it is certainly forbidden to have flowers at a Jewish funeral, it is also forbidden to hurt the feelings of well-meaning people. We should place the flowers at a proper distance or out of sight; the person sending them should be thanked and certainly not offended by informing him that what he has done is wrong. The same applies to gifts of non-kosher food from Gentile friends; we may not eat it, but we must be careful not to throw it out where the giver can see it.

Invitations to Gentile Religious Celebrations

Jews are not supposed to enter a church except in case of an emergency. When they are invited to baptisms, funeral masses, weddings, etc., it is usually possible to avoid the church ceremony and attend the reception or the burial, to condole the mourners at their home (a positive mitzva), etc. The sending of wedding and baptismal gifts is certainly permitted as is rejoicing at the wedding reception, if the dietary laws and other laws are kept by the Jew.

Insults to Gentiles

Insulting a Gentile is prohibited and not only because of darchei shalom. In the Sefer Chasidim it is stated that to ridicule a Gentile in a foreign language which he does not understand (such as Yiddish) while the Gentile thinks we are wishing him well is among the greatest of sins because it violates the prohibition against deceit, which includes the Gentiles. Now what about the word Goy? Is it an insult? The word *goy* literally means "kingdom" in the Bible and in the Talmud acquired the additional meaning not only of a kingdom but of a member of a kingdom, meaning a non-Jew. There is nothing offensive in referring to a Gentile as a Goy or to Gentiles collectively as the Goyim. Quite otherwise is the word *sheigetz* (pl. *shkotzim*) meaning a non-Jewish young man, or *shiksa,* meaning a non-Jewish young woman. These words are offensive and should not be used, either among Jews or in the presence of non-Jews. (Actually, the word sheigetz is frequently used to refer to an unmannerly *Jewish* boy!)

Jesus and the Christian Religion

Any discussion of the supposed debt owed Judaism by Christianity would be out of place in this book. In the opinion of a good many scholars, not a few of them Gentiles, it can be summed up in Israel Zangwill's mordant phrase: "Scratch a Christian and you'll find a pagan—spoiled." Judaism owes nothing to Christianity, quite obviously, but not so obvious is the fact that Christianity owes almost nothing to Judaism. The two religions have little if anything in common.

Jews are often asked by non-Jews, "What is the Jewish attitude toward Jesus?" The honest answer to this question is: The Jewish attitude toward Jesus is precisely the same as the Christian attitude toward Mohammed. This is an accurate answer and a valid parallel. Mohammed appeared when Christianity was several centuries old and claimed to be the last of the prophets. He recognized both the Bible and the New Testament as books of truth and both the Hebrew prophets and Jesus as holy men. Nonetheless he claimed that his revelation was the true and final one, supplanting all that had gone before. This is just about what Jesus, or at least his followers, did. They recognized the Bible, called the prophets and figures of the Torah bearers of truth, but ended up by saying that their revelation made the laws of the Torah a dead letter because the acceptance of Jesus took their place. The Christians' declarations culminated in the doctrine that Jesus was God incarnate, a claim no one ever made for Mohammed.

As for the relative importance of the two religions, it is reliably reported that Islam gains more converts every year than all other religions of the world combined, including all sects of Christianity. In spite of this and in spite of Islam's recognition of Jesus as a holy prophet, most Christians would be hard put to it to tell you in what year or even in what century Mohammed was born. That attitude, with modifications in the degree of awareness, describes the Jewish view of Jesus. We know he lived and have a vague idea of what he preached but there it ends. The widespread idea that the Jews, while rejecting Jesus' claim to divinity, consider him a great teacher and moral figure is completely false. We do not accept his claims and we are oblivious to his teachings; we are simply not interested in him nor in what he had to say, any more than Christians are interested in Mohammed.

As for the New Testament, Jews who have taken the trouble to read it find themselves in disagreement with much of what it contains. When we read in the Gospel according to St. Matthew,

8:21-22: "And another of his disciples said unto him, Lord, suffer me first to go and bury my father. But Jesus said unto him, Follow me; and let the dead bury their dead," we hardly know what to make of it. The idea that it is possible for a man to save his soul by leaving his father's body unburied is something the Jewish mind is unable to accept. To say that the end, in this case the salvation of the soul, justifies the means, elicits the Jewish answer that an end that employs such means is one in which we cannot share an interest.

There is little point in going further into the doctrines contained in the New Testament except to say that they account, to a large degree, for the signal lack of success the Christians have had in converting Jews to their religion. Actually, the paganism of the Greeks made greater inroads into Israel in its time than Christianity has ever been able to.

Other Religions

Of all the world's religions, the one that has had the most influence on Jewish customs and traditions and even, in isolated places and times, on Jewish religious thought, has been Islam. The *Sufists,* profound Moslem mystics, left traces of their thinking on certain Kabbalists, according to scholars of the subject, but no religious system has succeeded in modifying even slightly the basic religious beliefs of the Jews. The influence of Islam on Jewish custom and outlook is, of course, restricted to those countries dominated by that religion.

Actually, the attitude of the Jew in Moslem countries toward the religion of his neighbors is one of indifference, as it is in Christian countries, with the difference that the Moslems, because of their dietary laws and their strict monotheism—both acquired from the Jews—are not looked upon as Gentiles in the same sense that Christians are. In a purely religious sense, the gap between Moslems and Jews is narrower.

In the area of custom and morality, however, the Jew feels much closer to the Christian and to the Protestant more than the Catholic. This can be seen perhaps most clearly in the varying degrees of assimilation in North and Latin America. South of the border, Jews are far less assimilated and identify themselves less with the Gentiles among whom they live, than is the case in the United States and Canada. One important reason is the widespread custom in Catholic, that is to say, Latin Catholic, countries, of married men having mistresses. This is still to a large degree an accepted way of life for many Latins and a man known to have a mistress is welcome in decent homes and his presence in church on Sunday arouses no surprise. A Jew in Latin America known to have a mistress (and there are no secrets in Latin American life, particularly among the Jews) would be frozen out of the Jewish community in a matter of weeks. In the United States, whose orientation is basically Protestant and to a certain degree Irish Catholic, mistresses are rare indeed and the custom is by no means accepted.

This important difference between Jews and non-Jews in Latin America has done much to maintain Jewish integrity. In the United States, where this difference does not exist, Jews tend to think of themselves as being much more like their neighbors. This is only one instance; there are many others.

When my Sunday-school students in the States used to ask me, "Must we respect the religion of our neighbors?" my answer was, "Certainly not. But you must respect your neighbors themselves and for that reason you may not find fault with their religion because to do so would be disrespectful to them as people." Since there is almost no common ground between Christianity and Judaism, despite widespread misconceptions to the contrary, any discussion of religion with Gentiles is likely to be a waste of time and Jews are advised to abstain. Frankness in particular could easily lead to injured feelings; there are plenty of things that are better left unsaid.

Are the Jews a Superior People?

I don't suppose there exists a people that does not consider itself superior in some sense. Perhaps the best way to explain the Jewish attitude is through one of the blessings that form part of the prayers of every observant Jew every day of the year: *Baruch Ata Adonai, Elohenu Melech ha-olam, shelo asani Goy* (Blessed art thou, O Lord, our God, King of the universe, Who has not made me a Goy).

Our reason for being thankful is obvious: if the Jew saying the blessing were a Gentile he would not be privileged to obey the commandments God gave us when He chose us as His special people. But why is the blessing stated in a negative fashion? Why doesn't it say instead, "Who has made me a Jew"?

The answer casts light on our view of ourselves as compared with the rest of the world. The reason the blessing does not say, "Who has made me a Jew," is that being a Jew in its fullest sense is not something God does, but that we ourselves must do. God gives us a head start in not making us Gentiles, but making ourselves real Jews is up to us.

In other words, we have the possibility before us of making ourselves a "superior" people, and the Torah points the way to do it. If we follow the Torah's guidelines, we are justified in calling ourselves superior; if we do not, we have no right to consider ourselves above the peoples of the world.

Of course the reference is to Jews as individuals. As a people in its entirety, Israel is and will always remain the beloved of God, even when their conduct leaves much to be desired. Jeremiah (31:20) said it in a way that has become part of the High Holiday services as well as one of the most famous Chasidic songs. Efraim in the verse refers to the people of Israel:

"Is not Efraim my dear son, my beloved boy?
Even when I speak against him I remember him fondly.
Therefore my heart yearns for him and I will surely
show him mercy, says the Lord."

49

Enemies of the Jewish People

ALL the admonitions to help our enemies and try to conquer feelings of hatred refer to personal enemies—people we don't like. They do not refer to enemies of humanity, enemies of our country or enemies of the Jewish people; those we are commanded not to love but to hate, because they are also enemies of God.

We are told in the Bible how Amalek and his people followed us out of Egypt and killed the stragglers of our people: the old, the ill and the children, who could not keep up with the rest. A similar procedure was carried out in the concentration camps set up by the Germans. All arrivals were paraded past a German physician—in the Auschwitz camp his name was Josef Mengele—who picked from the line all who were old, ill or unable to keep up, including all small children. The Germans then killed them, before the day was out.

Regarding Amalek, the Torah's commandment is clear: "Blot out the remembrance of Amalek from under Heaven: *do not forget*" (Deut. 25:19). In the view of almost all Orthodox Jews, the same commandment must apply to the Germans in our time.

There can be no forgiveness for what they did and no consideration of pardon and certainly no forgetting.

Further, it is widely held among Orthodox Jews in particular,
that the entire German nation is guilty. The slaughter of Jews
took place without discrimination; its victims were men, women
and children. And just as every Jew was killed, without regard to
age or sex, so in the same measure are the Germans guilty of that
slaughter.

How real this is comes home in an incident that happened after
the war, told me by Rabbi Joseph W., one of the handful of survivors of Polish Jewry. On a flight between Israel and France his
plane was forced, by mechanical difficulties, to stop in a German
airport, and he had no alternative but to spend several hours on
German soil waiting for another plane. When the time for Mincha, the afternoon prayer, came around, he did not wish to pray
in public and asked a KLM Dutch Airlines officer, on whose
flight he was booked, if he could show him to a room where he
could pray in private. The Dutch captain immediately called over
an airport guard and asked him to escort the rabbi to a special
room used by KLM functionaries. The guard politely asked the
rabbi to accompany him, but the rabbi ignored him. The captain
asked, "Why won't you go with the guard, Rabbi?" and Rabbi
W. answered: *"How do I know he is not the man who killed my
mother?"*

This is something a Hollander understands immediately and
without another word he accompanied Rabbi W. personally.

I told this story to a highly assimilated German-Jewish neighbor and his comment was that perhaps Germany was no more to
blame than anyone else. "It could just as easily have happened in
the United States," he said. The answer to slanderous statements
like that is that it didn't happen in the United States, and nothing
like it or even distantly resembling it has ever happened in the
United States. Where it happened was Germany, and there it was
just the latest in a long series of similar "incidents" in German
history. And it was not even the last such incident. The wave of
anti-Semitism that swept Europe in the mid-fifties started with
the desecration of Jewish cemeteries in Germany. A Gentile edi-
torial writer in a prominent Latin American newspaper asked at

the time, "How is it possible that anyone can ask us to believe that this is a coincidence?"

As for people of German descent, born outside Germany, Judaism considers the Germans to be not a race but a people, in direct connection with their geographical homeland. Accordingly such people of German extraction are unconnected with what was done by the inhabitants of Germany and Austria and their Polish, Ukrainian, Lithuanian, Latvian, Hungarian, Romanian and Slovenian cohorts. To give but one example: General Dwight D. Eisenhower, during the entire course of the war, refused to allow a single captured German general to be brought to see him because, in his opinion, the Germans, and he made no distinction between "Nazis" and "non-Nazis," were not soldiers but common bestial murderers. General Eisenhower was of pure German extraction.

Do we feel the same way about the Arabs? We do not. The Arabs as a people have never been able to get together on anything, including the extinction of the Jews, and the Moslems as a religious group have never advocated a "final solution" either. Those Arab nations who have expressed their intention of "driving Israel into the sea" must be fought and defeated, but it is really not possible to consider their inhabitants enemies of the Jewish people. In our day the only Arab who has advocated the wiping out of Jews as Jews, wherever they may be found, was Haj Amin El-Husseini, the Grand Mufti of Jerusalem, who was an official ally of the Germans and supplied troops to the German army.

In reality, Jews and Arabs are always finding out how close they are to each other—sometimes closer than they think. At one time in my life I traveled constantly and on one flight found myself sitting next to a well-dressed, quiet man, obviously an Arab. When the stewardess brought our dinner to us, the Arab refused the meal, saying he wanted nothing. I turned to him and said, "Are you a Muslim?" Somewhat surprised, he answered that he was and I offered to share my kosher meal with him. "You can eat this," I said. "There is no *chanzir* [the Arabic word for pork] in it."

"Are you a Muslim?" he asked.

"No," I answered, "I'm a Jew."

"Oh, we are cousins," he said.

I agreed and we started talking. It turned out that he was the concessionaire of a large Japanese manufacturing firm in one of the Persian Gulf oil states. We were on our way to Japan, as I recall, and I gave him the name and address of a Moslem Chinese restaurant in Tokyo, which he wrote down gratefully. After a while he seemed to get quieter and quieter and finally blurted out, "The truth is this: my father is from Oman, but my mother is from Bahrein. And she is Jewish. . . ."

Closer to home, anti-Semites in our own country and elsewhere must also be hated. In the words of Menachem Begin, "If you love freedom, you must hate slavery; if you love your people, you cannot but hate the enemies that compass their destruction." It is not proper to look for anti-Semitism where none exists, and it is not correct to label a man an anti-Semite because he uses an expression like "Jewing down" for reducing a price. As inelegant as the expression is, it is simply a folk idiom and should be considered innocent until proven otherwise. But genuine anti-Semites must be recognized for what they are: enemies of the Jewish people. It is correct and desirable to boycott the products of anti-Semitic firms and refuse to do business with anti-Semitic banks, organizations and companies. It is a mitzva to refuse "made in Germany" products and to make one's objection known.

As for giving support of any kind to organizations that take an anti-Semitic stand, the Jew who would do this is a traitor to his people and a fool who "sharpens the axe for his own neck." It should also be remembered that the fact that an anti-Semite is himself a member of an oppressed minority, ethnic or economic, is no mitigation at all: two wrongs don't make a right.

Do the Orthodox Jews include missionaries among the enemies of the Jews? We certainly do, and any organization engaged in missionary activity to the Jews may receive neither support nor sympathy from us. They are enemies of the Jews in the most basic sense, since they deny our very reason for existing. Despite all the protestations of "ecumenism," certain clergymen continue to make every attempt to turn our children away from us and us away from the God of our fathers.

Finally, what about Russia and the Russians; must they be considered enemies of the Jewish people? This is a difficult question to answer. We cannot forget the centuries-long hatred of the Jews by the Russian people (albeit with honorable exceptions), a hatred to which a long series of pogroms and persecutions give adequate witness. At the same time we cannot forget that over thirty generations of our ancestors lived in Russia and that great numbers of Jews were saved by the Russians from the Germans during a period extending from the Crusades to the Second World War.

We cannot forget that Russia voted in the United Nations in favor of the partition of Palestine and the formation of a Jewish state, and then permitted their slave-state, Czechoslovakia, to supply the newly born republic with arms while the rest of the world put an embargo on the weapons Israel needed to defend itself against the Arabs.

But neither can we forget what is going on in Russia today. In addition to forcibly keeping two million Jews captive in the vast prison that is the Soviet Union, there is active persecution of Jewish religious and cultural activity. While many Christian sects as well as Moslems are permitted to make religious pilgrimages, to train their clergy and publish religious and ethnic texts, the Soviet government, according to the way they feel in any given year, makes even the baking of matzos a crime. Further, there is a determined attempt to wipe out Judaism at all levels. There is no publication of books or periodicals in Yiddish or Hebrew, no Jewish schools or institutions to which Jewish children may be sent. All other ethnic minorities in the Soviet Union enjoy these privileges; only the Jews are excluded. Of course, if the Jews are denied recognition as an ethnic minority in every other sense, they are conceded it in one: every Jew is perforce identified as such in the internal "passport" that all Russians must carry. If the yellow star is not sewn on their clothing, it *is* stamped on their identification papers. Present-day Russian support of the Arabs against Israel is so well known as to require no comment. Perhaps what it all comes down to is that birds of a feather flock together: dictatorships are dictatorships, whether of the right or the left, and have more in common with each other than either has with a democracy. In the entire Middle East there is only one real democracy: Israel.

50

Friends
of the Jews

JUST as we must not forgive the enemies of our people, so must we remember in gratitude those who have helped us. The Danes, that nation of heroes, can never be forgotten for defying the Germans and refusing to accept the Nuremberg laws, which classified the Jews as a sub-people. When the Germans finally, by force, put in effect their program of annihilation, the Danes managed to rescue well over eighty percent of their Jewish community by smuggling them into Sweden in fishing boats. More than one Dane lost his life in this fearless act. King Christian and the Royal Family of Denmark, as the spearheads of this great-hearted defense of a defenseless people, merit our special gratitude, but their valor was shared by all the King's subjects.

Alexander the Great was such a friend of the Jews that when he entered Jerusalem, the rabbis of the Holy City decreed that every boy born during the following year should be named Alexander and Alexander is still a common and accepted "Jewish" name. Had the heroic King of Denmark been named anything but Christian, it is more than likely that Jewish boys would be bearing his name with honor today.

Holland is another country in which the local population risked and often lost their lives in the attempt to rescue Jews from German hands. During the Yom Kippur war and afterwards, Holland defied the Arab oil boycott in affirming its friendship with Israel and showed the bravery of its great people by undergoing severe hardships in the frightful cold of a European winter without oil. This is, in fact, the continuance of a long tradition which goes back to the days of the Spanish Inquisition, when Holland was one of the few countries in the world and the only one in Europe to which Jews could turn for refuge. (People who maintain that "race" is responsible for national temperament should take note of the fact that racially the Dutch, Danes and Germans are indistinguishable. They speak closely related languages and are all Teutons.)

And there are others. When President Lyndon B. Johnson was asked in 1967 by Russian Premier Kosygin why the United States backed three million Jews against forty million Arabs, Johnson answered: "Because it is right." He spoke for his country.

Yad V'shem, the worldwide organization formed to make us remember the German destruction of European Jewry, also has a section dedicated to the remembrance of those noble Gentiles who, with everything to lose and nothing to gain but the gratitude of what then looked like a doomed people, nevertheless put their very lives and those of their families on the line to save their Jewish neighbors, and often, Jews they had never seen before. These are the *Chasidei Umot Ha-olam*, the Righteous Gentiles, and we must never forget them.

51

Alcohol, Tobacco and Drugs

ALCOHOL

CONCERNING alcohol, Jews are agreed on its benefits and place high value on alcoholic drinks, from beer to *bronfen* (brandy). For example, when a person offers a *kiddush* to the congregation after prayers, it usually consists of cake and liquor. The reason given by many rabbis for this custom is that it would be best to offer a complete meal, but since one cannot afford to do that for the entire congregation, we substitute whiskey.

For the purpose of saying kiddush, which means "sanctification," or making holy, we should use kosher wine, but if no wine is available, any other beverage containing alcohol is permissible. The drinking of a glass of *mashke* (any liquor) with the rest of the congregation after morning prayers, when one is offered, is considered an important religious act, since in order to do so we must first thank God by saying the proper blessing and then wish our fellow Jews good health by saying *L'chaim*! (To life) as we drink.

Wine is put into the mouth of a boy on his eighth day, at the time of his circumcision, and special rules apply to the drinking of wine, most of which are covered in the section on the dietary laws (chapter 21). Among the Jewish lore connected with wine is the belief that spilling it is a good omen. I first heard this at the table of the Bobover Rebbe, one of the great living saints of Judaism, where I inadvertently knocked over a wineglass. The Rabbi saw this and called to me from the end of the long table, "Mechel; giessen vain iz a gitte simen" (Michael, spilling wine is a good sign).

It was not until twenty-five years later, in a synagogue in Rio de Janeiro, Brazil, that I was given an explanation of why this should be so. Rabbi Abraham Anidjar, of Tangiers, a long way in time and distance from the Polish village of Bobov (Bobowa), explained to me, after someone else had spilled wine and I remarked on its being a good omen, that wine is given to one who is of heavy heart, to cheer him up. A mourner is given wine so that his sadness will not overcome him. If wine is spilled, this is an indication that it is not going to be needed, and we may expect no sorrow. (The source of this explanation is found in Prov. 31:6.)

These two men, one speaking in Yiddish and the other in Spanish, one from a tiny village in the Polish countryside and the other from a teeming city in North Africa, outwardly so dissimilar in physical appearance, language, dress, diet and custom, still share a common tradition that extends from the essential religious concepts to the most casual folklore. They would, if they were ever to meet, feel quite at home in each other's company; their differences would be minor compared with what they have in common, and one of the links between them is the Jewish attitude toward wine as a bringer of cheer and disperser of sorrow.

On the eight days preceding the fast of Tisha B'av, the saddest day in the Jewish year, it is forbidden to drink wine, so that our mourning for the destruction of the Temple may be intensified.

As for the extent to which alcohol is consumed among Jews, it is commonly accepted that the more religious a Jew is, the more likely he will be to enjoy a snifter on the appropriate occasion. Really, that is the key to Jewish drinking: "on the appropriate occasion." A Jew is generally not a man to drink in a bar or among strangers. Jews tend to enjoy a drink (or two) in their own homes, at the home of a friend, at a party among other Jews or on any of the occasions when a drink is not only allowed but encouraged: weddings, brisses, bar mitzvas, Sabbaths and holidays.

Drunkenness is rare among Jews, although occasionally one may take a drop too much; but alcoholism is almost unknown. It is true, nevertheless, that most sizeable Jewish communities will usually have one alcoholic who is the equivalent of the "town drunk" in small towns. In one large Latin American city where I lived, there were two: one Sephardic and the other Ashkenazic. It appears that the tendency of the two great Jewish communities to maintain their own separate identities extends even to that! Extensive studies done in the United States among different ethnic groups show that the lowest indices of alcoholism are found among Jews, Chinese and Italians. Chinese alcoholics are rare and Jewish alcoholics even rarer, although I have known both. I must say, with admiration, that I have never known an Italian alcoholic and I have a great many Italian friends.

TOBACCO

Tobacco is considered a legitimate pleasure among Jews. There is now extremely strong medical evidence that smoking, particularly cigarette smoking, is inextricably linked with both cancer and heart disease so we may see a change in the traditional Jewish attitude. Observant Jews who are heavy smokers, and they are far from few, must, of course, refrain from smoking on the Sabbath. Many will take snuff on Shabbat in substitution, and older Jews from all parts of the world are partial to a *shmeck tabak* from time to time.

DRUGS.

The use of drugs, and this includes marijuana and hashish as well as "hard" drugs, is rare in traditional Jewish communities, and this includes such areas as North Africa where marijuana is legal and where the Jews reached a high degree of assimilation to the local population in many other respects. In the United States and most other countries, the use of drugs is totally forbidden by Jewish law because it violates the law of the land, and it is a fundamental principle that *Dina d'malchuta dina:* the law of the land is the law.

If marijuana, for example, were to be legalized in the United States, as some people advocate, it is possible that rabbinical authorities might find grounds for prohibiting its use to Jews, but this seems unlikely or such prohibitions would have been forthcoming in the past since the weed has been in common use in the Middle East since time immemorial. It just seems to be a thing that, like wife-beating, is "not done in Israel." The existence of Jewish addicts and "heads" does not change this: they are few and in almost every case have abandoned Judaism as a way of life.

52

Charity

THE English word "charity" has no equivalent in Hebrew. The word used is *tzedaka*, which means "justice." To the Jew there is no choice involved in giving charity: he is not at liberty to say no.

As far as his means permit, the Jew is obliged to give *tzedaka*, unless, of course, he receives it. By the same token, the Jewish recipient of charity does not feel any particular obligation to thank the giver, any more than the average American thinks to thank his state government for providing his children with an education. It is expected that the state will educate its citizens and it is expected, among the Jews, that the community will look after those who cannot look after themselves.

Communities that have few or no indigent members are still under the obligation to give toward the maintenance of the indigent members of other communities, as well as support of the State of Israel. In this respect, statistics seem to show that the community which gives most, per capita, to Israel, is that of South Africa. In second place is the community of Venezuela, and in third place, Switzerland. In addition to their contributions to the Jewish state, all of these countries have numbers of poor Jews who are supported and whose children are educated at the expense of the community.

This is not to say that all Jews give charity equally according to their means. Some give more than others and just as every sizeable community has its alcoholic, so every community has its Jew who gives little or nothing to charity. Such a person is usually more pitied than hated; like the alcoholic, he is considered abnormal.

Maimonides lists several degrees of charity, of which the highest is helping another to help himself. This particular form of tzedaka is usually an interest-free loan to help a Jew start a business so that he can support himself and his family. It has, among Jews, the special name of *gemilat chesed*, a deed of lovingkindness. Jewish free-loan societies are an outgrowth of the *gemilat chesed* fund traditionally maintained in Orthodox congregations of a certain size.

In regard to giving charity to individuals, it is a general rule that if someone comes to you with his hand held out, you must put something in it. This rule applies to non-Jewish as well as Jewish supplicants. In the synagogue, when pledging a contribution, charity is often given in multiples of 18, since that number is numerically equivalent to the letters chet and yud which spell *chai*—life.

I recall once reading an essayist—I think it was the late Bob Considine—who said he was sick of hearing certain people say that they did not give to beggars or to certain charities "as a matter of principle." What he wanted to see, he said, was the occasion on which these people *gave* as a matter of principle, implying that they never did.

The essayist was more than likely right, but if he wanted to see people give as a matter of principle, any ordinary Jew would fulfill his wish. Giving, with Jews, is not a matter of choice and they do so even when they are not particularly inclined, or even when they suspect that the money is not going into the designated charitable organization as much as into the collector's pocket. If this is suspected to be the case and their attention is called to it, they may give less, but they are likely to shrug and say, "What can you do? They come and ask, you gotta give something"—as a matter of principle.

53

Sex

SEX IN MARRIAGE

As we have seen in the section on marriage, the husband is obliged to guarantee his wife a normal sex life. At the same time, the same Talmudic source states emphatically that a man should never attempt to oblige his wife to have intercourse with him at a time when he "is hateful to her"; in other words, when she is angry with him. At one point the Talmud has a good deal to say about how often a man should have sexual relations with his wife, stating that a young and vigorous man should do so every night, while a poor man who labors hard and is ill-fed should do so once a week. These passages in the Talmud have been misinterpreted by dilettantes; they contain no laws and no regulations. They are simply aggada: observations which can be taken into account or ignored as one wishes, and are simply another indication that Judaism leaves no aspect of life uncommented upon.

In regard to the above suggestions, however, the Talmud goes on to say that in the case of a couple who have the custom of having intercourse only on certain nights, if the husband sees his wife dressing attractively, putting on perfume or otherwise acting in such a fashion as to attract his attention on a night which is not an "appointed" night, he must not deny her the comfort she obviously seeks. Scholars and religious men in general are accustomed to have intercourse with their wives on Friday nights, since this is the holiest night of the week. To the joy of Shabbat is added the "holy joy" that only a devoted husband and wife can know. To the mitzva of observing Shabbat is added the mitzva of marital relations.

SEX OUTSIDE MARRIAGE

Extra-marital sex is forbidden by Jewish law and it is not looked upon tolerantly. It is, however, divided into two classifications of seriousness: casual sex among the unmarried, consorting with prostitutes, etc., on the one hand, and adultery on the other.

The first sort of extra-marital sex is severely censured. Married men among Jews do not keep mistresses, and traditionally Orthodox Jews are encouraged to marry young so that they will not be forced by nature into sex outside marriage. The Talmud says, "Eighteen is the age for marriage." This is suggestion, not law, but among observant Jews early marriage is to be desired.

If the prohibition against sex outside marriage is transgressed, the world obviously does not come to an end, but in the case of young people, genuine shame is felt by the families involved. The greatest shame is felt by the boy's family, since it is assumed he has taken advantage of the girl and in any event should have been strong enough to refrain from what he knew to be improper.

This is in direct contrast to the attitude of Latin American parents. In a similar case the boy's father is more than likely to boast of his son's "virility" among his own friends, another factor in the lower level of assimilation in Latin America.

In general it can be said that in the Jewish view, sex is too important a thing to be exercised outside of the ample framework God has given us for it in the Torah.

Adultery, the second classification, is something quite different. In the first place we must understand that, according to Jewish law, the term adultery refers exclusively to sexual relations between a married woman and a man not her husband. It does not refer, for example, to sexual relations between a married man and a woman not his wife, unless the woman is married as well. While forbidden and roundly condemned, this is not adultery.

Adultery is one of the most horrifying of sins in Jewish eyes. In the case that it occurs, the man is felt to be the greater sinner, but both are equally guilty unless, of course, rape is involved. Perhaps the most frightening thing about an adulterous relationship is the possibility of a child resulting from it. Such a child would be a *mamzer* and forever disqualified from marrying any Jew not himself a mamzer.

Nor is the situation much different when the married woman involved is not Jewish. It is still a terrible sin, not only against the woman's husband, but against God who has prohibited this act in His Torah. For proof we need go no further than Genesis 39, where the story of Joseph and Potiphar's wife demonstrates that Joseph preferred to risk death rather than betray the woman's husband and "sin against God."

If the woman with whom the Jew has sexual relations is an unmarried Gentile, it is obviously not adultery, but there is still an absolute prohibition for many reasons, not the least of which must be wronging or cheating Gentiles, since there is no doubt that a woman's worth, both to herself and others, is diminished by illegal, casual sex. In addition it is prohibited because of the great danger that the Jew may be led into *avoda zara*, the worship of idols.

HOMOSEXUALITY

It appears that certain Christian denominations have now taken the attitude that homosexual acts between consenting adults are not a sin and not to be condemned. This is rejected by traditional Jews, whose guideline is the Torah in which (Lev. 18:22) such acts are defined as "abomination." It is also rejected by the anti-religious kibbutz and moshav movements in Israel as well, of course, as the religious kibbutzim and moshavim. Condemnation is absolute and it is not tolerated.

In fact, homosexuality is largely ignored in the Talmud,

although other sexual offenses against the Torah such as adultery and rape are discussed at length. Rabbinical and scholarly opinion is that its incidence was so low that no point was seen in discussing it. The enormous post-Talmudic responsa literature, which extends over fourteen centuries into the present, contains almost no reference to homosexuality for the same reason: it has never been a significant factor in Jewish life.

54

Science and Evolution

DESPITE the "fundamentalist" stand taken by some Orthodox figures, there is no conflict between science and religion in Judaism. One of the greatest thinkers in Jewish history, Saadia Gaon (882-942 C.E.), stated this clearly: "There are two sources of the knowledge of God: nature and the Torah, the book of the created world and the book of revelation. Both, as coming from God, must be in agreement. If they seem to disagree, it must be due to the fact that we misread the testimony in one or the other of them."

There are, nonetheless, unresolved problems and the age of the world is, to the minds of many, one of them. As of this writing the creation of the world is calculated, according to the Jewish calendar, to have taken place 5738 years ago. Faced with the apparent impossibility of this date, Jewish thinkers long ago reasoned that the six days of creation referred to in the Torah have no relation to days as we understand them. Each "day" of creation, they reason, may have covered millions of years.

Corollary to this, it was postulated that the date of creation refers not to the period encompassed in the first five "days," but to the final day alone, on which mankind was created. Moshe Kohn, in one of his widely read articles in The Jerusalem Post, puts it that, ". . . the year begins on Rosh Hashana, the 'anniversary' of God's creation of the human race late one Friday afternoon, nearly 5737 years ago (and not even 'Orthodox' scholarship requires us to understand this 'Friday,' 'afternoon,' '5737' and 'years' in the way these terms are used today)."

While this is accepted and was even before science began to have an idea of the great age of the universe, it is not universally accepted. Certain Orthodox thinkers insist that we must interpret the Jewish date literally and that no more than 5738 calendar years have elapsed since the creation of Man. Unfortunately, there is overwhelming scientific evidence that man in civilized form has existed longer than 5738 years and early man much longer than that. The famous cave paintings at Lasceaux have been dated by the carbon-14 method to 15,000 years ago. The men who executed those beautiful works of art were skeletally almost indistinguishable from modern man and of their intelligence and humanity there can be no doubt. The statements that carbon-14 dating is hypothetical—made by certain rabbis learned in the revealed Torah but ignorant of "the book of the created world"—are untrue: it is based on the firmest of scientific evidence.

The discoveries of the archeologists are explained by some Jewish intellectuals as the remains of worlds that God created and then destroyed before He created the world of Adam. This explanation comes from the Midrash. Others say that the fossil remains of dinosaurs, carbon-14 dated artifacts of early man and similar finds, were placed in the earth for reasons we cannot know and serve to deceive us because we give them an interpretation which is not the correct one. Even those who offer this explanation do so with some diffidence; most people simply ignore it.

In any event, it would appear to be a fact that the uninterrupted history of man extends back well over 5738 years, and how this squares with the "creation" date has yet to be explained. Perhaps the answer lies in acknowledging, with Saadia Gaon, the possibility that the testimony of the revealed Torah may have been misinterpreted, and recalculating the date or admitting that no real calculation is possible.

To tell the truth, it is not a subject that occupies the minds of many Jews. When God created the universe is something we may eventually know, but until we do, it is enough for us to know He did, and of that we have no doubt at all: the testimony of the Torah in that respect admits of no misinterpretation in its basic meaning. From the times of the earliest Jewish commentators on the Bible, the story of Creation has been understood in a symbolic sense, as is much of what we read in the first part of Genesis. Rabbi Leo Jung explains in the introduction to one of his books the wide variety of interpretations of the story of Creation by Orthodox commentators: "The basis of all scholars' views was the belief that God created the world. An infinite margin is left to individual ingenuity." It is a Jewish axiom that "the Torah speaks in the language of men." This means that the Torah uses images and symbols which men can understand for events and processes which man would otherwise have no way of comprehending. An example of this is the commonly found expression, "God spoke." The Jews have always maintained that God has no form that we can begin to understand, and certainly no mouth, tongue or vocal cords. God's way of communicating with Moses is, of course, unknown to us, but the Torah puts it in a form we can understand. It is well to keep this in mind when studying the Torah, although it is by no means universally applicable.

The question of the evolution of mankind from lower animals is a difficult but by no means an insoluble one. There appears now to be little doubt that humans did evolve physically from beings which were less than human. It is even possible that all living beings have, as the scientists suppose, a common ancestry.

But what is also evident is that at that point where man became human, as distinguished from animal, something radical and drastic took place, because no one can deny that men and animals are radically different creatures.

The basic difference between men and beasts is that men have souls while beasts do not. The earlier Jewish thinkers had no illusions about the common features shared by men and animals, but they were quick to spot the one difference between them which accounts for man's incredibly rapid progress from one generation to the next, while even the most intelligent animals have remained fixed in the place they had reached on the scale of evolution at the time of man's creation as man. That difference is *speech*; and the rabbis took speech as the physical evidence of the presence of a soul in man and its absence in all other creatures. No animal has ever been able to pass on to a succeeding generation the "experience" it has acquired; all animals start from scratch and whatever they "learn" dies with them, for none possesses genuine speech.

Casual observation will show the immense, unbridgeable gap that exists between the most primitive of men and the most advanced of animals. We can attribute this only to man's soul. The theory of evolution is acceptable, perhaps, if we recognize that at some point in the process of evolution, man was separated in a basic sense from the other living beings by God, who gave him a soul and made him human. God may have chosen evolution as the means of arriving at the concrete, physical form of man, but man's humanity is a *direct* gift from God which was given him at a distinct moment in time, not as a gradual development over generations or even years, months or hours. That moment, perhaps, was the real creation of man.

And there is a very clear indication that this view of man's creation has long existed in the minds of the greatest of the analysts of the Torah. Gen. 1:26 says, "And God said, let Us make man in Our image." Nachmanides says in his commentary on this verse that the plural form, "let *us* make man," refers to God and the earth, because man's body comes from the earth and his soul from God. In other words, the earth "created" man's body and God gave him his soul. Ibn Ezra, in his commentary on the same passage, says, "All other life was brought forth by the earth and the water; but regarding man, God said, to His angels, 'We Ourselves will engage in his creation.' " The description of living beings having been brought forth by the earth sounds like a rather clumsy but not at all roundabout way of describing the process of evolution, centuries before Darwin!

As to the words, "in Our image," all Jewish commentators are agreed that this refers to the soul of man, which shares the characteristics of immortality with its Creator.

In the case of other aspects of Biblical history, such as Adam and Eve, the Flood, the Tower of Babel, the age of Methuselah, etc., we may suspect that here again the Torah is speaking in the language of men. There are Orthodox figures who will state flatly that while some of the Torah can be explained in symbolic terms and indeed must be—anthropomorphisms, for instance—the advanced age reached by early figures in the Torah must be taken literally and not questioned. Others will say that the figures themselves are symbolic. The story of the Tower of Babel in which it is said, "The whole world was of one language and one speech," is interpreted by Ibn Ezra to mean that whereas in our day the ignorant and the learned do not speak the same language, in those days all spoke alike. A literal interpretation of the verse apparently never occurred to him. And of course, Ibn Ezra was right. In Peru, for example, even today the illiterate population speak Quechua or Aymara, and the literate population Spanish. Similar situations exist in many countries all over the world, not excepting our own, but in pre-literate times all socio-economic levels of a given society spoke the same language.

What we can say without hesitation is that while the generation of Noah may have been more symbolic than concrete, and while there may be room for uncertainty concerning the nature of the succeeding generations up to Terah, the father of Abraham, from that point on all Orthodox Jews accept the historicity of the Bible and the people in it. Whether Abraham lived 175 years or whether this means that the virtue accumulated by him in his lifetime was the equivalent of what an ordinary man could accumulate only if he lived that long, I do not feel qualified to say. But that Abraham lived and that his story was exactly as the Torah relates it, I have not the slightest doubt, nor does any Orthodox Jew.

And those happenings described in the Torah as miraculous hold no difficulty for me, who have seen with my own eyes the coming into being of the State of Israel after two thousand years of the exile of her people.

והיה כאשר ירים משה ידו וגבר ישראל וגו'
(שמות י'ז:י'א)
וכי ידיו של משה עושות מלחמה או שוברות מלחמה?
אלא לומר לך כל-זמן שהיו ישראל מסתכלים כלפי
מעלה ושעבדין את לבם לאביהם שבשמים היו מתגברין
ואים לאו היו נופלין.
(מֹשניֹת, מסכת ראש הֹשֹנה ג:ח)

"And it came to pass when Moses held up his hand that Israel prevailed" (Ex. 17:11).

But could the hands of Moses wage a war or lose a war? This rather tells you that as long as Israel looked on high and subjected their heart to their father in heaven, they prevailed; but if not they fell (Mishna, Tractate Rosh Hashana 3:8).

Appendix I

Suitable Names for Jewish Children

The following lists of names are by no means complete. There are many names not on them that are acceptable, particularly among Sephardim. If there is doubt about any name not on the lists, any Orthodox rabbi of one's own tradition may be consulted. As explained in chapter 7, many of these names are not of biblical or even of Hebrew origin, but by custom have come to be accepted as suitable names for Jews.

Missing from the lists are a great many "new" names, most of them given to girls, now in vogue in Eretz Israel. Far from being new, most of these names are Hebrew words that had never been used as names in the past, such as *Tikva* and *Kadima*, or had fallen into disuse and are now, happily, being revived. While quite acceptable in any part of the world, their use appears to be restricted mostly to Israel, so I have not attempted to compile a list of them here.

The names themselves are listed in alphabetical order, following the Latin alphabet, with the common or Yiddish pronunciation first. The English or Spanish equivalent is then given, followed by the Hebrew equivalent, where these exist. Finally the accepted Hebrew spelling is given.

Names for Males

Common or Yiddish Pronunciation	English or Spanish	Hebrew Equivalent	Hebrew or Yiddish Spelling
Aaron	Aaron	Aaron	אהרן
Abba	Abba	Abba	אבא
Ada	–	Ada	אדא
Ahuvia	Teófilo	Ahubia	אהוביה
Akiva	–	Akiba	עקיבה
Alexander	Alexander	–	אלכסנדר
Alter	–	–	אלטער
Amiel	–	Amiel	עמיאל
Amihud	–	Amihud	עמיהוד
Aminadab	–	Aminadab	עמינדב
Amram	–	Amram	עמרם
Anshel	Anselm(o)	Asher	אנשיל
Arieh	Leo/León	Ariah	אריה
Asher	Felix	Asher	אשר
Aviezer	Abiezer	Abiezer	אביעזר
Avigdor	Victor	Avigdor	אביגדור
Avisholom	Absolom	Abishalom	אבישלום
Avner	Abner	Abner	אבנר

Avrom	Abraham	Abrahm	אברהם
Azarieh	—	Azariah	עזריה
Azriah	—	Azriah	עזריה
Azriel	—	Azriel	עזריאל
Beinish/			
Bonush	Benjamin	Benyamin	בינוש
Bendit	Benedict	Baruch	בענדיט
Bentzion	Ben Zion	Ben Tzion	בן ציון
Benyomin	Benjamin	Benyamin	בנימין
Ber/Berel	Bruno	Dov	בער, בעריל
Bera	Isaac	Yitzchak	בערא
Betzalel	Bezalel	Betzalel	בצלאל
Bontche	—	—	בונטשע
Boruch	Benedict/		
	Benito	Baruch	ברוך
Buna	—	—	בונא
Bunim	—	Simcha/	
		Yechiel	בונים
Chabia	Rehabia	Rehavia	חביה
Chaim	Vidal/Jaime	Chaim	חיים
Chamia/			
Chemioh	Nehemiah	Nechemiah	חמיה
Chananel	Hananiel	Chananel	חננאל
Chananioh	Hananiah	Chanania	חנניה
Chanon/Chonon	Hanon	Chanon	חנן
Chanoch	Enoch	Chanoch	חנוך
Chaskel/			חצקאל
Chatzkel	Ezekiel	Yecheskel	חזקאל
Chemele	Nehemiah	Nechemiah	חמעלע
Chezkia	Hezekiah	Chezekia	חזקיה
Chiel	—	Yechiel	חיאל
Chiyya	—	Chiyya	חייה
Chomel/			חמל
Chomke	Nahum	Nachum	חמקע
Daniel	Daniel	Daniel	דניאל
Don	Dan	Dan	דן
Dov/Dovber	Bruno	Dov	דוב/דובער
Dovid	David	David	דוד
Eber	Abraham	Abrahm	אבר
Efroim	Efraim	Efraim	אפרים
Elchanon	Elhanan	Elchanan	אלחנן
Eldad	—	Eldad	עלדד
Elimelech	Elimelech	Elimelech	אלימלך
Elioh	Elias	Elia	אליה
Eliyohu	Elijah	Eliyahu	אליהו
Elkana	—	Elkana	אלקנה

Elozor	Eliezer	Elazar	אלעזר
Elyakim	Godfrey	Elyakim	אליקים
Emanuel	Emmanuel	Emanuel	עמנואל
Ezra	Ezra	Ezra	עזרא
Faitl	Vito/Vitus	—	פייטל
Feivish/Fybush	Phoebus	—	פייבוש
Fishl/Fishke	—	—	פישל
Gam'liel	Gamaliel	Gam'liel	גמליאל
Gavriel	Gabriel	Gabriel	גבריאל
Gedalioh	Gedaliah	Gedalia	גדליה
Gershom/Gershon	Gerson	Gershom	גרשם
Getz/Getzel	Godfrey	Elyakim	געץ/געצל
Gimpel/Gumpel	Mordechai	Mordechai	גומפיל
God/God'l	Gad	Gad	גד
Gotlieb/	Teófilo/		
Gutlieb	Theophilus	Yedidiah	גאטליב
Gronam	Jerome/		
	Gerónimo	Samuel	גרונם
Grossman	Gedaliah	Gedalia	גרוסמן
Gutkind/			
Gutman	Tobias	Tobiah	גוטקינד
Hashke	Joshua	Yehoshua	האשקע
Hendel	Manoah	Manoach	העגדל
Henech	Enoch	Chanoch	חנוך
Hermaln	Aaron	Aaron	הערמאלן
Hersh/Hershel	Nephtali	Naftali/Tzvi	הירש
Heshel	Joshua	Yehoshua	העשל
Hillel	Hillel	Hillel	הילל
Hillman	Samuel	Shmuel	הילמן
Hirsh/Hirshel	Nephtali	Naftali/Tzvi	הירש
Hirtz	Nephtali	Naftali/Tzvi	הירץ
Hoishe	Hosea	Hoshe	הושע
Huna	—	Huna	הונא
Idel	Judah	Yehuda	אידל
Isomar	Ithamar	Itamar	יתמר
Isser/Isserel	Israel	Yisrael	איסר
Itshe	Isaac	Yitzchak	איטשע
Itzel/Itzik	Isaac	Yitzchak	איצל/איציק
Izah	Isaac	Yitzchak	איזה
Kahana	—	Kahana	כהנה
Kalman	Kalonymus	—	קלמן
Karmi	Moses	Moshe	כרמי
Karpl	Nathan	Natan	קארפל
Kasriel	Kathriel	Katriel	כתריאל
Kehos	Kehath	Kehat	קהת

Kelev	Caleb	Keleb	כלב
Ketzel	Moses	Moshe	קעציל
Kibeh	Akiba	Akiva	קיבא
Kloinimos/			
Kalonimos	Kalonymus	—	קלונימוס
Koifman	—	Yekutiel	קויפמן
Koppel	Jacob	Yaacov	קאפל
Koppelman	—	—	קופילמן
Kushe	—	Yekutiel	קושא
Kusiel	—	Yekutiel	קותיאל
Laib/Laibel	Leo/Leon	Ariah/Yehuda	לייב/לייבל
Laibush	Leo/Leon	Ariah/Yehuda	לייבוש
Laizer	Eliezer	Elazar	לייזער
Lapidos	—	Lapidot	לפידות
Lebel/Lepke	Leo/Leon	Ariah/Yehuda	לייבקע
Lemel	—	—	לעמל
Levi	Levi	Levi	לוי
Lezer	Eliezer	Elazar	ליזר
Libbe	Judah	Yehuda	ליבא
Liberman	Eliezer/Judah	Elazar/Yehuda	ליברמן
Lippe	Eliezer	Elazar	ליפע
Lippmen	—	—	ליפמן
Lozor	Eliezer	Elazar	לאזער
Mair/Meir	Mayer	Mair	מאיר
Maitshe	Mordechai	Mordechai	מייטשע
Maizel	Mordechai	Mordechai	מייזל
Man/Manne	Menahem	Menachem	מן
Manish/Monish	Menahem	Menachem	מניש
Mannye	Mannie	Mannieh	מני
Manzur	Eliezer	Elazar	מנזור
Matisyohu	Matthew/		
	Matthias	Matityahu	מתתיהו
Matzliach	—	Matzliach	מצליח
Mechel	Michael	Michael	מיכאל
Melech	Rex/Rey	Melech	מלך
Menachem	Menahem	Menachem	מנחם
Menashe	Manasseh	Menashe	מנשה
Mendel	Menahem	Menachem	מענדעל
Menoach	Manoah	Manoach	מנוח
Meshulam	Meshulam	Meshulam	משלם
Mesod	—	—	מסוד
Michoel	Michael	Michael	מיכאל
Mikoh	Micah	Mika	מיכה
Moishe	Moses	Moshe	משה
Moneh/Monem	Mordechai	Mordechai	מונע/מונם
Mordechai	Mordechai	Mordechai	מרדכי
Moshke	Moses	Moshe	משקע
Mote/Motke	Mordechai	Mordechai	מאטע/מוטקע

Mottel/Motye	Mordechai	Mordechai	מוטיע/מאטל
Nachman	Nahaman	Nachman	נחמן
Naftoli	Nephtali	Naftali	נפתלי
Natan	Nathan	Natan	נתן
Nataniel	Nathaniel	Nataniel	נתנאל
Nechemioh	Nehemiah	Nechemia	נחמיה
Nisan	—	Nisan	ניסן
Nissele	—	Nisan	ניסעלע
Nissim	—	Nissim	ניסים
Nochum	Nahum	Nachum	נחם
Nossen	Nathan	Natan	נתן
Note	Nathan	Natan	נטע
Nuche	Menahem	Menachem	נוחע
Obadía	—	Obadia	עבדיה
Oizer	—	Ozer	עוזר
Oshiah	—	Oshia	אושיה
Ozer	—	Ozer	עוזר
Paishe/Paishke	—	Pesach	פיישע/פיישקע
Palti	—	Palti	פלטי
Paltiel	Phillip	Paltiel	פלטיאל
Peretz	—	Peretz	פרץ
Pesach	Pascual	Pesach	פסח
Petachioh	—	Petachia	פתחיה
Pinchas	Phineas	Pinchas	פינחס
Pinieh	Phineas	Pinchas	פיניע
Rafoel	Raphael	Rafael	רפאל
Ruven	Reuben	Ruven	ראובן
Saadia	—	Saadia	סעריה
Sander/Sender	Alexander	—	סנדר
Senderman	—	—	סנדרמן
Shabbsai	Sabbatai	Shabtai	שבתי
Shachne	—	Shachna	שכנא
Shammai	—	Shammai	שמאי
Shaya	Isaiah	Yeshaia	שיע
Shebtel	Sabbatai	Shabtai	שבתל
Shemtob	—	Shemtob	שמטוב
Shepsel	Sabbatai	Shabtai	שעפסל
Sheshet	—	Sheshet	ששת
Shevach	—	Shevach	שבח
Shiah	Joshua	Yehoshua	שיא
Shikeh	Joshua	Yehoshua	שיקע
Shimon	Simon	Shimon	שמעון
Shimshon	Samson	Shimshon	שמשון
Shloime	Solomon	Shelomo	שלמה
Shmaioh	—	Shemaia	שמעיה

Shmarioh	—	Shemaria	שמריה
Shmeelik	Samuel	Shemuel	שמוליק
Shmerel	—	Shemaria	שמערעל
Shmul/Shmil	Samuel	Shemuel	שמואל
Shnieur	—	—	שניאור
Shochor	Issachar	Yissachar	שחור
Shol	Saul	Shaul	שאול
Sholom	—	Shalom	שלום
Shraga	Phillip	Shraga	שרגא
Shullam	—	Meshulem	שלם
Simcha	—	Simcha	שמחה
Sinai	—	Sinai	סיני
Sonderman	—	—	סנדרמן
Tanchum	—	Tanchum	תנחום
Tevye	Tobias	Tevia	תביה
Todros	Theodore	Menachem	טודרוס
Traitel	Judah	Yehuda	טרייטל
Tuvia	Tobias	Tuvia	טוביה
Tzadok	—	Tzadok	צדוק
Tzelel	Betzalel	Betzalel	צלאל
Tzemach	—	Tzemach	צמח
Tzvi	Hirsch	Tzvi	צבי
Uri	—	Uri	אורי
Uziel	—	Uziel	וזיאל
Vaiber	—	Elyakim	ווייבר
Vigdor	Victor	Avigdor	ביגדור
Volf	Wolf	Zev	וואלף
Yakir	Jakkir	Yakir	יקיר
Yakov/Yankev	Jacob	Yaacov	יעקב
Yankel	Jacob	Yaacov	יאנקעל
Yechezkel	Ezekiel	Yechezkel	יחזקאל
Yechiel	—	Yechiel	יחיאל
Yedidiah	Jedidah	Yedidia	ידידיה
Yehoiash	Jehoash	Yehoash	יהואש
Yehoishua	Joshua	Yehoshua	יהושע
Yehonoson	Jonathan	Yehonatan	יהונתן
Yehuda	Judah	Yehuda	יהודה
Yehudi	Judah	Yehudi	יהודי
Yekel	Jacob	Yaacov	יעקל
Yekusiel	Jekutiel	Yekutiel	יקותיאל
Yerachmiel	—	Yerachmiel	ירחמיאל
Yermiohu	Jeremiah	Yermiyahu	ירמיהו
Yeruchem	—	Yerucham	ירוחם
Yeshaiah	Isaiah	Yeshaia	ישעיה
Yishmael	Ismael	Yishmael	ישמעאל
Yisroel	Israel	Yisrael	ישראל

Yissachar	Isahar	Yisachar	יששכר
Yitzchok	Isaac	Yitzchak	יצחק
Yochanan	Jochanan	Yochanan	יוחנן
Yoiel	Joel	Yoel	יואל
Yoilish	Joel	Yoel	יואליש
Yoina	Jonah	Yona	יונה
Yoisef	Joseph	Yosef	יוסף
Yoizel	Joseph	Yosef	יוזל
Yomtov	—	Yomtov	יומטוב
Yona	Jonah	Yona	יונה
Yontel	—	Yomtov	יאנטל
Yoshe/Yoshke	Joseph	Yosef	יאשקע
Yossel	Joseph	Yosef	יאסל
Yuda	Judah	Yehuda	יודא
Yudel/Yidel	Judah	Yehuda	יודל
Yukl	Jacob	Yaacov	יוקל
Zachai	Zakkai	Zachai	זכאי
Zainvil/Zanvil	Samuel	Shemuel	זנויל
Zalkin	Isaac	Yitzchak	צאלקין
Zalkind	Solomon	Shelomo	זלקינד
Zalman	Solomon	Shelomo	זלמן
Zavel	Wolf	Zev	זוול
Z'bulun	Zebulon	Z'bulun	זבולון
Zecharioh	Zachariah	Zecharia	זכריה
Zela	—	Shneiur	זלא
Zelig	Zelig	Zelig	זעליג
Zeligman	Hezekiah	Chezekia	זעליגמן
Zerach	Zarah	Zerach	זרח
Zev	Wolf	Zev	זאב
Zimel	Simon	Shimon	זימל
Zishe	—	Meshulam	זישע
Zundel	Enoch	Chanoch	זונדל
Zussel/Zissel	—	Shneiur	זוסל
Zusskind	—	Shneiur	זוסקינד
Zusslin	Isaac	Yitzchak	זוסלין
Zussman	Eliezer	Elazar	זוסמן
Zussya	—	Meshulam	זוסיא

Names for Females

Common or Yiddish Pronunciation	English or Spanish	Hebrew Equivalent	Hebrew or Yiddish Spelling
Achseh	—	Achsa	עכסה
Alta/Alte	—	—	אלטע
Alterke	—	—	אלטערקע
Asna	—	Asna	אסנה
Asnas	Asenath	Asnat	אסנת
Avigail	Abigail	Avigail	אביגיל
Badana	Theodora	—	באדאנא
Bashe/Basieh	Bithiah	Batya	בתיה
Bas-sheva	Bathsheba	Batsheva	בת שבע
Batya	Bithiah	Batya	בתיה
Beile	Blanche	—	בילא
Beilke	Blanche	—	בילקע
Bisieh	Bithiah	Batya	בתיה
Blima/Bluma	Flora/Flor	—	בלימא/בלומא
Blimele	Flora/Flor	—	בלימעלע
Breindel	—	—	ברײנדל
Breine	—	—	ברײנא
Brocho	Beatrice/ Benita	Beracha	ברכה
Broyna	—	—	ברױנא
Buna	Bona	—	בונא
Bunieh	Bona	—	בוניא
Buntzeh	Bona	—	בונצא
Chana	Hannah	Chana	חנה
Chasheh	Hannah	Chana	חאסיע/חאשע
Chasida	Pia	Chasida	חסידה
Chava	Eva/Eve/Ava	Chava	חוה
Chaya	Vivian	Chaya	חיה
Cheneh	Grace	Chena	חנה
Chinna	Grace	Chena	חנה
Chissa	—	—	חיסא
Chvolash	Leonie/Leona	—	חװלש/חװאלס
Dana	Theodora	—	דאנא
Deiche	Judith	Yehudit	דײכע
Dinoh	Dinah	Dina	דינה
Doba	Bona	—	דאבא
Dobra	Bona	—	דאברא
Dobrusha	Bona	—	דאברושא
Dreiza	Drusilla	—	דרײזא
Dreizel	Drusilla	—	דרײזל

Dvoira	Deborah	D'vora	דבורה
Dvoshe	Deborah	D'vora	דוואשע
Eidel	–	–	אידל
Eidla	–	–	אידלא
Etta/Ettel	Esther	Ester	עטא/עטל
Elkeh	Esther	Ester	עלקע
Eshkeh	Esther	Ester	עשקא
Ester	Esther	Ester	אסתר
Esti	Esther	Ester	עסטי
Feige	Robin	Tzippora	פייגא
Feigel	Robin	Tzippora	פייגל
Feygu	–	–	פיגו
Fradl	–	–	פרדל
Fraidel	–	–	פריידל
Frieda	Joy/Alegria	–	פרידא
Friedel	Frieda/Allegra	–	פרידל
Frima	Pia	Chasida	פרומא
Fruma	Pia	Chasida	פרומא
Geila	Joy	Gila	גילה
Gella	–	–	געלא
Gittel	Bona	Tova	גיטל
Glicka	Felicia	Mazal	גליקא
G'nendel	Agnes	–	גינענדל
G'nessieh	Agnes	–	גינעסיא
Golda	Aura/Aurelia	–	גאלדא
Gruna	–	–	גרונא
Gutta	Bona	Tova	גוטע/גוטא
Hadassa	Esther	Hadassa	הדסא
Hagar	Hagar	Hagar	הגר
Hena	Hannah	Chana	כענא
Hendl	Hannah	Chana	העֿנדל
Henieh	Hannah	Chana	העניע
Hessieh	Hannah	Chana	כסיא
Hinda	–	–	הינדל
Hindele	–	–	הינדעלע
Hoda	Esther	Ester	האדא
Hodel	Esther	Ester	האדל
Hodes	Esther	Ester	האדעס
Itta	Judith	Yehudit	איטא
Keila	–	–	קילא
Kendl	–	–	קענדל
Klara	Clara	–	קלארא
Kreindel	–	–	קריינדל

Kroina	—	—	קרוינא
Kunieh	—	—	קוניע
Leah	Leah	Leah	לאה
Leyke	Leah	Leah	לאה'סע
Libba	Libby	—	ליבא
Libke	Libby	—	ליבקע
Liuba	Luba	—	ליובא
Loytza	—	—	לויצא
Machla	Mahlah	Machla	מחלה
Malka	Regina/Reina/ Sultana	Malka	מלכה
Margolis	Margaret/ Pearl/Perla	Margalit	מרגלית
Maryashe	Mary	Miriam	מאריאשע
Mattel	Virginia	—	מאטל
Mattla	Virginia	—	מאטלא
Mazal	Fortuna	Mazal	מזל
Meitel	Virginia	—	מייטל
Menieh	Menuha	Menucha	מעניע
Menucha	Menuha	Menucha	מנוחה
Mereh	Miriam	Miriam	מערע
Merima	Miriam	Miriam	מרימה
Merkeh	Miriam	Miriam	מערקע
Michla	—	—	מיכלה
Milka	—	Milka	מילכה
Mindl	—	—	מינדל
Minkeh	—	—	מינקע
Minna	Wilhelmina	—	מינא
Mirele	Myhrra	—	מירעלע
Miriom	Miriam	Miriam	מרים
Mirra	Myhrra	—	מירא
Nechama	Consuelo	Nechama	נחמה
Necheh	Consuelo	Nechama	נעכע
Nechele	Consuelo	Nechama	נעכעלע
Noemi	Naomi	Naemi	נעמי
Nucheh	Menuha	Menucha	נוכע
Nushe/Nusieh	—	—	נוסיע/נושע
Perl	Pearl/Margaret	Margalit	פערל
Pesha	Pearl/Margaret	Margalit	פעשא
Peshke	Pearl/Margaret	Margalit	פעשקע
Peya	Robin	Tzipporah	פייע
Rachman	Mercy/Piedad	Rachman	רחמן
Rala	Rachel	Rachel	ראלא
Rashel	Rachel	Rachel	ראשל
Rechuma	—	Rechuma	רחמה

Reicha	—	—	רייכא
Reichel	—	—	רייכל
Reina	—	—	ריינא
Reitza	Grace	Chena	רייצא
Reitzel	Grace	Chena	רייצל
Reizel	Rose/Rosa	Shoshana	רייזל
Rella	—	—	רעלא
Reshka	—	—	רעשקא
Riba	Rebecca	Rivka	ריבא
Rickel	—	—	ריקל
Rickla	—	—	ריקלא
Rissa	Rebecca	Rivka	ריסא
Rivka	Rebecca	Rivka	רבקה
Roche	Rachel	Rachel	ראכע
Rochel	Rachel	Rachel	רחל
Roda	Rose/Rosa	Shoshana	רודא
Roiza	Rose/Rosa	Shoshana	רויזא
Roizel	Rose/Rosa	Shoshana	רויזל
Ronieh	Rose/Rosa	Shoshana	רוניע
Rus	Ruth	Rut	רות
Sheina	Linda	Yaffa	שיינא
Sheindel	Linda	Yaffa	שיינדל
Shelomis	—	Shelomit	שלומית
Sheva	Bathsheba	Batsheva	שבע
Shevaleh	Bathsheba	Batsheva	שבע'לע
Shifra	Bella	Shifra	שפרה
Shprintel	Hope/Esperanza	Tikva	שפרינטל
Shprintza	Hope/Esperanza	Tikva	שפרינצא
Shulamis	Shulamit	Shulamit	שולמית
Sima	—	Simcha	סימא
Simcha	—	Simcha	שמחה
Slava	Leonie	—	סלאווא
Slova	Leonie	—	סלאווא
Soro	Sarah	Sara	שרה
Sossieh	Sarah	Sara	סוסיא
Sosskeh	Sarah	Sara	סוסקע
Stireh	Stella	—	סטירא
Tamara	Tamara	Tamar	תמרה/תמר
Tana	—	—	טאנא
Teibele	Paloma	—	טייבעלע
Temma	Tamara	Tamar	טעמא
Tila	—	Tehila	טהילה
Tirtza	Tirsa	Tirtza	תרצה
Toiba	Paloma	—	טויבא
Toiva	Bona	Tova	טובה
Toltza	Dulcia/Dulce	—	טאלצא
Treina	Catherine	—	טריינא
Troila	—	—	טרוילא

Tsartel	—	—	צארטל
Tseitel	—	—	צייטל
Tsharne	Bruna	—	טשארנע
Tsinna	—	Ketsina	צינא
Tsippeh	Robin	Tzippora	ציפע
Tsira	Sarah	Sara	צירע
Tsirele	Sarah	Sara	צירעלע
Tsiviah	—	—	צביה
Tzipporah	Robin	Tzippora	צפורה
Vichneh	—	—	וויכנע
Yache	Johebed	Yocheved	יאכע
Yachne	Johebed	Yocheved	יאכנע
Yehudis	Judith	Yehudit	יהודית
Yenta	Gentille	—	ינטא
Yetta	Judith	Yehudit	איטא
Yitta	Judith	Yehudit	איטא
Yittke	Judith	Yehudit	איטקע
Yoche	Johebed	Yocheved	יאכע
Yocheved	Johebed	Yocheved	יוכבד
Yuta	Judith	Yehudit	יוטא
Yutelin	Judith	Yehudit	יוטעלין
Zelda	—	—	זלדא
Zelma	Selma	—	זעלמא
Zilpah	Zilpah	Zilpa	זלפה
Zissa	Dulcia/Dulce	—	זיסא
Zissele	Dulcia/Dulce	—	זיסעלע
Zlatta	Aura/Aurelia	—	זלאטא
Zussa	Dulcia/Dulce	—	זוסא

Appendix II

Jewish Calendar – 5661 to 5760 with Corresponding Dates
On the Civil Calendar – 1900 to 2000

The nature and constitution of the Jewish calendar is explained in chapter 38. The following table shows the equivalent dates on the Jewish calendar to the years 1900 to 2000 C.E.

To determine a birthday, yohrtzeit or other date on the Jewish calendar when all you know is the civil date, simply find the nearest date on the table and figure either backward or forward to the date you want.

For example, say you want to know on what Jewish date July 19, 1936, fell. You will find that the nearest date on the table is July 20, 1936, corresponding to the first day of Av, 5696. Accordingly, the 19th of July, the preceding day, is the last day of Tamuz, which always has 29 days. Thus July 19, 1936, corresponds to the 29th day of Tamuz, 5696.

To take another case, say you want to know the equivalent Jewish date to the 27th of November, 1943. On the Jewish calendar, the nearest date is the 28th of November, which is the first day of Kislev, 5704. Here we cannot work backward since the preceding month of Cheshvan can have either 29 or 30 days, so we must work forward from the first day of Cheshvan, which fell, according to the table, on the 30th of October. Working forward from that date, we see that the 29th day of Cheshvan fell on the 27th of November, the date we are seeking. Obviously, in the year 5704, Cheshvan had only 29 days.

The Jewish months have the following number of days:

Tishri	30 days
Cheshvan	29 or 30 days
Kislev	29 or 30 days
Tevet	29 days
Shvat	30 days
Adar	29 days except on a leap year when it has 30 days
Adar Sheni	29 days
Nisan	30 days
Iyyar	29 days
Sivan	30 days
Tamuz	29 days
Av	30 days
Elul	29 days

	5661	5662	5663	5664	5665	5666	5667	5668	5669	5670	5671	5672
TISHRI	9 24 00	9 14 01	10 2 02	9 22 03	9 10 04	9 30 05	9 20 06	9 9 07	9 26 08	9 16 09	10 4 10	9 23 11
CHESHVAN	10 24 00	10 14 01	11 1 02	10 22 03	10 10 04	10 30 05	10 20 06	10 9 07	10 26 08	10 16 09	11 3 10	10 23 11
KISLEV	11 23 00	11 12 01	12 1 02	11 20 03	11 9 04	11 29 05	11 18 06	11 7 07	11 25 08	11 14 09	12 2 10	11 22 11
TEVET	12 23 00	12 11 01	12 31 02	12 20 03	12 9 04	12 29 05	12 18 06	12 6 07	12 25 08	12 13 09	1 1 11	12 22 11
SH'VAT	1 21 01	1 9 02	1 29 03	1 18 04	1 7 05	1 27 06	1 16 07	1 4 08	1 23 09	1 11 10	1 30 11	1 20 12
ADAR	2 20 01	2 8 02	2 28 03	2 17 04	2 6 05	2 26 06	2 15 07	2 3 08	2 22 09	2 10 10	3 1 11	2 19 12
ADAR SHENI	—	3 10 02	—	—	3 8 05	—	—	3 4 08	—	3 12 10	—	—
NISAN	3 21 01	4 8 02	3 29 03	3 17 04	4 6 05	3 27 06	3 16 07	4 2 08	3 23 09	4 10 10	3 30 11	3 19 12
IYYAR	4 20 01	5 8 02	4 28 03	4 16 04	5 6 05	4 26 06	4 15 07	5 2 08	4 22 09	5 10 10	4 29 11	4 18 12
SIVAN	5 19 01	6 6 02	5 27 03	5 15 04	6 4 05	5 25 06	5 14 07	5 31 08	5 21 09	6 8 10	5 28 11	5 17 12
TAMUZ	6 18 01	7 6 02	6 26 03	6 14 04	7 4 05	6 24 06	6 13 07	6 30 08	6 20 09	7 8 10	6 27 11	6 16 12
AV	7 17 01	8 4 02	7 25 03	7 13 04	8 2 05	7 23 06	7 12 07	7 29 08	7 19 09	8 6 10	7 26 11	7 15 12
ELUL	8 16 01	9 3 02	8 24 03	8 12 04	9 1 05	8 22 06	8 11 07	8 28 08	8 18 09	9 5 10	8 25 11	8 14 12

JEWISH CALENDAR – 1900 TO 2000 C.E.

THE DATE SHOWN OPPOSITE THE JEWISH MONTH IS THE FIRST DAY OF THAT MONTH. NUMBERS OF CIVIL DATE INDICATE MONTH, DAY AND YEAR STARTING WITH 1900 C.E.

	5673			5674			5675			5676			5677			5678			5679			5680			5681			5682			5683			5684		
TISHRI	9	12	12	10	2	13	9	21	14	9	9	15	9	28	16	9	17	17	9	7	18	9	25	19	9	13	20	10	3	21	9	23	22	9	11	23
CHESHVAN	10	12	12	11	1	13	10	21	14	10	9	15	10	28	16	10	17	17	10	7	18	10	25	19	10	13	20	11	2	21	10	23	22	10	11	23
KISLEV	11	11	12	11	30	13	11	19	14	11	8	15	11	26	16	11	16	17	11	5	18	11	23	19	11	12	20	12	2	21	11	21	22	11	9	23
TEVET	12	11	12	12	30	13	12	18	14	12	8	15	12	26	16	12	16	17	12	4	18	12	23	19	12	12	20	1	1	22	12	20	22	12	9	23
SH'VAT	1	9	13	1	28	14	1	16	15	1	6	16	1	24	17	1	14	18	1	2	19	1	21	20	1	10	21	1	30	22	1	18	23	1	7	24
ADAR	2	8	13	2	27	14	2	15	15	2	5	16	2	23	17	2	13	18	2	1	19	2	20	20	2	9	21	2	1	22	2	17	23	2	6	24
ADAR SHENI	3	10	13	—	—	—	—	—	—	3	6	16	—	—	—	—	—	—	3	3	19	—	—	—	3	11	21	—	—	—	—	—	—	3	7	24
NISAN	4	8	13	3	28	14	3	16	15	4	4	16	3	24	17	3	14	18	4	1	19	3	20	20	4	9	21	3	30	22	3	18	23	4	5	24
IYYAR	5	8	13	4	27	14	4	15	15	5	4	16	4	23	17	4	13	18	5	1	19	4	19	20	5	9	21	4	29	22	4	17	23	5	5	24
SIVAN	6	6	13	5	26	14	5	14	15	6	2	16	5	22	17	5	12	18	5	30	19	5	18	20	6	7	21	5	28	22	5	16	23	6	3	24
TAMUZ	7	6	13	6	25	14	6	13	15	7	2	16	6	21	17	6	11	18	6	29	19	6	17	20	7	7	21	6	27	22	6	15	23	7	3	24
AV	8	4	13	7	24	14	7	12	15	7	31	16	7	20	17	7	10	18	7	28	19	7	16	20	8	5	21	7	26	22	7	14	23	8	1	24
ELUL	9	3	13	8	23	14	8	11	15	8	30	16	8	19	17	8	9	18	8	27	19	8	15	20	9	4	21	8	25	22	8	13	23	8	31	24

	5685	5686	5687	5688	5689	5690	5691	5692	5693	5694	5695	5696
TISHRI	9 29 24	9 19 25	9 9 26	9 27 27	9 15 28	10 5 29	9 23 30	9 12 31	10 1 32	9 21 33	9 10 34	9 28 35
CHESHVAN	10 29 24	10 19 25	10 9 26	10 27 27	10 15 28	11 4 29	10 23 30	10 12 31	10 31 32	10 21 33	10 10 34	10 28 35
KISLEV	11 28 24	11 18 25	11 7 26	11 25 27	11 14 28	12 3 29	11 21 30	11 11 31	11 30 32	11 19 33	11 8 34	11 27 35
TEVET	12 28 24	12 18 25	12 6 26	12 25 27	12 14 28	1 1 30	12 21 30	12 11 31	12 30 32	12 19 33	12 7 34	12 27 35
SH'VAT	1 26 25	1 16 26	1 4 27	1 23 28	1 12 29	1 30 30	1 19 31	1 9 32	1 28 33	1 17 34	1 5 35	1 25 36
ADAR	2 25 25	2 15 26	2 3 27	2 22 28	2 11 29	2 1 30	2 18 31	2 8 32	2 27 33	2 16 34	2 4 35	2 24 36
ADAR SHENI	– –	– –	3 5 27	– –	3 13 29	– –	– –	3 9 32	– –	– –	3 6 35	– –
NISAN	3 26 25	3 16 26	4 3 27	3 22 28	4 11 29	3 30 30	3 19 31	4 7 32	3 28 33	3 17 34	4 4 35	3 24 36
IYYAR	4 25 25	4 15 26	5 3 27	4 21 28	5 11 29	4 29 30	4 18 31	5 7 32	4 27 33	4 16 34	5 4 35	4 23 36
SIVAN	5 24 25	5 14 26	6 1 27	5 20 28	6 9 29	5 28 30	5 17 31	6 5 32	5 26 33	5 15 34	6 2 35	5 22 36
TAMUZ	6 23 25	6 13 26	7 1 27	6 19 28	7 9 29	6 27 30	6 16 31	7 5 32	6 25 33	6 14 34	7 2 35	6 21 36
AV	7 22 25	7 12 26	7 30 27	7 18 28	8 7 29	7 26 30	7 15 31	8 3 32	7 24 33	7 13 34	7 31 35	7 20 36
ELUL	8 21 25	8 11 26	8 29 27	8 17 28	9 6 29	8 25 30	8 14 31	9 2 32	8 23 33	8 12 34	8 30 35	8 19 36

JEWISH CALENDAR – 1900 TO 2000 C.E.

THE DATE SHOWN OPPOSITE THE JEWISH MONTH IS THE FIRST DAY OF THAT MONTH.
NUMBERS OF CIVIL DATE INDICATE MONTH, DAY AND YEAR STARTING WITH 1900 C.E.

	5697	5698	5699	5700	5701	5702	5703	5704	5705	5706	5707	5708
TISHRI	9 17 36	9 6 37	9 26 38	9 14 39	10 3 40	9 22 41	9 12 42	9 30 43	9 18 44	9 8 45	9 26 46	9 15 47
CHESHVAN	10 17 36	10 6 37	10 26 38	10 14 39	11 2 40	10 22 41	10 12 42	10 30 43	10 18 44	10 8 45	10 26 46	10 15 47
KISLEV	11 15 36	11 5 37	11 24 38	11 13 39	12 1 40	11 21 41	11 10 42	11 28 43	11 17 44	11 6 45	11 24 46	11 14 47
TEVET	12 15 36	12 5 37	12 23 38	12 13 39	12 31 40	12 21 41	12 9 42	12 28 43	12 17 44	12 5 45	12 24 46	12 14 47
SH'VAT	1 13 37	1 3 38	1 21 39	1 11 40	1 29 41	1 19 42	1 7 43	1 26 44	1 15 45	1 3 46	1 22 47	1 12 48
ADAR	2 12 37	2 2 38	2 20 39	2 10 40	2 28 41	2 18 42	2 6 43	2 25 44	2 14 45	2 2 46	2 21 47	2 11 48
ADAR SHENI	— —	3 4 38	— —	3 11 40	— —	— —	3 8 43	— —	— —	3 4 46	— —	3 12 48
NISAN	3 13 37	4 2 38	3 21 39	4 9 40	3 29 41	3 19 42	4 6 43	3 25 44	3 15 45	4 2 46	3 22 47	4 10 48
IYYAR	4 12 37	5 2 38	4 20 39	5 9 40	4 28 41	4 18 42	5 6 43	4 24 44	4 14 45	5 2 46	4 21 47	5 10 48
SIVAN	5 11 37	5 31 38	5 19 39	6 7 40	5 27 41	5 17 42	6 4 43	5 23 44	5 13 45	5 31 46	5 20 47	6 8 48
TAMUZ	6 10 37	6 30 38	6 18 39	7 7 40	6 26 41	6 16 42	7 4 43	6 22 44	6 12 45	6 30 46	6 19 47	7 8 48
AV	7 9 37	7 29 38	7 17 39	8 5 40	7 25 41	7 15 42	8 2 43	7 21 44	7 11 45	7 29 46	7 18 47	8 6 48
ELUL	8 8 37	8 28 38	8 16 39	9 4 40	8 24 41	8 14 42	9 1 43	8 20 44	8 10 45	8 28 46	8 17 47	9 5 48

	5709			5710			5711			5712			5713			5714			5715			5716			5717			5718			5719			5720		
TISHRI	10	4	48	9	24	49	9	12	50	10	1	51	9	20	52	9	10	53	9	28	54	9	17	55	9	6	56	9	26	57	9	15	58	10	3	59
CHESHVAN	11	3	48	10	24	49	10	12	50	10	31	51	10	20	52	10	10	53	10	28	54	10	17	55	10	6	56	10	26	57	10	15	58	11	2	59
KISLEV	12	3	48	11	22	49	11	10	50	11	30	51	11	19	52	11	8	53	11	26	54	11	16	55	11	5	56	11	24	57	11	13	58	12	2	59
TEVET	1	2	49	12	21	49	12	10	50	12	30	51	12	19	52	12	7	53	12	26	54	12	16	55	12	5	56	12	24	57	12	12	58	1	1	60
SH'VAT	1	31	49	1	19	50	1	8	51	1	28	52	1	17	53	1	5	54	1	24	55	1	14	56	1	3	57	1	22	58	1	10	59	1	30	60
ADAR	2	2	49	2	18	50	2	7	51	2	27	52	2	16	53	2	4	54	2	23	55	2	13	56	2	2	57	2	21	58	2	9	59	2	29	60
ADAR SHENI	—	—	—	—	—	—	3	9	51	—	—	—	—	—	—	3	6	54	—	—	—	—	—	—	3	4	57	—	—	—	3	11	59	—	—	—
NISAN	3	31	49	3	19	50	4	7	51	3	27	52	3	17	53	4	4	54	3	24	55	3	13	56	4	2	57	3	22	58	4	9	59	3	29	60
IYYAR	4	30	49	4	18	50	5	7	51	4	26	52	4	16	53	5	4	54	4	23	55	4	12	56	5	2	57	4	21	58	5	9	59	4	28	60
SIVAN	5	29	49	5	17	50	6	5	51	5	25	52	5	15	53	6	2	54	5	22	55	5	11	56	5	31	57	5	20	58	6	7	59	5	27	60
TAMUZ	6	28	49	6	16	50	7	5	51	6	24	52	6	14	53	7	2	54	6	21	55	6	10	56	6	30	57	6	19	58	7	7	59	6	26	60
AV	7	27	49	7	15	50	8	3	51	7	23	52	7	13	53	7	31	54	7	20	55	7	9	56	7	29	57	7	18	58	8	5	59	7	25	60
ELUL	8	26	49	8	14	50	9	2	51	8	22	52	8	12	53	8	30	54	8	19	55	8	8	56	8	28	57	8	17	58	9	4	59	8	24	60

JEWISH CALENDAR – 1900 TO 2000 C.E.

THE DATE SHOWN OPPOSITE THE JEWISH MONTH IS THE FIRST DAY OF THAT MONTH.
NUMBERS OF CIVIL DATE INDICATE MONTH, DAY AND YEAR STARTING WITH 1900 C.E.

	5721	5722	5723	5724	5725	5726	5727	5728	5729	5730	5731	5732
TISHRI	9 22 60	9 11 61	9 29 62	9 19 63	9 7 64	9 27 65	9 15 66	10 5 67	9 23 68	9 13 69	10 1 70	9 20 71
CHESHVAN	10 22 60	10 11 61	10 29 62	10 19 63	10 7 64	10 27 65	10 15 66	11 4 67	10 23 68	10 13 69	10 31 70	10 20 71
KISLEV	11 20 60	11 9 61	11 28 62	11 17 63	11 6 64	11 25 65	11 14 66	12 3 67	11 22 68	11 11 69	11 29 70	11 19 71
TEVET	12 20 60	12 8 61	12 28 62	12 17 63	12 6 64	12 24 65	12 14 66	1 2 68	12 22 68	12 10 69	12 29 70	12 19 71
SH'VAT	1 18 61	1 6 62	1 26 63	1 15 64	1 4 65	1 22 66	1 12 67	1 31 68	1 20 69	1 8 70	1 27 71	1 17 72
ADAR	2 17 61	2 5 62	2 25 63	2 14 64	2 3 65	2 21 66	2 11 67	2 1 68	2 19 69	2 7 70	2 26 71	2 16 72
ADAR SHENI	—	3 7 62	—	—	3 5 65	—	3 13 67	—	—	3 9 70	—	—
NISAN	3 18 61	4 5 62	3 26 63	3 14 64	4 3 65	3 22 66	4 11 67	3 30 68	3 20 69	4 7 70	3 27 71	3 16 72
IYYAR	4 17 61	5 5 62	4 25 63	4 13 64	5 3 65	4 21 66	5 11 67	4 29 68	4 19 69	5 7 70	4 26 71	4 15 72
SIVAN	5 16 61	6 3 62	5 24 63	5 12 64	6 1 65	5 20 66	6 9 67	5 28 68	5 18 69	6 5 70	5 25 71	5 14 72
TAMUZ	6 15 61	7 3 62	6 23 63	6 11 64	7 1 65	6 19 66	7 9 67	6 27 68	6 17 69	7 5 70	6 24 71	6 13 72
AV	7 14 61	8 1 62	7 22 63	7 10 64	7 30 65	7 18 66	8 7 67	7 26 68	7 16 69	8 3 70	7 23 71	7 12 72
ELUL	8 13 61	8 31 62	8 21 63	8 9 64	8 29 65	8 17 66	9 6 67	8 25 68	8 15 69	9 2 70	8 22 71	8 11 72

	5733			5734			5735			5736			5737			5738			5739			5740			5741			5742			5743			5744		
TISHRI	9	9	72	9	27	73	9	17	74	9	6	75	9	25	76	9	13	77	10	2	78	9	22	79	9	11	80	9	29	81	9	18	82	9	8	83
CHESHVAN	10	9	72	10	27	73	10	17	74	10	6	75	10	25	76	10	13	77	11	1	78	10	22	79	10	11	80	10	29	81	10	18	82	10	8	83
KISLEV	11	7	72	11	26	73	11	15	74	11	5	75	11	23	76	11	11	77	12	1	78	11	21	79	11	9	80	11	27	81	11	17	82	11	7	83
TEVET	12	6	72	12	26	73	12	15	74	12	5	75	12	22	76	12	11	77	12	31	78	12	21	79	12	8	80	12	27	81	12	17	82	12	7	83
SH'VAT	1	4	73	1	24	74	1	13	75	1	3	76	1	20	77	1	9	78	1	29	79	1	19	80	1	6	81	1	25	82	1	15	83	1	5	84
ADAR	2	3	73	2	23	74	2	12	75	2	2	76	2	19	77	2	8	78	2	28	79	2	18	80	2	5	81	2	24	82	2	14	83	2	4	84
ADAR SHENI	3	5	73	—	—		—	—		3	3	76	—	—		3	10	78	—	—		—	—		3	7	81	—	—		—	—		3	5	84
NISAN	4	3	73	3	24	74	3	13	75	4	1	76	3	20	77	4	8	78	3	29	79	3	18	80	4	5	81	3	25	82	3	15	83	4	3	84
IYYAR	5	3	73	4	23	74	4	12	75	5	1	76	4	19	77	5	8	78	4	28	79	4	17	80	5	5	81	4	24	82	4	14	83	5	3	84
SIVAN	6	1	73	5	22	74	5	11	75	5	30	76	5	18	77	6	6	78	5	27	79	5	16	80	6	3	81	5	23	82	5	13	83	6	1	84
TAMUZ	7	1	73	6	21	74	6	10	75	6	29	76	6	17	77	7	6	78	6	26	79	6	15	80	7	3	81	6	22	82	6	12	83	7	1	84
AV	7	30	73	7	20	74	7	9	75	7	28	76	7	16	77	8	4	78	7	25	79	7	14	80	8	1	81	7	21	82	7	11	83	7	30	84
ELUL	8	29	73	8	19	74	8	8	75	8	27	76	8	15	77	9	3	78	8	24	79	8	13	80	8	31	81	8	20	82	8	10	83	8	29	84

JEWISH CALENDAR – 1900 TO 2000 C.E.

THE DATE SHOWN OPPOSITE THE JEWISH MONTH IS THE FIRST DAY OF THAT MONTH. NUMBERS OF CIVIL DATE INDICATE MONTH, DAY AND YEAR STARTING WITH 1900 C.E.

	5745	5746	5747	5748	5749	5750	5751	5752	5753	5754	5755	5756
TISHRI	9 27 84	9 16 85	10 4 86	9 24 87	9 12 88	9 30 89	9 20 90	9 9 91	9 28 92	9 16 93	9 6 94	9 25 95
CHESHVAN	10 27 84	10 16 85	11 3 86	10 24 87	10 12 88	10 30 89	10 20 90	10 9 91	10 28 92	10 16 93	10 6 94	10 25 95
KISLEV	11 25 84	11 14 85	12 3 86	11 22 87	11 10 88	11 29 89	11 18 90	11 8 91	11 26 92	11 15 93	11 4 94	11 24 95
TEVET	12 25 84	12 13 85	1 2 87	12 22 87	12 9 88	12 29 89	12 18 90	12 8 91	12 25 92	12 15 93	12 4 94	12 24 95
SH'VAT	1 23 85	1 11 86	1 31 87	1 20 88	1 7 89	1 27 90	1 16 91	1 6 92	1 23 93	1 13 94	1 2 95	1 22 96
ADAR	2 22 85	2 10 86	2 2 87	2 19 88	2 6 89	2 26 90	2 15 91	2 5 92	2 22 93	2 12 94	2 1 95	2 21 96
ADAR SHENI	—	3 12 86	—	—	3 8 89	—	—	3 6 92	—	—	3 3 95	—
NISAN	3 23 85	4 10 86	3 31 87	3 19 88	4 6 89	3 27 90	3 16 91	4 4 92	3 23 93	3 13 94	4 1 95	3 21 96
IYYAR	4 22 85	5 10 86	4 30 87	4 18 88	5 6 89	4 26 90	4 15 91	5 4 92	4 22 93	4 12 94	5 1 95	4 20 96
SIVAN	5 21 85	6 8 86	5 29 87	5 17 88	6 4 89	5 25 90	5 14 91	6 2 92	5 21 93	5 11 94	5 30 95	5 19 96
TAMUZ	6 20 85	7 8 86	6 28 87	6 16 88	7 4 89	6 24 90	6 13 91	7 2 92	6 20 93	6 10 94	6 29 95	6 18 96
AV	7 19 85	8 6 86	7 27 87	7 15 88	8 2 89	7 23 90	7 12 91	7 31 92	7 19 93	7 9 94	7 28 95	7 17 96
ELUL	8 18 85	9 5 86	8 26 87	8 14 88	9 1 89	8 22 90	8 11 91	8 30 92	8 18 93	8 8 94	8 27 95	8 16 96

	5757			5758			5759			5760		
TISHRI	9	14	96	10	2	97	9	21	98	9	11	99
CHESHVAN	10	14	96	11	1	97	10	21	98	10	11	99
KISLEV	11	12	96	11	30	97	11	20	98	11	10	99
TEVET	12	11	96	12	30	97	12	20	98	12	10	99
SH'VAT	1	9	97	1	28	98	1	18	99	1	8	00
ADAR	2	8	97	2	27	98	2	17	99	2	7	00
ADAR SHENI	3	10	97	—	—	—	—	—	—	3	8	00
NISAN	4	8	97	3	28	98	3	18	99	4	6	00
IYYAR	5	8	97	4	27	98	4	17	99	5	6	00
SIVAN	6	6	97	5	26	98	5	16	99	6	4	00
TAMUZ	7	6	97	6	25	98	6	15	99	7	4	00
AV	8	4	97	7	24	98	7	14	99	8	2	00
ELUL	9	3	97	8	23	98	8	13	99	9	1	00

Appendix III

Civil Dates of Jewish Holidays, 1975-1999

Year	Rosh Hashana	Yom Kippur	Sukkot	Sh'mini Atzeret	Chanuka	Year	Tu B'Shvat	Purim	Passover	Lag B'omer	Shavuot	Tisha B'av
1975	Sep 6	Sep 15	Sep 20	Sep 27	Nov 29	1976	Jan 17	Mar 16	Apr 15	May 18	Jun 4	Aug 5
1976	Sep 25	Oct 4	Oct 9	Oct 16	Dec 17	1977	Feb 3	Mar 4	Apr 3	May 6	May 23	Jul 24
1977	Sep 13	Sep 22	Sep 27	Oct 4	Dec 5	1978	Jan 23	Mar 23	Apr 22	May 25	Jun 11	Aug 13
1978	Oct 2	Oct 11	Oct 16	Oct 23	Dec 25	1979	Feb 12	Mar 13	Apr 12	May 15	Jun 1	Aug 2
1979	Sep 22	Oct 1	Oct 6	Oct 13	Dec 15	1980	Feb 2	Mar 2	Apr 1	May 4	May 21	Jul 22
1980	Sep 11	Sep 20	Sep 25	Oct 2	Dec 3	1981	Jan 20	Mar 20	Apr 19	May 22	Jun 8	Aug 9
1981	Sep 29	Oct 8	Oct 13	Oct 20	Dec 21	1982	Feb 8	Mar 9	Apr 8	May 11	May 28	July 29
1982	Sep 18	Sep 27	Oct 2	Oct 9	Dec 11	1983	Jan 29	Feb 27	Mar 29	May 1	May 18	Jul 19
1983	Sep 8	Sep 17	Sep 22	Sep 29	Dec 1	1984	Jan 19	Mar 18	Apr 17	May 20	Jun 6	Aug 7
1984	Sep 27	Oct 6	Oct 11	Oct 18	Dec 19	1985	Feb 6	Mar 7	Apr 6	May 9	May 26	Jul 28
1985	Sep 16	Sep 25	Sep 30	Oct 7	Dec 8	1986	Jan 25	Mar 25	Apr 24	May 27	Jun 13	Aug 14
1986	Oct 4	Oct 13	Oct 18	Oct 25	Dec 27	1987	Feb 14	Mar 15	Apr 14	May 17	Jun 3	Aug 4
1987	Sep 24	Oct 3	Oct 8	Oct 15	Dec 16	1988	Feb 3	Mar 3	Apr 2	May 5	May 22	Jul 24
1988	Sep 12	Sep 21	Sep 26	Oct 3	Dec 4	1989	Jan 21	Mar 21	Apr 20	May 23	Jun 9	Aug 10
1989	Sep 30	Oct 9	Oct 14	Oct 21	Dec 23	1990	Feb 10	Mar 11	Apr 10	May 13	May 30	Jul 31
1990	Sep 20	Sep 29	Oct 4	Oct 11	Dec 12	1991	Jan 30	Feb 21	Mar 30	May 2	May 19	Jul 20
1991	Sep 9	Sep 18	Sep 23	Sep 30	Dec 2	1992	Jan 20	Mar 9	Apr 18	May 21	Jun 7	Aug 8
1992	Sep 28	Oct 7	Oct 12	Oct 19	Dec 20	1993	Feb 6	Mar 7	Apr 6	May 9	May 26	Jul 27
1993	Sep 16	Sep 25	Sep 30	Oct 6	Dec 9	1994	Jan 27	Feb 25	Mar 27	Apr 29	May 15	Jul 17
1994	Sep 6	Sep 15	Sep 20	Sep 27	Nov 28	1995	Jan 16	Mar 16	Apr 15	May 18	Jun 4	Aug 5
1995	Sep 25	Oct 4	Oct 9	Oct 16	Dec 18	1996	Feb 5	Mar 6	Apr 4	May 7	May 24	Jul 25
1996	Sep 14	Sep 23	Sep 28	Oct 5	Dec 6	1997	Jan 23	Mar 23	Apr 22	Mar 25	Jun 11	Aug 12
1997	Oct 2	Oct 11	Oct 16	Oct 23	Dec 24	1998	Feb 11	Mar 11	Apr 11	May 14	May 31	Aug 1
1998	Sep 21	Sep 30	Oct 5	Oct 12	Dec 14	1999	Feb 1	Mar 2	Apr 1	May 4	May 21	Jul 22
1999	Sep 11	Sep 20	Sep 25	Oct 2	Dec 4	2000	Jan 22	Mar 21	Apr 19	May 24	Jun 9	Aug 10

All holidays start at sundown on the day preceding the dates listed above. Hoshana Rabba is the day before Shemini Atzeret, and Simchat Torah is the day after Shemini Atzeret

Appendix IV

THE blessings most often used by the Jew in his daily life are found below, translated into English and transliterated into Latin letters in the Sephardic pronunciation used in Israel. The Hebrew text is not given, since it can be found in any siddur.

While blessings as well as prayers can be said in any language, there is a positive benefit in saying them in Hebrew. First, because tradition is continued and strengthened in every house in which the holy language is used, and second, because the use of Hebrew in the blessings will help the person saying them to familiarize himself with the language. Even if at first the words are just sounds, unrelated to sense, in time the individual words will be recognized and the language take shape.

As for the longer blessings, such as the Sabbath Kiddush, the fact that the father of the house might read Hebrew with difficulty should not stop him from reciting the Kiddush in Hebrew, which he can read in the alphabet with which he is most familiar. In time, of course, he will know it by heart.

Blessings for Food

1. BLESSING ON WASHING THE HANDS PRIOR TO EATING. After making sure the hands are clean by thoroughly washing them, the washing should be ritually concluded by pouring over them water from a glass or other vessel. As explained elsewhere, this is to assure that no contaminating substances are in the water, which we can see in the vessel. After pouring water over the hands, they must be dried—this is an integral part of the process of washing them—and the blessing said. This blessing must be said before eating bread and it is forbidden to speak until the blessing for bread has been recited.

Baruch Ata Adonai, Elohenu Melech ha-olam, asher kidshanu b'mitzvotav, v'tzivanu al netilat yadaim.

Blessed art Thou, O Lord, our God, King of the universe, who has sanctified us in His commandments and commanded us to raise up our hands. (The expression, "raise up our hands," refers to raising the hands after washing them, in order to dry them.)

2. BLESSING FOR BREAD. As explained above, the hands must first be correctly washed and the blessing said. After saying the blessing for bread, put a little salt on the bread before eating it: this is explained in chapter 26. Only bread made of the "five species" of grain requires the *hamotzi* blessing. These grains are wheat, rye, barley, oats and spelt, a kind of red wheat. Other foods made out of these grains, such as cakes, cereals, etc., require the *m'zonot* blessing (no. 4).

Since bread is taken to represent food in general, after saying this blessing, no other blessings need be said for any other food during the meal. If wine is brought to the table, however, the proper blessing for wine (no. 3) must be said.

Baruch Ata Adonai, Elohenu Melech ha-olam, hamotzi lechem min ha-aretz.

Blessed art Thou, O Lord our God, King of the universe, who brings bread out of the earth.

3. BLESSING FOR WINE. This blessing may be said only over kosher grape wine. All other beverages require the *shehakol* blessing (no. 5).

Baruch Ata Adonai, Elohenu Melech ha-olam, boreh pri ha-gafen (Sephardim say, *boreh pri hagefen*).

Blessed art Thou, O Lord our God, King of the universe, who creates the fruit of the vine.

4. BLESSING FOR FOODS, OTHER THAN BREAD, MADE FROM FLOUR OR GRAIN. This includes cookies, cake, wheatflakes, spaghetti, noodles etc. but does not include whiskey or vodka, which are beverages.

Baruch Ata Adonai, Elohenu Melech ha-olam, boreh minei m'zonot.

Blessed art Thou, O Lord our God, King of the universe, who creates different kinds of food.

5. BLESSING FOR MEAT, MILK, FISH, ALL BEVERAGES EXCEPT WINE AND FOR MISCELLANEOUS FOODS. This blessing is said before drinking anything but wine, including water, and for foods such as candy, sugar, honey, etc., which do not fit into any of the other categories.

Baruch Ata Adonai, Elohenu Melech ha-olam, shehakol nihieh bidvaro.

Blessed art Thou, O Lord our God, King of the universe, by whose word all things exist.

6. BLESSING FOR FOODS FROM THE GROUND. This includes all foods which must be dug up from the ground such as potatoes, carrots etc., and all other fruits or vegetables which grow on a plant that produces fruit only once in its lifetime. This includes beans, strawberries, bananas, pineapple, rhubarb, spinach, corn-on-the-cob, sugarcane (eaten raw) etc.

Baruch Ata Adonai, Elohenu Melech ha-olam, boreh pri ha-adama.

Blessed art Thou, O Lord our God, King of the universe, who creates the fruits of the earth.

7. BLESSING FOR THE FRUIT OF TREES. This includes apples, nuts, oranges (but not orange juice, which is a beverage), grapes, avocados, etc.

Baruch Ata Adonai, Elohenu Melech ha-olam, boreh pri ha-etz.

Blessed art Thou, O Lord our God, King of the universe, who creates the fruit of the tree.

Other Blessings

8. BLESSING FOR PUTTING UP A MEZUZA. The laws concerning the placing of the mezuza as well as the blessing, will be found in chapter 20.

9. BLESSING FOR BURNING DOUGH WHEN MAKING BREAD.
Before putting the bread in the oven, a piece of dough the
size of an olive should be taken and burned after saying
the following blessing.

*Baruch Ata Adonai, Elohenu Melech ha-olam, asher
kidshanu b'mitzvotav v'tzivanu lehafrish challa.*

Blessed art Thou, O Lord our God, King of the
universe, who has sanctified us in His commandments and
commanded us to separate dough.

10. BLESSING WHEN PUTTING ON NEW CLOTHES FOR THE
FIRST TIME.

*Baruch Ata Adonai, Elohenu Melech ha-olam,
malbish arumim.*

Blessed art Thou, O Lord our God, King of the
universe, who clothes the naked.

11. SHEHECHEYANU: the blessing for buying new clothes
or vessels, entering into the possession of a house, tasting
fruit for the first time in the season, arriving in Israel for
the first time and for any "new thing."

This blessing thanks God for permitting us to live long
enough to enjoy whatever new thing it is that we are
enjoying. It is also said on all holidays after lighting the
holiday candles, and is a part of the holiday kiddush.

*Baruch Ata Adonai, Elohenu Melech ha-olam,
shehecheyanu, v'kimanu v'higgiyanu lazman ha-zeh.*

Blessed art Thou, O Lord our God, King of the
universe, who has kept us alive and preserved us and
enabled us to reach this time.

Sabbath Blessings

12. BLESSING FOR LIGHTING THE SABBATH CANDLES. The
laws concerning the Sabbath lights as well as the blessing
can be found in chapter 23.

13. BLESSING ONE'S CHILDREN ON FRIDAY NIGHT. As
described in chapter 23, the father, on returning home
from the synagogue on Friday night, blesses the children.

He places his hands on their heads and, looking at the Shabbat candles, says the following blessing.

Blessing for a boy:

Y'simcha Elohim k'Efraim v'chi-Menasheh.

God make thee as Efraim and Manasseh.

Blessing for a girl:

Y'simech Elohim k'sara, Rivka, Rachel v'Leah.

God make thee as Sara, Rebecca, Rachel and Leah.

Blessing for boys and girls:

Y'varech'cha Adonai v'yishm'recha: yaer Adonai panav elecha viyichunecha: yisa Adonai panav elecha v'yasem l'cha shalom.

May the Lord bless thee and keep thee: may the Lord make His face shine upon thee and be gracious to thee: the Lord turn His face to thee and give thee peace. (This is the *Birchat Cohanim*—the Priestly Blessing.)

14. KIDDUSH FOR FRIDAY NIGHT. This is described in detail in chapter 23. The entire kiddush is as follows.

(in a low voice): *Vayhi erev vayhi voker*

Yom hashishi: vaychulu ha-shamaim v'ha-aretz v'chol tzevaam: vaychal Elohim bayom ha-shviyi m'lachto asher asa, vayishbot bayom ha-sh'viyi mikol melachto asher asa vayvarech Elohim et yom ha-sh'viyi vaykadesh oto ki vo shavat mikol melachto asher bara Elohim la-asot.

(On wine: *Sav'ri maranan v'rabotai. Baruch Ata Adonai, Elohenu Melech ha-olam, boreh pri hagafen.*

On challa: *Birshut maranan v'rabotai. Baruch Ata Adonai, Elohenu Melech ha-olam hamotzi lechem min ha-aretz.)*

Baruch Ata Adonai, Elohenu Melech ha-olam, asher kidshanu b'mitzvotav v'ratza vanu. V'Shabbat kadsho b'ahava u-v'ratzon hinchilanu, zikaron l'maaseh b'reshit. Ki hu yom t'chila l'mikraeh kodesh, zecher liytziyat Mitzraim. Ki vanu vacharta v'otanu kidashta mikol ha-amim, v'Shabbat kodshecha b'ahava u-v'ratzon hinchaltanu: baruch Ata Adonai, mikadesh ha-Shabbat.

And it was morning and it was evening. Sixth day: And the heaven and the earth were finished and all their host. And on the seventh day God had finished His work which He had made; and He rested on the seventh day from all His work which He had made. And God blessed the seventh day and He hallowed it because He rested thereon from all His work which God had created and made (Gen. 1:31, 2:1-3).

(On wine: If it please my masters. Blessed art Thou O Lord our God, King of the universe, who creates the fruit of the vine.

On challa: With permission of my masters Blessed art Thou O Lord our God, King of the universe, who brings bread out of the earth.)

Blessed art Thou O Lord our God, King of the universe, who has sanctified us in His commandments and has taken pleasure in us and in love and favor has given us the holy Sabbath as an inheritance, as a memorial of creation, that day being also the first of the holy convocations in remembrance of the Exodus from Egypt. For Thou hast chosen us and sanctified us above all nations and in love and favor hast Thou given us the holy Sabbath as an inheritance. Blessed art Thou O Lord, who sanctifies the Sabbath.

15. KIDDUSH FOR SATURDAY NOON.

V'shomru b'nei Yisrael et ha-Shabbat la-asot et ha-Shabbat l'dorotam brit olam; beyni u-veyn bnai Yisrael ot hi le-olam, ki sheshet yamim asa Adonai et ha-shamaim v'et ha-aretz u-vayom hashviyi shavat vaynafash.

Zechor et yom ha-Shabbat l'kadsho: sheshet yamim ta-avod ve-asita kol m'lachtecha; v'yom hashviyi Shabbat'Adonai Elohecha, lo ta-aseh kol m'lacha ata u-vincha u-vitecha, avdecha va-amatcha u-v'hemtecha v'gerecha asher b'sharecha: ki sheshet yamim asa Adonai et ha-shamaim v'et ha-aretz et ha-yam v'et kol asher bam, vayanach bayom hashviyi. Al ken berach Adonai et yom ha-Shabbat vayikodshecha.

(On wine: *Baruch Ata Adonai, Elohenu Melech ha-olam, boreh pri ha-gafen.*)

Wherefore the children of Israel shall keep the Sabbath, to observe the Sabbath throughout their generations, for a perpetual covenant. It is a sign between Me and the children of Israel forever; for in six days the Lord made heaven and earth and on the seventh day He ceased from work and rested (Exod. 31:16-17).

Remember the Sabbath day to keep it holy. Six days shalt thou labor and do all thy work, but the seventh day is a Sabbath unto the Lord thy God; in it thou shalt not do any kind of work, thou, nor thy son, nor thy daughter, nor thy servant, nor thy maid-servant, nor thy cattle nor the stranger that is within thy gates. For in six days the Lord made heaven and earth, the sea and all that is in them and rested on the seventh day; wherefore the Lord blessed the Sabbath day and hallowed it (Exod. 20:8-11).

(On wine: Blessed art Thou O Lord our God, King of the universe, who creates the fruit of the vine.)

Holiday Blessings

16. BLESSING FOR LIGHTING THE HOLIDAY CANDLES. The following blessing is said after lighting the candles or other lights on all holidays. The words in parentheses are added if the holiday falls on Friday night.

Baruch Ata Adonai, Elohenu Melech ha-olam asher kidshanu b'mitzvotav v'tzivanu l'hadlik ner shel (Shabbat v-) yom tov. (On Rosh Hashana, instead of *yom tov,* say *yom ha-zikaron.* On Yom Kippur, instead of *yom tov,* say *yom ha-kippurim.*)

Blessed art Thou O Lord our God, King of the universe, who has sanctified us in His commandments and commanded us to light the (Sabbath and) holiday lights. (On Rosh Hashana instead of holiday, say "day of remembrance." On Yom Kippur, instead of holiday, say "day of atonement.")

After this blessing the *shehecheyanu* blessing (no. 11)
is said. Shehecheyanu is omitted on the last two nights of
Passover.

17. KIDDUSH FOR ROSH HASHANA. This kiddush is
recited at the holiday meal in the evening on returning
from the synagogue at the commencement of Rosh
Hashana. If this happens to be a Friday night, start the
kiddush with the first paragraph of the Sabbath kiddush,
starting with (in a low voice) *Vayhi erev vayhi voker* until
bara Elohim la-asot. Then recite the rest of the kiddush
as follows. Words in parentheses are said when the
holiday falls on Friday night.

(On wine: *Baruch Ata Adonai, Elohenu Melech ha-
olam, boreh pri hagafen.*

On any other liquor: *Baruch Ata Adonai, Elohenu
Melech ha-olam, shehakol nihieh bidvaro.)*

*Baruch Ata Adonai, Elohenu Melech ha-olam, asher
bachar banu mikol am v'rom'manu mikol lashon
v'kidshanu b'mitzvotav v'titen lanu, Adonai Elohenu,
b'ahava et yom (ha-Shabbat ha-zeh v'et yom) ha-zikaron
ha-zeh, yom (zichron) terua (b'ahava) mikra kodesh
zecher liy-tziat Mitzraim. Ki vanu vacharta v'otanu
kidashta mikol ha-amim. U-dvarecha emet v'kayam la-
ad. Baruch Ata Adonai, Melech al kol ha-aretz
m'kadesh (ha-Shabbat v-) Yisrael v'yom ha-zikaron.*

Blessed art Thou, O Lord our God, King of the
universe, who has chosen us from all people and exalted
us above all languages and sanctified us in His
commandments and has given us in love, O Lord our
God (this Sabbath day and), this day of remembrance, a
day (of remembering) of blowing the shofar (in love), a
holy convocation as a memorial of the Exodus from
Egypt. For He has chosen us and sanctified us above all
nations. And thy word is truth and endures forever.
Blessed art Thou O Lord, King over all the earth, who
sanctifies (the Sabbath and) Israel and the day of
remembrance.

18. KIDDUSH FOR PASSOVER, SHAVUOT AND SUKKOT.
This kiddush is recited at the holiday meal in the evening
after the holiday has begun. If the holiday falls on Friday
night, start with the first paragraph of the Sabbath
kiddush, starting with (in a low voice) *Vayhi erev vayhi
voker* until *bara Elohim la-asot.* Then recite the rest of
the kiddush as follows. (Words in brackets are said when
the holiday falls on Friday night.)

(On wine: *Baruch Ata Adonai, Elohenu Melech ha-
olam, boreh pri hagafen.*

On any other liquor: *Baruch Ata Adonai, Elohenu
Melech ha-olam shehakol nihieh bidvaro.)*

*Baruch Ata Adonai, Elohenu Melech ha-olam, asher
bachar banu mikol am v'rom'manu mikol lashon
v'kidshanu b'mitzvotav v'titen lanu Adonai Elohenu,
b'ahava [Shabbatot limnucha u-] moadim l'simcha;
chagim u-zmanim l'sason; et yom [ha-Shabbat ha-zeh
v'et yom].*

On Passover: *Chag ha-matzot ha-zeh, zman
cherutenu.*

On Shavuot: *Chag ha-Shavuot ha-zeh, zman matan
Toratenu.*

On Sukkot: *Chag ha-Sukkot ha-zeh, zman simchatenu.*

On Sh'mini Atzeret and Simchat Torah: *Ha-sh'mini
chag ha-atzeret ha-zeh, zman simchatenu.)*

*[B 'ahava] mikra kodesh zecher liy'tziat Mitzraim ki
vanu vacharta v'otanu kidashta mikol ha-amim
[v'Shabbat] u-moadei kadshecha [b'ahava u-v'ratzon]
b'simcha u-v'sason hinchaltanu. Baruch Ata Adonai,
m'kadesh [ha-Shabbat v-] Yisrael v-ha-zmanim.*

Blessed art Thou O Lord our God, King of the
universe, who has chosen us from all people and exalted
us above all languages and sanctified us in His
commandments and has given us in love, O Lord our
God [Sabbaths for rest], appointed times for gladness,
festivals and seasons for joy [this Sabbath day and] this
day of

(Passover: the feast of the matzot, season of our
freedom.

Shavuot: the feast of Shavuot, the season of the giving
of our Torah.

Sukkot: the feast of Sukkot, season of our rejoicing.

Sh'mini Atzeret and Simchat Torah: the feast of the
solemn assembly on the eighth day, season of our
rejoicing.)

[in love] a holy convocation as a memorial of the
Exodus from Egypt; for He has chosen us and sanctified
us above all people and Thy holy [Sabbath and]
appointed times hast Thou caused us to inherit [in love
and favor] in joy and gladness. Blessed art Thou, O Lord,
who sanctifies [the Sabbath and] Israel and the festive
seasons.

Other blessings are given throughout the book and a complete
list will be found in any siddur.

Appendix V

All About Tcholent

As we saw in chapter 23, tcholent was invented in order to increase our enjoyment of the Sabbath without breaking its laws. Accordingly it behooves us to take care that both these conditions are met: the tcholent must be a *m'chaya* and the Sabbath must not be violated in its making.

To consider the second point first, once all the ingredients are in the pot on Friday afternoon, it is usually cooked on a low flame on the back burner of the stove before the Sabbath candles are lit. It is then transferred to the oven where it cooks slowly all night and the next morning. Experience has shown that the best temperature for the oven is 220° Fahrenheit, give or take a couple of degrees. If the family has no oven, the tcholent will cook very nicely on top of the stove with the flame adjusted so that the liquid in the pot is barely at simmering point. The best way to make sure it won't burn is to put an asbestos or metal plaque—a *blech*—between the pot and the flame.

Once Shabbat has started, the tcholent, whether in the oven or on the stove, may not be stirred nor may the pot be shaken, since this would constitute your participating in cooking it, a forbidden activity on Shabbat. To be strictly observant, the top of the tcholent pot should not even be lifted.

If, however, you have reason to suspect that the liquid is consumed or close to it and that the tcholent will burn, you are permitted to look at it and, if you find that to be the case, water can be added. It is important that any water added must have been brought to the boiling point for a few seconds before Shabbat starts and kept hot until it is used. This can be done by putting the kettle on the lid of the tcholent pot (if it is on the stove) or on a blech with a low flame if the tcholent is in the oven.

Now, for the tcholent itself, the best I can do is give you my own recipe, basically a combination of Moroccan and Polish

tcholentry and the fruit of thirty years of constant experimenting
in search of the perfect Sabbath meal. Modesty prevents me from
telling you how great it is, but my friend Herman Kugler, who is
reputed to know more about migraine than practically anyone, is
also an outstanding tcholent *meyvin*. Dr. Kugler, whose experience (in both neurology and Jewish food) covers four continents,
has been eating tcholent in our house for over twenty years and
invariably, on finishing his third helping, lowers his fork gently to
his plate and declares, in a rich Czernowitz-German accent,
"This is *noble* tcholent!"

Let the reader decide for himself next Shabbat.

Michael Asheri's Noble Tcholent

To start with, a heavy aluminum or cast iron pot is best, but
any good solid vessel of sufficient size will do. There is no fixed
quantity for any of the ingredients; it will depend on how many
people you plan to have at the table.

First slice up a couple of onions and brown them in a little oil
(not olive oil) or chicken fat in the bottom of the pot. When the
onions are medium brown, put some bones in the bottom of the
pot with them. Marrow bones are best, but any bones you can get
will give a particularly rich flavor to the tcholent.

Then take a small or medium-sized head of garlic, trim off the
roots at the bottom (they are usually dirty), and put the entire
head into the pot without peeling it. This is a Moroccan trick and
it makes the difference between tcholent and *noble* tcholent.

Next put one or two small, very hot red chili peppers in. If your
taste doesn't run to anything this violent, take some black pep-
percorns (ten or twelve) and sprinkle them in as you add the other
ingredients.

The next thing to add is a few raw eggs in the shell, taking care
not to break the shells. The eggs can be added at any time while
you are putting in the other ingredients, but I have found it easier
to place them carefully on top of the bones. When the time comes
to eat them, you will, if you've never lived among Sephardim, get
quite a surprise. While the shells are still white, the eggs inside
have turned a rich brown color and will taste quite unlike any egg
you have ever eaten before. They are called *Huevos Aljamiados*

in Jaquetía and *Huevos Jaminados* in Ladino. To all Sephardim they are a highly esteemed delicacy, but I know Ashkenazim who consider them an acquired taste (and have taken very little trouble to acquire it).

Now come the main ingredients. These are peeled white potatoes, cut into large pieces (halved or quartered), barley, large broad beans (large dried limas will do if you can't get the other kind, called *havas* in Spanish) which have been soaked since some time in the morning, and beef. The meat should be the toughest cut you can get and should have some fat on it or in it. The toughest cut is specified because the long cooking will make any cut tender and tough meat provides better flavor. The fat is also necessary to ensure full flavor for the tcholent.

These ingredients can be put in in any order, but I have found the best way to put half the potatoes in first, together with some of the beans and part of the barley. Then put the meat in—cut into chunks or as is—and follow it with the rest of the potatoes, beans, and barley. While you are doing this, sprinkle in three or four good pinches of savory. If you can't get savory, its close relative thyme will do almost equally well. If you are not using beans, substitute one bay leaf for the savory or thyme.

A good two or three teaspoons of salt should then be sprinkled over the top of everything and enough boiling water to cover poured on top of the salt. Put the lid on the pot and start cooking. Check just before Shabbat to see if there is enough liquid.

Many people like an additional dish to eat on the side with the tcholent. Among the Ashkenazim this is likely to be a *kishke*, stuffed intestine. You can buy ready-made kishke from your kosher butcher, possibly frozen. The way to handle it is enclose it in aluminum foil and seal it in by carefully folding the edges over (the edges of the foil, that is; kishke doesn't have edges). It can then be placed on top of the other ingredients and left to cook with the tcholent.

A second side dish is *oriza*, a Moroccan specialty. Oriza is whole wheat and it used to be hard to get, but nowadays there are health food stores all over the place that carry it. It is prepared as follows:

Chop fine a few cloves of garlic and fry them in a tablespoon or two of olive oil. When the garlic starts to brown, add one cup of whole wheat which has been washed and drained after inspecting it for weevils. Fry the wheat in the oil until it begins to darken in color (it is best to stir it frequently while it is frying) and then add one and one-half cups of water into which a teaspoonful or so of mild paprika has been stirred. Add salt and pepper to taste (I add salt but no pepper at all) and cook on a low flame, covered, until all the water has been absorbed.

Then, if you are a Moroccan, you will put the oriza into a small aluminum pot with a tight fitting top, tie the top in place, and put it in the middle of the tcholent, except that you would call it *adafina* and would use *garbanzos* (chickpeas) instead of beans and would leave out the barley. If you are not Moroccan, the chances of your having a special pot for oriza are small, so you will make an envelope of heavy aluminum foil and pour the oriza into it, folding all the edges carefully and sealing it off. Put it on top of the tcholent, put the lid of the tcholent pot on, and forget about it until the next day at noon.

And remember: When you take the tcholent out at noon on Saturday, don't turn off the oven! For that you have to wait until Shabbat is over.

B'teavon! (An expression lacking in English, so we say it in French: *bon appetit!*)

Glossary

Unless otherwise noted, all words are Hebrew. Y.-Yiddish; Sp.-Spanish; Aram.-Aramaic; A.-Ashkenazic; S.-Sephardic

AARONITES. (Eng.) Descendants of Aaron; Cohanim.

ADAFINA. (Sp.) see Tcholent.

ADAR SHENI. "Second Adar"; the extra month in the Jewish leap year.

ADLOYADA. Purim carnival celebrated in Israel.

ADONAI. Literally, "Lord"; the pronunciation given the Name of God spelled with the Hebrew letters yud, heh, vav, heh, the proper pronunciation of which is forbidden to Jews.

AGGADA. Non-legal matter contained in the Talmud, as opposed to Halacha (q.v.).

AGUDA. A woven palm-leaf holder for the Hadassim and Aravot, held together with the Lulav.

AGUNA. A woman whose husband has disappeared but who has no proof that he is dead. She may not remarry until proof is forthcoming.

AKDAMOT. A special Shavuot prayer.

ALFA BETA. A collection of psalms and hymns recited in Sephardic congregations on Saturday afternoon.

ALIYA. Literally, "going up." (a)The honor and act of going to the Torah to read a portion publicly; (b)Emigration to Israel.

ALMEMOR. See Bima.

AMIDA. An important series of prayers, said standing and in silence.

AMUD. A column; used by Sephardim to describe one of the posts used in building the Sukka according to their tradition.

ARAVOT. Willow branches, held together with the lulav.

ARBA KANFOT. Literally, "four corners"; a garment with tsitsit (ritual fringes), usually worn under the shirt by men. Also called Tallit Katan.

ARBA KOSOT. "Four cups"; the four cups of wine which must be drunk during the Passover Seder.

ARBIT. The evening prayer; also called Maariv.

ARK. The Aron Kodesh.

ARON KODESH. The cabinet or "Ark" in which the scrolls of the Torah are kept in the synagogue.

ASHKENAZI. Originally, German; now refers to all European Jews not specifically Sephardic, and their descendants.

ASSERET Y'MEI T'SHUVA. The ten days of repentance between Rosh Hashana and Yom Kippur.

AVEIRA. A sin.

AVIN HARA. The evil eye.

AVODA ZARA. Worship of strange gods; idol worship.

AVRAM AVINU. Literally, "Our Father, Abraham": Abraham.

AZHAROT. Literally, "Warnings"; special Sephardic prayers recited on Shavuot.

BAAL HAGGADA. Leader of the Seder ceremony of Passover.

BAAL KOREH. The reader of the Torah scroll in the synagogue service.

BAAL MUSAPH. The Sheliach Tzibbur for the Musaph service.

BAAL SHACHRIT. The Sheliach Tzibbur for the Shachrit service.

BAAL T'FILLA. The Sheliach Tzibbur (q.v.).

BAGHDADI. Certain Jews of Iraqi origin living in India.

BARCHES. The German name for Challa; the Sabbath loaf.

BAR MITZVA. Literally, "son of the commandment"; a Jewish boy who has
reached his thirteenth birthday according to the Jewish calendar.

BARUCH SHEPTARANI. Brief blessing said by the father of a bar mitzva.

BAT. (pl. Banot) Daughter; daughter of.

BAT MITZVA. A ceremony in some Reform and Conservative congregations,
analogous to that held for a bar mitzva, but for a twelve-year-old girl.

B.C.E. Before the Common Era; equivalent to B.C. in Christian reckoning.

B'CHOR. (pl. B'chorim) A woman's firstborn son.

BEDIKAT CHAMETZ. Ceremonial search for leaven on the night before Passover.

BEN. Son; son of.

BENE-ISRAEL. Marathi-speaking Jews of Bombay, India.

BET DIN. A three-man rabbinical court.

BET HA-KNESSET. Literally, "house of assembly"; a synagogue.

BET-HA-MIDRASH. (A. Besmedrash) Literally "house of study"; a synagogue.

BET HA-MIKDASH. The Holy Temple in Jerusalem.

BET OLAM. Literally "eternal house"; a Jewish cemetery.

BETSA. (Aram.) An egg. Refers to the egg on the Passover Seder plate. Also the
name of a tractate of the Talmud.

BET T'FILLA. Literally "house of prayer"; a generic name for the synagogue.

B'EZRAT HA-SHEM. "With God's help"; used at the head of correspondence.

BIKKUR CHOLIM. The mitzva of visiting the ill.

BILBUL DAM. The blood libel.

BIMA. Table from which the Sefer Torah is read in the synagogue; usually a
raised platform.

BIRCHAT COHANIM. The Priestly Blessing (Num. 6:22-27).

BIRCHAT HA-MAZON. The grace after a meal in which bread has been eaten.

BIZ HUNDERT UN TZVANTZIG. (Y.) "Till one hundred and twenty"; said after
mentioning someone's age.

B'LI NEDER. Literally, "without vowing"; said when making an appointment for a future time.

BLINTZES. (Y.) A cheese-filled fried pancake.

BOKSER. (Y.) The carob bean or St. John's bread (*Ceratonia siliqua*).

BOREKES. (Turkish) A cheese-filled pastry—Sephardic.

B'RACHA. A blessing.

BRISS. The Ashkenazic pronunciation of Brit (Mila); used to describe the ceremony and celebration of a circumcision.

BRIT MILA. Literally, "Covenant of Circumcision"; ritual circumcision.

BRONFEN. (Y.) Brandy.

B'SAMIM. Spices; the spices used for the Havdala ceremony.

B'SOMIM BICKSEL. (Y.) The spice box used to hold the spices for Havdala.

CARAITES. See Karaim.

CARDIAC JUDAISM. An ironic phrase describing the religion of those who say that all one needs is to have "a Jewish heart."

C.E. Common Era; equivalent to A.D. in Christian reckoning.

CHACHAM. Literally, "a wise man"; the term Sephardim use for their rabbis.

CHAI. Literally "life"; has the numerical value 18.

CHALALA. The daughter of a Cohen and a divorced woman or a chalutza.

CHALAT. A robe used by Chasidim.

CHALEV ISRAEL. Cow's milk which has been milked and processed under rabbinical supervision.

CHALILA. "God forbid!"

CHALITZA. A ceremony whereby a man refuses to wed his childless brother's widow, thus freeing her for remarriage.

CHALLA. Literally, "dough"; the twisted Sabbath loaf.

CHALUTZ. A pioneer in the settlement of Israel.

CHALUTZA. A widow who has undergone the chalitza ceremony.

CHAMETZ. Leaven; anything made of fermented grain and by extension non-useable on Passover.

CHAMETZDIK. (Y.) (adj.) Non-useable on Passover by reason of leaven.

CHAMIN. See Tcholent.

CHANUKA GELT. (Y.) Money given children on the fifth night of Chanuka.

CHANUKAT HA-BAIT. Housewarming.

CHANUKIYA. Chanuka lamp; a menora.

CHAROSET. A paste made of apples, nuts, wine, etc., used on the seder plate for Passover.

CHASID. Member of an Orthodox sect founded by Rabbi Israel Ben Eliezer, the Baal Shem Tov (died 1760 C.E.).

CHASIDEI UMOT HA-OLAM. Literally, "The righteous among the peoples of the world." Today this phrase is used to describe Gentiles who aided Jews during the German genocide.

CHAS V'SHALOM. "God forbid!"

CHATAN. A bridegroom.

CHATAN B'RESHIT. "Bridegroom of Genesis"; the man chosen to read the opening verses of the Torah on Simchat Torah.

CHATAN TORAH. "Bridegroom of the Torah"; the man chosen to read the concluding verses of the Torah on Simchat Torah.

CHATZI KADDISH. A short version of the Kaddish prayer.

CHAZAK U'BARUCH. Literally, "strong and blessed"; a phrase used by Sephardim to mean, "congratulations!"

CHAZAN. A cantor.

CHEDER. A Jewish elementary school, usually open after regular school hours. (U.S.A.)

CHEREM. Excommunication; a ban.

CHEREM OF RABBENU GERSHOM. A ban on polygamy put into effect for one thousand years in the 10th century C.E. It is obligatory only for Ashkenazim.

CHEVRA KADISHA. Burial society.

CHEVRA SHASS. Talmud study society.

CHEVRA SHEL EMET. Literally, "Brotherhood of Truth"; another name for the burial society.

CHEVRA TEHILLIM. A society for study and recitation of psalms.

CHILAZON. A mollusk used to make the dye with which the "blue thread" of the tsitsit was colored. No longer identifiable.

CHILIBON. (Ladino) A second name given a posthumous child by Sephardim. Pron. Tchilibon.

CHILUL SHABBAT. Violation of the Sabbath.

CHOK. A commandment whose reason we cannot guess at.

CHOL HA-MOED. The intermediate days of the holidays Sukkot and Passover.

CHUETA. A group of people of Jewish extraction living in Majorca, Spain; they are Roman Catholics.

CHUKOT HA-GOY. A commandment (Lev. 20:23) forbidding Jews from following the customs of the Gentiles, insofar as they involve idolatry.

CHUMASH. The Pentateuch.

CHUPPA. The marriage canopy.

CHURBAN BET HA-MIKDASH. The destruction of the Temple in Jerusalem.

CHURBAN EUROPA. The destruction of European Jewry by the Germans, 1939-1945.

CHUTZ LAARETZ. In the diaspora; outside Eretz Israel.

COHEN. A (Jewish) priest; a descendant of Aaron.

COHEN GADOL. The High Priest of the Temple in Jerusalem.

DAM. Blood.

DAM HA-BRIT. Literally, "blood of the covenant"; the drop of blood taken from the place the foreskin would be in the case of converts who are already circumcised, or children born without a foreskin.

DARCHEI SHALOM. Literally, "ways of peace"; a phrase referring to keeping peace with our non-Jewish neighbors.

DAVVEN. (Y.) To pray.

DIBBUK. The malicious spirit of a dead person, possessing a living person.

DIN. Law.

DINA D'MALCHUTA DINA. (Aram.) Literally, "The law of the land is the law"; there can be no conflict between civil and religious law.

DIVREI TORAH. Literally, "words of Torah"; exegetical talk given by a learned man on religious subjects.

DOENMEH. Turkish converts to Islam who maintain a secret "Judaism."

DREDEL. The "put and take" top used for gambling on Chanuka.

DUCHAN. The platform in front of the Aron Kodesh.

DUCHENEN. (Y.) To give the Priestly Blessing.

ELIYAHU HA-NAVI. The Prophet Elijah.

ERETZ ISRAEL. Israel; the Holy Land.

EREV. Evening; the eve of Sabbath or a holiday.

EREV SHABBAT. Friday afternoon; the eve of a Sabbath.

ERUV TAVSHILIN. Food, prepared on the eve of a holiday followed by Shabbat, and set aside.

ESHET CHAYIL. "A woman of valor"; verses (Prov. 31:10-31) recited by the husband in praise of his wife before Friday night kiddush.

ESNOGA. See Snoga.

ETROG. The citron; held with the lulav on Sukkot.

EZRAT NASHIM. The women's section of the synagogue.

FALASHA. A sect of Negro Jews, native to Ethiopia.

FLEISHIG. (Y.) Food containing meat.

FRANKISTS. Followers of the Sabbatean, Joseph Frank, who eventually converted to Catholicism.

GABBAI. President or officer of a congregation.

GAN EDEN. The Garden of Eden; Paradise.

GAON. Literally, "Eminence"; a title given to a few particularly outstanding rabbis in our times.

GARTEL. (Y.) A woven sash worn by Chasidim at prayers.

GEFILLTE FISH. A chopped fish dish basic to Eastern European Jewish cuisine.

GEHINNOM. Gehenna; the Jewish word for Hell.

GELILA. The binding and covering of the Sefer Torah after it has been read from.

GEMARA. The completion of the Mishna; the Talmud.

GEMATRIA. The reckoning of the numerical value of Hebrew words for purposes of interpretation.

GEMILAT CHESED. An interest-free loan; literally, "deed of lovingkindness."

GENIZA. A burial place for papers on which God's Name appears.

GER. A convert to Judaism.

GERUT. Conversion to Judaism.

GESHEM. A prayer for rain said on Shemini Atzeret.

GETT. A Jewish divorce.

GETT CHALITZA. A document releasing the widow of a childless man from the duty of marrying her husband's brother.

GILGUL HA-NESHAMOT. The reincarnation of souls.

GITTIN. A general term for divorces; a tractate of the Talmud.

GOMEL. A prayer of thanks on escaping from danger; said in the synagogue in the presence of a minyan.

GOY. A Gentile.

GRAGER. A Purim noisemaker.

GUT SHABBOS. (Y.) "Good Sabbath"; a Sabbath greeting.

GUT VOCH. (Y.) "Good week"; a Saturday night greeting.

GUT YOHR. (Y.) "Good year"; a New Year (Rosh Hashana) greeting.

GUT YOMTOV. (Y.) "Good holiday"; a holiday greeting.

GYORET. A female convert to Judaism.

HA-BACHUR HA-CHATAN. "Bachelor and bridegroom"; a phrase used in calling up a bridegroom to the Torah on the Sabbath before his wedding.

HACHNASOT KALA. Provision of dowries to poor or orphaned brides.

HADAS. A spice box used for Havdala.

HADASSIM. Myrtle branches held with the lulav on Sukkot.

HAFTARA. A section from the Prophets, read as a supplement to the weekly Torah portion on Shabbat and on holidays.

HAGBA. The raising of the open Sefer Torah before (Sephardim) or after (Ashkenazim) reading it.

HAGGADA. A book recited in its entirety at the Passover Seder.

HAKAFA. Circuit made around the inside of the synagogue with the lulav (Sukkot) or the Sifrei Torah (Simchat Torah).

HALACHA. That part of the Talmud which constitutes law which Jews are obliged to observe, as opposed to Aggada (q.v.).

HALLEL. A prayer of praise recited on holidays.

HAMOTZI. The blessing said before eating bread.

HA-SHEM. Literally, "The Name"; used to refer to God.

HASHGACHA. Religious supervision, particularly of food preparation.

HASHKABA. Memorial prayer said in Sephardic congregations.

HATIKVA. "The Hope"; the Israeli national anthem.

HAVDALA. Literally, "Separation"; a ceremony held on Saturday night at the end of the Sabbath.

HAZKARAT N'SHAMA. See Yizkor.

HECHSHER. Certificate of kashrut on food.

HEICHAL. Sephardic term for the Aron Kodesh.

HILULA. Commemoration of the death of a parent or of a famous man (Sephardic).

HOMENTASHEN. (Y.) Literally, "Haman's pockets"; a filled pastry eaten on Purim.

HOSHANOT. Hymns sung during the hakafot on Hoshana Rabba.

HOSHIANA. Hymn sung during the hakafot of Simchat Torah.

IMBESHREER. (Y.) Literally, "unbewitched"; said when complimenting a child.

IM YIRTZEH HA-SHEM. "If God wishes."

ISRAEL. (a) The Holy Land; (b) the Jewish people; (c)Jews who are neither Cohen nor Levi.

JAQUETÍA. (Sp.) Dialect of archaic Spanish spoken by North African Jews (pron. Hock-et-EE-ya).

JUDEO-GERMAN. Yiddish.

JUDEO-SPANISH. Ladino.

JUDEZMO. (Ladino) Ladino.

KABBALA. The mystic tradition in Judaism.

KABBALAT MITZVOT. Acceptance of the commandments; a necessary prelude to conversion to Judaism.

KABBALAT SHABBAT. Prayer service preceding Maariv on Friday evening.

KADDISH. Prayer said by mourners for eleven months following the death of a near relative.

KAFTAN. A type of coat, worn by Chasidim.

KAL. A congregation (Sephardic).

KALA. A bride.

KAPPAROT. Ritual sacrifice of chickens before Yom Kippur.

KARAIM. Sectarians who broke away from Judaism in the 8th century C.E.

KARPAS. Green vegetable eaten at the Passover seder.

KASHER. (adj.) Fit, proper or useable by Jews; (vb.) to make kasher—refers to soaking and salting of meat and purging of vessels; kosher.

KASHER L'PESACH. Useable on Passover.

KASHRUT. Kosherness; the laws and regulations pertaining to what is kosher.

KEHILLA. A congregation.

KEIN AYIN HARA. Literally, "no evil eye"; said to ward off bad luck.

KEPPALEH. A skullcap.

KETUBA. The marriage contract.

KHAZARS. A Tataric people who converted to Judaism in the 8th century C.E.

KIBBUTZ. An Israeli collective farm.

KIBBUTZ GALUYOT. The ingathering of the exiles; the return of Jews to Israel from the diaspora.

KIBBUTZNIK. A resident of a kibbutz.

KIDDUSH. Literally, "sanctification"; a blessing said over wine or liquor in honor of the Sabbath, a holiday, a yohrtzeit, etc.

KIDDUSH HA-SHEM. Literally, "Sanctification of the Name"; martyrdom; being put to death for being Jewish; a martyr.

KIDDUSHIN. The wedding ceremony.

KIDDUSH LEVANA. The blessing of the new moon, said between the third and sixteenth days of the Jewish month.

KINNOT. Mourning prayers and hymns recited on Tisha B'av.

KINUI. The name by which a Jew is known in non-Jewish life; not his "Jewish" name.

KINYAN. The formal closing of a contract of agreement, done by both parties grasping a garment at the same time.

KIPA. A skullcap.

KISEH SHEL ELIYAHU HA-NAVI. The "Chair of the Prophet Elijah" on which a boy is placed before his circumcision.

KITNIOT. The lesser grains such as rice, beans, maize, etc.; forbidden to Ashkenazim on Passover but permitted to most sephardim.

KITTEL. (Y.) A white robe worn by men on the High Holidays and at the Passover seder.

KOL HA-NEORIM. "All the lads"; a collective aliya for boys under thirteen on Simchat Torah.

KOL NIDREI. Literally "all vows"; an Aramaic-Hebrew prayer which initiates the Yom Kippur service.

KOSHER. (A.) adj.; kasher.

KOTEL HA-MAARABI. Literally "West Wall"; the remaining wall of the Bet Ha-Mikdash; the Wailing Wall.

KREPLACH. (Y.) Boiled dumplings, usually cheese-filled.

K'RIAH. Tearing of the clothing in sign of mourning.

K'RIAT HA-TORAH. The public reading of the Torah from the Sefer Torah, or Torah scroll.

K'RIAT SHEMA. Recitation of the Shema Israel; by extension any of the daily prayer services: Shachrit, Mincha and Arbit (Maariv).

K'RIAT SHEMA AL HA-MITTA. The bedtime prayer.

KRIMCHAKS. Tatar-speaking Jews of the Crimean Peninsula.

KVATTER. (Y.) The man who brings the child to the sondek at the time of circumcision.

KVATTERIN. The kvatter's wife.

K'ZAIT. A piece (usually of food) the size of an olive; the minimum required for certain blessings.

LADINO. Archaic Spanish dialect spoken by Sephardim in the Near East, Serbia and Greece.

LASHON KODESH. Literally, "holy language"; Hebrew.

LASHON TARGUM. Aramaic.

LATKES. (Y.) Potato pancakes traditionally eaten on Chanuka.

L'CHAIM. Literally, "To life!"; a toast, said before drinking liquor or wine.

LEKACH. (Y.) A sweet cake; usually a honeycake.

LEVI. Descendant of the Tribe of Levi; assistants to the Cohanim.

L'SHEM GERUT. Referring to circumcision; for the purpose of conversion to Judaism.

LUACH. A Jewish calendar.

LULAV. A palm branch, held on Sukkot.

MAARIV. The evening prayer, also called Arbit.

MACHZOR. The holiday prayer book.

MAFTIR. The last section of the Sabbath or holiday Sedra, or portion of the Torah.

MAMZER. A child born of a forbidden union or born in adultery.

MAMZERUT. Bastardy; the condition of being a mamzer.

MA'OT CHITTIM. Money collected before Passover to buy matzot and wine for needy Jews.

MAPPAH. Literally, "a tablecloth"; the gloss to the Shulchan Aruch, making it useable by Ashkenazim.

MAROR. Bitter vegetable eaten at the Passover Seder.

MARRANO. A Spanish Jew converted to Catholicism but secretly remaining Jewish.

MASECHTA. A tractate of the Mishna.

MASHGIACH. Ritual supervisor, particularly of food.

MASHIACH. The Messiah.

MASHKE. Any alcoholic liquor. In modern Hebrew, any beverage.

MATZA. Unleavened bread eaten on Passover.

MATZA SH'MURA. Matza made under specially rigorous supervision.

MATZEVA. A tombstone.

MATZOT SHEL MITZVA. The three matzot eaten at the beginning of the Seder ceremony.

MAYIM ACHRONIM. Water used to wash the fingertips prior to saying the grace after meals when three men or more have eaten together.

MAZZELTOV. "Congratulations!" "Good luck!"

MEA SHEARIM. Literally, "Hundred Gates"; the extreme Orthodox quarter of Jerusalem.

MECHITZA. A panel or curtain separating men from women, particularly in the synagogue.

MEGILLA. A scroll.

MEGILLAT ESTER. The book of Esther in scroll form; read on Purim.

MELDADO. (Ladino) A get-together at which readings from religious literature are featured (Sephardic).

MELDAR. (Ladino) (vb.) To read Hebrew.

MENORA. The Temple candelabrum; also used for the Chanuka lamp.

METIVTA. An academy for higher studies in the Talmud.

MET MITZVA. An unclaimed Jewish corpse whose burial is the responsibility of the community.

MEZONOT. Literally, "food"; used to refer to foods made of the five species of grain.

MEZUZA. A parchment with biblical verses written on it, placed on the door-post.

MIDRASH. A homiletic commentary on the Bible.

MIKRA. The Written Torah.

MIKVA. A ritual bath.

MILA. Circumcision.

MILCHIG. (Y.) Food containing milk.

MIMISHPACHAT. "Of the family of . . ."

MIMONA. See Noche de Mimona.

MINCHA. The afternoon prayer.

MINHAG. Custom.

MINYAN. Religious quorum of ten males, thirteen years old or more.

MIRTZESHEM. A corruption of Im Yirtzeh Ha-Shem (q.v.).

MI-SHEBERACH. A prayer in which blessings are called down on a person by name.

MISHNA. The first part of the Talmud.

MITNAGED. A non-Chasidic Orthodox Jew.

MITZVA. A commandment; by extension, an act performed in observance of a commandment.

MIZRACH. East.

MIZRACH BILD. (Y.) A calligraphic picture hung on the east wall of a house.

MIZRACH VANDT. (Y.) The east wall of the synagogue.

M'LAVEH MALKA. Feast held after the conclusion of the Sabbath.

MODEH ANI. Prayer said before opening one's eyes in the morning.

MOHEL. A ritual circumciser.

MOSHAV. A modified form of collective farm: not a kibbutz.

MOSSER. An informer; stool pigeon.

MOTZEI SHABBAT. Saturday night.

M'SADER GITTIN. A rabbi specialized in writing divorces.

M'SADER KIDDUSHIN. A man qualified to perform marriages.

M'SHUMAD. An apostate from Judaism.

M'TZITZA. The sucking of blood from the wound left by circumcision.

MUKTZEH. Forbidden to be touched on Shabbat.

MUSAPH. The additional prayer service following Shachrit on Sabbaths and holidays including Rosh Chodesh.

MUTER. Permitted on Shabbat.

M'ZUMEN. Three adult males (or more) who have eaten together (for grace after meals).

NACHALA. Death anniversary (Sephardic).

NEDAR. A pledge; money pledged on Shabbat or a holiday to be paid later; a pledged contribution to the congregation or to charity.

NEFESH. One of the three components of the soul; the life-spark.

NEILA. The concluding prayer service of Yom Kippur.

NER TAMID. The light left burning in front of the Aron Kodesh.

NESECH. Referring to wine, not useable by Jews.

NESIAT KAPPAYIM. The Birchat Cohanim, or Priestly Blessing.

NETOREI KARTA. Literally, "Guardians of the City" (Aram.); a group of anti-Zionist, extreme Orthodox Jews.

NIDDA. A menstrually unclean woman.

NIGUN. A wordless Chasidic melody.

NOCHE DE MIMONA. Moroccan feast of sweet foods, held on the last night of Passover.

N'SHAMA. Man's eternal soul.

N'SHAMA YETARA. The "extra soul" received by Jews on Shabbat.

NUSACH. The order of prayers according to different traditions: Nusach Ashkenaz, Nusach Sepharad, etc.

N'VIIM. The Prophets (in the Bible).

OIFRIFUNG. (German, Aufrüfung); the calling to the Torah of a bridegroom on the Sabbath before his wedding.

OMED. The lectern before which the Sheliach Tzibbur stands in Ashkenazi synagogues.

OMER. Literally, "sheaf of grain"; refers to the seven-week period between Passover and Shavuot.

ORAL TORAH. The Talmud, including Mishna and Gemara.

OTO HA-ISH. Literally, "that man"; Jesus.

OZNEI HAMAN. Literally, "Haman's ears"; Homentashen, the word commonly used in Israel.

PARASHA. A section or part of a text. Among Sephardim, the weekly Sedra.

PARDESI. Certain light-skinned Jews of Cochin, Malabar Coast, India.

PAREVEH. (Y.) Food which is neither milchig nor fleishig.

PARNASS. The president of a congregation.

PAROCHET. The curtain hung in front of the Aron Kodesh.

PASUL. Disqualified; not ritually useable, in reference to things other than food; the opposite of kasher.

PAYES. (A.) Hair left to grow long at the temples; (S.) Payot.

PEKESHEH. (Y.) A festive robe worn by Chasidim.

PESACH. Passover.

PESADIK. (Y.) Kosher for Passover.

PIDYON HA-BEN. Redemption of the firstborn sons.

PIKUACH NEFESH. Preservation of (human) life.

PITAM. The button-like protuberance on the etrog.

PIYYUT. Liturgical poem.

PIZMON. Hymn, particularly the hymns sung on Saturday night by Sephardim (pizmonim l'motzei Shabbat).

POSEK. A learned rabbi, noted for his decisions on difficult questions of Jewish law.

P'RIAH. The uncovering and bandaging of the glans penis at the time of circumcision.

PRIESTLY BLESSING. The Birchat Cohanim (Numb. 6:24-26) given by the Cohanim on holidays and among the Sephardim on Sabbath as well.

P'SHAT. The plain meaning of the Torah text.

P'TIL TECHELET. The blue thread of the tsitsit: no longer used (except by Bratzlaver Chasidim).

PURIM SHPIEL. (Y.) A Purim masquerade play.

RASHI. (a) Rabbi Shelomo Yitzchaki, author of the basic commentary on the Torah and the Talmud; (b) the modified form of the Hebrew printed alphabet, used for printing Rashi's commentary and other rabbinical matter.

REB. An honorific title, similar to "Don" in Spanish (used with a man's first name).

REBBE. A Chasidic rabbi.

REFUA SHELEMA. Complete recovery from an illness.

REMEZ. A hint; refers to implied meanings in the text of the Torah, in particular.

RESPONSA. Answers by learned rabbis to questions submitted them on Jewish law. In Hebrew, shaalot u-t'shuvot.

RIMMONIM. Literally, "pomegranates"; silver ornaments placed on the upper handles of the Torah scroll.

ROSH CHODESH. The first day of a Jewish month.

RUACH. The spirit; one of the three components of the soul; also, spirit in general.

SABBATEANS. See Doenmeh.

SAKKANAT NEFASHOT. Danger to life.

SAMARITANS. See Shomronim.

SANCTIFICATION OF THE NAME. See Kiddush ha-Shem.

S'CHACH. Green branches used to cover the roof of the Sukka.

SCHALET. See Tcholent.

SEDER. Literally, "order"; refers to the ceremony held in the home on Passover.

SEDRA. The portion of the Torah read on Sabbaths and holidays. (The proper pronunciation is Sidra, but Sedra is more often heard).

SEFER. A book. Refers to a book written in Hebrew on a religious subject.

SEFER TORAH. The parchment, handwritten scroll containing the text of the Pentateuch, or Written Torah (pl. Sifrei Torah).

SEFIRA. Literally "counting"; refers to the seven-week period between Passover and Shavuot.

SEFIRAT HA-OMER. See Sefira.

SELAIM. (pl.) Ancient Jewish coins, today used in the measure of the "five selaim" necessary to redeem the firstborn son. (In the U.S.A., five half-dollars.)

SELICHOT. Penitential prayers said before Rosh Hashana and between Rosh Hashana and Yom Kippur.

SEMANADA BUENA. (Ladino) Sephardic Saturday night greeting.

SEPHARDIC. From Sepharad, Spain; (adj.) referring to Jews of Spanish origin, but now applied to most non-Ashkenazic Jews, regardless of origin. (Also, Sephardi.)

SEUDA HA-SHELISHIT. The third meal of the Sabbath, eaten by the men in the synagogue.

SEUDAT MITZVA. A feast, at which food is served, in honor of the performance of a commandment.

SHAALOT U-T'SHUVOT. See Responsa.

SHAATNEZ. The forbidden mixture of linen and wool in clothing.

SHABBAT. The Sabbath.

SHABBAT HAGADOL. Literally, "The Great Sabbath"; the Sabbath before Passover.

SHABBAT SHALOM. Literally, "Peaceful Shabbat!"; Sephardic and Israeli Sabbath greeting.

SHABBOS GOY. (A.) A Gentile, hired in advance, to do work on Sabbath prohibited to Jews (mostly lighting fires, and in former times, bringing the tcholent home from the baker's oven).

SHACHRIT. The morning prayer service.

SHALACH MANOT. The sending of gifts (usually pastry) on Purim.

SHALOSH REGALIM. The three holidays of Sukkot, Passover and Shavuot.

SHALOSH SEUDA. See Seuda ha-Shelishit.

SHAMASH. (A. Shammos) Beadle. Synagogue caretaker and assistant.

SHASS. Acronym of Sisha Sedarim (Six Sections); the Talmud, including Mishna and Gemara.

SH'CHITA. The slaughter of animals according to Jewish law.

SHECHINA. The Divine Presence.

SHEHAKOL. The blessing said over liquids, meats and several other types of food.

SHEIGETZ. A non-Jewish young man or boy; an insulting term.

SHEITEL. (Y.) A wig, worn by married women among the Orthodox.

SHELIACH TZIBBUR. Literally, "Envoy of the congregation"; the reader or Baal T'filla at the prayer service.

SHEMA ISRAEL. The central declaration of the Jewish faith: "Hear, O Israel, the Lord our God, the Lord is One."

SHEVUA TOV. "Good week!"; a Saturday night greeting.

SHIKKER. (adj. and noun) Drunk.

SHIKSA. A non-Jewish young woman; an insulting term.

SHIR HA-SHIRIM. The Song of Songs.

SHIVA. The seven-day period of mourning.

SH'LOSHIM. The thirty-day period of mourning (includes Shiva).

SHMAD. Apostasy from Judaism.

SHMEK TABAK. (Y.) A pinch of snuff.

SH'MIRAT SHABBAT. Observation of the Sabbath.

SH'MONEH ESSREH. See Amida.

SH'MURA MATZA. See Matza Sh'mura.

SHNUDDER. (Y.) To pledge a contribution when called to the Torah.

SHOCHET. Ritual slaughterer.

SHOFAR. The trumpet made of a ram's horn, blown on Rosh Hashana.

SHOMER. A watchman or guardian (particularly of a corpse).

SHOMER SHABBAT. A Sabbath observer (also an adjective).

SHOMRONIM. Samaritans; a group of Jewish sectarians; a people living on the West Bank of the Jordan who practice a primitive Judaism.

SH'TAR. A contract or other Jewish legal document.

SH'TAR GERUT. Certificate of conversion to Judaism.

SHTREIMEL. (Y.) A round fur hat, worn by Chasidic rabbis.

SHUL. (Y.) A synagogue.

SHULCHAN ARUCH. The basic code of Jewish law in everyday practice.

SIDDUR. The Jewish prayerbook.

SINAT CHINAM. Groundless hatred (specifically between Jews).

SIYYUM. A celebration honoring the termination of the study of a tractate in the Talmud.

SLIVOVITZ. (Slavic) Plum brandy.

S'MICHA. Rabbinical ordination.

SNOGA. (Ladino) A synagogue.

SOFER. A Jewish scribe.

SONDEK. (S., Sandek) Godfather of a boy at the time of his circumcision. The word, considered Hebrew, is actually of Greek origin.

SPODEK. A high velvet or fur hat worn by certain rabbis, particularly on weekdays.

SUFISTS. Moslem mystics.

SUKKA. A temporary dwelling built for the Sukkot holiday.

S'VIVON. See Dredel.

TAAM SHABBAT. The special taste food has on Shabbat.

TAANIT. A fast.

TACHANUN. Pentitential prayers said during the weekday service.

TACHRICHIM. The burial shroud.

TAHARAT MISHPACHA. Literally, "family purity"; the use of the mikva by married women to remove menstrual uncleanness.

TAKKANA. Any special regulation instituted by a community or congregation.

TAL. A prayer for dew, said on Passover.

TALLIT. The prayer shawl.

TALLIT KATAN. See Arba Kanfot.

TALMUD. In English this word is used to refer to the Oral Torah, including Mishna and Gemara. Properly it refers only to the Gemara.

TALMUD BAVLI. The Babylonian Talmud.

TALMUD YERUSHALMI. The Jerusalem Talmud.

TANACH. The Bible; the Old Testament.

TARGUM. A translation.

TARGUM ONKELOS. The Aramaic translation of the Pentateuch by Aquilas, the convert.

TASHLICH. Prayers said by a body of water on the first day of Rosh Hashana.

TAT. A Persian dialect spoken by the "Mountain Jews" of the Caucasus.

T'CHIAT HA-METIM. The resurrection of the dead.

TCHOLENT. A dish consisting of meat and some grain or legume, placed in the oven on Friday afternoon and left to cook until Saturday noon when it is eaten on returning from the synagogue. Called Shalet or Sholet by German-speaking Jews and Adafina or Chamin by Sephardim.

TEBA. See Bima; Teba is the Sephardic term.

T'EFILAT HA-DERECH. The prayer said before starting a journey.

TENAIM. The Ashkenazic pre-matrimonial engagement agreement.

T'FILLA. Prayer. Among the Sephardim, also Shachrit (q.v.).

T'FILLIN. The phylacteries; boxes mounted on leather straps worn during weekday morning prayer.

T'FILLIN SHEL ROSH. T'fillin worn on the head.

T'FILLIN SHEL YAD. T'fillin worn on the arm and hand.

TIKKUN. A devotion or devotional prayer service.

T'KIAH. The blowing of the shofar.

TORAH. The Jewish law and doctrine as contained in the Pentateuch and the Talmud.

TORAH SH'B'AL PEH. The Oral Torah.

TORAH SH'B'KTAV. The Written Torah.

TREF. (Also Trefa) Ritually unfit for Jews to eat. Non-kosher, referring to food.

TREIBER. (Y.) To remove the sciatic nerve and certain other vessels and tendons from the hindquarter of an animal, rendering it kosher. The Hebrew verb is Nikker.

T'SHUVA. Literally, "turning"; repentance and abandonment of former improper practices.

TSITSIT. The ritual fringes attached to the tallit and arba kanfot (q.v.).

TUCH. (Y.) A kerchief, used to cover the hair of Orthodox married women.

TZADDIK. Literally, "A man of justice"; a saint, particularly a Chasidic saint.

TZEDAKA. Literally, "justice"; charity and the giving of charity.

TZELEM. An image; refers to the crucifix.

TZOM. A fast.

UMOT HA-OLAM. "The peoples of the world"; Gentiles.

USHPIZIN. (Aram.) Literally, "guests"; prayers said to welcome the Patriarchs into the Sukka.

V'ADAR. See Adar Sheni.

VIDDUI. The confession of sins made to God on Yom Kippur and on the deathbed.

WEISSE ZEKELACH. (Y.) The white stockings worn by certain Chasidim.

WISHNIAK. (Slavic) Cherry brandy.

WRITTEN TORAH. The Pentateuch; the first five books of the Bible.

YAALEH V'YAVO. An additional prayer recited during the Amida and the grace after meals on holidays.

YARMULKEH. (Y.) A skullcap.

YASHER KOYACH. (A.) "Congratulations!" (Literally, "May your strength increase!").

YASHKE BUBIK. (Y.) Jesus.

YAYIN NESECH. Non-kosher wine.

YESHIVA. A school where Torah is studied.

YIDDISH. The common language of Eastern European Ashkenazim.

YISHUV B'ARETZ. The mitzva of residing in Israel.

YIZKOR. The memorial prayer for parents recited four times a year by Ashkenazim.

Y'MACH SH'MO. Literally, "May his name be blotted out!," said after mentioning an enemy of Israel.

YOHRTZEIT. (Y.) The death anniversary of a parent or of a famous rabbi; any death anniversary.

YOHRTZEIT LICHT. (Y.) A twenty-four-hour candle or lamp burned on a yohrtzeit.

YOM HA-ATZMAUT. Israel Independence Day.

YOM HA-DIN. A day of judgment, such as Yom Kippur.

YOMIM NORAIM. Literally, "Days of Awe"; the High Holidays.

YOM TOV. A major holiday, on which work is forbidden.

YOTZEI SIN. Jews formerly resident in China, now living elsewhere; not Chinese Jews.

ZERO'A. The bone placed on the Seder plate on Passover.

ZHUPETZEH. A robe worn by Chasidim.

Z'MIROT. (sing. Zemer) Hebrew and Aramaic hymns sung at the Sabbath table.

ZOHAR. Literally, "splendor"; the principal text of the Kabbala (q.v.).

ZUZIM. Babylonian coins referred to in the Passover song, "Chad Gadya."

Index

This is a functional, rather than an exhaustive index. Its main purpose is to help the reader find quickly those subjects regarding which he wants information or instruction.